Canada and International Affairs

Series Editors
David Carment, NPSIA, Carleton University,
Ottawa, ON, Canada
Philippe Lagassé, NPSIA, Carleton University,
Ottawa, ON, Canada
Yiagadeesen Samy, NPSIA, Carleton University, Norman Paterson,
Ottawa, ON, Canada

Palgrave's Canada and International Affairs is a timely and rigorous series for showcasing scholarship by Canadian scholars of international affairs and foreign scholars who study Canada's place in the world. The series will be of interest to students and academics studying and teaching Canadian foreign, security, development and economic policy. By focusing on policy matters, the series will be of use to policy makers in the public and private sectors who want access to rigorous, timely, informed and independent analysis. As the anchor, Canada Among Nations is the series' most recognisable annual contribution. In addition, the series showcases work by scholars from Canadian universities featuring structured analyses of Canadian foreign policy and international affairs. The series also features work by international scholars and practitioners working in key thematic areas that provides an international context against which Canada's performance can be compared and understood.

More information about this series at
http://www.palgrave.com/gp/series/15905

David Carment · Richard Nimijean
Editors

Political Turmoil in a Tumultuous World

Canada Among Nations 2020

palgrave
macmillan

Editors
David Carment
Norman Paterson School
of International Affairs
Carleton University
Ottawa, ON, Canada

Richard Nimijean
School of Indigenous and
Canadian Studies
Carleton University
Ottawa, ON, Canada

ISSN 2523-7187   ISSN 2523-7195   (electronic)
Canada and International Affairs
ISBN 978-3-030-70685-2   ISBN 978-3-030-70686-9   (eBook)
https://doi.org/10.1007/978-3-030-70686-9

This Palgrave Macmillan imprint is published by the registered company Springer Nature
Switzerland AG
The registered company address is: Gewerbestrasse 11, 6330 Cham, Switzerland

For William and Anna
—David Carment

For Danita, Alexander, and William
—Richard Nimijean

ACKNOWLEDGMENTS

The editors wish to acknowledge the contributions of our colleagues. Not only have they provided high-quality and timely analyses of Canada's evolving place in the world; they did so under extremely challenging circumstances. We are grateful that they promptly responded to our many requests for updates as conditions changed, which was not always easy since we all have to deal with the pandemic.

We also wish to acknowledge the outstanding contributions of Sydney Stewart. She has done a first-rate job at communicating and working with authors on their chapters and in managing the collection. Her dedicated and flawless research and editorial contributions made this volume possible.

The editors would like to thank Carleton University and the Social Sciences and Humanities Research Council for their support in this research.

We are especially grateful for Palgrave Macmillan's continuing support of the Canada Among Nations series and wish to especially acknowledge our editor Anca Pusca, who has provided us with invaluable support and guidance.

Ottawa, Canada   David Carment
Bottmingen, Switzerland   Richard Nimijean

CONTENTS

Notes on Contributors

Lloyd Axworthy P.C., C.C., O.M. has a B.A. from United College now the University of Winnipeg, M.A. and Ph.D. from Princeton University and an extensive record of public service. He is the Chair of the World Refugee Council, an international body established to develop solutions to problems in the current refugee system. He led Canada's election observation mission to Ukraine in 2019. He served as Board Chair of CUSO International and is on the executive committee of the International Institute of Sustainable Development. He is past member of the Boards of the MacArthur Foundation and Human Rights Watch. From 2004 to 2014, Dr. Axworthy was the President and Vice Chancellor of the University of Winnipeg. He served seven years as a member of the Legislative Assembly of Manitoba and twenty-one years as an elected member of the Canadian Parliament, holding several Cabinet posts, including Minister of Employment and Immigration, Western Diversification and Minister of Foreign Affairs. In that position, he was known for his work in advancing the Human Security agenda that included the Treaty on anti-personnel land mines, the International Criminal Court, and the Protocol on Child Soldiers. In 1997, he was nominated by United States Senator Patrick Leahy for the Nobel Peace Prize for his work on banning land mines. In 2002, he was awarded the Order of Canada and in 2016, he was made a Companion—the highest rank of the Order. In August 2017, The American Political Science Association awarded him the Hubert H. Humphrey award for notable public service. The United

Nations Association awarded him the Lester B. Pearson Pearson Medal. He has received sixteen honorary doctorates since leaving government. Dr. Axworthy is the author of *Navigating a New World: Canada's Global Future* (Toronto: Alfred A. Knopf Canada, 2003).

Duane Bratt is a Political Science Professor in the Department of Economics, Justice, and Policy Studies at Mount Royal University (Calgary, Alberta). He has written extensively on aspects of Canadian foreign policy including co-editor of a three-volume series entitled Classic Debates and New Idea: Readings in Canadian Foreign Policy.

Stephen Brown is a Professor of Political Science at the University of Ottawa. His research examines the intersection of the policies and practices of Northern countries and other international actors with politics in Southern countries, especially in sub-Saharan Africa. His recent work focuses on foreign aid, especially Canadian aid policy, and international LGBTI rights.

David Carment is a Full Professor of International Affairs, NPSIA, Carleton University, Ottawa. He is Editor of *Canadian Foreign Policy Journal* and Fellow of the Canadian Global Affairs Institute. His research focuses on Canadian foreign policy, fragile states, ethnic conflict and diaspora politics. He is the author, editor or co-editor of 15 books and has authored or co-authored over 60 peer-reviewed journal articles and book chapters.

Paul Gecelovsky is a Faculty Member at the University of Windsor and former book review editor for the Canadian Foreign Policy Journal. He has published extensively in CFPJ and in various edited volumes on Canadian Foreign Policy. He has also held positions at Western University and University of Lethbridge.

Frank Graves is the Founder of EKOS Research Associates and is a leading public opinion, social policy, and public policy expert. He has directed hundreds of large-scale studies of Canadian attitudes to a vast array of issues. He is an Honorary Fellow with the Calgary School of Public Policy and sits on the Advisory Board of the Sprott School of Business at Carleton University.

Robert Huish is an Associate Professor in International Development Studies at Dalhousie University in Halifax, Nova Scotia. Dr. Huish's research covers a wide range of topics such as global health, social justice, and the consequences of sanctions and embargoes. His global health work focuses on South-South Cooperation, notably between Cuba and other countries in the Global South. He is the Author of *Going Where No Doctor Has Gone Before: Cuba's Place in the Global Health Landscape*, and numerous articles on global health, Dr. Huish's research looks at how good health is often the product of social justice. Dr. Huish was named one of Canada's most innovative educators in the *Globe and Mail's* "Our Time to Lead" series. He is also the host of the podcast "GDP: The Global Development Primer" which is available on podcast platforms everywhere.

Chris Kilford is a Member of the National Board of the Canadian International Council (CIC) and President of the CIC Victoria branch. Besides a long career in the Canadian Armed Forces with postings in Germany, Afghanistan and Turkey, he holds a Ph.D. in history from Queen's University with a focus on civil-military relations in the developing world. He is also a Fellow with the Queen's Centre for International and Defence Policy.

Samuel MacIsaac is a Ph.D. Candidate at the Norman Paterson School of International Affairs (NPSIA). Prior to joining the Ph.D. program, he worked as an Economist for Statistics Canada. He was until recently the Managing Editor of the *Canadian Foreign Policy Journal* and completed a short contract for Global Affairs Canada relating to remittance policy in late 2019. He was awarded several scholarships—most notably SSHRC's Joseph-Armand Bombardier CGS award (2017–2020), TD's graduate fellowship for diaspora and migration studies (2019–2020), and the Ontario Graduate Scholarship (awarded but declined in 2017 and accepted for 2020–2021).

Michael W. Manulak is an Assistant Professor at the Norman Paterson School of International Affairs, Carleton University, and a Fellow at the Balsillie School of International Affairs and the Canadian Global Affairs Institute. He is a Former Analyst in the Government of Canada.

Alex Marland is a Professor of Political Science at Memorial University. He researches political marketing in Canada. His book *Brand Command: Canadian Politics and Democracy in the Age of Message Control* (UBC Press, 2016) won the Donner Prize for best public policy book by a Canadian.

Nelson Michaud is a Full Professor of political science and international relations at the École nationale d'administration publique. His work covers the disciplines from which he comes: history, political science, and law. Recipient of prestigious research awards, he has extensively published: peer-reviewed papers, chapters and several books including *Diplomatic Departures: The Conservative Era in Canadian Foreign Policy 1984–1993* (UBC Press, coedited with Kim Richard Nossal), *Global Media Perspectives on the Crisis in Panama* (Ashgate, coedited with Howard Hensel), the *Handbook of Canadian Foreign Policy* (Lexington, coedited with Pat James and Marc O'Reilly) and *Nouvelle politique étrangère* followed by La politique étrangère contemporaine en bons termes (PUQ with Charlie M'Balla).

Milana Nikolko, Ph.D. is an Adjunct Professor at the Institute of European, Russian and Eurasian Studies (EURUS), Carleton University (Canada). From 2005 to 2014, Nikolko was an Associate Professor of Political Science (Docent) at V. Vernadsky Taurida National University (Ukraine). In 2008, she was appointed as a Visiting Professor at Political Science Department, Valdosta State University (USA). She has published extensively on topics of Ukraine's nation-building process, mediation of grey zone conflicts (case Ukraine), political narratives of victimization among ethnic minorities, migrants and diasporas groups from the post-Soviet countries.

Richard Nimijean is a Member of the School of Indigenous and Canadian Studies at Carleton University, Ottawa and in 2020–2021 is a Visiting Professor in the Department of English and American Studies at Masaryk University in Brno, Czech Republic. His research and teaching focus on the branding of Canada, the politics of the brand state, the relationship between Canada's role as a global actor and the Canadian identity, Canada-US relations, and approaches to the study of Canada. He is a Co-editor (with David Carment) of *Canada, Nation Branding and Domestic Politics* (2019: Routledge).

Kari Roberts is an Associate Professor at Mount Royal University's Department of Political Studies, and the department chair of Economics, Justice, and Policy Studies. Dr. Roberts' research concerns Russian foreign policy toward the United States specifically and the West more broadly. She is specifically focused on Russia's interests in the Arctic and how it affects relations with Canada and the US. She has published widely on these issues including *Canadian Foreign Policy Journal.*

Sydney Stewart is a first year M.A. Candidate at Carleton University's Norman Paterson School of International Affairs. She completed a Bachelor of Arts with Honours Specialization in International Relations at Western University. Her research interests include intersections of gender, health and conflict, and women in security.

Rebecca Tiessen is a Professor and Deputy Director in the School of International Development and Global Studies and University Chair in Teaching at the University of Ottawa. Her areas of specialization include gender equality and women's empowerment, Canadian foreign aid policy, and the roles and impacts of development actors. Her current SSHRC-funded research (2019–2024) examines the contributions of international aid workers (international volunteers) to gender equality outcomes in 10 countries in the Global South.

List of Figures

LIST OF TABLES

PART I

Political Turmoil in a Tumultuous World

CHAPTER 1

Divided in a Dangerous World?

David Carment and Richard Nimijean

DIVIDED IN A DANGEROUS WORLD

The polarizing outcome of the 2019 Canadian federal election—the Liberals forming a minority government despite receiving fewer votes than the Conservative party of Canada—brought to light growing and deep divisions in the country. It raised questions not only of national unity not seen for decades but also of Canada's ability to act in the world, including how it manages its relationship with the USA. In this volume of

D. Carment (✉)
Norman Paterson School of International Affairs, Carleton University, Ottawa, ON, Canada
e-mail: david.carment@carleton.ca

R. Nimijean
School of Indigenous and Canadian Studies, Carleton University, Ottawa, ON, Canada

Department of English and American Studies, Masaryk University, Brno, Czech Republic

R. Nimijean
e-mail: richard.nimijean@carleton.ca

© The Author(s), under exclusive license to Springer Nature Switzerland AG 2021
D. Carment and R. Nimijean (eds.), *Political Turmoil in a Tumultuous World*, Canada and International Affairs, https://doi.org/10.1007/978-3-030-70686-9_1

Canada Among Nations, our colleagues explore how Canada's domestic divisions affect Canada as a global actor, from development assistance and Canada's feminist foreign policy to multilateralism and Canada's brand in the world.

This is not simply a matter of domestic politics; the world itself faces major challenges while embroiled in great tension and conflict: a stand-off between China and the USA; the unpredictability of the North Korean regime; a European Union struggling to maintain unity in the face of growing ethnonationalism and authoritarianism; a climate crisis that many leaders continue to refuse to take seriously; and, to top it all off, a serious global health crisis linked to the spread of COVID-19. This situation is likely to continue despite Joe Biden's victory over Donald Trump in the 2020 American presidential election. With this in mind, we identify the rationale for the volume in this introductory chapter.

THE LUCK OF THE LIBERALS DESPITE DIVISIONS AT HOME

The 2019 election produced a maze of distortions and divisions. The governing Liberal party received a lower share of the popular vote than the Conservatives yet won 36 more seats because the Conservatives lost ground in the vote-rich provinces of Ontario and Québec. The Green Party had nearly the same share of the popular vote as the Bloc Québécois but 29 less seats, while the NDP had twice the popular vote of the Bloc but 8 fewer seats. This lopsided and uneven outcome altered the country's political dynamics for the worse. The leader of the reinvigorated Bloc, Yves-François Blanchet, remarked on election night that his job was "not to make federalism work" but to get as much as his party could for Québec without compromising its values. Meanwhile, Alberta and Saskatchewan did not elect any Liberal members to the House of Commons, spawning a new wave of western alienation, calls for increased provincial autonomy, and a renascent Alberta separatism movement. These tensions were inflamed by the Trudeau government's attempt to promote the energy sector. Widespread protests by Indigenous peoples and environmentalists shut down major infrastructure across the country. In turn, this raised the spectre of a resurgent white supremacist vigilante movement. A February 2020 poll indicated that a majority of Canadians believed that "Canada is broken" and headed in the wrong direction under Trudeau's leadership (Thomson 2020).

This reflected ever-increasing rhetoric-reality gaps between big promises and government actions that diminished the prime minister's credibility, none more than his promise that the 2015 election would be the last one to use a "first past the post" system. When the parliamentary committee considering alternatives rejected Trudeau's preferred model, the Liberals quickly dropped electoral reform. Trudeau's optimistic outlook ("sunny ways") gave way to politics as usual, deepening mistrust even further. While scandals on the home front divided the country, geopolitical rifts abroad tore asunder the Liberal's so-called progressive and multilateralist agenda (Carment and Belo 2020). Trudeau's 2017 commitment to increase military spending in response to criticism from Trump disappointed those who supported Trudeau's alleged liberal internationalism, resulting in diminished commitments to peacekeeping and development assistance.

Despite many contradictions and scandals, the Liberals often met good fortune, though it happened more through serendipity than carefully crafted policy. For example, while Trudeau's promise to increase military spending to satisfy Trump only resulted in small nominal increases, Canada's spending as a percentage of GDP actually increased, due to the COVID-19 pandemic-induced contraction of the economy. Trudeau's climate change agenda, coupled with a contradictory pipeline policy, appeared to be the straw that would break Confederation's back. Alberta under Jason Kenney saw a resurgence of separatist and autonomist sentiments. When not taking on the federal government, Kenney attacked the "green Left" and bickered with BC and Québec over pipelines and energy policy. These clashes also affected the Liberal's ambitious agenda for national reconciliation, with a growing number of Indigenous peoples losing faith in Trudeau and his ability to deliver on his promises. Only a poor campaign by Conservative leader Andrew Scheer, which saw his party lose much support outside of its western Canadian base, allowed the Liberals to salvage a minority government in 2019. Scheer's fate as leader was sealed when he lost a winnable election, especially following the stunning mid-campaign revelation that Trudeau, who always proclaimed that diversity was Canada's strength, had appeared in blackface and brownface on several occasions.

COVID-19's Impact on a Divided Canada

The COVID-19 pandemic reached Canada in early 2020. Its arrival fundamentally altered these dynamics not only because of the very real public health crisis; it followed a significant shift in the political sphere as well. The most important and obvious shift domestically was its impact on politics and governance, as the federal election revealed the country to be politically and ideologically divided. Between the election and the arrival of the pandemic, the Trudeau government was very unpopular, sinking to less than 30% in some polls, and was confronting several nationwide protests. Yet less than two months into the pandemic, a "Team Canada" approach emerged. Liberal support rebounded while support for the Conservatives collapsed. This was compounded by the fact that the opposition Conservatives were in turmoil as they began the process of replacing their leader Andrew Scheer.

Despite the best efforts to bring the country together, the sheer length of the pandemic has produced growing cracks in unity and somewhat shaken Canadians' trust. As the second wave of COVID-19 hit in late 2020, more public protests against pandemic measures took place. Public opinion of the government's handling of the pandemic is divided along political and regional lines. Conservatives and residents of Alberta and Saskatchewan are most critical, reflecting post-election tensions (Angus Reid Institute 2020). "Corona fatigue" is due not only to the health, psychological, and economic tolls of the pandemic; the lack of a coherent nation-wide strategy has led to increased federal-provincial tensions over the funding of health care and the coordination of pandemic responses. The stop-start nature of containment and preventative measures combined with incoherent messaging both inside and across provinces has produced growing dissatisfaction with government efforts.

The federal Liberals initially received praise for taking the pandemic seriously, including regular briefings from the prime minister, and they developed generous economic relief programmes. However, Liberal strategy enraged critics who accused them of bypassing parliament and suppressing debate and scrutiny of its actions both before and during the pandemic. This included not maintaining an adequate supply of personal protective equipment prior to the current pandemic and changes to the administration and funding of the Public Health Agency of Canada, which led to a "breakdown" of Canada's pandemic early warning system (Robertson 2020). Canada's initial reaction was deemed "scattered and slow" (Doolittle et al. 2020); quicker action to contain the spread of the virus might have saved Canadian lives (Maher 2020; Cardoso and Wang 2020). This is not simply a matter of opponents scoring political points; the WE Charity scandal followed by stalling tactics in parliamentary committees and the sudden proroguing of parliament revealed the need for ongoing political accountability of the government; however, the Liberals and Conservatives instead bicker over who is to blame for the fact that Canada lost the ability to produce a COVID-19 vaccine. Thus, the pandemic reinforces the core question this volume looks to answer: How does an increasingly divided country engage a world that is itself divided?

The pandemic has reinforced the core challenges facing Canada: an underperforming economy marked by socioeconomic inequality, national disunity, and a tendency to engage in domestic politics rather than strategizing Canada's future. Recent political events regarding climate change, energy, racism (especially in the aftermath of the George Floyd murder in May 2020 in the USA), and the presidential election in the USA, all compounded by COVID-19, indicate that Canada will continue to face a crisis of governance. Threats to national unity undermine Canada's ability to engage as an effective international actor and its ability to promote its values and interests. This task is all the more complicated by the fact that global responses to the pandemic are all over the map, ranging from Germany's and South Korea's clinical and scientific approach to the incoherent and politically driven responses in the USA, the UK, and Brazil. By late 2020, several Asian countries were on track to improve their economic performance while North America and Europe experienced a crippling second wave of the pandemic, resulting in more lockdowns.

This was the inevitable outcome of the politicization of the pandemic, as it increasingly became enmeshed in China-US tensions. Even at the initial stages of the outbreak, extreme measures taken by China to contain the spread of the virus were roundly criticized. President Trump took to using racist tropes like "the China virus" and "Kung flu". He called the World Health Organization "very China-centric" and ultimately stopped American funding of the WHO. Trump and many governors "slow walked" the crisis to protect the US economy and secure votes in the November presidential, congressional, and state elections, even if the lives of hundreds of thousands of their fellow citizens were put at risk. Given that the USA is the world leader in health spending, the Trump administration seemingly believed it could manage the pandemic without resorting to costly options like containment and quarantine, ignoring that the American healthcare system was unequal, decentralized, and not efficient despite significant spending (Schneider et al. 2017).

Events in the USA have disproportionately affected Canada, given the close ties between the countries, and Canada's ability to respond is in many ways constrained by diminishing sovereignty vis-à-vis the USA (Carment and Sands 2019). Many of the most important decisions taken in response to COVID-19, such as reducing air traffic, restricting cross-border travel, and enforcing containment measures, were unprecedented. Some pundits could not understand the possibility that such extreme measures were appropriate to resilient Western political systems that placed individual freedom above all else (among others, see Black 2020). Even by November 2020, with the virus continuing to rage across the USA, Supreme Court Justice Samuel Alito stated that the pandemic has led to "previously unimaginable restrictions on individual liberty" (cited in Chappell 2020).

The politicization of the pandemic affected Canada and Canadians and how their governments responded to the pandemic. While Canadians are gravely concerned with the chaotic situation to the south, Canadian public opinion has also become very anti-China in recent years. Indeed, many Canadians are sceptical of the leadership of China, the USA, and Russia (Anderson 2020). Thus, the federal government has had to carefully calibrate its response between two broad outlooks.

On the one hand, the pandemic provided an opportunity for some to draw a favourable comparison between "our" political system and "theirs". Conservative leader Erin O'Toole has used the crisis as an opportunity to promote a hardened agenda against "communist China", who some blame for the outbreak, and thus want to delink from China economically and politically. Alberta premier Jason Kenney claimed that China would face a "reckoning" for how it handled the outbreak of the virus; he used the crisis as an opportunity to promote North American energy integration and the "reshoring" of manufacturing in Canada. Critics (among others, see Burney 2020) concerned about defence, intelligence, and security in the context of China-US tensions used the pandemic to criticize Canada for seemingly "kowtowing" to "bullies" like China, arguing that it is in Canada's interest to work alongside the US administration in its efforts to re-establish America's political and economic hegemony pre-crisis. COVID-19 has proven to be a policy tool to drive a deeper wedge between states rather than bringing them together. At the core is a need to ensure that America—and by extension

Canada—does not falter, and that any advantage that China might enjoy post-crisis is weakened.

On the other hand, polls regularly show that Canadians overwhelmingly rejected Trump's handling of the pandemic and would have voted for Joe Biden in the US election if given the chance; they also favoured keeping the border closed for an indeterminate period despite the importance of an open border for the economy, tourism, and family reasons. The Liberals have used the pandemic as an opportunity to reinforce Canada's commitment to multilateralism and engagement with the world, claiming that now is not the time to turn inwards. Emergency government activity and spending also means that this can be the perfect time to embrace a post-carbon economy while promoting economic nationalism. This desire for an economic shift long predates COVID-19 but is now catalysed and more unified due to some harsh realities, not the least of which is the extremely unattractive pricing of Alberta oil and its impact on the national economy. Thus, partly environmentally driven and partly driven by the view that confrontation is counterproductive to problem-solving a global crisis, there is a desire to invest more resources in health and economic well-being.

These are not "either/or" positions. Both conservatives and critics of neoliberalism, for example, see the pandemic as the opportunity to rethink globalization. COVID-19 thus poses several challenges for Canada, which has historically presented a united front globally that tends to ebb and flow, even in times of crisis. For example, the Spanish Flu (H1N1) pandemic of 1918 occurred at the tail end of World War I. Canadian deaths (55,000) nearly matched Canadian loss of life in World War I (60,000). A disproportionate number of the dead came from Indigenous communities, Labrador, and Québec. At the time, the government of Robert Borden did not offer a coherent response to the pandemic. In response, Canadians defied government orders to delay celebration of the end of World War I while municipalities set in motion a linked system of domestic healthcare initiatives. Similarly, in both world wars, Canadian domestic politics affected how Canada supported the war effort. Notably, two conscription crises, linked to the national question in Québec, showed how division affects Canada as a global actor.

The current pandemic has, in essence, put a pause on the sordid affairs of a country in disarray. Canadian leaders, provincial and federal, have begun to get along. Over the course of the spring and summer of 2020, they set aside their differences to face a common enemy. Provincial leaders, notably Premiers Legault of Québec and Ford of Ontario, who talked honestly and forthrightly to Canadians and even admitted that their actions were not always perfect, saw their popularity rise. Prime Minister Trudeau's Team Canada approach signalled the need to work together and support for the governing Liberals increased. Even Doug Ford and Chrystia Freeland claimed they were friends. Canadians placed their trust in science and public servants, many of whom are women, including Dr. Theresa Tam, Canada's Chief Public Health Officer. Unlike Donald Trump, Justin Trudeau's approval ratings soared after the pandemic began.

Nevertheless, division remains, notably from some pundits and opposition politicians. Among the more egregious, Trudeau's response to the crisis was said to reveal his "true authoritarian colours" (de Souza 2020). Beyond these superficial pronouncements, deep divisions endured. Conservative criticism of Canada's Chief Public Health Officer, Dr. Theresa Tam, was rooted not in policy debates but in politics. Dr. Tam and her colleagues became a proxy for criticizing the federal Liberal's handling of the crisis and to attack China. Outgoing federal Conservative leader Andrew Scheer and leadership hopefuls Peter Mackay and Erin O'Toole, along with Alberta premier Jason Kenney, voiced concerns about the WHO and China, echoing sentiments expressed by leading members of the Trump administration, most notably Secretary of State Michael Pompeo. Scheer also claimed that the opposition was ignored in Trudeau's Team Canada approach, even as the Liberals continued to modify pandemic responses due to opposition demands.

Politics as Usual: Unprepared for a More Dangerous World

The pandemic is forcing Canadians to debate their future in terms of health care, economic strategies, the role of government in the economy, and Canada's international affairs. However, as the pandemic endures, "politics as usual" informs the debate and federal-provincial tensions mount. Trudeau's ongoing commitment to building the Trans Mountain pipeline confounds environmentalists who say it will undermine Canada's climate change goals. Alberta Premier Kenney continues to push the federal government, noting how his commitment to building the Keystone XL pipeline (threatened by Joe Biden's promise to stop the project) was driven by his lack of trust in Trudeau's commitment to complete Trans Mountain. Right after Alberta announced a strategy for diversifying the petrochemical industry by recycling plastic, the federal government announced a ban on single-use plastics. Rumours that the September Speech from the Throne would feature a major green transformation initiative proved unfounded, perhaps connected to the fact that a major government survey showed that most Canadians did not see a green recovery plan as a priority (Akin 2020). Trudeau told the premiers to not prioritize the economy over the health of Canadians, while they responded by saying that the federal government needs to stay within its constitutional jurisdiction; if the federal government was concerned about the health of Canadians, it should transfer more money to the provinces. Trudeau in return said that there are limits to how much Canada can spend.

In brief, while the pandemic temporarily brought together the country at a time of great fear and uncertainty, underlying tensions persist and will worsen over time. Canada's reckoning is still to come. The pandemic has provoked a wide-ranging series of policy and political issues that must be addressed.[1] Not only is its long-term relationship with the USA being questioned (Nimijean and Carment 2020), so too is its position as an energy and natural resource exporter and its commitment to multilateralism. The pandemic has shone a light on ongoing systemic inequalities in Canadian society, given its unequal impact on Canadians, disproportionately affecting women, racial and ethnic minorities, Indigenous peoples, salaried workers, and people receiving social assistance.

Failure to seriously tackle these issues means that Canada was unprepared for the rapid pace of change experienced since Trudeau assumed office late in 2015. Consider the road travelled thus far since the hopeful and somewhat outdated optimism of the 2017 volume of *Canada Among Nations*: the rise of Donald Trump's iconoclastic demagoguery, his vision of "America first", and the shattering of traditional political norms domestically and in alliances; deep rifts in Canadian national unity, sharpened by a Trudeau minority in 2019; a destabilized system of international relations due to the actions of the USA; and an unchartered world beset by pandemic that also must deal with an urgent climate change crisis. After his presidential victory, Joe Biden, borrowing a line from Justin Trudeau, proclaimed that America was back, though given the failure of Democrats

---

[1] *Policy Options* has an ongoing excellent series on the pandemic and Canadian policy debates: see https://policyoptions.irpp.org.

to make inroads in congressional and state elections, it is hard to see how Biden's election alone will change this state of affairs.

If it is true, as Trudeau claimed in 2015, that Canada was back on the world stage, it has been a journey like no other. In hindsight, Trudeau's claim was more political posturing to distinguish his party from the preceding Harper government than a serious commitment to reinvigorate if not redefine Canada's place in the world (Nimijean 2018). With a shaky minority in hand, the governing Liberals now find themselves with the immense and important challenge of doing just that. Rhetoric alone will not address how a Liberal minority defines and enacts its commitments to multilateralism, respect for human rights, and support for the rule of law, all the while reclaiming Canada's position as a middle power with influence and pride of place. While substance, not style, will matter more than ever, there is no sign that the Liberals have given any serious thought about how to engage the world. Despite comprehensive defence and aid policy reviews, the Liberals have so far not seen the need to conduct a parallel foreign policy review to recalibrate Canada's national interests in an increasingly complex world. Former Foreign Affairs Minister Chrystia Freeland mostly played on the margins, making passing reference to the end of the liberal international order in speeches to parliament and American think tanks while devoting most of her energies to finalizing the Canada-EU trade deal and renegotiating NAFTA. Her successor François-Philippe Champagne made only indirect remarks to reengaging Canada globally at the onset of the pandemic and has been relatively quiet since then.

It is telling that more than five years after claiming that Canada *is back*, we continue to think about *how to be back*. 2015's election promised a shift to loftier values, a more open and transparent government, and a country where Canada could make a difference in the world. Trudeau's message that diversity was Canada's strength, combined with his declaration that Canada was back, came to a crashing and abrupt conclusion when the 2020 competition for a seat on the United Nations Security Council revealed that just a few countries took Trudeau and his promises seriously.

More disturbingly, the Liberals have still not clarified what a revitalized Canadian foreign policy strategy might look like. Instead, Canadians continue to be treated to "Brand Canada", even if the image has been tarnished greatly. This is because Trudeau's emerging global celebrity initially helped raise Canada's foreign policy agenda to lofty unobtainable virtues and values (Marland and Nimijean this volume). It was often said that Canada in 2015 stood out as "a beacon of hope" in an age of growing global discontent, a message Trudeau conveyed when Canada celebrated the 150th anniversary of Confederation in 2017. Geography allowed Trudeau to stand in stark contrast to new American president Donald Trump. Peak Trudeaumania followed Donald Trump's election as American president. There was the obvious contrast between the young, dapper, and emoting Trudeau and his belief in internationalism and social equality, versus the ageing, outspoken, and nativist Trump who believed in America First and believed that borders needed walls and other barriers to keep people and threats out (Carment and Sands 2019). When Trump immediately tried to implement an Executive Order banning people from seven Muslim-majority countries from entering the USA, Trudeau in response tweeted that Canada was a welcoming country. Trudeau's popularity soared following Trump's personal insults against Trudeau in the summer of 2018 during contentious NAFTA negotiations, with American opponents of Trump asking why Trudeau could not be their president (Nimijean 2017).

However, just a few short years after Trump's election, Canada became a very different, inward-looking, and arguably more cynical country, far from the optimistic one that celebrated its Centennial of Confederation in 1967. The political landscape changed dramatically, but so too did the rhetoric. The corrosive effects of Trump-style populism took root in Canada. MAGA spawned a "Make Canada Great Again" movement. 2017 Conservative leadership hopeful Kelly Leitch promised a Canadian values test for immigrants, a view supported by many Canadians at the time (CROP 2017). While Canadians decried racism in the USA, overt acts of racism towards Asian-Canadians increased once the pandemic began. New Conservative leader Erin O'Toole, a former corporate lawyer and son of a long-time provincial politician, promised to "take Canada back" from elites with a "Canada First" approach that would be tough on China while promoting national economic self-sufficiency.

While Trudeau has rebranded as the silent, serious leader with a greying beard and O'Toole is now softening the harder edges of his leadership campaign platform to increase his party's appeals to Canadians, where this leads, nobody knows. The only certainty is that division and uncertainty will reign for the foreseeable future.

CANADA IN A POST-PANDEMIC WORLD?

As the chapters in this volume argue, these divisions, whether reflected in political or economic instability or international uncertainty, will affect Canada's domestic situation and its ability to engage as an effective global actor. In reviewing the contributions to this volume, we begin with a far-reaching and comprehensive overview of Canada's place in the world by Lloyd Axworthy, "Reflections on 2020: Awakening to a World at Risk". Drawing on a lifetime of experience in international affairs and politics, Axworthy sets the stage for the chapters that follow. Rather than looking at divisions at home and thinking about how this affects our ability to act in a dangerous world, this chapter presents to the reader how a prepared Canada can make a difference. To make this change we will need determined and thoughtful leadership, parliamentary discussion, and an informed public. Throughout the chapter, Axworthy seeks answers to his core question: Can we overcome the frailties of a minority government, divided federalism, burgeoning budgets, and weakened diplomatic and defence assets? In answering this question, the chapter comprehensively sets the scene through a personalized and human-centred perspective.

In the second section of the volume, we review how deep divisions at home impact foreign policy and Canada's place in the world. Chapter two, "Rebranding Brand Trudeau" by Alex Marland and Richard Nimijean, examines how Trudeau's brand image evolved since 2015 and explores the implications of a diminished brand for Canada's place in the world in 2020. Though Canada consistently ranks high in terms of national brand, that brand has not played out in terms of re-establishing Canada's place as a player in international affairs. A case in point was the disastrous UNSC seat bid in which a majority of UN members said no to the Trudeau government. One of the reasons for this and other turnarounds is that Canada's brand has suffered due to political scandal, policy shortcomings, and poor expectations management. The authors examine the implications of contrasting brands in the context of the new dynamics of a minority parliament and the government's ability to address global challenges.

In his chapter "Balancing Interests and Constraints: The Role of Provinces in the Shaping of Canadian Foreign Policy", Nelson Michaud asks whether the COVID-19 crisis has dampened the increasingly influential role provinces play in the making and implementation of foreign policy. This rise is not without its problems as tensions between the provinces and Liberals on the foreign policy front were also on the upswing. Showing that the growth of parastatal foreign policy and globalization worked hand in hand, Michaud notes the domination of the current agenda by the national government as COVID-19 peels back many of the perceived gains that globalization engendered. Indeed, the COVID-19 crisis has encouraged the federal government to dominate the stage on many policy issues. Exploring international law, constitutional frameworks, provincial administration of international issues, and paying special attention to Québec, the most active province in this regard, Michaud concludes that provincial actors prefer to face this tumultuous world by putting aside long held antagonistic views on climate change, pipelines, and the environment as a more efficient way to advance their mainly economic interests.

In his chapter, "Beneath the Skin: Canadian Global Health Policy in the time of a Pandemic", Robert Huish argues that COVID-19 will have a lasting impact on Canada's place in the world. Like Michaud, Huish believes the federal government has been front and centre in terms of health care since the pandemic began. However, Huish argues there will be considerable room to advance provincial leadership, creating new opportunities to not only bring a distinctly Canadian approach to health care but to distance Canada from the USA, whose pandemic strategy thus far appears to be in disarray if not an outright failure. The tumultuous and divisive US election only heightens the need for Canada to chart its own course even more. Huish also raises the question as to whether provinces, especially those in the increasingly fragile "Atlantic bubble", should pursue their own foreign relations by partnering with other countries, or intra-national jurisdictions, that have similar numbers of COVID-19.

In her chapter, "Geopolitics and Diplomacy in Canadian Arctic Relations", Kari Roberts advances the argument that with climate change, Canada will increasingly find itself competing with three great powers in the region—the USA, Russia, and China. The current Liberal government, which has not emphasized Arctic policy nearly as much as Harper and the Conservatives, will need to harness the economic potential the Arctic holds and protect the region from potential geopolitical conflict. To complicate matters, Canada faces its own set of challenges with all three countries. It is all the more surprising that Trudeau's Liberals have de-emphasized Arctic policy, especially when it comes to critical and overlapping issues such as energy, climate change, and Indigenous communities. The COVID-19 pandemic further complicates inaction on this file, as it has forced many nations, including Canada, to scale back or even suspend key initiatives.

In his chapter on identity and global populism, Frank Graves draws on recent polling data to get a sense of how divided Canada really is. Graves shows that despite assertions to the contrary from all levels of government, authoritarian populism is a major new force in Canadian society, reinforced by the US election which clearly showed that Trumpism is no aberration or ephemeral force in US politics. Populism, it seems, is here to stay, at least south of the border. Indeed, the same authoritarian reflex which has reshaped Western democracies in recent years (e.g. the election of Donald Trump, Brexit, and beyond) has found a foothold in Canada for many of the same reasons. Not only are we experiencing intense new levels of political polarization, the traditional left-right axis has shifted to an open-ordered axis. The contest for the future now revolves around whether to turn back the clock and pull up the drawbridge or to embrace a more open-cosmopolitan posture. Clearly, this will have profound implications for how Canada constructs its foreign policy in the near future. Not only is the country deeply divided in an arguably unprecedented fashion, but the broad issue of how we see our place in the world is at the centre of this debate.

In writing on the future of the Conservative Party of Canada, Paul Gecelovsky provides an interesting and important contrast to chapters in this book which are focused primarily on the Liberal party and how it has helped shape the future of Canada in a divided world. Instead, Gecelovsky examines the foreign policy platform of the Conservative Party of Canada and in doing so demonstrates that a grass-roots, populist-oriented agenda portends the future for the Conservative party if not Canada. Indeed, while many may regard Trumpian (and Harperian) politics as passé, Gecelovsky shows that the Conservatives intend to tap into much of the sentiment if not the strategies espoused by Trump and his followers. His study builds on prior ideas such as personal responsibility and the end of the Laurentian elite that emerged under the Harper government, reflecting an increasing disenchantment with elitist, progressive, and centralized politics in favour of a common-sense agenda grounded in the day-to-day experiences of ordinary Canadians. Such ideas tap into the perceived alienation many Canadians feel from the Liberal agenda and express a desire to regroup under a national and potentially "delinked" political and economic agenda.

The third section of the volume examines how Canada acts in this divided world. Chris Kilford examines Canada's diplomatic and military presence in the Middle East, arguably the most divided region of the world and one that Canada has tried to stay involved in since advancing a peacekeeping agenda in the 1950s. Kilford's chapter broadly examines Canada's contemporary strategic engagement in the Middle East and North Africa and provides policy options and advice in support of Canada's future national interests. Kilford shows that the long-term effort of engagement may well pay off as the region overcomes the frailties brought upon it by climate change, political upheaval, and civil strife. Indeed, Canadian citizens and businesses are becoming increasingly engaged in the region while immigrants, political refugees, and students flow in the other direction seeking new opportunities in Canada

In his chapter, Michael Manulak shows that an important part of the Trudeau government's international policies has been its embrace of informal international institutions. Manulak argues that the choice of informal institutions has been driven by geopolitical shifts. For example, the creation of the Ministerial Coordination Group on COVID-19 (MCGC) is a means of generating an international response to the obstruction of global supply-chains and transportation hubs. According to Manulak, this institution offers a flexible vehicle for managing uncertainty and addressing a fast-moving crisis. Such informal institutions are likely to become an increasingly prevalent mode of international cooperation in a post-COVID-19 world.

In a much-needed update to current assessments of the Liberal party's feminist agenda, Rebecca Tiessen examines the global context in which feminist foreign policy is becoming increasingly popular; the current state of Canada's feminist foreign policy; and considerations for Canada's next steps in the creation of an expanded vision of a feminist foreign policy in light of the COVID-19 pandemic. Tiessen concludes that it is too early to say if Canada has achieved the traction on this file to claim a leadership role. This is in part due to the distraction that COVID-19 poses to the Liberal agenda, but also because Trudeau himself has recast his image as inward-looking and almost patriarchal.

Building on insights from the Tiessen chapter, Stephen Brown examines Canada's all-important aid envelope in the context of the global COVID-19 pandemic. COVID-19 not only forced the Liberals to rethink their development policies in general terms, it also stressed government expenditures as new priorities quickly piled up in the most dire regions of the world. Despite multiple government announcements proclaiming Canada's leadership role, the shift in financial priorities has been modest at best. Brown concludes that the Liberals continue to use aid policy primarily for domestic political purposes rather than significantly stepping up their efforts to meet global development challenges.

Duane Bratt digs through the controversies embedded in the unravelling China-Canada relationship. As we showed above, COVID-19 has fundamentally changed the relationship between Canada, China, and the USA. It has led to rising anti-China sentiment, calls for re-shoring essential products, and pledges in both the USA and Canada to hold China "accountable" for the pandemic. However, the relations between China and Canada/USA were problematic before COVID-19. Bratt's chapter examines Canada's economic, diplomatic, and security relations with China in the context of a series of clashes between the USA and China. It also considers the situation of Huawei and Canada's 5G network; the arrest of Meng Wanzhou on a US extradition request; Chinese trade embargoes in pork, beef, and canola; the collapse of free trade talks; and the imprisonment of prominent Canadians in China.

In their chapter on mobilizing Canada's diaspora during crisis, Milana Nikolko, Sam MacIsaac, and David Carment advance an understanding of the limitations and strengths of Canada's diaspora support to improving gender dynamics in situations of state fragility. Drawing on studies by Tiessen and others, the authors argue that though the Canadian government frequently cites the correlation between gender empowerment and stability, the impact that Canada is having on gender dynamics is not as strong as it could be. In particular, they argue that Ukraine poses a number of challenges to Canada's gender-based policies. Ukrainian women have become a crucial part of the informal economy, dependent on remittances but also increasingly present in a variety of informal activities. This suggests an expanded gender-driven policy that includes the foreign activities of labour migrants, remittance flows, household work, and other labour roles, including traditionally unpaid or self-employed work performed by women. The authors conclude by suggesting that Canada's diaspora can help encourage Ukrainian women to take on a more significant role in the formal economy.

In their concluding chapter, the editors and Sydney Stewart show that Canada is not fully prepared to engage a divided world, as seen in the numerous political, economic, and social challenges that continue to keep Canadians from pursuing an interest-based foreign policy agenda. Indeed, it can be convincingly argued that for the last 40 years or so, so-called Canadian values have substituted for promoting Canada's interests. They argue that this approach and the lack of a strategic vision for Canada's place in the world has left Canada ill-equipped to deal with these tumultuous times, never mind a leading or coordinating role. Canada's election loss at the UNSC is reflective of a stark reality: the world wants Canada to act, not just talk.

Canada is in a difficult spot: hobbled by and dependent on America's political and economic self-interests, on the one hand, while unable or unwilling to engage rising powers economically and politically, on the other. When asked what the Liberals should do to achieve an effective foreign policy, former Prime Minister Jean Chrétien advised that they must "talk to everybody and offer a solution" (Quoted in CTV News 2015). Since Stéphane Dion was removed from Foreign Affairs in 2016, the Liberals have tended to avoid this advice, and Canada is paying the price for not confronting growing tensions between China and the USA. Unable to articulate its own clear path ahead, the major power standoff has exposed Canadian economic and security vulnerabilities; a Biden presidency, while welcomed by Canadians, will not fundamentally alter the situation. A tumultuous 2020 has put Canada at a crossroads, thus necessitating a serious examination of Canada's role in the world and a commitment to act to promote its interests.

References

Akin, David. 2020. "Coronavirus: As Canadians Huddled at Home, Feds Found Meagre Support for Green Recovery Plan." *Global News*, October 18. https://globalnews.ca/news/7402329/coronavirus-canadian-green-recovery-poll/.

Anderson, Bruce. 2020. "The New World Order Is Disorder." *National Observer*, May 25. https://www.nationalobserver.com/2020/05/25/opinion/new-world-order-disorder.

Angus Reid Institute. 2020. "Most Say Trudeau Government Handling COVID-19 Crisis Well, But Liberals, Cpc Remain in Virtual Tie on Vote Intent." http://angusreid.org/wp-content/uploads/2020/11/2020.11.09_Nov_Federal_Politics.pdf.

Black, Conrad. 2020. "Conrad Black on COVID-19: The World Succumbed to a Pandemic of Hysteria, More Than a Virus." *National Post*, March 27. https://nationalpost.com/opinion/conrad-black-on-covid-19-the-world-succumbed-to-a-pandemic-of-hysteria-more-than-a-virus.

Burney, Derek H. 2020. "Derek H. Burney on COVID-19: It's Hard for Canada to Stand Up to China While It's Bowing." *National Post*, May 14. https://nationalpost.com/opinion/derek-h-burney-on-covid-hard-for-canada-to-stand-up-to-china-while-its-on-its-knees-bowing.

Cardoso, Tom, and Chen Wang. 2020. "'We Could Have Saved Lives': Did Ottawa's Spring Break COVID-19 Travel Advisory Come Too Late?" *Globe and Mail*, May 4. https://www.theglobeandmail.com/canada/article-we-could-have-saved-lives-did-ottawas-spring-break-covid-19-travel/.

Carment, David, and Christopher Sands, eds. 2019. *Canada–US Relations: Sovereignty or Shared Institutions?* Springer.

Carment, David, and Dani Belo. 2020. "Security First in a Post-Pandemic World? Grey-Zone Conflict and Shifting Alliances." *Canadian Global Affairs Institute*. https://www.cgai.ca/security_first_in_a_post_pandemic_world_grey_zone_conflict_and_shifting_alliances.

Chappell, Bill. 2020. "Justice Alito: Pandemic Has Brought 'Unimaginable Restrictions' On Freedoms." *NPR*, November 13. https://www.npr.org/2020/11/13/934666499/justice-alito-pandemic-has-brought-unimaginable-restrictions-on-freedoms?t=1605351798954.

CROP. 2017. "LES CANADIENS, LE POPULISME ET LA XÉNOPHOBIE." Radio Canada. https://ici.radio-canada.ca/nouvelles/special/2017/03/sondage-crop/Sondage%20CROP-Radio-Canada.pdf.

CTV News. 2015. "Chretien's Advice to Trudeau on Foreign Policy: 'Talk to Everybody'." *CTV News*, October 25. https://www.ctvnews.ca/politics/chretien-s-advice-to-trudeau-on-foreign-policy-talk-to-everybody-1.2626606.

De Souza, Raymond J. 2020. "Raymond J. de Souza: When the Going Got Tough Due to COVID-19, Justin Trudeau Showed His True Authoritarian Colours." *National Post*, May 27. https://nationalpost.com/opinion/raymond-j-de-souza-when-the-going-got-tough-due-to-covid-19-justin-trudeau-showed-his-true-authoritarian-colours.

Doolittle, Robyn, Michelle Carbert, and Daniel Leblanc. 2020. "Canada's Lost Months: When COVID-19's First Wave Hit, Governments and Health Officials Were Scattered and Slow to Act." *Globe and Mail*, June 25. https://www.theglobeandmail.com/canada/investigations/article-canadas-lost-months-when-covid-19s-first-wave-hit-governments-and/.

Maher, Stephen. 2020. "Where Canada's Coronavirus Response Wasn't Good Enough." *Maclean's*, April 14. https://www.macleans.ca/opinion/where-canadas-coronavirus-response-wasnt-good-enough/.

Nimijean, Richard. 2017. "A Portrait of Justin Trudeau." *The Monitor*, August 24. https://www.policyalternatives.ca/publications/monitor/portrait-justin-trudeau.

Nimijean, Richard. 2018. "Introduction: Is Canada Back? Brand Canada in a Turbulent World." *Canadian Foreign Policy Journal* 24 (2): 127–138.

Nimijean, Richard, and David Carment. 2020. "Rethinking the Canada-Us Relationship After the Pandemic." *Policy Options*, May 7. https://policyopt ions.irpp.org/magazines/may-2020/rethinking-the-canada-us-relationship-after-the-pandemic/.

Robertson, Grant. 2020. "Ottawa Names Three Experts to Review Breakdown of Pandemic Early Warning System." *Globe and Mail*, November 18. https://www.theglobeandmail.com/canada/investigations/article-ottawa-names-three-experts-to-review-breakdown-of-pandemic-early/.

Schneider, Eric C, Dana O. Sarnak, David Squires, Arnav Shah, and Micelle M. Doty. 2017. "Mirror, Mirror 2017: International Comparison Reflects Flaws and Opportunities for Better U.S. Health Care." The Commonwealth Fund. https://interactives.commonwealthfund.org/2017/july/mirror-mirror/.

Thomson, Stuart. 2020. "'Canada Is Broken,' Say Majority of Canadians in Poll Taken in Wake of Rail Blockades." *National Post*, February 28. https://nationalpost.com/news/one-thing-canadians-arent-div ided-on-blaming-the-government.

CHAPTER 2

Reflections on 2020: Awakening to a World at Risk

Lloyd Axworthy

INTRODUCTION

This chapter begins with a wakeup call: 2020 has ushered in a confluence of global threats creating an uncharted and hazardous landscape that Canada must navigate. Big power realignments, weakening of the international liberal order, economic doomsday on the horizon and loss of trust in governments cause added handicaps. Our recent foreign policy performances will be examined to suggest ways to move forward by building on our experience as a respected global player carefully treading the role of good ally and independent middle power. This will be followed by a proposition on how Canada should address an interlace of domestic and international reforms enabling the country to continue playing an effective role in the world. Finally, I lay out a set of choices this country might make to travel a secure, sensible, successful, sustainable pathway in this time of global existential risk. COVID-19 should not become a justification for delaying a game plan for the global future. I use as a mantra what

L. Axworthy (✉)
Chair, World Refugee and Migration Council, Winnipeg, MB, Canada

© The Author(s), under exclusive license to Springer Nature   23
Switzerland AG 2021
D. Carment and R. Nimijean (eds.), *Political Turmoil
in a Tumultuous World*, Canada and International Affairs,
https://doi.org/10.1007/978-3-030-70686-9_2

Toby Ord (2020: 14) argues in his book *The Precipice*, "safeguarding humanity is the defining challenge of our time."

WINNIPEG, MANITOBA, AUGUST 2020

On a sunny morning several months into the COVID-19 pandemic, I begin to ruminate on the text of this essay. Normally a time of late summer respite from winter bundling up. Now a time of angst, uncertainty and a growing sense of dread as the disease surges throughout the globe. My wife Denise and I have begun our morning routine of coffee and semi-masochistic perusal of news, first checking on the latest epidemic announcements from Manitoba, Canada and then horrifyingly, the myriad of hot spots in the United States and around the world.

It's sobering. Optimistic hopes of a month ago have relapsed into reports of new outbreaks in places like Germany, Taiwan, Korea and in our own provincial and national bailiwicks that had seen to be on a positive downward curve. Our neighbour to the South is plagued by an out-of-control pandemic and the flailings of an out-of-control president. The global economy is volatile, likely heading into a deep recession. There is evidence of global disarray and disillusionment. The World Health Organization President appears on the screen, dishevelled and distraught as he warns of the risk of "response fatigue" given the socio-economic pressures on most countries and the anticipated lengthy duration of COVID-19.

Equally threatening is the hovering shadow of climate change. UN reports released this summer forecast severe weather impacts resulting in the migration of displaced persons. The Head of UNHCR, Fillipo Grande intones "The world needs to prepare for millions of people being driven from their homes by the impact of climate change" (CBC NEWS 2020). There is a dire warning from one of the world's recognized experts on infectious diseases; "Fauci and epidemiologist David Morens, his National Institute of Allergy and Infectious Diseases (NIAID) colleague, foresee an accelerating rate of pandemics in the years ahead driven largely by deforestation, urban crowding, and wet markets for wild game, which will make increasing environmental degradation worldwide in this century" (Vergano 2020). A long-term cocktail of calamity is in the offing.

Add to the brew is the imminence of a new nuclear arms race as the Americans, Russians and Chinese modernize their arsenals. The smaller nuke wannabees like North Korea and Iran flex their muscles. Arms control agreements are being shredded.

It's not a world well prepared to cope. Great power strife is on the rise and there is a posse of political leaders who exploit the worst angels of our nature, abetted by a social media that fosters the resentments of growing numbers of disaffected citizens. Anna Applebaum (2020: 102) in her book *The Twilight of Democracy* describes how the algorithms of social media "encourage false perceptions, fostering polarized emotions, leading to hyper partisanship that feeds distrust of mainstream politics and promotes extremism and fragments common purpose or consensus."

THE YEAR OF THE BLACK SWANS

In 2007, Nassim Nicholas Taleb used the concept of "Black Swans" to explain unpredictable events that have massive impacts on human society. They are the "unknown unknowns" for which even our most comprehensive models can't account. He warns about the "naïve empiricists"—who think that our tomorrows are likely to be pretty much like our yesterdays and fail to understand the magnitude of change that's underway (Avishai 2020).

It is a precarious perch upon which to pivot forward, especially as the horizon is so murky. Many people are dispirited. They want to escape the lockdowns, the closed temples of sports, entertainment and religion, and desire a return to normalcy of work, school, travel and personal contact. The impulse to ignore public health precautions and urge undisciplined re-opening is the propaganda of a cadre of populist opportunists who disregard science and the welfare of their own people.

Fortunately, they are not the only voices. There is a rising chorus of calls proposing a post-epidemic recovery strategy that fosters a sustainable development agenda. A group of twenty-two prominent economists wrote that:

> Even as climate breakdown looms around the corner, the pressure to return to the old carbon-based economy is real – and all the more dangerous, given the fundamental instability of an economy rooted in injustice. Sources of large-scale human suffering, such as crop failures, water shortages, rising tides, wildfires, severe weather, forced migration and pandemics, go hand-in-hand with a warming world. (Sachs et al. 2020)

The deep discrimination in our global economic system has been exposed, revealing global patterns of trade, taxation, supply chains and investment that foster inequality. UN Secretary General Guterres in this year's Mandela lecture pointed out,

> The expansion of trade, and technological progress, have contributed to 'an unprecedented shift in income distribution'. Low-skilled workers are bearing the brunt, he warned, and face an "onslaught" from new technologies, automation, the offshoring of manufacturing and the demise of labor organizations. (UN News 2020)

This global septic tank is full of casualties. The UN Security Council is paralysed. Humanitarian agencies are woefully underfunded. Demagogues attack international governance on peacemaking, conflict resolution, migration management, refugee protection and development aid. Some regional bodies like the African Union show resilience, and others such as the OAS and the Commonwealth are hollow shells. Institutions established to further strengthen the rule of law such as the International Criminal Court struggle against attacks from the United States, Russia and China. The G-7 and G-20 have become annual showcases with little to show in real achievements.

The geopolitical situation throughout most of 2020 has been marked by conundrums. Canadians have been perplexed and worried by the unravelling of the American polity, verging on a breakdown of democratic norms and the undermining of international cooperative action. The Biden election has given respite to such concerns and opened up possibilities of a return to a more compatible relationship with Americans. There is an opportunity to initiate joint efforts on key global challenges such as the epidemic, climate change, trade, energy, security cooperation and hopefully migration and refugee issues. However, the Canadian government would be wise not to return to a pre-COVID-19 playbook. As argued earlier, it is time to re-set, not fall into old ruts. The Biden administration will have its hands full in meeting domestic expectations and dealing with the defeated but not repudiated former president. There will continue to be deep political divisions fuelled by Trump's administration and supporters' efforts to de-legitimize Biden just as they did with Obama. It is in our interest to carefully use the time of transitioning into January 20th to work on our mutual priorities. A continental strategy among the NAFTA partners on climate, conservation and energy incorporating differences on a cross border fossil fuel tax and the XL pipeline would be welcome, as would be an upgrading of Canada/US efforts on Arctic security, transportation and sustainable development and a re-thinking of border controls including the Third Party Agreement on refugees.

The same broad-based policy development is needed in China. The present situation is a Gordian Knot. The government's acquiescence to American demands to extradite Madame Meng Wanzhou and China's retaliatory imprisonment of Canadians Michael Kovrig and Michael Spavor have resulted in a diplomatic box and an ethical quandary. I was signatory to a letter to the Prime Minister from over twenty diplomats/academics and former politicians experienced in consular negotiations and hostage situations and that urged a diplomatic exchange, rebuffed by the Prime Minister and latched onto by various right-wing commentators as giving into China, just the opposite of our intentions. The standoff has not only resulted in continuing suffering of the two men and their families but a handcuffing of Canadian policy. The growing aggressiveness of China and the countermeasures of the United States require skilful manoeuvring by Canada, not bromides and slogans. It would be very helpful if the new American administration would withdraw the Trump request for the extradition of Madam Weng.

The stifling of minority rights and takeover of Hong Kong should be front and centre on our foreign policy screen. What's clear is the need to open alternate tracks of discussion especially in the context of the powerful surge of Asian countries and our need to be in concert with this shift of economic, security and environmental centres of power. The braggadocio tough line of the new Official Opposition leader is a reprise of Cold War rhetoric. Canadian diplomacy vis a vis China is at a tipping point and we need a balanced, skilful mix of containment/engagement initiatives.

The Chinese strategy to make an imprint on the UN should bear special attention from Canada. Its goal is to enforce a strict observance of non-interference in sovereign matters which runs totally counter to our interests in promoting accountability for violence against citizens and human rights transgressions (Lee 2020). This should inspire to join an effort with other UN members, particularly the Americans, to organize against this scheme. Bringing the large-scale abuse of the Uyghurs to the attention of the UN Human Rights Council would be a start, seeing as China has just become a member.

One arena where the big power rivalry will directly impinge on our interests is in the Arctic. There is already security, environmental and economic competition in the region with growing evidence of Russian militarization, unilateral US defence preparation and Chinese assertion of the area as part of their Silk Road strategy (see Roberts this volume). There are warnings of thawing permafrost releasing unknown pathogens, drawing further urgency to cooperate on science and health initiatives among the polar communities (Heffernan 2018). As the ice continues to melt, it will be important to update the architecture of the Arctic Council in order to promote further cooperation on climate issues and offset unilateral expansion of security grabs by the "Bully Battalions."

The voice of Black Lives Matter has brought further exposure to the inequity of racial discrimination, a movement that has worldwide manifestations. In Canada, it has thrown a new light on the human rights abuses against Indigenous peoples, African-Canadians and other minority communities. The tardiness in implementing the recommendations of the Missing and Murdered Indigenous Women inquiry is a negative factor affecting our perception abroad.

One of the pluses arising out of the protests on racial inequities in the midst of the pandemic is the catapulting into public awareness a new generation of woman leaders. The victory of Kamala Harris as a black woman candidate for Vice President is an inflection moment. Angela Merkel has shown the value of experience, skill and empathetic instincts in leading her country on a principled refugee policy in 2015 and then laying out a series of effective COVID-19-related actions as have the prime ministers of New Zealand, Denmark, Finland and Taiwan. *NY Times* headlined the effectiveness of women in dealing with coronavirus, employing a style based on developing trust, showing empathy, being evidence savvy and taking tough decisions (Taub 2020). It stands in stark contrast to the conniving buffoonery and savagery of Trump, Bolsonaro, Johnson and other of their ilk.

The Good, the Bad and the Ugly governmental performances bared open in the last several pandemic months underscore the singular importance of good governance. The attack against public institutions that Reagan, Thatcher and their followers unloosed on the world in the early 1980s dismissed the constructive role that governments can and must play in defending the common good. The pandemic has exposed how autocratic, corrupt, nationalist government are the ones screwing the works.

Social media has given a powerful tool to disrupt traditional election practices and leads to centralized authority bordering on fascism and certainly unaccountability. The emergence of AI poses serious threats to algorithms ruling the world. But there is a push back. The power of the street, civil non-violent protest and digital networks that give voice to ordinary citizens is showcasing how to govern more openly and democratically. It opens possibilities of transformative reform. Marilynne Robinson (2020: 1) has set out this proposition:

> Without an acknowledgment of the grief brought into the whole world by the coronavirus, which is very much the effect of sorrows that plagued the world before this crisis came down on us, it might seem like blindness or denial to say that the hiatus prompted by the crisis may offer us an opportunity for a great emancipation, one that would do the whole world good... Options now suddenly open to us would have been unthinkable six months ago.

WAYFARING: LOOKING BACK TO LOOK AHEAD

In her book, *The Next Great Migration*, Sonia Shah (2020: 217) describes how in the 1770s Polynesian adventurers traversed 2700 miles of open ocean between Tahiti and Hawaii in thirty-four days. Drawing on the sun, moon, stars, winds, currents, flights of birds and making thousands of observations a day, they used a form of navigation called wayfaring. It is a good way to understand how to navigate our present unknowns. Tap into the knowledge of previous generations and seek out coordinates guided by careful study of the lessons imbedded in the inherent wisdom of nature and history. It means jettisoning the prevailing practice of governance by sleight of hand, secrecy, spin and self-serving transactions.

I make a case that since World War II until the early 2000s Canada had been following a form of wayfarer's navigation, rooted in a set of historical values, current interests determined by a reading of our expansive geography, a small but shifting demographic reality and diverse religious and cultural experiences. It was a pathway originally constructed around its sharing of North America with an Alpha country, the continuing ties with Great Britain and Europe, the Commonwealth and the Atlantic-euro centric connection. Then came a layering in of the emerging salience of post-colonial Southern nations and people.

As a high school student in the multi-cultural North end of Winnipeg, I was taken by the words of Lester Pearson in a speech in the old Winnipeg Auditorium. He set out how Canada is distinct: active participation in multilateral cooperation, promoting diplomacy to resolve conflicts, maintaining a friendly but independent relationship with the Americans, engaging in efforts to reduce the risks of nuclear weapons and pioneering development initiatives such as the Colombo plan; in effect being global citizens was our kismet.

There were pivotal moments when Canada showed spunk and innovation. Trap lines were laid that gave purpose and guidance to our foreign policy. Pearson's 1956 UN leadership on peacekeeping during the Suez crisis, his opposition to the Vietnam War and his dedication to the 0.7% of GDP goal on international aid set down important markers. Pierre Trudeau established international institutions such as CIDA and IDRC to build bridges with developing countries, co-chairing the historic North-South Summit. He travelled to the portals of great powers to restart nuclear arms control talks. His government made major changes in refugee policy including the unique private refugee sponsorship programme. John Turner led the charge on using an election to debate the proposed Free Trade deal, thus showing that democratic decisions on international priorities can be the focus of an election campaign. Brian Mulroney's break with Thatcher on apartheid in South Africa was a significant move. He authored our participation in the first sustainable development conference in Rio and negotiated the Acid Rain agreement with United States. Jean Chrétien's government undertook the Team Canada trade initiatives and the application of a human security thrust that led to the Anti-Personnel Land Mines Treaty and the International Criminal Court. His decision to stay out of the American invasion of Iraq was a smart and brave move. The Canadian public was generally supportive of Canada's course of international leadership and applauded these activist foreign policy initiatives.

Constraints are constant. Our federalist constitution requires an honouring of provincial positions, especially of Québec's interests. Business pressure to integrate economically with the Americans is a given. The emergence of the Global South led to important revisions in aid, immigration and refugee policies requiring a clear definition of multi-cultural rights. The reach of our diplomatic network in a more diverse global landscape ran up against fiscal restraints. The tricky issues of intervention to meet civil genocide and oppression in places like Rwanda, Timor-Leste and Kosovo were a domestic challenge that became significant in the 1990s, giving forth the Canadian sponsored R2P concept adopted by the UN Leaders' Summit in 2005. It won for Canada respect and soft power influence. But the world was about to shift.

The shock of 9/11 and the threat of terrorism created a new set of security risks and the arrival of a more muscular military approach to our international persona. Paul Martin's government negotiated a far-reaching set of border arrangements, including the controversial Safe Third Party Agreement that has entangled us in the punitive refugee policies of the Trump administration ever since. He brought Canada into the Afghan war and his Defence Chief, General Rick Hillier, downgraded peacemaking efforts and pushed the notion of Canada as a warrior nation. The Afghan involvement dominated Canadian thought and action for over a decade, sidelining other critical concerns. To Martin's credit, aided by Ambassador Allan Rock, he became an ardent advocate of the R2P concept at the UN.

In 2006, Stephen Harper became Prime Minister, inheriting the Afghan mission. He found this military-dominated policy compatible with his rejection of human security concepts and his anti-internationalist approach. He was disdainful of the UN, froze foreign aid, abandoned a balance to Middle East issues and eviscerated our diplomatic presence while muzzling our diplomats and ignoring African and Latin American states. It was not just a course correction but a juncture towards foreign policy instructed increasingly by ideology and religion. The internationalist chronicle lost salience with Canadians and our range of policy options languished.

The 2015 election saw the Liberals return to power under Justin Trudeau. He immediately announced that Canada was back as an internationally committed player. And, in his early years, he walked the talk by his actions to resettle Syrian refugees. Of particular note was his dedication to becoming a feminist PM, resulting in a gender-balanced cabinet and shifting focus of foreign development assistance towards promoting empowerment of women and girls. He was greeted on the world stage as a fresh, charismatic leader.

Then, in 2016, Americans elected Donald Trump. Canadians soon learned that they now shared the North American rock with a government that saw Canada through the lens of being a liberal, internationalist proponent/opponent. Trump demanded the renegotiation of NAFTA[1] and then imposed tariffs on Canadian exports on the pretext that we were a "security risk." Another prop pulled out was the ferocious attack by Trump on multilateral arrangements, pulling out of the Iran nuclear arms agreements, and withdrawing from the Trans-Pacific Trade Partnership and Paris Climate Accords. His only appearance on Canadian soil was a cameo appearance at the G7 meetings in Charlevoix where he roiled the meeting and on his plane ride back, tweeted unseemly comments about his Canadian host. Wariness and watchfulness became the watchword in Ottawa. Living next to a contentious neighbour for the past four years prompted a reset of US relations even before COVID-19. Trump became an Ottawa preoccupation, leading to reduced activity on a range of other files. Canada has had a diminished voice on human rights issues, plight of refugees and disarmament. Our international preparation for epidemics was severely downgraded. Relations and diplomatic presence with NAFTA partner Mexico, African, and Mid-East states were at a low ebb. Exception to that was a strategy to diversify trade connections, highlighted by the trade deal with the European Union.

This hiatus of Canadian independent activism could be lifted following the defeat of Trump in the November election. The Biden victory should restore a compatibility between our two nations on a variety of issues other than trade. But even that could be frustrated by post-election challenges being mounted by Trump and his enablers. Jennifer Rubin (2020) of the Washington Post writes "the damage that Trump and his fellow Republicans have done — by not recognizing the results of the election, by casting the media as an 'enemy of the people,' by stoking racism, by violating the human rights of refugees and by enabling human rights abusers — should not be underestimated." She goes on to suggest that it will be important for Biden's foreign policy to signal a dramatic break with Trump policies desecrating human rights issues and returning to "a humane, responsible refugee policy." Here is a political space for making common cause with the new administration, offering our support and showing how we can be a partner in areas where we have capability and commitment. It will also be important for Canada to continue its full recognition of the legitimacy of the American voting results as Prime Minister Trudeau did with his early congratulations to Joe Biden. The

---

[1] Editors' note: Prime Minister Trudeau offered to renegotiate NAFTA soon after Trump's victory.

democratic members of the international community must be clear in their rejection of any further skulduggery by Trump.

"Never Let a Good Crisis Go to Waste"

2020 has not been a propitious time for Canadians to undertake a redefined role in the world. The electoral setback in late October 2019 made for a weakened Liberal minority government. Trudeau lost experienced cabinet members such as Ralph Goodale in Regina and Jim Carr, the Trade Minister, was furloughed with a serious illness. The Conservatives emerged from the election winning the popular vote and they, with the Bloc and the NDP, now held a majority of seats, wielding a sword of Damocles over the government. Furthermore, seven of the ten provinces were now governed by opposition parties, several of which were distinctly unfriendly. It was a fragmented and fractious political landscape.

In early 2020, COVID-19 arrived on our shores. By late February, it had become an all-engulfing storm, and Canadians were ushered into a series of tough measures limiting travel, shutting businesses and schools, lockdowns and strict orders on public gatherings. Travel and mobility have fallen precipitously. Good news was that provincial and municipal governments all showed unusual unity with Ottawa in mounting countermeasures to the virus. Canadians have been approving of these combined efforts and responded with a high level of compliance with the tougher restrictions. Canada was seen both at home and abroad to have been successful in its government interventions meeting the first epidemic surge (our universal healthcare system was the foundation of the response).

Unfortunately, the trust earned by Trudeau through his government's epidemic management has been impaired by revelations that the WE charitable organization, with close contacts with the Prime Minister and the Finance Minister Bill Morneau, might have received preferential treatment in being awarded a sole source contract worth hundreds of millions of dollars. The resignation of Morneau and the ensuing Throne Speech outlining a recovery package might assuage some criticism but the government itself must lance the "mistrust boil" by setting out a comprehensive reform proposal restoring the integrity of the government and the importance of parliament. Announcing a prorogation, silencing parliament, limiting debate and using a non-confidence designation have not been sterling ways to start.

As the second epidemic wave takes over in the final quarter of 2020, our governance will be further stressed by recurring demands on our health system, increasing financial outlays and population exhaustion over ongoing uncertainty and further restrictions. Global demands will accelerate as the virus begins advancing in Southern regions, invading highly vulnerable populations such as refugee camps and undermining the already precarious position of the global poor.

2020 has been a revelatory period. The epidemic has been a prism, throwing refracted light on many outworn conventional assumptions, revealing major flaws and failures of present practices. The importance of essential workers has shown how much our labour laws, income security programmes and treatment of migration workers are in need of an overhaul. The serious outbreaks in nursing homes demonstrated a lack of oversight and the absence of effective home care in our health system. Plane travel has been shown to be a carrier of pathogens and a more visible source of carbon emission excesses. Global supply lines are interrupted by the increasing inward-looking positions of most countries. Canadian internal border barriers between provinces and regions undermine concerted action, and in the case of the previously undefended frontier with the United States, most Canadians want it to stay closed. The dilemma is how do you keep the virus out but maintain an open movement of people, commerce and ideas.

The COVID-19 experience has driven home the importance of collaboration in international public health governance, risk intelligence, disaster relief management and innovative international development policy. Climate migration, refugee policy refit, and cleaning up corruption are really just a few important vectors needing new direction. And there is the Fauci warning of the need to change deeply entrenched patterns of human behaviour.

Calls from conservative think tank commentators and right-wing media to abandon multilateralism in favour of a bilateral relation with the United States are becoming more insistent, if less persuasive. A re-setting of our narrative with more, not less, international engagement must begin with changes in Canada that can skilfully weave together our domestic and international priorities. Ambassador Bill Burns (2020) of the Carnegie Endowment for International Peace got it right in a recent *Atlantic* magazine article: "Smart foreign policy begins at home, with a strong democracy, society, and economy. But it has to end there too—with more and better jobs, greater security, a better environment, and a more inclusive, just and resilient society."

2020-Call for Renewal

Part of the soft power influence of Canada over the years has been a perception of Canada as a nation with a stable, responsible, well-managed, non-corrupt government, able to advance the rights of people, as was done with the advancement of Charter of Rights and Freedoms, as a beacon for human rights around the world and a commitment to progressive policies on foreign aid and trade. Refurbishment of our democratic governance, streamlining bureaucratic programme delivery and fixing our foreign policy tool kit is in order if Canada is to play an effective role in helping with the reconstruction of a collaborative international system capable of taking on the autocrats, the kleptocrats, the oligarchs and meeting the transformative changes underway.

More than ever, parliament must be seen by Canadians not as a handmaiden to the central executive but as a body with independent oversight capacity. One way to emphasize the importance of revivifying parliament's watchdog/policy role would be to set at work amending the Charter of Rights and Freedoms "Section Five" with a clause that parliament must sit for a minimum of twenty days every calendar quarter, compared to the present requirement of one sitting a year. A process of that kind led by civil society and caring parliamentarians would send the right message.

Operationally, parliament must come into the modern age by using digital technology to enhance its ability to broaden and deepen the reach of parliamentarians with each other, with the Canadian public and to network with their counterpart parliamentarians around the world. Sergio Marchi and Allan Rock (2020) wrote in the *Ottawa Citizen* that parliament should be the crucible for renewing our foreign policy, seeking more inclusive sources of ideas from diverse sources across Canada and in the global sphere.

I would add that parliamentarians themselves must become, on a bipartisan basis, much more focused on reforming their institution. This is hard to do with the present levers of power so concentrated and our politics so divisive. But, surely, the unfolding events of 2020 that have shown an erosion of democratic institutions throughout the globe should be cause for deep soul searching on how to sturdy our own democratic institutions. Paradoxically, the epidemic can be the catalyst that spurs renewed commitment to reform and instils a sense of obligation for MPs and Senators as representatives of the people to take steps to strengthen the process of parliamentary responsibility.

Our federalism needs renewal. Professor Donald Savoie has long argued that the present system does not have any mechanism through which regions can be represented at the federal level. Speaking from my experience as an elected member from the Prairies at both provincial and federal levels for close to three decades, I attest to that verity. There is a fundamental regional imbalance in the way national policy and programmes are developed and delivered. The disproportionate weight of seats in Ontario and Québec without any mechanism of regional balance is at the heart of the problem, as are entrenched attitudes of control in Ottawa ministries. For example, in 1992, Jake Epp, Minister of Health and a Conservative MP from Manitoba, opened the National Virology Lab in Winnipeg, heralding it as the only level 4 infectious disease lab in Canada. Since that time, there have been reductions in funding, a shrinkage of mandate, closure of its international agency, and an increasing bureaucratic management. Because of this control freak mentality in the Ottawa-based Public Health Agency, it has played a muted role in the coronavirus epidemic. The defunding of the Agency's international work must be corrected.

Regional inequity was certainly a feature of our political scene before COVID-19. The epidemic has simply cast a harsher light on serious inequities and distribution of responsibilities across regions and social classes. As studies on the rise of populism show a sense of not being listened to, feeling left behind is the source of resentments that express themselves in more extreme political action. The higher rates of infection in minority populations, marginalized low-paid frontline workers, the economic fragility of small businesses and the impact on service workers, especially women, have revealed serious gaps in our economic, social and political system. Equalization payments have been written into our constitution giving a base for future amplifying of services and income security. Home care needs to be written into our national healthcare system. Federal-based labour standards including a minimum wage regime need to be upgraded along with joint employment especially for young people designed to protect and conserve our environment. Recruitment of young men and women into a Service Corps to work tracing the virus, supporting food banks, building water infrastructure, rehabbing our

Boreal Forest (in partnership with other Northern countries) would be a major restorative.

An altered Employment Insurance system can provide short-term relief, but there needs to be a serious conversation on a basic minimum income system. Germany is setting up pilot projects to examine the outcomes of such a reform. Political architecture that incorporates cities and municipalities into collaborative trilevel agencies to collaborate on crucial areas of local concern such as immigration, infrastructure, poverty and education should be part of our rebuilding agenda. Broadband service across rural and Northern regions, and Indigenous communities, often promised but infrequently delivered, is an imperative in overcoming the digital divide. At the core of our present condition is the weakening of a common purpose and unity of action. Rebuilding will take institutional reform, federalist redefinition, and an affirmation not just of the middle class but of "Ordinary Life", to use Charles Taylor's prescriptive tenet for our secular age. He puts the case this way,

> The purposes of God were narrowed to this one goal of sustaining human life. The continuing power of this idea is perhaps evident in the contemporary concern to preserve life, to bring prosperity, to reduce suffering worldwide which is I believe without precedent. (Taylor 2007: 370)

One area begging for attention is the need for a national food security strategy. As one of the world's agricultural powerhouses, we must mobilize food producers, labour, provincial, municipal, and Indigenous governments, environmentalists and universities to engage in a combined effort to mount a Food Security Marshall plan both at home and abroad. The awarding of the 2020 Nobel Peace Prize to the UN's World Food Program highlights the importance of the issue and opens a venue for an expanded role for Canada. One important contribution by Canada would be a targeting on freshwater conservation, quality and distribution. Initiatives addressing these issues are imperative as waterborne diseases kill millions, especially children, and water scarcity often leads to violent conflict. The proposed National Water Agency must have an international mandate and be involved in convening collaborative efforts linking water to food supply.

This has special import for Indigenous peoples. There are over 600 million Indigenous persons in the world, most on the bottom rungs of poverty but with a generic science that understands water as a life-giving gift. A Human Rights Watch (2020: 9) report finds, "nearly one in two households in First Nations are food insecure, compared with one out of nine white Canadian households." The federal government must respond immediately to this crisis.

It must also reform its approach to resource management especially as it affects Indigenous rights. The Trudeau government's intent to move towards a green economy must include a transfer of the very large subsidies paid to oil companies to renewal energy development, training and re-employment projects, particularly in Western Canada, and major water infrastructure for reserves and rural communities. The energy sector has a capacity to shift its know-how to develop non-fossil fuel alternatives. This structural change in our federal system is a worthy task for a Royal Commission, perhaps chaired by professor Savoie. It could be a modelling of a form of decentralized, community power that would be a beacon for joining with other global partners aiming at the same green recovery agenda.

Equally, the recommendations of the Commission of Inquiry on Murdered and Missing Women and the ratification of the International Convention of Indigenous Rights point to the need to reform our judicial and law enforcement systems to expunge systemic discrimination. This would set the stage for Canada to take a more active role in the advancement of Indigenous issues globally. As Foreign Affairs Minister, I appointed, in collaboration with then National Assembly Grand Chief Phil Fontaine, an Ambassador of Indigenous Matters (Saskatchewan chief Blaine Favel) to spur involvement with Indigenous peoples around the world on matters of rights, closer trade ties, cultural exchanges and human security issues. Canada was the leader in establishing the Arctic Council, the only multilateral institution with designated membership of Indigenous people. It too is a model of Indigenous participation in determining foreign policy issues.

Often overlooked in assessments of our governance system has been the diminution of the political parties as agencies of international policy development. They have become election and financial machines. Before the 1993 election, my own party held a series of party discussions on international issues. When I became Foreign Affairs Minister, I was able to draw upon the findings of these fora. The last policy discussion on things international I attended in Convention was an hour and a half mid-morning session. I believe the same acts of omission to be true of the other parties.

The Trudeau government in its first term promised a significant reform in the traditional first-past-the-post election system, subsequently dropped. It's time to return to that objective and overhaul the election system to be more representative of our diversity, protect against abuse and be able to tackle increasing cyber interference from other governments and extremist groups. An effective and fair electoral system is the essential foundation of representative democracy. It is of prime essence that our commitment to democratic reform be a centre point in defining our role in the world.

This takes me to a disconcerting reality; the political/bureaucratic class in our capital is not sufficiently engaged internationally. Global Affairs has been eviscerated by a series of financial reductions. Our diplomatic network has been shrunk and its central, coordinating role on international matters diminished. There is benign neglect when it comes to actually expediting development aid or intelligence capability. A report from Geoffrey York (2020) in the *Globe and Mail* revealed the dysfunctional performance of the bureaucracy in spending only $120,000 of a $1.5 billion development aid initiative over three years. It is indicative of how a crucial element of Canada's role in the world is being hamstrung by mismanagement. What's also in short shrift is the increasing shortfall for supporting the work of Canadian NGOs. The processing of grants and proposals often takes years to be approved. In general, there is an animus towards the promotion of volunteerism opportunities using ordinary Canadians as ambassadors for Canada abroad. As head of the Canadian election monitoring mission to Ukraine in 2019 that involved over 200 Canadians, I was conscious of how effective and well received they were and how their commitment and enthusiasm for democracy were carried back to their communities in Canada. Presently, this is not a priority. The experiment of folding the former CIDA into Global Affairs, a move I initially supported in the hope of there being a coherent melding of development and diplomacy, has failed. Time for a reconstruction of the development delivery apparatus.

This last June, I was asked to appear on a network news show to discuss the defeat of Canada for a seat on the UN Security Council. The segment before was a panel made up of Ottawa lobbyists. Their response to this setback was to dismiss its importance with the offhand view that foreign policy doesn't interest Canadians, reflecting a shallowness in assessing every event by its impact on opinion polls. Canada's unsuccessful bid for a Security Council seat this past June is itself a product of the reduced attention in concrete terms to our role in the world and a sign of attenuation of our diplomatic capacity. Blaming the loss solely on a late start in the campaign excluded consideration of more significant structural reasons. What weighed more was our low level of development aid, the reluctance to upgrade our peacemaking commitments, the absence of diplomatic presence in the Southern part of the globe and the lack of a coherent platform on what we would do as a Security Council member (see the chapter by Marland and Nimijean).

Yet in a way, not being on the Security Council may be a blessing. It might emancipate thinking both in policy terms and in being able to devote scarce resources to other international initiatives without being tied to the machinations of great power politics presently stymying the Council.

I believe that if the government afforded far more attention to human rights, this opportunity to act innovatively could be realized. Full marks are deserved for strong language and appropriate actions in dealing with empowerment of women and girls. There is a mixed response on refugee matters—an A for dealing with the Rohingya situation, a D for not acceding to the Federal Court decision rescinding the Third Party Agreement and buying into the Trump anti-refugee posture, and an outright F for expanded arms sales to the Saudis, silence on the Trump administration's attacks on the International Criminal Court, and the tepid response on Chinese disbandment of rights in Hong Kong, breaking an agreement signed with Canada in 1997 protecting dual citizenry rights. Coherence and commitment to human rights need to be a basic goal, followed by effective action. A recent report from Amnesty International gives further evidence to a lackadaisical interest in human rights, showing the paucity of efforts to apprehend and try war criminals, an oversight that ignores parliamentary legislation (The Canadian Press 2020). The same can be said for the hall pass being given to money laundering and hiding of purloined foreign assets. A report by Transparency International (TI) (2020) puts Canada at the bottom of the list of countries prosecuting bribery, and further, Canada is now included on TI's list of "countries to watch."

The strengthening of our capacity to advance Human Rights could begin with the appointment of a Minister of Human Rights that would take on the oversight and coordination of the government's various human rights agencies and commissions. She or he could be mandated to develop a global human rights education strategy that would encompass both domestic and international partners. And, there would be someone at the cabinet table that had the responsibility to signal sins of commission/omission on human rights issues and coordinate responses to domestic and international transgressions.

Refurbishing and re-thinking of the diplomatic toolkit are part of buttressing our role in the world. As Foreign Affairs Minister, I found a highly professional foreign service and an infrastructure of public diplomacy enabling an outreach and influence that connected in Canada and the globe. The last three deputy ministers in the ministry have not been foreign service officers. My deputy minister at the time, Gordon Smith, was an early advocate on the emerging possibilities of digital diplomacy, bristling with ideas on how information technology could become an important tool of soft power. That mission needs to be recaptured. Going forward a keyword for Canadian diplomacy is Connectivity. The foreign policy toolkit must re-build around digital networking and virtual participation. The advent of global digital technology opens new channels of direct participation of ordinary people in decisions that affect them, creating a powerful new dynamic of democratic policy-making both in Canada and around the world.

Essential to a new toolkit are ideas. In the past, there have been various ways for the government to reach out of the box to enrich their options and see the world through clearer lens. There was a small, agile unit within DFAIT called the Center for Foreign Policy Development led by Steve Lee, responsible for generating broad public interchange and often offering ideas different from those of officialdom. There were the Pearson Peacekeeping Centres in Nova Scotia and Montreal that were training grounds for peacekeepers and a source of research on peacekeeping including the role of women in peacekeeping, a joint initiative with Secretary of State Madeleine Albright. The Rights and Democracy Center led by outstanding parliamentarians like Ed Broadbent and Warren Allmand cut an intellectual swath around the world until it was defunded. There has been an ongoing pattern by successive governments of shutting down modalities that enhanced our capacity to engage Canadians and global citizens.

Canada's branding is now very centred on the personality of the Prime Minister, a formidable asset. But it is not enough. A rebooting of our foreign policy capability to direct an advancement out of the COVID-19 period that can create agile networks of nation states, civil society and business groups, international agencies, universities and foundations is a prerequisite for a renewed role in the world. Canada must aim for a broadening and deepening involvement in a process through which people are active participants in decisions that affect them. The recent efforts at the UN Assembly, marking the 75th anniversary, to be more participatory were not very successful. The institution needs champions to open its political arteries. Canada should be in the vanguard in shaping a more fluid, flexible, democratic global system.

CHOICES

Let's start with an example of a recent Canadian diplomatic initiative, courtesy of Adam Chapnick's (2020) Blog that shows the kind of role we're good at:

> Diplomats set the conditions for national success by building relationships, nibbling around the edges of conflict, and reaching obscure agreements with allies, associates, and sometimes even adversaries, to preserve a system of rules and laws that is consistent with Canadian national interests.

Discussions towards the Multiparty Interim Appeal Arbitration Arrangement (MPIA) were launched in Davos in January 2020. It effectively prevented the World Trade Organization (WTO) from imploding, for the time being. What's the takeaway? It was Canadian diplomatic leadership that mobilized a mixed group of countries into signing an agreement that short circuited the efforts by the Trump administration to paralyse the WTO. It grew out of a ministerial initiative launched in Ottawa in 2018 by then Trade Minister Jim Carr devoted to reform of the WTO. Discussions on how to address the Appellate Body impasse in the Ottawa Group led to a spin-off process to set up an alternate trade dispute resolution. It targeted a special niche problem leading to an innovative solution. As Chapnick (2020) concludes, "it is a prime example of Canadian diplomacy at its best." It showed that you don't need big power involvement to work out a solution to a serious issue.

This model of middle power—Convenor, Matchmaker, Innovator, and Reformer—is one that I've long believed to be a distinctive Canadian role. It was the mode of mobilizing support for the Treaty on Land Mines, the International Criminal Court and the adoption of the R2P concept by the UN Leaders' Summit in 2005. It should be a model for setting priorities as we exit 2020 with so many uncertainties. Wayfaring navigation comes into play. Set out goals, tap into where the currents are running, tack when the winds change, be open and agile in choosing navigable channels. Canada post the Security Council defeat is now in the words of a senior official "unshackled" to take on a more independent and innovative leadership role without worrying about where the votes will come from. So we can make choices.

COVID-19 AND PUBLIC HEALTH

The epidemic demonstrates the need for building a more robust and collaborative public health system with stronger ties internationally. The Public Health Agency needs an overhaul and a reinvigoration, especially in its international capacity (including the Winnipeg Virology Lab), and a much clearer accountability to parliament. There certainly needs to be better coordination and integration of public health research, supply management, and treatment between the different partners in our federal system. Intelligence services must be more effective in ascertaining the security risks attached to disease. Ambassador Bob Rae (2020) recommends in his recent report on humanitarian assistance that more funding is needed for an international COVID-19 response:

> These funds should be additional to current commitments and estimated spending and support a balance of multilateral partners and local, national and international NGOs, all while continuing to prioritize the needs of women and girls and ensuring gender-responsiveness in their approaches. Canada could significantly alleviate suffering and help build a bridge to recovery.

An idea worth considering that has appeared in both UN and the OECD reports is to look at schemes for multilateral digital taxation to apply accountability to the telecom giants. Proceeds from such a tax could begin to finance the post-COVID-19 needs of millions of marginal population groups.

Another tack is to begin advancing innovative means of direct economic assistance to the countries undertaking adaptation work to offset the ravages of climate-related effects. The Ottawa Group that has been working on WTO reform should follow the recommendations of the World Economic Forum's (WEF) Global Future Council on International Trade and Investment. In a recent briefing paper, the council argues "It is no longer a choice but, rather, an imperative to make international trade a central part of the solution to the environmental challenges we face" and that trade must align with the SDGs (Weder et al. 2020: 3).

The World Bank estimates that every year, corrupt officials worldwide steal US$20 billion to US$40 billion from money intended as development support. The amount of purloined funds will increase exponentially as new sums are allocated to deal with epidemic recovery and climate change remedial costs. These transgressions can be offset by a very rigorous attack on the billions in stolen money while breaking the immunity of the criminals, kleptocrats, warlords and others of their kind.

Canada can make a meaningful difference by supporting efforts to ensure those dollars get to where they are needed most. At a recent webinar sponsored by the World Refugee and Migration Council (WRMC) and the International Integrity Initiative, innovative measures were discussed. Countries should freeze purloined assets found in their jurisdictions and adopt legislation permitting a court order confiscating those assets and their repurposing for the benefit of refugees and displaced persons. The second proposal is to create a coalition of interested governments, civil society and international agencies to promote the establishment of an International Anti-Corruption Court (IACC). It would have authority to investigate, prosecute and punish grand corruption. IACC would prosecute only if a country was found to be unable or unwilling to initiate prosecutions itself. The United Nations is planning a special session on corruption in 2021. This presents an opening for Canada to become a champion of these new institutional vehicles for buttressing the rule of law in a very concrete way. Peter Donolo (2020) in a *Toronto Star* op-ed makes the case that new Finance Minister Chrystia Freeland, with her background as a journalist writing about corruption, could exercise effective leadership.

In a digital global conference that the WRMC organized in partnership with the Global Independent Women's Refugee Leadership, hundreds of refugee women throughout the globe told of an increasing breakdown of rules, governance and law enforcement in refugee concentrations. They voiced a fear that women and girls refugee and displaced persons will always be last in the queue when it comes to distribution of COVID-19 remedies. Canada can help open doors for participation in COVID-19-related decisions that affect them. The Trudeau government is showing leadership in providing support for COVAX, an international coalition to ensure poor populations are part of an equitable distribution of COVID-19 remedies (Blanchfield 2020). They should use that leverage to insure the inclusion of refugee and displaced persons in the scheme. They have no governments representing them, so they must be given a voice. We should be partnering with the African Union, which is organizing regional remedial actions on COVID-19. The ASEAN group at its summit in June issued a statement calling for cooperative effort among its members. Central and Latin American countries are in dire need of both health and economic assistance. The epidemic is writing a new script for global cooperation.

COVID-19 and Climate

Scientists are increasingly drawing attention to the interaction between climate and disease, a syndrome running through human history. Among the areas of vital concern to Canadians is the thawing permafrost in Northern and Arctic regions that not only releases carbon and methane gases but also various toxins and pathogens that can lead to serious infection in the Arctic food chain and even become potential carriers of epidemics. A further warning comes from increasing reports of the transmission of infectious diseases from animals to human, accounting for 75% of new outbreaks. Experts are advising a grassroots, bottom-up approach to tackle this issue: "When communities and civil society are engaged, they bring their lived experience, expertise, policy knowledge and health responses that are informed, effective and sustainable" (Bambara 2020).

There is a Canadian answer. The Arctic Council, founded in 1996, is a multilateral regional organization that uniquely includes direct seating of Indigenous organizations and supports community-based solutions. In a report released in June 2020, it outlined a comprehensive assessment of COVID-19 impacts and how the Council can coordinate responses to guard against epidemic spread, encourage food security and advance infrastructure and bandwidth improvements. Canada should and can provide leadership on Council efforts to limit COVID-19 and climate impacts. The community approach is one that already is being applied through the Council.

Climate, Borders and Migration

In a recent Brookings Report, John Podesta (2019) writes that "In 2018, the World Bank estimated that three regions (Latin America, sub-Saharan Africa, and Southeast Asia) will generate 143 million more climate migrants by 2050." It is not a country-specific challenge however; it is a global challenge requiring the best in humanity to seek sustainable solutions and to accelerate planning and protection for these millions uprooted from the destruction of their living environments. The 1951 Refugee Convention did not contemplate climate refugees when the world came together to protect those who had been displaced during World War II. Now we need new agreements to respond to the growing numbers of people in need of protection.

Here's a glimmer of hope. One Kiribati family fled to New Zealand claiming refugee status. While the New Zealand courts rejected their refugee claim and deported them, a landmark decision by the United Nations Human Rights Committee in January of 2020 said that rising sea levels and other climate change impacts did necessitate a broadening of refugee law. The principle of non-refoulement is a cornerstone of international refugee law (United Nations Human Rights 2020). The Committee has opened a rethink of the global governance of refugees. The status quo is inadequate for the size and scale of the humanitarian crisis looming. Forced displacement due to climate/epidemic impact is a communal threat.

It is a phenomenon that can no longer be dictated solely by the caprice of national governments but needs an active involvement of those who are being forced to move. There are core problems in the structure of the global refugee system that impedes effective leadership. One is the anachronism of the legal framework defining who is a refugee. The 1951 Refugee Convention definition, "one escaping political persecution," is a reflection of the movement of people from the Soviet Union post-World War II. Equally problematic is the dependence of the refugee system on voluntary contributions. Unlike UN peacekeeping, which is funded by a compulsory assessed fee to member states, the budget for UNHCR relies on contributions from governments. For all the dire warnings on the climate impact affecting millions of people and the related consequence of fostering further disputes and conflicts, the UN has not found the governance system to bring together the respective agencies and political bodies to address the human security crisis at hand. There is a degree of muddling through and therefore a vacuum in the ability to cope with the triple whammy of COVID-19 and climate, and mass migration. One important step is to bring together as partners the civil networks that respectively advocate for climate and refugees to mount a joint campaign for change. Canada has an opportunity to forge an international dialogue and consensus that breaks new ground. We have the ability to be a catalyst in rescuing the present refugee/migration system that is in a state of atrophy.

A Nuclear Winter

The Book of Revelation warns of the "four horsemen of the apocalypse." This chapter has enumerated at least that number. But the one that has been out there the longest and remains perhaps the most deadly of them all is the nuclear overhang. Our age evades its potential terror at our peril. It is time for Canada to resume a multi-decade long commitment to reduce the risk of nuclear holocaust. The Nuclear Ban Treaty came into effect in late October with fifty ratifications. Canada was not among them, even though we were the very first country to decide against becoming a nuclear weapon nation.

McGeorge Bundy, the long-time US diplomat in describing a meeting between the Americans, Canadians and British to discuss post war nuclear policy commented:

> the role of Canada in the history of nuclear weapons is unique, and it seems appropriate here to remark that Canadian good sense and moderation are visible at many points in the nuclear age ....Canada was the first country to decide clearly that it would not itself become a nuclear weapons state, reaching that conclusion openly, and with no voice on the other side, in 1945. The Canadians had everything at hand – the uranium, the science, and the technical head start – everything except the desire. (Bundy 1988: 149)

That decision taken in 1945 by the Canadian government has always intrigued me and certainly underscores the moral case for Canada undertaking an active position on controlling the spread of nuclear arsenals. We were the first to espouse a non-nuclear posture and in following eras made good on our dedication to limit the threat of nuclear weapons. Prime Minister Pierre Trudeau made a bold effort to kick-start nuclear disarmament talks in the mid-1980s. In the mid-1990s, Canada proposed at the NATO Summit meeting in Washington that the organization drops its stated position of first use of nuclear weapons. Nova Scotia is home to the Pugwash Conference, a leading international scientific group working on nuclear disarmament issues. Nobel Laureate in physics, John Polanyi is an internationally recognized expert on nuclear issues. It's been part of Canada's DNA for decades.

That mission is not being exercised today. Canada has been missing in action on the global talks for a nuclear ban treaty. Silent on the efforts underway on great powers forays into making space a nuclear platform. Non-obtrusive on efforts by the Americans and Russians to scupper long-standing disarmament treaties. Yet, the risk to the planet is heightened by excessive new efforts to re-stock nuclear arsenals and produce new nuclear weaponry. As Canadians reboot in face of present calamities, we must re-enter the arena of nuclear arms discussions and ultimately make the case for a nuclear ban. The place to start is to have a special House of Commons Committee undertake a current scan on our nuclear stand, similar to what the Hon Bill Graham presided over in the mid-1990s prior to the NATO Summit. To quote Lester Pearson's (1957) Nobel Lecture, "Today, less than ever can we defend ourselves by force, for there is no effective defence against the all-destroying effect of nuclear missile weapons. Indeed, their very power has made their use intolerable, even unthinkable, because of the annihilative retaliation in kind that such use would invoke."

The point is that nowhere in the world is there immunity from disaster and disruption. Policymakers who believe that borders are all we need must unlearn such folly. It is a complex intermixed system of dangers, transcending borders, drawing us all into the vortex and requiring our best efforts. Canada's role in the world as viewed at the end of 2020 is a complex passage of careful manoeuvring through a dangerous set of global risks, avoiding the shoals of power rivalries and unleashed passions of nationalism but freed of restrictive anachronisms to search out openings for applying skill and knowledge to help solve unattended global inequities and threats. It will require integrated, intertwined reforms of our domestic and international capabilities.

In his Grammy award-winning country music song, George Jones (1999) poignantly vocalized that he was "living and dying with choices I've made." Dramatic as that sounds, it's not too far-fetched in the age of existential risk to suggest that we are in a world where choices are so consequential. As we exit from 2020, Canadians have choices that will affect our future and help shape the directions being made in a global context. Canadians must rise to the occasion and seize the moment to set out on a voyage of discovery not unlike that taken by Tahitian wayfarers of the eighteenth century, heading into the unknown by putting their ears to the currents and their eyes on a new horizon.

References

Applebaum, Anna. 2020. *Twilight of Democracy: The Seductive Lure of Authoritarianism*. Canada: Penguin Random House.

Avishai, Bernard. 2020. "The Pandemic Isn't a Black Swan But a Portent of a More Fragile Global System." *The New Yorker*, April 21. https://www.newyorker.com/news/daily-comment/the-pandemic-isnt-a-black-swan-but-a-portent-of-a-more-fragile-global-system.

Bambara, Carine. 2020. "Leave No One Behind: 3 Ways Governments Can Engage with Communities on One Health." *Bond News*, September 22. https://www.bond.org.uk/news/2020/09/leave-no-one-beh ind-3-ways-governments-can-engage-with-communities-on-one-health.

Blanchfield, Mike. 2020. "Trudeau Pledges Extra $400 Million in Humanitarian Aid to Fight COVID-19." *New Westminister Record*, September 29. https:// www.newwestrecord.ca/trudeau-pledges-extra-400-million-in-humanitarian-aid-to-fight-covid-19-1.24211735.

Bundy, McGeorge. 1988. *Danger and Survival: Choices About the Bomb in the First Fifty Years*. New York: Random House.

Burns, William J. 2020. "The United States Needs a New Foreign Policy." *The Atlantic*, July 14. https://www.theatlantic.com/ideas/archive/2020/07/uni ted-states-needs-new-foreign-policy/614110/.

CBC. 2020. "World Needs to Prepare for Millions of Climate Displaced UN Says." *CBC News*, January 22. https://www.cbc.ca/news/technology/cli mate-refugees-un-1.5435843.

Chapnick, Adam. 2020. "A Canadian Foreign Policy Victory at the WTO." *Adam Chapnick's Blog*, August 10. http://www.adamchapnick.ca/adam-cha pnicks-blog/a-canadian-foreign-policy-victory-at-the-wto.

Donolo, Peter. 2020. "It's Time for United Global Action to Stem Corruption." *The Toronto Star*, August 28. https://www.thestar.com/opinion/contribut ors/2020/08/28/its-time-for-united-global-action-to-stem-corruption.html.

Harper, Kyle. 2017. *The Fate of Rome: Climate, Disease and the End of Empire*. Princeton, NJ: Princeton University Press.

Heffernan, Claire. 2018. Climate Change and Multiple Emerging Infectious Diseases. *Veterinary Journal* 234: 43.

Human Rights Watch. 2020. "My Fear Is Losing Everything: The Climate Crisis and First Nations' Right to Food in Canada." https://www.hrw.org/ report/2020/10/21/my-fear-losing-everything/climate-crisis-and-first-nat ions-right-food-canada.

Jones, George. 1999. "Choices." *The Cold Hard Truth*. Written by Billy Wayne Yates and Michael Curtis. https://www.azlyrics.com/lyrics/georgejones/cho ices.html.

Lee, Kristine. 2020. "It's Not Just the WHO: How China Is Moving on the Whole U.N." *Politico*, April 15. https://www.politico.com/news/magazine/2020/04/15/its-not-just-the-who-how-china-is-moving-on-the-whole-un-189029.

Marchi, Sergio, and Allan Rock. 2020. "Canada Should Draw Key Lessons from UN Defeat." *Policy Options*, June 22. https://policyoptions.irpp.org/magazi nes/june-2020/canada-should-draw-key-lessons-from-the-un-defeat/.

Ord, Toby. 2020. *The Precipice-Existential Risk and the Future of Humanity*. New York: Hachette Books.

Pearson, Lester Bowles. 1957. "Nobel Lecture: The Four Faces of Peace." https://www.nobelprize.org/prizes/peace/1957/pearson/lecture/.

Podesta, John. 2019. "The Climate Crisis, Migration, and Refugees." *Brookings Report*, July 25. https://www.brookings.edu/research/the-climate-crisis-mig ration-and-refugees/.

Rae, Bob. 2020. "A Global Crisis Requires a Global Response." Government of Canada. Last modified August 31. https://www.international.gc.ca/world-monde/issues_development-enjeux_developpement/response_conflict-rep onse_conflits/crisis-crises/global_crisis-crise_mondiale.aspx?lang=eng#a7.

Robinson, Marilynne. 2020. "What Kind of Country Do We Want?" *New York Review of Books*, June 11.

Rubin, Jennifer. 2020. "Five Big Challenges for the Biden Foreign Policy Team." *Washington Post*, November 10. https://www.washingtonpost.com/opinions/2020/11/10/four-big-challenges-biden-foreign-policy-team/.

Sachs, Jeffrey, Joseph Stiglitz, Mariana Mazzucato, Clair Brown, Indivar Dutta-Gupta, Robert Reich, Gabriel Zucman and Others. 2020. "Letter from Economists: To Rebuild Our World, We Must End the Carbon Economy." *The Guardian*, August 4. https://www.theguardian.com/commentisfree/2020/aug/04/economists-letter-carbon-economy-climate-change-rebuild.

Shah, Sonia. 2020. *The Next Great Migration: The Beauty and Terror of Life on the Move*. New York: Bloomsbury.

Taub, Amanda. 2020. "A New Leadership Style Offers Promise for a New Era of Global Threats." *The New York Times*, May 15. https://www.nytimes.com/2020/05/15/world/coronavirus-women-leaders.html.

Taylor, Charles. 2007. *A Secular Age*. Cambridge: Harvard University Press.

The Canadian Press. 2020. "Canada Failing to Bring Suspected War Criminals to Justice: Amnesty International." *Global News*, September 8. https://glo balnews.ca/news/7320946/canada-failing-bring-war-criminals-justice-amn esty-international/.

Transparency International. 2020. "Exporting Corruption: Progress Report 2020: Assessing Enforcement of the OECD Anti-Bribery Convention." https://www.transparency.org/en/projects/exporting-corruption.

UN News. 2020. "'Inequality Defines Our Time': UN Chief Delivers Hard-Hitting Mandela Day Message." *UN News*, July 18. https://news.un.org/en/story/2020/07/1068611.

United Nations Human Rights. 2020. "Historic UN Human Rights Case Opens Door to Climate Change Asylum Claims." *United Nations Human Rights, News*, January 21. https://www.ohchr.org/en/NewsEvents/Pages/DisplayNews.aspx?NewsID=25482&LangID=E#.

Vergano, Dan. 2020. "COVID-19 Might Mean Humanity Has Entered An Age of Pandemics, Tony Fauci Warned." *Buzzfeed News*, September 1. https://www.buzzfeednews.com/article/danvergano/more-coronavirus-pandemics-warning.

Weder, Ghislaine, Janet Whittaker, Penelope Naas, and Sarah Thorn. 2020. "How Can Trade Rules Support Environmental Action? Global Future Council on International Trade and Investment." World Economic Forum. http://www3.weforum.org/docs/WEF_GFC_Briefing_on_Trade_and_Environment_Report_2020.pdf.

York, Geoffrey. 2020. "Ottawa's $1.5-Billion Foreign Aid Initiative Has Spent Only $120,000 So Far." *The Globe and Mail*, October 8. https://www.theglobeandmail.com/world/article-ottawas-15-billion-foreign-aid-initiative-has-spent-only-12000/.

PART II

Deep Divisions

CHAPTER 3

Rebranding Brand Trudeau

Alex Marland and Richard Nimijean

INTRODUCTION

Historically, few Canadian politicians achieve international recognition outside of confined elite circles. Consequently, Canada must compete for a voice in global forums and its prime ministers must reassure Canadians that the country is an effective player in international affairs. On the rare occasion that a Canadian leader achieves global fame, it must not be squandered.

Enter Justin Trudeau. The charismatic son of a transformative prime minister, Trudeau, ascended to power as a bastion of hope and reform, positioning himself as a unifier after the divisive politics of Conservative

A. Marland (✉)
Memorial University, St. John's, NL, Canada
e-mail: amarland@mun.ca

R. Nimijean
School of Indigenous and Canadian Studies,
Carleton University, Ottawa, Canada

Department of English and American Studies,
Masaryk University, Brno, Czech Republic

© The Author(s), under exclusive license to Springer Nature
Switzerland AG 2021
D. Carment and R. Nimijean (eds.), *Political Turmoil
in a Tumultuous World*, Canada and International Affairs,
https://doi.org/10.1007/978-3-030-70686-9_3

Prime Minister Stephen Harper. Trudeau became leader of the Liberal Party of Canada at a young age, proved to be adept with image management, and in 2015 propelled the Liberals to a shocking electoral victory. Years later, Canada's 23rd prime minister had a record of accomplishments, shortcomings, and failures that provides a basis upon which to judge his leadership on the global stage. At times, the telegenic leader has attracted international attention as a darling of progressives and the political left; other times, his dubious political acumen has impugned both his and Canada's brand image. More often than not, Trudeau's image has been an asset for the Liberal government; however, the Liberals are discovering that celebrity politics is not enough to deal with pressing global challenges.

How has Justin Trudeau's and—by extension, Canada's—brand evolved since 2015? Trudeau's instant global celebrity initially improved his political fortunes and increased Canada's global profile. However, blunders, controversy, and shortcomings have damaged his reputation. This chapter combines insights from political marketing and critical nation branding analyses to examine the implications for both brands and show how the Liberals' approach to governance and politics makes it more difficult to address domestic disunity and global challenges like the COVID-19 pandemic in the context of a minority parliament after the 2019 federal election. We begin by explaining what public sector branding is.

Public Sector Branding

Branding is a tool of communications efficiency that is highly attractive to politicians, political parties, and governments. Boiling down messaging to core values and themes saves time, effort, and money, and delivers value by harmonizing all messaging and communications touchpoints. Advantages include simplifying information processing for citizens, generating trust through standardized interactions, creating positive feelings, and offering authenticity (Needham 2006: 179). To accomplish this, brand enthusiasts demand a relentless commitment to message repetition, including visuals, as marketers strive to craft a strategic image and persuade audiences to form an emotional connection. There must be message consistency, both in terms of congruence between promises, brand values and delivery, and the reiteration of information that contributes to a strategic frame. Success is achieved when supporters prefer the brand to alternatives even when those alternatives would potentially better meet their needs and wants. Branding is therefore a strategic asset in politics and public administration.

However, a brand is a problematic psychological construct, and brand management requires centralized control. Snippets of information prevail over details; images can highlight the superficial. Journalistic scrutiny is avoided through cameras-only photo-ops, spin, message repetition and direct marketing. The commodification of political leaders shifts public attention away from policy towards personality and image, resulting in "the simulation of an ideal image rather than an ideal leader" (Zavattaro 2010: 124). The fusion of a prime minister's brand with that of the government exacerbates the problems of centralization and politicization of the public service (Marland et al. 2017).

The branding strategies of some recent progressive leaders offer an image management roadmap. Jack Layton, who led the New Democratic Party of Canada from 2003 to 2011, thrust a regimented focus on political marketing upon a dishevelled caucus and transformed it into a cohesive group with leader-centric brand positioning and a message of positive change (McGrane 2019). Layton's aspirational messaging of love, hope, and optimism resulted in an electoral breakthrough in 2011 and a playbook for the Trudeau Liberals to emulate. Both Trudeau and Layton were inspired by Barack Obama's message of hope that resonated with Americans seeking a unifier. The 2008 Democratic presidential candidate's image-centric campaign harnessed social media to build an inclusive political movement and enabled him to carry on personified communication from the Oval Office. That President Obama's international celebrity reflected well on global evaluations of the United States demonstrates how a high-profile political actor can prime the opinions of the foreign public (Dragojlovic 2011). But as he and other heads of government have experienced, controversies pile up, and leaders who project great optimism must recalibrate their brand to reconnect with voters. Seeking a third straight election victory, in 2005 UK Prime Minister Tony Blair was vulnerable to impressions of lacking credibility because of heightened expectations and frustrations with spin. Some voters continued to see optimism and enthusiasm; many others felt pessimism and anger. The Labour Party rebranded Blair's tarnished image into a more mature leader who headed up a competent cabinet team, which involved empowering spokespeople to draw public attention away from the prime minister, and a recognition that citizens were angry. The intent was to recalibrate the brand to make it "about *we*, not *me*" (Scammell 2007: 185; emphasis in original). Many of these aspects of the progressive brand strategy apply to Justin Trudeau and the Liberal Party of Canada.

The Government of Canada is an ardent enthusiast of branding. Historically, ambassadors were at the forefront of Canadian trade diplomacy; today, the foreign service's activities are wrapped up in consistent messaging (Potter 2004). The federal identity programme anchors all government communications guidelines, including a Treasury Board-mandated requirement that departments use a single corporate image—the ubiquitous logo of "Canada" with the maple leaf flag above the final letter—to impose message unity throughout public administration (Way 1993). The cabinet and public service attempt to apply a strategic frame on the country's image for economic activities such as tourism, international trade, food quality, and natural resource development, resulting in clearly positioned competitive messaging that has been dubbed "Brand Canada" (Hudson and Ritchie 2009). The financial expense of exemptions can add up; for example, in 2017 an international anti-poverty organization within Export Development Canada spent half a million dollars on a name, logo, brand and website (Curry 2018). Furthermore, blunders can disrupt the government's communications agenda, as occurred in 2017 with a controversial tweet from the Minister of Environment and Climate Change that praised Syria for joining the Paris climate change agreement despite Canada's concerns about "the dismal human rights records of [the Syrian] government" (Beeby 2017a). Ministers, ministerial staff, and senior public servants in Canada are acutely aware that problems result from incongruent government messaging.

The prime minister is Canada's chief international spokesperson and determines the political values that inform brand messaging. Anchoring Canada's brand is the country's very identity. Internal disputes, shifting economic and social priorities, latent nationalism, free trade, and global forces all inform the governing party's foreign policy stance. Some brand commonalities exist regardless of leadership, with Canada exerting limited international influence as a middle power under Liberals and Conservatives alike, even though it is an advanced economy with membership in the Group of Seven. The international brand of a Canadian prime minister is underpinned by "pre-existing impressions...decades or centuries in the making" (Rose 2010: 261) such as politeness, perceptions of natural terrain, symbols such as the Royal Canadian Mounted Police, cold temperatures and a love of winter sports particularly hockey. Nuances in Brand Canada foremost arise depending on which party is in power, as prime ministers play to the party's base of supporters. Liberals are more likely to approve of peacekeeping and foreign aid than Conservatives are (Gravelle et al. 2014), and Liberal governments direct foreign aid to Africa and, under Trudeau, towards programming to help women and girls, whereas the Harper Conservatives excluded funding for abortion services (Brown 2018). Regardless of these partisan variances, in Canada foreign policy is largely a moot issue where prospecting for votes is concerned (Landriault 2016).

The rise of political branding coincided with the emergence of nation branding—the effort to promote national economic and political interests as international relations and the global economy were experiencing transformation following the demise of the Soviet Union and the rise of globalization. Asserting national brand identities, it was believed, could increase a country's influence and attract foreign direct investment and skilled labour (van Ham 2001). However, nation branding efforts can devolve into propaganda, and brands are subject to rhetoric-reality gaps when a country does not live up to its values (Anholt 2009: 88). Country brands are often tools for governments to project ideological messages and policies that may or may not reflect national values (Curry Jansen 2008) and, arguably, competing brands have replaced classic ideologies as the primary source of competition and differentiation in Canadian politics and public policy (Nimijean 2005: 28–29). Here we see the connection between domestic politics that focus on image and a country's brand. While political brands seek to move attention away from policies rooted in ideology, rhetoric-reality gaps return the attention to policy. Such inconsistency erodes trust and damages the country brand.

BRAND TRUDEAU AND CANADA'S BRAND

Justin Trudeau's global celebrity fundamentally changed Brand Canada, if temporarily. His international political fame is matched only by that of his father, Pierre Trudeau, who hobnobbed with pop culture stars in the late 1960s and 1970s, and whose brand turned on national unity and "holding Canada together" (Hunt 2003: 88). Canadian politicians simply do not grace the cover of *Rolling Stone* or *Vanity Fair* as the current prime minister did early in his tenure.

From his first day in office, the younger Trudeau's international brand took shape through policy priorities such as feminism and migration. The triumph of vaulting the Liberals from the third-most seats in the House of

Commons to a majority of seats after the 2015 federal election generated additional international interest when he presented a cabinet comprised of an equal number of men and women. More headlines arose at a photo-op when Trudeau personally greeted Syrian refugees arriving in Canada, visually reinforcing a campaign pledge to increase the number of displaced Syrians that the government would allow into the country. He proclaimed "Canada is back" as though the country had gone missing under the Conservatives—never mind that the Harper Conservatives likewise used the expression when they replaced the Liberals.

During his first year in office, Trudeau was a social media darling: a stream of photos of the prime minister in Hallowe'en costume, cuddling pandas and performing a peacock yoga pose were interspersed with serious images of meeting with world leaders (Lalancette and Raynauld 2017). He was celebrated at global forums, including images of Trudeau and premiers of various partisan allegiances smiling at the United Nations climate change conference (COP 21) in late 2015, which were a powerful blend of progressive politics, youthful optimism, and cross-partisan unity. The message of Canada as a "helpful fixer" boosted the country's brand at a time of simmering international turmoil as other countries were turning to populism, conservatism, and xenophobia (Nimijean 2018: 128).

By 2017, the prime minister was an inspiring northern beacon of stability. His progressive values and cheery demeanour stood in sharp contrast with the erratic diplomacy of US President Donald Trump, who refreshed the Republican brand in his image and that of the American past (Cosgrove 2018). Enthusiasm for Brand Trudeau arguably peaked when it was revealed that Canadian diplomatic missions in the United States were displaying life-size cardboard replicas of him so that visitors could take selfies (Beeby 2017b).

Despite his relative comfort with journalists and social media, Trudeau sometimes offered glib, simplistic, or confusing thoughts. In his first year as Liberal leader, he expressed admiration for China because its "basic dictatorship is actually allowing them to turn their economy around on a dime" (quoted in CBC News 2013). In power, the first significant dent in Trudeau's international image occurred in late 2016 when he expressed sadness over the death of Cuban dictator Fidel Castro. Canadian diplomats scampered to request message lines as Trudeau—and therefore Canada—endured social media mocking, political criticism, and negative headlines (Campion-Smith 2017). It was a moment that transformed him from "Disney prince" to "international laughingstock" (Glavin 2016);

however, internationally he had built a sufficient reservoir of goodwill that the snafu was soon forgotten. Nevertheless, at times a penchant for virtue signalling has been mocked internationally, such as when he suggested that an audience member at a town hall use "peoplekind" instead of "mankind" (The Guardian 2018).

Domestically, the remarks added to cracks that had begun to show in Brand Trudeau. In 2017, the ethics commissioner ruled that the prime minister had violated Canada's ethics law for accepting helicopter flights as part of two all-expenses paid family vacations on the Aga Khan's private island. Aside from raising red flags about Trudeau's political judgement, which weakens brand trust, the wealthy elitism was at odds with his efforts to connect with average Canadians. More brand incongruence followed. In February 2018, the prime minister and his family made a disastrous eight-day trip to India that was widely portrayed as a celebrity jaunt because they hammed it up for the cameras. They overdid dressing up in traditional Indian clothing. Trudeau was fêted in Canada House in New Delhi where he danced the bhangra. Most ominously, Sophie Grégoire Trudeau had her photograph taken with a Sikh extremist. The Prime Minister's Office had invited the convicted murderer to attend an event, ostensibly at the suggestion of a Liberal MP who took the blame, raising serious questions about security protocols. Politically, the focus on celebrity and creating photo-ops aimed at an important voting bloc in Canada (Dutt 2018) was poorly received by India, a growing market and influential international player. Together, such incidents portrayed the prime minister as placing greater weight on image than substance (Marland 2018).

The SNC-Lavalin Affair
and the 2019 Canadian Election

In early 2019, as the Liberals were turning their sights to a Fall election campaign, the government endured two months of negative headlines over its handling of the criminal prosecution of SNC-Lavalin. Efforts to bend the rule of law for the Montreal-based international engineering company in the name of protecting jobs culminated in two high-profile ministers and Trudeau's former parliamentary secretary sitting as independents (Marland 2020: 280–318). The prime minister's personal brand endured serious damage because the dispute and loss of three women MPs cut to the core of his government's values of feminism, Indigenous reconciliation, and diversity, as well as his commitment to doing politics differently. Furthermore, the SNC-Lavalin affair tarnished Canada's reputation as a country that follows the rule of law. On the one hand, the Prime Minister's Office had urged the Attorney-General to pursue a remediation agreement with SNC-Lavalin, while on the other it claimed that following the rule of law prevented the government from intervening in the detention case of Huawei executive Meng Wanzhou (see Bratt in this volume).

Thus, while Trudeau's celebrity once again served to get Canada noticed on the world stage, it also meant that rhetoric-reality gaps damaged both brands. The SNC-Lavalin affair challenged the message that "low corruption" was a reason to pursue economic ventures in Canada (Invest in Canada 2020). Indeed, in the ensuing annual global corruption rankings, Canada registered its lowest net score since the metric was created in the mid-1990s, slipping four spots from 8th to 12th, and was one of the countries experiencing the biggest drops in its performance over the past eight years (Transparency International 2020).[1] Canadians also believed that Canada's global reputation had taken a hit. While Canada scored better on this metric during Trudeau's first three years as prime minister than it had under Harper, in 2019 the country registered a six-year low, prompting a pollster to observe that Trudeau always seems to have diversions associated with his successes (Hahn 2020).

Foreign policy was a key part of the rise of Trudeau's brand, yet by the time of the 2019 election campaign, internationalism was squarely focused on climate change. Canadian elections rarely command international media attention; this one was different precisely because of Trudeau's celebrity and a betrayal of his carefully honed image as a champion of diversity and inclusion. The SNC-Lavalin affair prompted a significant drop in Liberal support, especially among women (Hahn 2019), contributing to an extremely competitive election. One week into the campaign, *Time* magazine revealed that Trudeau, before he became a Member of Parliament, had worn blackface and brownface. Other media ran images showing that he had done so multiple times. The racist photographs rocketed around the world. The prime minister's image was

---

[1] While this drop would seemingly indicate poor performance, *Invest in Canada* uses the same ranking as a positive: "Canada is seen as the second least corrupt country among G20 members and 12th globally" (Invest in Canada 2020).

irrevocably tarnished and the Liberals were often on the defensive for the balance of the campaign.

The election results were a comeuppance. The Conservatives won the popular vote (34.3%) and the Liberals were reduced to a minority of seats with the lowest vote share (33.1%) of any government in Canadian history. Deep regional divides were exposed, with the Liberals shut out in Alberta and Saskatchewan, and the Bloc Québécois resurrected from a vanishing force to holding the third-most seats. Anger at Trudeau was palpable, salvaged only by widespread mistrust of Conservative leader Andrew Scheer, who had his own brand image problems. In the aftermath, *Politico* proclaimed that both Canada's and Trudeau's brand reputations were "on the line" (Heath 2019).

The election results led to a new strategy. Much as Tony Blair had done years ago, Trudeau sought a brand re-set after the election by purposely staying out of the public eye and deferring to other government spokespersons: "'The place that the visuals or the role that I took on in leading this government sometimes interfered with our ability to actually talk about the really substantive things we were able to get done,' Trudeau said. 'I think a lot of the time, politics has become very leader-centric in terms of the visuals...[the] extraordinary team of ministers who weren't always given the attention or visibility that we would all have benefited from'" (quoted in Bryden 2019). Of course, Trudeau and the PMO were partly responsible for exploiting and intensifying a leader-centric focus, such as by disseminating a stream of digital visuals taken by his official photographer. Regardless, it was an admission that Canadians had grown tired of celebrity politics, and mimicked the "low bridge" strategy of staying out of the public eye that Pierre Trudeau followed in the 1980 election campaign after voters had enough.

Chrystia Freeland assumed much of the media limelight after her promotion as deputy prime minister following the election; this reflected Trudeau's recognition that he was overexposed. Often portrayed as one of the government's most competent frontbenchers and the subject of favourable profiles (e.g. Kinsman 2020), Freeland was initially minister of international trade, becoming minister of foreign affairs in 2017 until the cabinet reset after the 2019 election. Freeland's role in renegotiating the North American Free Trade Agreement contributed to her being entrusted as minister of intergovernmental affairs to resolve post-election regional tensions. She garnered laudatory headlines for meeting with premiers that harkened to the salad days of Brand Trudeau, and even referred to Ontario Progressive Conservative premier Doug Ford as her "therapist" when commenting on their new friendship (Delacourt 2020a). However, for all the hagiography, Freeland's international profile was confined to elite political circles.

When Trudeau reappeared in January 2020, his metamorphosis was marked with a greying beard, widely interpreted as an image shift designed to signal a more experienced head of government. Such is the hyper-mediatized nature of contemporary politics that pundits world-wide could interpret facial hair as indicating a new approach to politics (e.g. Vieira 2020). Nevertheless, the new brand was working. The prime minister's newfound seriousness was on full display that month after Iranian forces shot down a Ukrainian jet, killing 176 people including 57 Canadians. Trudeau's stern demand for Iran to provide answers and to compensate victim's families contributed to higher approval ratings (EKOS Politics 2020). However, he committed a diplomatic blunder when he was caught on camera smiling and shaking the hands of Iran's foreign minister soon afterwards. Once again, a Trudeau gaffe undermined his public relations achievements.

COVID-19

Despite this gaffe, Trudeau's popularity once again rose, this time due to his leadership during the COVID-19 crisis, though again his standing with the public was weakened by controversy. His approval ratings have generally been high, as his communication style during the pandemic enabled him to recast his public image after the problems of 2019. The Trudeau government received high marks for taking the pandemic seriously and acting quickly to address public health and economic issues. This was aided by the fact that the height of the health crisis marked a rare moment of cross-partisan consensus in Canada (Merkley et al. 2020). Canadians displayed a willingness to accept large-scale spending and forgave occasional problems in delivering support to Canadians, given the urgency of the situation. Trudeau not only conveyed a serious image; he came to personify the Canadian response, including deferring getting a haircut and wearing a face mask. Trudeau's near-daily press conferences allowed him to speak directly to Canadians, without questioning from the opposition, thus salvaging his brand, an approach that also worked for premiers across the country.

Trudeau's management of the crisis was not without criticism or controversy. Speaking directly to Canadians and often bypassing parliament allowed him to avoid persistent questions from the opposition, giving the government considerable power despite its minority status. Only outrage from the opposition led the government to not table its March 2020 proposal to give the finance minister the right to implement tax, borrowing and spending measures for nearly two years without parliamentary approval. Some policy analysts and pundits raised concerns about deficit and debt levels and unchecked government spending; however, there was broad political consensus that the social safety net was ill-equipped for the disruption wrought by the pandemic.

Trudeau's management skills and brand were again questioned in the summer of 2020, when news broke that the government had awarded a sole-sourced contract to the WE Charity to deliver a $912 million student service grant programme. This set off political fireworks in the capital, given that the prime minister and his wife were actively involved in the charity, prompting the Ethics commissioner to launch another investigation of the prime minister. It was discovered that the prime minister's mother and brother had received considerable speaking fees for speaking at WE events, raising the spectre of serious conflict of interest, with a subtext of rekindling the morality of Trudeau charging charities tens of thousands of dollars to hire him to speak when he was a backbencher MP (Mas 2013). Finance Minister Bill Morneau and other family members were also involved with the charity, prompting the commissioner to also launch an investigation of Morneau. Neither Trudeau not Morneau recused themselves from cabinet deliberations of the programme, raising the spectre of both men having conflicts of interest, for which Trudeau apologized. A parliamentary committee investigated, and we witnessed the extraordinary spectacle of the prime minister testifying and accepting some blame for the problematic rollout of the programme's approval process. It was later revealed that Morneau had failed to properly document expenses incurred when travelling for the charity. This contributed to the minister's resignation, which was an astounding turn of events.

The emerging political scandal again tarnished Trudeau's brand and drew unwanted international attention. It raised issues of political control and the centralization of power in the PMO, in contrast to the Trudeau brand promise of doing politics differently. The concentration of power that supported the Trudeau brand and contributed to the SNC-Lavalin affair was still there when Trudeau was caught in the WE Charity scandal

(Bryden and Bronskill 2020). The governor general agreed to Trudeau's request to prorogue parliament in August; the prime minister's rationale was that the government's last throne speech had not mentioned COVID-19, so a new mandate was needed. Critics noted that this move shut down the parliamentary committee that was probing the WE controversy and whose findings could provide more political problems for the Liberals. When parliament resumed, Liberal MPs on the Ethics Committee continued to throw up obstacles to Conservative attempts to investigate Trudeau family speaking appearances at WE events and any fees and expenses they received.

Lost in the political turmoil is the pandemic's uneven impact on Canadians—especially women, Indigenous peoples, racial and ethnic minorities, and lower-income Canadians—and how this challenges the prime minister's brand. The Trudeau government offered mixed messaging in the name of expediency, for example by providing a one-time tax free payment for seniors, many of whom are financially solvent. It is not clear that the government's emergency measures will fundamentally alter the situation of such Canadians, laying bare the rhetoric-reality gaps between the prime minister's brand of inclusiveness and his government's inability to effect profound change.

Some of Trudeau's actions during the pandemic also undermined his personal brand. Why could he cross provincial boundaries to go to the prime minister's cottage in Québec during the Easter holidays when Canadians were told to stay home? Why did he attend a June anti-racism protest on Parliament Hill when Canadians were still being encouraged to stay away from mass gatherings? Like other protesters, Trudeau took a knee. While appreciated by some, others dismissed it as more virtue signalling. Critics used social media to recall the 2019 revelations that Trudeau wore brownface and blackface (Ruiz 2020). Accusations were made that his government had failed to substantively follow through on his condemnation of anti-Black and anti-Asian Canadian racism or address questions of police violence (Cecco 2020). Canadian reaction to anti-racism demonstrations in the USA also challenged Canada's myth of racelessness—that racism is an American problem, not a Canadian problem. The head of the RCMP had trouble defining systemic racism and later said that it does not exist in the force, which coincided with video of the assault of an Indigenous leader. The PMO stated that it had confidence in the commissioner, but did not offer more specifics on police reform, prompting NDP leader Jagmeet Singh to say that Trudeau had to do more than take a knee (see Kirkup and Walsh 2020).

Meanwhile, Trudeau refused to criticize President Trump's controversial tactics for dealing with Black Lives Matters protesters, instead using a press conference to "perform" his answer with a 21-second delay when asked about his erratic American counterpart. Conveying disapproval in this manner meant that he could not be accused of criticizing the president, a new twist in his ongoing strategy for dealing with Trump by avoiding controversy. Trudeau may have avoided an awkward situation, but his inaction on addressing grievances and his refusal to discuss the values of others when they were controversial was noted, this despite the fact that part of Trudeau's brand strategy is values projection and connecting them to Canadian values.

Trudeau's strategic silence towards the Trump administration's bullying tactics towards Canada is noteworthy. Typically, Canadian politicians display anti-Americanism during election season (Doran and Sewell 1988), but in 2020, it was President Trump who repeatedly criticized Canada, not the other way around. Trudeau reportedly told his team to avoid commenting on the US election, even to the point of not congratulating Kamala Harris for being the first African-American vice-presidential nominee (Delacourt 2020b). The rationale is that criticism is unnecessary and jeopardizes Canadian interests, though it is unclear how this meshes with a brand strategy based on values projection, especially given that polls repeatedly showed that Canadians overwhelmingly disapproved of Trump and his handling of the pandemic. For example, Ontario did not experience political backlash when Ontario premier Doug Ford complained that the president's attempt to prevent 3M from shipping respirator masks to Canada was no way to treat friends.

Prime Minister Trudeau's management of Canada's COVID-19 response will ultimately be judged by how he delivers on his promises and actions that uphold his brand values, not by his rhetoric or performance. The government is faced with developing post-pandemic strategies for rebuilding the economy and the social safety net, including health care, as the world processes the implications of the pandemic. As well, the Canadian government will be pressed to rethink its confidence in global trade rules and its role in global health diplomacy, among other international agreements.

CANADA IN THE WORLD

The case of Brand Trudeau illustrates the opportunities and peril of celebrity branding for nation brands. After winning the 2015 federal election, Trudeau briefly caught the attention of global elites, boosting Canada's profile and raising hopes in some quarters that Canada was prepared to act constructively. However, gaps between political rhetoric promoting the brand versus policy and programme delivery produced a disconnect that weakened Trudeau's political capital.

Just as a political brand can raise a country's profile, a tarnished political brand can drag it down. While brand indexes are broader than the image of a national leader, rankings align with impressions of Brand Trudeau initially infusing positive effects on Canada's international image, which then receded because of negative publicity. One international index ranked Canada as the world's 8th most valuable nation brand in 2016 and 2019, and the globe's 7th most valuable in 2017 and 2018, switching spots each time with India (Brand Finance 2019). Another global index ranked Canada's brand as 5th in the world in 2014 and 8th in 2019, remarking that "much-loved Prime Minister Justin Trudeau has taken a beating lately in the press" (FutureBrand 2019: 85).

After the humbling of the 2019 election campaign, Trudeau's brand reset was a response to serious political divisions at home and a recognition of his overexposure. The reset might help the prime minister navigate challenging global issues, given that many require international cooperation despite increasing nationalist impulses (see the chapters by Axworthy and Manulak, this volume). As in Canada, internationally the initial Trudeau brand held less sway because of his habit of accumulating baggage as he becomes more experienced running a government. Concern about too much attention focused on the prime minister vanished when the COVID-19 pandemic called for urgent measures and daily media updates, for which Trudeau received considerable praise.

That the Trudeau brand had relinquished international lustre was evident when Canada lost its bid for a seat on the United Nations Security Council in mid-2020. Election to the seat is a status symbol for the political elites of a middle power like Canada. When Canada's bid was unsuccessful in 2010, Liberals decried the miss as a global indictment of Conservative foreign policy under Harper. That Canada obtained more first-round votes then was a stinging rebuke of the Trudeau brand and arguably that of Canada. Trudeau's celebrity could not overcome the fact that Canada, despite its rhetoric, had not delivered on international assistance (Brown, this volume) and peacekeeping, as had its competitors Norway and Ireland. Furthermore, Trudeau's virtue signalling at COP 21 of promising to take bold action on climate change was laid bare when Greta Thunberg, the Swedish climate activist, wrote to all of the United Nations' permanent missions to oppose Canada's bid (Blanchfield 2020).

Moreover, despite Trudeau's lofty liberal internationalist rhetoric, foreign policy after Freeland became Foreign Affairs minister had become more hard power than it sounded, and the Liberals continued the Harper government's propensity to favour Israel (Seligman 2018), alienating a number of countries. Canada was reduced to promoting its celebrity prime minister and his/Canada's values. François-Philippe Champagne, the Foreign Affairs minister, argued, "our reputation and credibility rest on our ability to demonstrate to our partners and allies how - in concrete terms - our principles and values guide our diplomacy" (Global Affairs Canada 2020). But what values, exactly? A last-minute push for votes led to awkward moments for the Trudeau government, given that he and his ministers were cozying up to regimes with regressive human rights and social policies. The prime minister claimed that the United Nations needed Canada on the Security Council post-pandemic because of the country's historic role in supporting the UN and contributing to post-World War II reconstruction. This response to critics who argued Canada did not deserve to win because of its lack of international engagement in recent years (Blanchfield 2020) did not convince member nations, perhaps because Canada's promises to act internationally on the COVID-19 pandemic were not significant (Brown, this volume).

Trudeau's questionable political judgement in openly pursuing the Security Council campaign (Chapnick 2020) reveals the extent to which the Trudeau team seemed to believe that a liberal internationalist rhetoric and a progressive image carried weight, and that other countries would simply ignore Canada's tendency under Trudeau and Freeland to support the Trump administration's views on international issues. This message also ignores the government's mixed record in international engagement, marked by conflicting messages at home and abroad. Trudeau promoted reconciliation with Indigenous peoples and action on climate change, but protesters had blocked railways to stop the construction of a natural gas pipeline through territory unceded by the Wet'suwet'en First Nation. His government had spent $4.5 billion to purchase the Trans Mountain pipeline and committed billions more as the project's cost ballooned, while failing to keep up with obligations made at the COP 21 conference. Trudeau fashioned an image as a champion of feminism and LGBTQ+ rights, yet Canada had sold armaments to countries with poor human rights records and stood accused of selling arms used in the war in Yemen, in contradiction of its support for a rules-based international order (Chase 2020). The Liberals returned the Canadian military to a peacekeeping role, yet the peacekeeping missions dwindled, and when the United States launched airstrikes on Syria in 2017, Trudeau called for a UN investigation, but then he publicly supported the unilateral action after speaking with President Trump (Rabson 2017). Canada's foreign aid spending was anaemic by comparative standards (Brown, this volume). Such inconsistencies between rhetoric and action produce cognitive dissonance that weaken public brands.

CONCLUSION

A diminished image globally undermines the overall branding effort to attract foreign direct investment and reduces Canada's influence in the world. Some Liberal politicians are fond of saying that "the world needs more Canada". However, the government led by Justin Trudeau has more often than not committed to contributing values, and at times its actions have been misaligned with those values.

Trudeau came to power in 2015 promising change and committing Canada to re-engaging with the world, yet there has been considerable continuity between the Harper and Trudeau foreign policies (Carment and Nimijean 2020). Five years later, the Angus Reid Institute noted that Canada, far from being "back"—in the Liberal sense—has not moved, as partisan differences mark perceptions of how Canada is seen in the world. It found that 45% of Liberals believed that Canada's international reputation was better than a decade ago, while 71% of Conservatives thought it was worse (Korzinski 2020). This reflects the phenomenon that governments in power seek to redefine Canada's international identity in partisan terms to nurture their base (Brown 2018). Despite initial plans to refocus after a rebuke in the 2019 election, the Liberal Party's brand image continues to be leader-centric and communicates values that Liberal partisans perceive as authentic but others view as hypocritical.

The COVID-19 pandemic laid bare the problem of messaging that emphasizes values while ignoring the policy requirements needed to uphold those values. Prime Ministers Jean Chrétien and Paul Martin were masters of this approach, arguing that the "Canadian Way" revealed Liberals as believers in caring and sharing and taking care of the less fortunate even as their neoliberal policies accentuated inequality (Nimijean 2006), and led governments that transformed the health care and unemployment systems, programmes now revealed to be inadequate for responding to the pandemic. The September 2020 Throne Speech, initially expected to be an ambitious blueprint for a green transformation of the economy, instead focused on addressing immediate economic concerns. The resumption of Trudeau speaking directly to Canadians, which began with a primetime televised address to Canadians immediately after the throne speech, reinforces the leader-centric brand.

For most of his prime ministership, Justin Trudeau has been omnipresent and has led a government that is indelibly shaped in its leader's image. Daily press conferences during the pandemic rejuvenated his brand and helped him navigate challenging global issues—many requiring international cooperation despite increasing nationalist impulses (see the chapters by Axworthy and Manulak, this volume). However, inconsistent messaging impedes his ability to capitalize on an unprecedented level of global celebrity by Canadian standards. For example, just as gains in recharging his domestic image were frittered away by the WE Charity fiasco and a third ethics investigation, similarly Trudeau's renewed commitment to the United Nations, multilateralism and helping the less fortunate stand in contrast to Canada's relatively sparse contributions to the developing world during the pandemic (Brown, this volume).

Following the Tony Blair communications playbook of projecting an image of seasoned leadership requires more than Prime Minister Trudeau growing a beard or empowering Minister Freeland as a government spokesperson. Internationally, Trudeau's celebrity is both a sensation and a squandered opportunity. The Canadian leader is held back by an alarming propensity to score own-goals that have repeatedly stained his brand with ethical lapses. It is difficult for him to preach progressive values or criticize moralistic actions of international leaders when his own record, and that of his government, are coloured by inconsistency between political messaging, values and actions.

References

Anholt, Simon. 2009. "Nation 'Branding': Propaganda or Statecraft?" *Public Diplomacy Magazine* (Summer): 88–90.

Beeby, Dean. 2017a. "Environment Minister's Staff Signed Off on Tweet Praising Syria for Joining Paris Accord." *CBC News*, October 25. https://www.cbc.ca/news/politics/paris-tweet-mckenna-syria-environment-social-media-raitt-climate-change-1.4876305.

Beeby, Dean. 2017b. "Cut out the Cardboard Cut-Outs of Trudeau, Canadian Diplomats Told." *CBC News*, March 20. https://www.cbc.ca/news/politics/trudeau-cut-outs-global-affairs-canada-conservative-harper-diplomats-1.4033120.

Blanchfield, Mike. 2020. "UN Security Council Needs Canada Post-Pandemic, Akin to Second World War: PM." *CTV News*, May 19. https://www.ctvnews.ca/politics/un-security-council-needs-canada-post-pandemic-akin-to-second-world-war-pm-1.4944971.

Brand Finance. 2019. "Nation Brands 2019." https://brandirectory.com/download-report/brand-finance-nation-brands-2019-preview.pdf. Accessed on September 22, 2020.

Brown, Stephen. 2018. "All About That Base? Branding and the Domestic Politics of Canadian Foreign Aid." *Canadian Foreign Policy Journal* 24 (2): 145–164. https://doi.org/10.1080/11926422.2018.1461666.

Bryden, Joan. 2019. "Trudeau Vows to Step Back from Limelight in Second Mandate." *Globe and Mail*, December 20. https://www.theglobeandmail.com/politics/article-trudeau-says-hes-taking-a-lower-profile-more-businesslike-approach/.

Bryden, Joan, and Jim Bronskill. 2020. "Documents Suggest Bureaucrats Were Nudged to Look to We Charity for Student Program." *CBC News*, August 19. https://www.cbc.ca/news/politics/we-charity-pmo-documents-1.5691699.

Campion-Smith, Bruce. 2017. "Prime Minister Justin Trudeau's Controversial Castro Tribute Left Bureaucrats Scrambling." *The Star*, March 10. https://www.thestar.com/news/canada/2017/03/10/prime-minister-justin-trudeaus-controversial-castro-tribute-left-bureaucrats-scrambling.html.

Carment, David, and Richard Nimijean. 2020. "Assessing Canada's Liberal Internationalism: Where Is Canada Headed on the Global Stage?" In *Canadian Political, Social and Historical (Re)Visions in 20th and 21st Centuries*, edited by Marcin Gabryś, Magdalena Marczuk-Karbownik, and Magdalena Paluszkiewicz-Misiaczek. Berlin: Peter Lang, 13–44.

CBC News. 2013. "Justin Trudeau's 'Foolish' China Remarks Spark Anger." *CBC News*, November 9. https://www.cbc.ca/news/canada/toronto/justin-trudeau-s-foolish-china-remarks-spark-anger-1.2421351.

Cecco, Leyland. 2020. "Justin Trudeau Takes a Knee But Is Silent on Reforms to Policing." *The Guardian*, June 6. https://www.theguardian.com/world/2020/jun/05/justin-trudeau-takes-a-knee-but-is-silent-on-reforms-to-policing.

Chapnick, Adam. 2020. "Ottawa's Ill-Fated Quest for a UN Security Council Seat." *Policy Options*, June 19. https://policyoptions.irpp.org/magazines/june-2020/ottawas-ill-fated-quest-for-a-un-security-council-seat/.

Chase, Stephen. 2020. "Canada Is Fuelling War in Yemen with Arms Sales, UN Report Says." *Globe and Mail*, September 9. https://www.theglobeandmail.com/politics/article-un-experts-report-on-yemen-war-names-canada-as-one-of-arms-suppliers/.

Cosgrove, Ken. 2018. Trump and the Republican Brand Refresh. In *Political Marketing in the 2016 U.S. Presidential Election*, edited by Jamie Gillies. Cham: Springer International Publishing.

Curry, Bill. 2018. "A Federal Agency, Created to Fight Poverty, Spent $500,000 on a Name, Logo and Branding." *Globe and Mail*, November 23. https://www.theglobeandmail.com/politics/article-sounds-like-deficit-how-a-federal-agency-created-to-fight-poverty/.

Curry Jansen, Sue. 2008. "Designer Nations: Neo-Liberal Nation Branding—Brand Estonia." *Social Identities* 14 (1): 121–142.

Delacourt, Susan. 2020a. "'He's My Therapist': How Chrystia Freeland and Doug Ford Forged an Unlikely Friendship in the Fight Against COVID-19." *The Star*, April 3. https://www.thestar.com/news/insight/2020/04/03/hes-my-therapist-how-chrystia-freeland-and-doug-ford-forged-an-unlikely-friendship-in-the-fight-against-covid-19.html.

Delacourt, Susan. 2020b. "Here's Why Justin Trudeau Told His MPs to Stop Tweeting About Kamala Harris." *The Star*, August 23. https://www.thestar.com/politics/political-opinion/2020/08/23/heres-why-justin-trudeau-told-his-mps-to-stop-tweeting-about-kamala-harris.html.

Doran, Charles, and James Sewell. 1988. "Anti-Americanism in Canada?" *The Annals of the American Academy* 497 (May): 105–119.

Dragojlovic, Nicolas Isak. 2011. "Priming and the Obama Effect on Public Evaluations of the United States." *Political Psychology* 32 (6): 989–1006. https://doi.org/10.1111/j.1467-9221.2011.00849.x.

Dutt, Barkha. 2018. "Trudeau's India Trip Is a Total Disaster—and He Has Only Himself to Blame." *Washington Post*, February 23. https://www.washingtonpost.com/news/global-opinions/wp/2018/02/22/trudeaus-india-trip-is-a-total-disaster-and-he-has-himself-to-blame/.

EKOS Politics. 2020. "Directional Outlook and Public Response to Growing Iran-U.S. Tensions." https://www.ekospolitics.com/index.php/2020/01/directional-outlook-and-public-response-to-growing-iran-u-s-tensions/. Accessed on January 18, 2020.

FutureBrand. 2019. "Country Index 2019." https://www.futurebrand.com/uploads/FCI/FutureBrand-Country-Index-2019.pdf. Accessed on September 22, 2020.

Glavin, Terry. 2016. "Trudeau's Turn from Cool to Laughing Stock." *Maclean's*, November 27. https://www.macleans.ca/news/trudeaus-turn-from-cool-to-laughing-stock/.

Global Affairs Canada. 2020. "Address by Minister of Foreign Affairs to the Montreal Council on Foreign Relations." Government of Canada. https://www.canada.ca/en/global-affairs/news/2020/02/address-by-minister-of-foreign-affairs-to-the-montreal-council-on-foreign-relations.html. Accessed on February 25, 2020.

Gravelle, Timothy B., Thomas J. Scotto, Jason Reifler, and Harold D. Clarke. 2014. "Foreign Policy Beliefs and Support for Stephen Harper and the Conservative Party." *Canadian Foreign Policy Journal* 20 (2): 111–130. https://doi.org/10.1080/11926422.2014.936477.

Hahn, Phil. 2019. "Support for Trudeau on the Decline Among Women: Nanos Tracking." *CTV News*, August 19. https://www.ctvnews.ca/politics/support-for-trudeau-on-the-decline-among-women-nanos-tracking-1.4559337.

Hahn, Phil. 2020. "Canadians Increasingly Negative on Government's Performance: 13-Year Nanos Study." *CTV News*, February 7. https://www.ctvnews.ca/politics/canadians-increasingly-negative-on-government-s-performance-13-year-nanos-study-1.4801766.

Heath, Ryan. 2019. "Canada's Brand Rose with Trudeau. Now Both Their Reputations Are on the Line." *Politico*, October 11. https://www.politico.com/news/2019/10/11/justin-trudeau-canada-image-044277.

Hudson, Simon, and J. R. Brent Ritchie. 2009. "Branding a Memorable Destination Experience. The Case of 'Brand Canada'." *International Journal of Tourism Research* 11 (2): 217–228.

Hunt, Wayne. 2003. "The 'Branding' of Trudeau." *London Journal of Canadian Studies* 18: 87–101.

Invest in Canada. 2020. "Why Invest in Canada?" https://www.investcanada.ca/why-invest. Accessed on September 22, 2020.

Kinsman, Jeremy. 2020. "The Many Stages of Chrystia Freeland." https://policymagazine.ca/the-many-stages-of-chrystia-freeland-2/. Accessed on January 6, 2020.

Kirkup, Kristy, and Marieke Walsh. 2020. "RCMP Commissioner Brenda Lucki Faces Calls to Resign over Comments on Systemic Racism in Force." *Globe and Mail*, June 15. https://www.theglobeandmail.com/politics/article-rcmp-should-institute-zero-tolerance-for-excessive-use-of-force-afn/.

Korzinski, Dave. 2020. "Five Years After Trudeau Promised Canada Was 'Back' on the World Stage, Many Canadians Say We're in the Same Place." Angus Ried Institute. http://angusreid.org/canada-international-reputation-un-security-council/. Accessed on July 16, 2020.

Lalancette, Mireille, and Vincent Raynauld. 2017. "The Power of Political Image: Justin Trudeau, Instagram, and Celebrity Politics." *The American Behavioral*

Scientist (Beverly Hills) 63 (7): 888–924. https://doi.org/10.1177/000276 4217744838.

Landriault, Mathieu. 2016. "Does Voting End at the Water's Edge? Canadian Public Opinion and Voter Intentions, 2006–2015." *Canadian Foreign Policy Journal* 22 (3): 249–261. https://doi.org/10.1080/11926422.2016. 1166143.

Marland, Alex. 2018. "The Brand Image of Canadian Prime Minister Justin Trudeau in International Context." *Canadian Foreign Policy Journal* 24 (2): 139–144. https://doi.org/10.1080/11926422.2018.1461665.

Marland, Alex. 2020. *Whipped: Party Discipline in Canada.* Vancouver: UBC Press.

Marland, Alex, J.P. Lewis, and Tom Flanagan. 2017. "Governance in the Age of Digital Media and Branding." *Governance* 30 (1): 125–141.

Mas, Susana. 2013. "Trudeau to Compensate Charities That Paid Him Speaking Fees." *CBC News*, June 16. https://www.cbc.ca/news/politics/trudeau-to-compensate-charities-that-paid-him-speaking-fees-1.1339441.

McGrane, David. 2019. *The New Ndp: Moderation, Modernization, and Political Marketing.* Vancouver: UBC Press.

Merkley, Eric, Aengus Bridgman, Peter John Loewen, Taylor Owen, Derek Ruths, and Oleg Zhilin. 2020. "A Rare Moment of Cross-Partisan Consensus: Elite and Public Response to the COVID-19 Pandemic in Canada." *Canadian Journal of Political Science* 53 (2): 311–318. https://doi.org/10.1017/s0008423920000311.

Needham, Catherine. 2006. "Brands and Political Loyalty." *Journal of Brand Management* 13 (3): 178–187. https://doi.org/10.1057/palgrave.bm.254 0260.

Nimijean, Richard. 2005. "The Paradoxical Nature of the Canadian Identity." *Teaching Canada* 23: 25–31.

Nimijean, Richard. 2006. "Brand Canada: The Brand State and the Decline of the Liberal Party." *Inroads* 19: 84–93.

Nimijean, Richard. 2018. "Introduction: Is Canada Back? Brand Canada in a Turbulent World." *Canadian Foreign Policy Journal* 24 (2): 127–138.

Potter, Evan H. 2004. "Branding Canada: The Renaissance of Canada's Commercial Diplomacy." *International Studies Perspectives* 5 (1): 55–60.

Rabson, Mia. 2017. "Trudeau's Stance on Syria Shows He Is Keen to Stay in Trump's Favour: Expert." *Global News*, April 12. https://globalnews.ca/news/3375146/trudeau-trump-syria-chemical-attack/.

Rose, Jonathan. 2010. "The Branding of States: The Uneasy Marriage of Marketing to Politics." *Journal of Political Marketing* 9 (4): 254–275.

Ruiz, Karen. 2020. "Justin Trudeau Kneels with Protesters During an Anti-Racism Rally in Ottawa—But Social Media Users Were Quick to Remind Him of His Blackface Photos." *Daily Mail*, June 5. https://www.dailym

ail.co.uk/news/article-8393515/Justin-Trudeau-takes-knee-protest-Twitter-immediately-calls-blackface-photos.html.

Scammell, Margaret. 2007. "Political Brands and Consumer Citizens: The Rebranding of Tony Blair." *The ANNALS of the American Academy of Political and Social Science* 611 (1): 176–192. https://doi.org/10.1177/000271 6206299149.

Seligman, Steven. 2018. "Canada's Israel Policy under Justin Trudeau: Rejecting or Reinforcing the Legacy of Stephen Harper?." *American Review of Canadian Studies* 48 (1): 80–95. https://doi.org/10.1080/02722011.2018.143 4552.

The Guardian. 2018. "Justin Trudeau Tells Woman to Say 'Peoplekind' Not 'Mankind.'" *The Guardian*, February 7. https://www.theguardian.com/world/2018/feb/07/justin-trudeau-tells-woman-to-say-peoplekind-not-man kind.

Transparency International. 2020. "Corruption Perceptions Index 2019." https://images.transparencycdn.org/images/2019_CPI_Report_EN_200 331_141425.pdf. Accessed on September 18, 2020.

van Ham, Peter. 2001. "The Rise of the Brand State: The Postmodern Politics of Image and Reputation." *Foreign Affairs* 80 (5): 2–6.

Vieira, Paul. 2020. "Can Justin Trudeau's Beard Overturn a Century of Politics?" *Wall Street Journal*, February 14. https://www.wsj.com/articles/can-justin-trudeaus-beard-overturn-a-century-of-politics-11581699766.

Way, Alan. 1993. "The Government of Canada's Federal Identity Program." *Design Management Journal*, Summer: 55–62.

Zavattaro, Staci M. 2010. "Brand Obama: The Implications of a Branded President." *Administrative Theory & Praxis* 32 (1): 123–128. https://doi.org/10.2753/atp1084-1806320108.

Balancing Interests and Constraints: The Role of Provinces in the Shaping of Canadian Foreign Policy

Nelson Michaud

INTRODUCTION

In his weekly column of April 30, 2020, Université de Montréal political scientist Pierre Martin underscored that "In the coronavirus crisis, many observers here deplore the Trudeau government's attempts to centralize certain powers under the guise of federal aid to the most affected provinces, including Québec" (Martin 2020). Of course, the COVID-19 pandemic has changed several of the parameters, the federal government even intruding in the area of health care for the elderly with the intent of implementing national norms (Buzzetti 2020) and in the field of primary education, probably the last domain where provincial jurisdictions are fully respected (Trudeau 2020).

N. Michaud (✉)
École nationale d'administration publique, Québec, QC, Canada
e-mail: Nelson.Michaud@enap.ca

© The Author(s), under exclusive license to Springer Nature   77
Switzerland AG 2021
D. Carment and R. Nimijean (eds.), *Political Turmoil
in a Tumultuous World*, Canada and International Affairs,
https://doi.org/10.1007/978-3-030-70686-9_4

An explanation given by some politicians in Ottawa is that in times of crisis, constitutional thresholds do not matter as much as the common good for all Canadians, notwithstanding their province of residence. In such circumstances, would it also be possible that provinces try to defend their interests abroad notwithstanding the prominent role of the federal government in the conduct of Canada's foreign policy? Do provinces simply influence Canada's stance? Is the crisis an enough serious matter that all governments rally around the Canadian flag and let Ottawa organize all foreign relations? In other words, in these times of uncertainty, do provinces in turn overstep a domain of federal jurisdiction?

To answer this question, one must determine how this potential role provinces play can be measured. I would suggest that first, we must take into account the difference that exists between international relations and foreign policy, for it is the policymaking power that is constitutionally framed. We understand that foreign policy must be a public policy, that is, the decision taken by a democratically representative governing body to do or not do something, and that this policy must be outward looking to distinguish it from domestic policy. Moreover, foreign policy must have an impact abroad, this impact being an influence in the shaping of international standards and legal norms. This influence in norm making is what differentiates implementing foreign policy from conducting international relations. Therefore, as long as provinces—or for that matter NGOs or corporations—conduct international relations, the level of interference with the federal government is minimal compared to their involvement in the realm of foreign policy.

This foreign policy role in turn depends largely on two factors. First, the more interests (I) a state has at stake in relation to an international issue, the more intensive its foreign policy role (R) will be. Second, states face constraints (C), internal and external, which will stall their efforts in trying to influence the shaping of international norms. Finally, a third factor is, at times, considered: the preferences expressed by the person who decides (p) could make a difference on specific policy issues. This relationship is illustrated by the equation:

$$R = I/C * p.$$

This foreign policy reading grid has the advantage of leaving the "schools" debate at the doorstep while it reaches the heart of what needs to be explained: why and how does a state intervene in the shaping of international norms in defence of its national interests? This magnifying glass is also useful to answer the question we are asking in this chapter: do provinces boost or hinder Canadian foreign policymaking? We will therefore look at the issues from this angle, mainly in terms of interests and constraints and, if appropriate, we will take into account the decider's preferences.

Looking at the province that has the longest history of challenging Ottawa's exclusive jurisdiction in the realm of foreign affairs helps in defining the furthest point to be reached or, in other terms, how far provinces wish to get involved. Consequently, this study provides also a reading of how the most active Canadian province on the international scene, namely Québec, is acting.

In view of appreciating the scope of this role, this chapter will first look at Canadian provinces' foreign policy potential position as framed by international law or the Canadian constitution, as well as the general practice some of them have adopted over the years. Then, since Québec's international presence is anchored on commitments dating back to the nineteenth century, an overview of this historical perspective will put into context Québec government's present action. The essential part of the chapter will then explore this latter theme, namely Premier François Legault's approach to Québec's international endeavours. We will finally focus on potential changes that may have appeared since the day the government has started to manage issues and to face challenges related the COVID-19 pandemic. We will see that the Québec government has expressed a noticeable doctrinal retreat which the 2020 context has not shaken.

PROVINCES AND FOREIGN POLICY

To fully appreciate how provinces can influence the shaping of Canadian foreign policy, a few remarks are in order. We must first look at the role the international as well as the constitutional environments allow them to play. Then, these roles must be referred to in terms of foreign policymaking inputs.

International Law

International law does not offer much to federated states that wish to play an international role. For all intents and purposes, "the state is the key subject of international law and the key actor in international relations, thus enjoying the ultimate degree of international legal personality" (Currie et al. 2014: 180), as recognized by the UN Charter.[1] And to the usual definition of a state, that is, a steady population living on a definite territory and politically organized, international law adds the sovereignty factor, which means that the state is an entity that is subordinate to no other member of the international community.[2] As a consequence, theoretically, federated states, not enjoying full sovereignty, cannot be considered as subjects of international law. We will see later why this factor is of importance and why provinces do not want to be merely viewed the same way multinational fora or INGOs are.

Although this conception of an international actor is of common knowledge and practice, an opening for federated states to express their own voice on the world scene exists. It is found in the *United Nations Convention on Jurisdictional Immunities of States and Their Property*.[3] This convention includes in its definition of a state "constituent units of a federal state or political subdivisions of the state, which are entitled to perform acts in the exercise of sovereign authority, and are acting in that capacity". This convention, however, is not yet in force for it has gathered only 22 of the 30 required instruments of ratification. Notably, Canada has neither signed nor ratified the convention although—or perhaps because—its provinces would qualify as states under this definition. Canadian provinces therefore cannot rely on international law to perform a formal international role.

Canadian Constitution

To make things more complex, the Canadian constitution does not address how Canada must face its own international responsibilities.

---

[1] S. 4, par.1. http://www.un.org/fr/charter-united-nations/.

[2] *Montevideo Convention on the Rights and Duties of States*, s.l.d. https://www.ilsa.org/Jessup/Jessup15/Montevideo%20Convention.pdf.

[3] S. 2, par. 1 b (ii) https://treaties.un.org/pages/ViewDetails.aspx?src=TREATY&mtdsg_no=III-13&chapter=3&clang=_en.

First, the *British North America Act* (BNAA) was adopted when Canada was not recognized as having autonomous international status since it was then a Dominion of the British Empire. Only Section 132 of the BNAA refers to foreign relations in stating that "The Parliament and Government of Canada shall have all Powers necessary or proper for performing the Obligations of Canada or of any Province thereof, as Part of the British Empire, towards Foreign Countries, arising under Treaties between the Empire and such Foreign Countries". This section of the Constitution has been challenged over the years.

First, provincial autonomy was recognized. In *Hodge* v *R*,[4] it was determined that provinces are in no way the delegates of the Imperial Parliament, nor do they act under any mandate received from the Imperial Parliament. In fact, the decision goes one step further in establishing that "subjects which in one aspect and for one purpose fall within Section 92 [provincial jurisdiction], may in another aspect and for another purpose fall within Section 91 [federal jurisdiction]".

Then, this principle was applied to Section 132 of the BNAA when the Judicial Committee of the Privy Council established that although it is up to the federal government to conclude treaties (including their negotiation, signature and ratification), their implementation comes under the purview of either provincial legislatures or the federal parliament depending on whether the subject is of provincial or federal jurisdiction according to the constitution.[5]

This means that provinces have a say in the implementation of treaties when these relate to their fields of jurisdiction. It offers them the possibility to influence, for instance, how Canada will negotiate a treaty bearing clauses that would have an impact on questions under provincial purview. Through their international actions, do provinces facilitate a strong Canadian foreign policy, or is this a way to dilute Canada's role in the world? On the one hand, there are instances when provinces are openly involved in the negotiation of treaties (Paquin 2019). On the other hand, examples abound to illustrate how the federal government is reluctant to share the international scene with provinces. We can therefore hypothesize that

---

[4] (1883) 9 A.C. 117.

[5] A case known as the *Labour Conventions Reference; Canada (AG)* v *Ontario (AG)*, 1937 A.C. 326.

there is a potential for division when provinces voice their foreign policy priorities. But is it still the case in 2020?

Provinces' International Actions

Provinces, over the years, have attempted to play a certain role in international relations. As we will see, Québec, since the inception of the Gérin-Lajoie doctrine, has been by far the most active province on the world stage. But other provinces are also present.

To give but a few examples, New Brunswick is probably the second most openly active province on the international scene. It benefits from an autonomous status in La Francophonie, the same that Québec enjoys. The province has also issued, a few years ago, an international relations statement or white paper (Government of New Brunswick 2003: 26).

In New Brunswick, the leadership belongs to the ministry of Intergovernmental Affairs and its policy serves the interests of the province in terms of economy and culture, reaching partners in the business sector as well as in academia (Government of New Brunswick 2020a). Recent announcements refer to participation in meetings with U.S. counterparts (Government of New Brunswick 2019c, f), or to maintaining relationships with La Francophonie or French regions (Government of New Brunswick 2019b, d, e). On the trade side, speaking about NAFTA negotiations, former Treasury Board President Roger Melanson made no mystery that "Our ultimate goal is to certify that New Brunswick's position continues to be reflected in the agreement as we work with the Government of Canada as the negotiator" (Government of New Brunswick 2017). The 2019 Speech from the Throne, delivered on November 19, refers to the Congrès mondial acadien as an international gathering the province takes advantage of, and to the "openness to the world" provided by the two linguistic communities (Government of New Brunswick 2019a). The COVID-19 outbreak challenged New Brunswick border towns and the province issued guidelines to supplement the federal restrictions (Government of New Brunswick 2020b).

In Alberta, international relations are strongly anchored in the economic dimension, as witnessed in the Ministry of Economic Development and Trade annual reports (Government of Alberta 2019). The province's efforts aim at representing Alberta's interests in Canada's international trade agreements (Government of Alberta 2020a); advancing international partnerships (Government of Alberta 2020c) in view of improving cooperation, trade and investment and identifying growth opportunities for local industries in foreign markets; organizing economic missions to reach priority markets for Alberta companies; and managing visits from foreign officials and industry partners (Government of Alberta 2020b). Alberta has opened offices in twelve cities, mainly located in Asia.[6] Actually, the province wishes to "aggressively compete" and position itself as "a global destination for petrochemical investment" through the Alberta Petrochemicals Incentive Program (APIP), as part of Alberta's Recovery Plan (Government of Alberta 2020d). In terms of culture, the Ukrainian community welcomes the province's efforts to maintain links abroad. However, according to the February 2020 Speech from the Throne, the only new endeavour with an international tone presented by the government is to adopt "amendments banning foreign money from Alberta politics by making it illegal for foreign entities to contribute to third party advertisers" (Government of Alberta 2020c).

The international relations division of Manitoba's ministry of Intergovernmental Affairs and International Relations concentrates on diplomacy and aid. On the diplomatic front, it builds "strategic relationships with governments outside of Canada, often resulting in bilateral international agreements" with countries from all continents. These range from economic development to agriculture, or from environment and science to education (Manitoba Ministry of Intergovernmental Affairs and International Relations 2020b). The province has also signed agreements with the United Nations (Manitoba Ministry of Intergovernmental Affairs and International Relations 2020a). Regarding aid, the ministry "facilitates the involvement of Manitoba firms and organizations and oversees the Government's involvement in international development projects" (Manitoba Ministry of Intergovernmental Affairs and International Relations 2020b). On top of a coordinating function that also monitors and reports on the province's international relations, the international relations division of the ministry offers strategic policy advice and support to the Premier's and the Minister's international activities.

The trade sector is also developed, but it operates under the jurisdiction of the Ministry of Economic Development and Training (Manitoba Ministry of Economic Development and Training 2020). In recent developments, we note that the post-COVID economy will benefit form "a

---

[6] Beijing, Guangzhou, Hong Kong, London, Mexico City, New Delhi, Seoul, Shanghai, Singapore, Tokyo, Taipei, and Washington, DC.

new, independent private sector-led economic development agency to attract investment and promote international trade for [the] province" as announced in the October 6, 2020 Speech from the Throne (Government of Manitoba 2020). The statement also mentions that the province will engage stakeholders, including from the international level, in the launch of "a challenge to build on, and enhance food security initiatives in northern Manitoba".

For its part, Ontario is a rather quiet province when it comes to international activities. The responsibility for international relations is managed from the ministry of Intergovernmental Affairs. Its motto, "Working with provincial, federal and international partners on issues that affect Ontario", broadcasts a cooperative agenda, but the level of information about the province's international role is shallow. For instance, the web page spends more time on protocol topics than on international relations *per se* (Ontario Ministry of Intergovernmental Affairs 2020). Moreover, the latest press release dates back to 2016 and is about electoral law, not international relations (Government of Ontario 2020). Doug Ford's government Speech from the Throne, delivered on July 12, 2018, keeps the same low profile as it does not refer to or even use the word "international" (Government of Ontario 2018). The province is no less involved, having offices in Canadian embassies.

This general picture of provincial international involvement refers to a common practice that is easily explained by the relationship we evoked earlier. These provinces wish to be present and play an international role in the promotion and defence of their interests, which are mostly of an economic nature. And in view of lowering the constraints the federal system presents, they prioritize their own issues, but they operate in conjunction if not in support of the Canadian foreign policy as defined by the federal government. Hence New Brunswick focusses on regional continental interests as well as its role in the French-speaking world community and it insures to have a say in key trade deals. In Alberta, the energy-based economy is at the fore while in Manitoba, a diversity of sectors coming under the provincial jurisdiction carry their weight.

QUÉBEC AND FOREIGN POLICY

Québec is by far the most active province in terms of international relations. This has obviously attracted a good amount of studies (Michaud 2016: 153–160) and it is no mystery if this chapter focusses on the province as the key analytical corpus to be considered. Moreover, Québec's international actions have often irritated Ottawa in the past to an extent no other province has ever reached. Examples abound in the fields of culture or education. For instance, the role Québec wanted to play in the newly organized post-colonial forum of French-speaking countries—the Agence pour la cooperation culturelle et technique—offered several occasions where both governments were at odds, even provoking a diplomatic clash with a third country, namely Gabon, over the participation of Québec's Minister of Education in an international conference (Morin 1987).

In his 1968 policy statement, Paul Martin Sr., (1968: 11) Secretary of State for External Affairs under Lester B. Pearson, attempted to stifle the initiative. He wrote: "The direction and conduct of foreign relations in federal states is recognized as under the control of central authorities. As a result, members of federal states do not have the independent and autonomous power to enter into treaties, to become full members of international bodies, or to accredit or receive diplomatic and consular officials". In a follow-up document released a few months later, Mitchell Sharp, Secretary of State for External Affairs under Pierre-Elliott Trudeau, offered a direct reply to Québec's initiatives when he added that the federal government is the only level of government that may represent Canada as a whole on the international stage even in regard to questions of provincial jurisdictions such as education (Sharp 1968; Jacomy-Millette 1979).

It was not until Brian Mulroney reached an agreement with Québec Premier Pierre-Marc Johnson that the question was settled. This agreement made the coming of La Francophonie possible (Michaud and Nossal 2001). However, the mistrust Ottawa had over Québec in terms of international involvement continued. It was even implicitly, but nevertheless clearly, underscored in Paul Martin Jr's foreign policy white paper in 2005 (Government of Canada 2005: 30–31).

Interestingly, there were also elements of convergence between Ottawa and Québec when some foreign policy issues were discussed. A clear example of such an agreement is offered by the strong support Québec gave to Canadian free trade initiatives, being it at the time of the original Free Trade Agreement with the United States in 1988 or in initiating the talks that resulted in the Canada-European Union Comprehensive Economic and Trade Agreement (CETA) signed on October 30, 2016, and entered into force provisionally on September 21, 2017.

Since past experience does not lead to predefined answers, this study is even more interesting. An overview of Québec's international role from a historical perspective is useful to understand its evolution at the beginning of the twenty-first century, and more specifically within the Legault-Trudeau relationship.

Historical Background

Québec's international involvement dates back almost 140 years ago when Hector Fabre was sent to Paris to ensure economic interests of the province would be taken care of overseas. In 1940, a delegation opened in New York City and is, as of today, Québec's longest serving office abroad. However, it is during the Quiet Revolution that things started to get organized through the opening of several delegations and the signing of agreements. This effort was framed within a doctrine that Québec Minister of Education and Deputy Premier, Paul Gérin-Lajoie, has formulated. This doctrine asserts "the external extension of Québec's internal jurisdictions". Up to the election of the Legault government, this doctrine prevailed, no matter which party was at the helm of the province.

Gérin-Lajoie has been carrying this idea since his days as a PhD student in Constitutional law at Oxford.[7] Once in office, Gérin-Lajoie met a devoted internationalist, André Patry, who had also thought about it (Aird 2005; Patry 1983; Patry 2006). Gérin-Lajoie "do[es] not dispute that the traditional content of foreign policy should remain in a federal state like ours in the hands of the central government. But when it comes to new areas to which international activity extends nowadays, the external jurisdiction of our Québec state must correspond to the fullest extent of our internal jurisdiction" (Assemblée nationale 1967). Premier Jean Charest will reformulate the doctrine a few years later in a speech at École nationale d'administration publique, stating that "what is of Québec's jurisdiction at home, is of Québec's jurisdiction abroad" (Charest 2004).

Namely, this means that Québec considers having the right to negotiate and implement agreements and other international arrangements in areas of jurisdiction that the Canadian Constitution grants to provinces under

---

[7] His thesis was published (Gérin-Lajoie 1950) and was awarded the Prix David in the field of Moral and Political Sciences by the Québec government the following year.

Section 92. As a result, according to Professor Richard Ouellet's assessment, Québec sometimes adopts the behaviour of "an actor who manages to conclude documents that produce effects in international law"(Ouellet and Beaumier 2016: 73).

In 1967, a ministry dedicated to "intergovernmental relations" was established, which was to become the current Ministry for International Relations and La Francophonie (MRIF). This allowed Québec to lower its constraints by expanding its network of representations abroad, signing agreements and adopting international relations policy statements. In 1985, Québec obtained an autonomous voice in the newly created Francophonie.

21st Century Initiatives

In a series of unanimously adopted amendments to the *Act Respecting the Ministère des Relations internationales* in 2002, the legislator established that "Every important international commitment, including the reservations relating thereto, if any, shall be tabled in the National Assembly by the Minister at the time deemed proper by the Minister".[8] This means that the approval of the National Assembly is needed before such pledge is enacted. Although this action comes after the ratification of an international agreement by Canada, it nevertheless means that the Canadian government, who has the obligation to guarantee the respect of this commitment, must take Québec's priorities into consideration even before agreeing on the content of any such agreement. This process lowers significantly the constraints Québec has to have an influence on the international order, but at the same time, heightens Canada's.

In 2005, the federal government recognized the legitimacy of Québec's international role (Michaud 2006). This recognition is explicitly formulated in the preamble to the *Canada-Québec Agreement on Representation at UNESCO*. The wording is unambiguous: both governments recognize that "in Canada, the specificity of Québec, based among other things on the use of the French language and a unique culture, leads it to play a particular role at the international level".[9]

---

[8] *Act respecting the Ministère des Relations internationales*, RLRQ, c. M-25.1.1, s. 22.2.

[9] *Accord Canada-Québec sur la représentation à l'UNESCO*, http://www.mrif.gouv.qc.ca/content/documents/fr/unesco.pdf.

This opening lessens considerably the level of constraints Québec faces when times come to intervene in international fora. For, although the nature of this recognition is disputed (Pelletier 2008), there are clues that lead to consider it as a constitutional convention. Henri Brun, Guy Tremblay, and Eugénie Brouillet (2014: 43) define the constitutional convention as "a rule developed empirically, by agreement between rulers or politicians, a rule that is not sanctioned by the courts, but enforced and respected by the parties because of a sense of political necessity". To qualify as such and to be part of the constitutional order of a state, an element must meet three criteria identified by Sir Ivor W. Jennings and taken up by the Supreme Court in references to the patriation of the Constitution: there must be precedents; actors in the precedent must have believed themselves bound by a rule; and the rule must have a purpose.[10]

When one applies these criteria to the preamble of the agreement, one notes that indeed there are precedents such as in La Francophonie, to name but one; the actors, that is, both Québec and the federal governments, consider themselves bound by this precedent since they recognize it; and the purpose, to give Québec its own voice in international fora, is unambiguous. Since this *Agreement* meets the test recognized by the Supreme Court to qualify as a constitutional convention, we may conclude that its impact on the international role Québec wishes to play is direct and important, as it lowers the level of constitutional constraints the province faces.

This agreement is the end result of the work done by Québec's most active premier on the international scene: federalist Jean Charest (Jeyabalaratnam and Paquin 2016). He transformed the Gérin-Lajoie doctrine by taking it one step further: not only are Québec's international actions concerned with questions of its own constitutional jurisdictions, but they also cover all questions related to Québec's interests (Charest 2020).

The Legault Government and Foreign Policy

The Legault government was elected on October 1, 2018. Premier François Legault is a former Parti Québécois minister who broke ranks to found a new party (Coalition avenir Québec—CAQ) by joining its forces with the Action démocratique, a party that blossomed when a

---

[10] *Renvoi: résolution pour modifier la Constitution*, [1981] 1 R.C.S. 753, p. 888 ss; *Re: opposition à une résolution pour modifier la Constitution*, [1982] 2 R.C.S. 793, p. 815 ss.

group of dissident Liberals left Robert Bourassa's formation. This meeting of disgruntled partisans gave birth to a nationalist party in the tradition of Québec's pledge for autonomy within the Canadian framework. This approach would normally clash with Justin Trudeau's preference for centralization. It might have been expected that international relations would figure prominently on the new government's agenda and present occasions when the two governments would ruffle feathers. However, this was not the case. Early on, the government sent strong signals that the economy—and especially trade—would be the prime objective of Québec's renewed international actions.

Administrative and Legislative Amendments

A few months after being sworn in as Minister of the Economy, Pierre Fitzgibbon made no secret that in the future, Québec's international strategy "will come from Investissement Québec[11]" (Presse canadienne 2019) and not from the Ministry of International Relations. In itself, this announcement was totally unconventional. Indeed, it is odd to think that a government was willing to subcontract one of its regal powers to an agency headed by a board of directors and a CEO.

Furthermore, the Ministry of International Relations has been, for all intent and purposes, second ranked. On June 12, 2019, Minister Fitzgibbon tabled Bill 27, *An Act respecting mainly government organization as regards the economy and innovation.*[12] This bill was enacted the following December 11. Some sections of this Bill transfer powers from the Minister of International Relations to the Minister of Economy and Innovation. Hence, political responsibility for Québec's international policy is now subject to the requirements of the Minister responsible for the Economy.[13] In other words, Québec's minister of International Relations answers, from now on, to the Minister of the Economy, concretely making the Ministry of International Relations a junior department. This

---

[11] Investissement Québec is a government agency whose mission is to stimulate growth and promote Québec's economic prosperity. To carry out its mandate, the organization has 30 offices in all regions of Québec and 12 offices elsewhere in the world.

[12] http://www.assnat.qc.ca/en/travaux-parlementaires/projets-loi/projet-loi-27-42-1.html?appelant=MC.

[13] Section 92 of the *Act*; which strikes out s.11, par.2 of the MRIF Act.

line of authority is also clearly established in sections 96 and 97 of the *Act*.

As recently as October 2020, the government gave further indication that a major makeover was underway to ensure that trade would be the foremost objective in Québec's international undertakings. This means that some offices and delegations will be closed and others will be moved. Based on several government sources, a journalist points to "the common denominator of this great game of musical chairs: the economic profitability, the strictly commercial interest of a Québec presence in a particular country or region of the globe. In the Caquist era, Québec celebrates business diplomacy" (Richer 2020). As expected, Investissement Québec heavily weighs in the redesigning of the map of where Québec's offices abroad will be located. As a practical consequence, Québec's international stance regarding its identity and culture, or in other words the defence of its jurisdictional responsibilities according to the Gérin-Lajoie doctrine, could be put on the back burner for a while.

Will this mean a lesser level of confrontation with Ottawa in the realm of foreign policy? In fact, we are facing an interesting paradox since, as we have seen, the regulation of trade and commerce is the only foreign policy aspect covered in the Canadian constitution and it is attributed to the federal level.[14] The strong accent put by Québec government on trade could very well be a source of tensions. Is it the case?

Trade Issues?

To answer this question, we must first look at what is understood by trade. Richard Ouellet correctly points out that, in principle, the Gérin-Lajoie doctrine, referring to Québec's internal competences (Section 92), does not touch on trade issues that fall under Section 91; he concludes that it "can apply only partially to the commercial domain" (Ouellet and Baeumier 2016: 79).

While it is important to keep this dimension in mind, we must also consider clarifications the Courts have brought. As early as in 1881, the Judicial Committee of the Privy Council gives the scope of this section,[15] specifying that it must be interpreted narrowly: in the event of

---

[14] *Constitution Act of 1867*, 30 & 31 Victoria, c. 3 (U.K.), s. 91 (2).

[15] *Citizens' and The Queen Insurance Cos.* v. *Parsons*, 4 SCR 215.

a jurisdictional dispute the federal government prevails. Hence, trade and commerce will include international trade, inter-provincial trade as well as general dominion-wide trade and trade regulation. The definition is therefore very clear: international trade is a matter of federal jurisdiction.

In a more recent decision however, the Supreme Court nuanced this standpoint when it stated that "A federal head of power cannot be given a scope that would eviscerate a provincial legislative competence. This is one of the principles that underlie the Constitution. The jurisprudence on the general trade and commerce power reflects this fundamental principle".[16]

The *General Motors* case[17] clarifies things. In this decision, Chief Justice Dickson echoes the argument developed in *Canadian National Transportation*[18] as he determines five criteria that indicate when Section 91 (2), that is, the federal jurisdiction, prevails:

- the impugned legislation must be part of a general regulatory scheme;
- the scheme must be monitored by the continuing oversight of a regulatory agency;
- the legislation must be concerned with trade as a whole rather than with a particular industry;
- the legislation should be of a nature that the provinces jointly or severally would be constitutionally incapable of enacting;
- the failure to include one or more provinces or localities in a legislative scheme would jeopardize the successful operation of the scheme in other parts of the country.

The decision specifically states that these criteria are not exhaustive and that not each of these needs to be present. It also notes that the last three criteria "are indications that the scheme of regulation is national in scope and that local regulation would be inadequate".[19] While this judgement

---

[16] Reference re *Securities Act*, 2011 SCC 66, [2011] 3 S.C.R. 837, par. 71–72.

[17] *General Motors of Canada Ltd.* v. *City National Leasing*, [1989] 1 S.C.R. 641.

[18] *Attorney General of Canada* v. *Canadian National Transportation, Ltd.*, [1983] 2 S.C.R. 206.

[19] Id.

deals with the appraisal of a law, its essence determines the share of international trade that cannot be attributed to a province, which is all that pertains to pan-Canadian dimensions of the measures considered.

A contrario, aspects of trade that are of specific interest to a province are therefore recognized. This is the ground on which provinces, and namely Québec, may adopt their own trade policies. These do not deal with regulations and their implementation, but rather with the development of trade as an economic tool to produce local wealth. They do not infringe on federal constitutional powers.

A reading of this setting in terms of interests and constraints underscores the former aspect, that is, the interest of producing wealth that will provide means to serve the common good. The constraints are high in terms of possibility to regulate trade, but they are low when prioritizing trade, for instance, is concerned. In fact, provinces—and Québec is no exception—take advantage and even support the coming of dynamic trade policies at the federal level. These are not perceived as constraints as much as they are used as levers to increase a province's prosperity level.

Policy Statements

This is the context in which the Québec government launched Minister Fitzgibbon's policy statement. The paper is published in French (Gouvernement du Québec 2019a) with a summary in both French and English (Gouvernement du Québec 2019b). For the first time, Québec's international policy has been largely crafted from priorities coming from outside of the Ministry of International Relations.[20] Nevertheless the document is signed, not by Minister Fitzgibbon, but by Minister Nadine Girault, Minister of International Relations and La Francophonie with a foreword by Premier Legault. Moreover, the document insists that it complements and extends Québec's International Policy adopted under Philippe Couillard's government (Gouvernement du Québec 2017) and which, we are reminded, is still in force.

Already, this 2017 policy statement's title leads to an important economic dimension: invest, perform, and prosper. Throughout the document, the trade aspect is very much present. And all mentions fall

---

[20] Parti Québécois Bernard Landry signed an international relations policy state that considered trade as of prime importance. However, trade was integral part of the ministry of international relations at the time (Gouvernement du Québec 1985: 204).

within the boundaries set for provincial involvement in trade issues. The policy covers Québec's role in multilateral trade treaties (pp. 14–17, 32–34) and the regulatory dimension of exports (p. 33), immigration (pp. 24, 45, 27), public procurement (p. 32), taxation (p. 41) or compliance with the Convention on the Protection and Promotion of Diversity of Cultural Expressions (p. 66). Elsewhere, the customary dimension is generally evoked ("economic challenges require cooperative mechanisms" (p. 11); "the Government of Québec subscribes to the principles and broad objectives of the multilateral trading system" (p. 33)) or is referred to in specific applications to the carbon market (pp. 10, 46–47), to the protection of its interests (in education (p. 31), in La Francophonie (pp. 40, 52), in relation to the responsibilities devolved to the Autorité des marchers financiers (p. 41) or to the regulations applicable to exports (p. 33)). Finally, positive references to Québec's interests and needs complement the policy. For instance, it is said that "The defense of Québec's economic, commercial and financial interests is central to the international action of the government and its representations abroad" (p. 24); "Representations abroad contribute to increasing Québec's attractiveness and to fostering adequacy with labour market needs" (p. 27; the idea is taken up at pp. 30, 31); or: "The Québec government continues to work on all fronts to improve the conditions for Québec businesses to access and integrate into global markets" (p. 31). Hence, the Couillard government international policy seemed to cover extensively trade issues, as far as provincial responsibility is concerned.

Why then the need for a complementary paper? First, issuing a specific policy is a means for the Legault government to leave its own imprint as the document bluntly refers to "the election of the Legault team" (p. 7). Then the policy upholds that, building on the traditional affirmation of Québec's values and specificity, it is now possible to aim at greater goals in the international context. This sets the table for a policy that is developed around three "action areas".

The first action area calls for the strengthening of Québec's economic role at the international level (pp. 15–36). It aims at attracting investments and increasing imports; recruiting labour and talent[21]; boosting

---

[21] It is important to remind that in Québec, through administrative agreements, immigration is a field of shared jurisdiction with the federal level.

Québec's innovation in international markets; opening the world to post-secondary institutions and young people; and contributing to the fight against climate change from a sustainable economic perspective.

The second action area also bears and promotes a strong economic complement as it asks to rely more fully on Québec networks and to use them as economic levers (pp. 37–46). In this realm, the government has particular goals regarding La Francophonie. It also presents an important soft power component (Mayer 2016) as it wishes to promote Québec's culture and artists internationally. It wants to consolidate Québec's standing as a world-class tourist destination, attract more international organizations and events and mobilize Québeckers who are active in international business networks.

Finally, it is late, in the third action area, that we find more traditional aspects of Québec's international policy. However, the Legault government does not want to project an image of "more of the same" since it underscores the need for modernizing Québec's international actions (pp. 47–53). This would be done through better high-level coordination, which means that a Cabinet-level Committee dedicated to Québec's international action will be statutory in nature; that Québec's representatives abroad will have a more direct input in establishing targets for their action; and that Minster-level delegations will be coordinated through a specific bureau within the department. As well, the "Québec brand" will be used as an international positioning strategy, to set the tone in all venues, being it traditional or virtual. The government will create an Institute of Diplomacy to ensure that its personnel will be better prepared to intervene abroad as it will redefine its presence considering delegations and bureaus as genuine economic and cultural hubs. Finally, it will also establish strategic international monitoring in the light of Québec's interests.

When one looks at the two policies, being it the Liberal policy of 2017 or the Caqist policy of 2019, it is hard to find elements that would initiate tensions between the federal and Québec governments. Québec's stance no doubt put the province at the centre of its endeavours. However, these interests do not clash with Canada's. Indeed, it would be hard for somebody in the Pearson building in Ottawa to advocate that these initiatives go against Canada's, or even the federal government's, interests. In fact, the latest Québec international policy statements correspond to the type of possible action allowed by the opening we identified at the legal level: they do not deal with trade regulations and their implementation, but rather with the development of trade as an economic tool to produce wealth. Both Ottawa and Québec aim in the same direction, as illustrated by Québec taking full advantage of the free trade agreements negotiated by Canada. As a result, it eliminates many of the constraints that the federal nature of the country, if not the political nature of the debates, usually place on this type of road.

COVID Developments

Has the situation caused by the COVID-19 pandemic impacted Québec from a Canadian foreign policy perspective? The question is worth asking since, at first, COVID-19 has been dealt with mainly as a domestic matter. It is true that provincial governments faced challenges in terms of supplies coming from abroad, but these issues were largely managed in conjunction with the federal government. For instance, talks with China regarding equipment availability were conducted by the federal government, but Québec, for whom China represents its second largest trading partner ($13.8 billions in 2016 [Gouvernement du Québec 2020]), backed the Canadian efforts through the relationships supported by its offices and antennas.[22] Moreover, although a trade dimension could be considered, this aspect of the crisis could hardly be seen as a contentious foreign policy question.

It is on another COVID-19 front that there was some foreign policy disagreement, although these were soon settled to the satisfaction of all. The Québec government as well as other politicians from the province pressured Justin Trudeau to close the borders early in the fight against the coronavirus (Lecavalier 2020a; TVA Nouvelles 2020; St-Pierre-Plamondon 2020). Québec's Ministry of Health even sent nurses and medical crews in airports to monitor the incoming passengers, even though airports are of federal jurisdiction (Lecavalier 2020b). Premier Legault was joined by Ontario Premier Doug Ford in this request (CBC News 2020).

A week later, Justin Trudeau finally adopted a series of Orders in Council that first closed the airports, banning entry of certain foreign nationals travelling to Canada by air from all countries with the exception of persons travelling from the United States (Government of Canada

---

[22] Bureaus are located in Beijing and Shanghai; antennas are located in Qingdao and Shenzhen.

2020a). He then closed the Canada-US border, with only a few exceptions justified by humanitarian or economic reasons (Government of Canada 2020b). Finally, by extending the Order in Council adopted four days earlier, he did the same for all foreign travellers entering Canada from foreign countries, notwithstanding their means of transportation (Government of Canada 2020c).

Premier Legault reiterated his concerns about opening the border as late as October, stating that "Instead of trying to tell Québec and the provinces how to run long-term care homes, Justin Trudeau should focus on ensuring the Canadian border stays closed until the end of the year" (Autier 2020).

BALANCING INTERESTS AND CONSTRAINTS: TOWARDS A CHANGE OF PARADIGM?

This chapter has explored the role of provinces in the shaping of Canadian foreign policy from the dual angle of the promotion of their own interests and the lowering of the constraints imposed on them regarding their international actions. The analysis rests on parameters, both from international law and the Canadian constitution, and it has explored how some provinces behave, with a particular accent on Québec. In these times of uncertainty, in a world where the number of international actors expand, and considering the autonomist trend provinces like Alberta, Québec, or even Saskatchewan are displaying, it could be conceivable that a clash might occur.

Our analysis demonstrates that this is not the case. From the sample of provinces we studied, we may conclude that provinces will generally promote their interests and try to lower their constraints while staying within the limits of their constitutional jurisdiction. As a matter of fact, even Québec, a province that has a long history of international involvement and that has acquired over the years doctrinal and quasi-constitutional tools to considerably lower its constraints, has taken a step back and has concentrated its efforts, under the Legault government, in the realm of international trade, understood as a means to promote a healthier economy; the province is not trying to infringe the federal power of norm setting in the domain, as defined by the Courts. Simply put, Québec, which is usually the more demanding province in terms of its international role, seems less vocal.

We did not pay a lot of attention to the role of individuals in this exercise. There are two reasons for this. First, we considered generic policy stances that define governments in the mid-term and not specific policies. It is true that the imprint of Justin Trudeau has an influence, and no doubt that Premier Legault's past experience as a businessman makes him look favourably at measures implemented to enhance trade and, consequently, the local economy. However, the mid-term perspective we adopted brought into light behaviours that are consistent from one government to the other within the same province. We have seen this in the case of New Brunswick, where the Liberal Gallant and Conservative Higgs governments followed the same line; and in Québec, where the Caqist Legault government builds on the Liberal Couillard government's international relations policy. In this study, the person's factor is therefore negligible.

As a general conclusion, one may say that Canadian foreign policy-making is not hindered by provincial claims, nor is it bound by some sort of veto provinces might raise. Although provinces were long ago legally recognized as the competent body to implement agreements signed by Canada, we have seen no recent traces of provincial claims that might have jeopardized a position Canada has defended. The free trade agreement with Europe is a prime example of cooperation between provinces and Ottawa. It is true that European countries, knowing very well that some aspects of the trade deal fell under provincial jurisdiction, wanted to hear provincial concerns directly before ratifying the deal. In the case of the free trade agreement with the United States and Mexico, although provinces were not at the table, they were consulted by federal negotiators throughout the process. This spirit seems to remain the general approach that is now taken by Canadian foreign policymakers when issues bear on provincial interests.

This does not prevent provinces from voicing their own concerns on the global stage. We have seen that it is obviously the case for Québec. However, we documented that New Brunswick and to some extent Manitoba also entertain an international activity in which they promote and defend their own interests. It is also the case with Alberta, but in a narrower spectrum. For its part, Ontario remains quiet, but nevertheless defends its economic interests abroad, without stating a specific policy to this effect. But in all cases, provinces will prefer to lower constraints by backing a Canadian position that is answering their needs.

Why is this level of agreement reachable? Part of the answer can be found in the fact that the Canadian government does not seem to pay a lot of interest to its foreign policy, notwithstanding the fact the Prime Minister claimed with eloquence that "Canada is back!". Not only has the Trudeau government neglected to issue a formal foreign policy statement, but its minimal participation in the peacekeeping operation in Mali, the failure of the G7 summit in Charlevoix that was not able to reach any sustainable conclusion, and the lack of international clout Canada now has, as demonstrated by the impossibility to get a seat at the United Nations Security Council, reveal the lesser attention the government pays to its foreign stance (see Marland and Nimijean, this volume). It is not unthinkable that this seeming lack of interest in foreign affairs also translates into some kind of *laissez-faire* towards provincial initiatives that former federal governments would never have authorized.

The COVID-19 pandemic has not modified this behaviour. Some provinces have pressured Ottawa to close the Canadian border, but it is hard to think that the federal government would have completely neglected this aspect in the long term, for most other countries around the world have done so at one point or another. It would therefore be farfetched to conclude that Ottawa's actions in this regard were the result of provincial pressures. Other provinces, like New Brunswick, issued criteria to be respected by people having to cross the border on a daily basis for their work or their need of essential goods, but within the framework designed by Ottawa.

Does this mean that we face a paradigmatic change? I would submit that it is too early to tell. The answer lies in large part in the evaluation one makes of Justin Trudeau's government: is it representative of future federal governments that will pay a less attention to world affairs, or is it typical of this particular government?

On the one hand, if we look at the Harper and Trudeau governments and their departure from Pearsonian internationalism that had characterized Canadian foreign policy for some time, we may say indeed that Canada, for the last fifteen years, has abandoned its middle power stance and decided to rank among the countries that put up with the influence of mightier powers. But on the other hand, one might say that Canada has already experienced a similar pattern: for most of his tenure, Pierre-Elliott Trudeau removed himself and his governments from Canada's traditional international role. This did not prevent the country from regaining respectful influence once he retired from politics (Hampson 2018). Here, the role of a specific individual might make a difference. It is true that the world has considerably changed over the last thirty-five years. It is also important to consider that the way provinces got themselves involved in the realm of international relations denotes a behaviour that will be hardly put aside, for their interests will not falter. We cannot read from the past what lies in the future. This means that Canada, more than ever, needs to redefine its foreign policy to take these new dimensions into account. The only ingredient that seems to be missing at this point is the political will to do so.

REFERENCES

Aird, Robert. 2005. *André Patry et la présence du Québec dans le monde*. Montréal, VLB éditeur.

Assemblée nationale du Québec. 1967. *Débats de l'Assemblée législative du Québec*, vol. 5, no 49, April 3.

Autier, Philip. 2020. "Legault Tells Trudeau to Focus on Keeping Canadian Border Closed." *Montreal Gazette*, October 28. https://montrealgazette.com/news/quebec/legault-tells-trudeau-to-focus-on-keeping-canadian-border-closed.

Brun, Henri, Guy Tremblay, and Eugénie Brouillet. 2014. *Droit constitutionnel*, 6th ed. Cowansville: Éditions Yvon Blais.

Buzetti, Hélène. 2000. "Normes nationales pour les soins aux aînés : Trudeau n'expose toujours pas son plan." *Le Devoir*, October 16. https://www.ledevoir.com/politique/canada/587963/point-de-presse-trudeau-16-oct.

CBC News. 2020. "Ford Open to Closing Borders to Visitors During Pandemic, Not to Commerce." March 16. https://www.cbc.ca/news/canada/toronto/ford-ontario-covid-19-borders-1.5499124.

Charest, Jean. 2004. "Allocution du Premier ministre à l'ENAP." Québec, ministère du Conseil exécutif. http://www.premier.gouv.qc.ca/general/discours/archives_discours/2004/fevrier/dis20040225.htm.

Charest, Jean. 2020. Interview with the author. June 15.

Currie, John H., Craig Forcese, Joanna Harrington, and Valerie Oosterveld. 2014. *International Law—Doctrine, Practice, and Theory*, 2nd ed. Toronto: Irwin Law.

Gérin-Lajoie, Paul. 1950. *Constitutional Amendments in Canada*. Toronto: University of Toronto Press.

Gouvernement du Québec. 1985. *Le Québec dans le monde. Le défi de l'interdépendance. Énoncé de politique de relations internationales*. Québec: Ministère des Relations internationales.

Gouvernement du Québec. 2017. *La politique internationale du Québec - Le Québec dans le monde : s'investir, agir, prospérer.* Québec: Ministère des Relations internationales et de La Francophonie. https://cdn-contenu.que bec.ca/cdn-contenu/adm/min/relations-internationales/publications-adm/politiques/PO-politique-internationale-du-Quebec-MRIF.pdf?1602012284.

Gouvernement du Québec. 2019a. *Le Québec: fier et en affaires partout dans le monde! Vision internationale du Québec.* Québec: Ministère des Relations internationales et de La Francophonie. https://cdn-contenu.quebec.ca/cdn-contenu/adm/min/relations-internationales/publications-adm/politiques/PO-vision-internationale-Quebec-FR-MRIF.pdf?1602012436.

Gouvernement du Québec. 2019b. *Québec: proud and doing business around the world! Summary.* Québec: Ministère des Relations internationales et de La Francophonie. https://cdn-contenu.quebec.ca/cdn-contenu/adm/min/rel ations-internationales/publications-adm/dossier/Relations_internationales/PO-vision-internationale-Quebec-summary-EN-MRIF.pdf?1576261620.

Gouvernement du Québec. 2020. *Secteurs de collaboration.* Québec: Ministère des Relations internationales et de la Francophonie. https://www.mrif.gouv.qc.ca/fr/relations-du-quebec/asie-pacifique/chine/secteurs-de-collaboration.

Government of Alberta. 2019. *Economic Development and Trade Report 2018–2019.* https://open.alberta.ca/dataset/ce036ce2-cea1-4e15-86c3-8c2a959f1 4ac/resource/8a111a82-0b39-4667-b56b-11eb7a2508e1/download/eco nomic-development-and-trade-nnual-report-2018-2019-web.pdf.

Government of Alberta. 2020a. "Alberta Trade Agreements." https://www.alb erta.ca/alberta-trade-agreements.aspx.

Government of Alberta. 2020b. *Country and Regional Relations.* https://www.alberta.ca/country-regional-relations.aspx#toc-0.

Government of Alberta. 2020c. "International Partnerships." https://www.alb erta.ca/international-partnerships.aspx.

Government of Alberta. 2020d. *Petrochemical Program Is Open for Business.* https://www.alberta.ca/release.cfm?xID=74587C34A7805-EB41-F08F-8C845801CF54F1FE.

Government of Alberta. 2020e. *Speech from the Throne.* February 25. https://www.alberta.ca/release.cfm?xID=68680E310C972-E5C9-BDB0-DCF1A7 8A225C7CC1.

Government of Canada. 2005. *Canada's International Policy Statement: A Role of Pride and Influence in the World—Diplomacy.* Ottawa: Department of Foreign Affairs and International Trade.

Government of Canada. 2020a. *Order in Council 2020-0157.* March 18. https://orders-in-council.canada.ca/attachment.php?attach=38952&lang=en.

Government of Canada. 2020b. *Order in Council 2020-0161.* March 20. https://orders-in-council.canada.ca/attachment.php?attach=38958&lang=en.

Government of Canada. 2020c. *Order in Council 2020-0162*. March 22. https:// orders-in-council.canada.ca/attachment.php?attach=38959&lang=en.

Government of Manitoba. 2020. "Speech from the Throne." https://www.gov. mb.ca/thronespeech/thronespeech-2020.html#jobs.

Government of New Brunswick. 2003. *Prospering in a Global Community: New Brunswick's International Strategy*. Fredericton: Province of New Brunswick.

Government of New Brunswick. 2017. "Government Seeks Feedback on Modernization of NAFTA." Ministry of Intergovernmental Affairs, August 17. https://www2.gnb.ca/content/gnb/en/news/news_release.2017.08. 1119.html.

Government of New Brunswick. 2019a. "2019 Speech from the Throne." https://www2.gnb.ca/content/gnb/en/corporate/promo/throne-speech/ 2019/2019-speech-from-the-throne.html.

Government of New Brunswick. 2019b. "Co-operation Agreement Renewed with the Département de la Vienne." Ministry of Intergovernmental Affairs, August 17. https://www2.gnb.ca/content/gnb/en/departments/intergove rnmental_affairs/news/news_release.2019.08.0463.html.

Government of New Brunswick. 2019c. "Eastern Canadian Premiers, New England Governors to Meet in Saint John." Ministry of Intergovernmental Affairs, July 31. https://www2.gnb.ca/content/gnb/en/departments/interg overnmental_affairs/news/news_release.2019.07.0441.html.

Government of New Brunswick. 2019d. "Minister responsible for La Francophonie visiting Paris." *Ministry of Intergovernmental Affairs*, February 12. https://www2.gnb.ca/content/gnb/en/departments/interg overnmental_affairs/news/news_release.2019.02.0074.html.

Government of New Brunswick. 2019e. "New Brunswick to Participate in Ministerial Conference of the Francophonie." Ministry of Intergovernmental Affairs, October 30. https://www2.gnb.ca/content/gnb/en/departments/ intergovernmental_affairs/news/news_release.2019.10.0562.html.

Government of New Brunswick. 2019f. "Premier Meeting with National Governors Association in Washington." Ministry of Intergovernmental Affairs and Office of the Premier, February 21. https://www2.gnb.ca/content/ gnb/en/departments/intergovernmental_affairs/news/news_release.2019. 02.0104.html.

Government of New Brunswick. 2020a. "International Relations." Ministry of Intergovernmental Affairs. https://www2.gnb.ca/content/gnb/en/dep artments/intergovernmental_affairs/partnerships_and_agreements/internati onal_.html.

Government of New Brunswick. 2020b. "Residents of Campobello Who Are Concerned About Access to Canada." Ministry of Intergovernmental Affairs. https://www2.gnb.ca/content/gnb/en/departments/intergovernm ental_affairs.html.

Government of Ontario. 2018. "Speech from the Throne." Premier's Office, July 12. https://news.ontario.ca/en/speech/49713/a-government-for-the-people.

Government of Ontario. 2020. "Newsroom." https://news.ontario.ca/newsroom/en.

Hampson, Fen Osler. 2018. *Master of Persuasion: Brian Mulroney's Global Legacy.* Toronto: signal—McClelland and Stewart.

Jacomy-Millette, Annemarie. 1979. "Le rôle des provinces dans les relations internationales." *Études internationales* 10 (2): 285–320.

Jeyabalaratnam, Gopinath and Stéphane Paquin. 2016. "La politique internationale du Québec sous Jean Charest: L'influence d'un premier ministre." *Revue québécoise de droit international, Special issue:* 165–183.

Lecavalier, Charles. 2020a. "François Legault demande à Trudeau de limiter l'entrée d'étrangers au Canada." *Le Journal de Québec,* March 13. https://www.journaldequebec.com/2020/03/13/francois-legault-demande-a-trudeau-de-limiter-lentree-detrangers-au-canada.

Lecavalier, Charles. 2020b. "Frontières: Legault s'impatiente avec Trudeau." *Le Journal de Québec,* March 15. https://www.journaldequebec.com/2020/03/15/frontieres-legault-simpatiente-envers-trudeau.

Manitoba Ministry of Economic Development and Training. 2020. "Trade Agreements and Negotiations." https://www.gov.mb.ca/jec/trade/index.html.

Manitoba Ministry of Intergovernmental Affairs and International Relations. 2020a. *International Agreements.* https://www.gov.mb.ca/fpir/intlrelations/agreements/index.html.

Manitoba Ministry of Intergovernmental Affairs and International Relations. 2020b. "International Relations." Government of Manitoba. https://www.gov.mb.ca/fpir/intlrelations/index.html.

Martin, Paul Sr. 1968. *Fédéralisme et relations internationales.* Ottawa: Ministère des affaires extérieures.

Martin, Pierre. 2020. "Un fédéralisme de tordage de bras." *Journal de Québec,* April 30. https://www.journaldemontreal.com/2020/04/30/un-federalisme-de-tordage-de-bras.

Mayer, Frédéric. 2016. "La Politique étrangère à l'épreuve du soft power." In *Nouvelle politique étrangère,* edited by Charlie Mballa and Nelson Michaud, 131–152. Québec: Presses de l'Université du Québec.

Michaud, Nelson. 2006. "Canada and Québec on the World Stage: Defining New Rules?" In *Canada Among Nations 2006: Minorities and Priorities,* edited by Andrew F. Cooper and Dane Rowlands, 232–249. Montreal and Kingston: McGill Queen's University Press.

Michaud, Nelson. 2016. *Cinquante ans de construction des administrations publiques: regards croisés entre la France et le Québec*. Québec: Presses de l'Université du Québec.

Michaud, Nelson, and Kim Richard Nossal, ed. 2001. *Diplomatic Departures: The Conservative Era in Canadian Foreign Policy, 1984–1993*. Vancouver: UBC Press.

Morin, Claude. 1987. *L'art de l'impossible*. Montréal: Boréal.

Ontario Ministry of Intergovernmental Affairs. 2020. "Ministry of Intergovernmental Affairs." Government of Ontario. https://www.ontario.ca/page/ministry-intergovernmental-affairs.

Ouellet, Richard, and Guillaume Beaumier. 2016. "L'activité internationale du Québec en matière de commerce international: de l'énonciation de la doctrine Gérin-Lajoie à la négociation de l'AECG." *Revue québécoise de droit international*, Special Issue: 67–79.

Patry, André. 1983. *La capacité internationale des États: l'exercice du jus tractatum*. Sillery: Presses de l'Université du Québec.

Patry, André. 2006. *Le Québec dans le monde*. Montréal: Éditions Typo.

Paquin, Stéphane. 2019. "From Gérin-Lajoie to USMCA: The Role of the Canadian Provinces in Trade Negotiation." In *Policy Transformation in Canada: Is the Past Prologue?*, edited by Carolyn Tuohy Hugues, Sophie Borwein, Peter John Loewen, and Andrew Potter, 159–166. Toronto: University of Toronto Press.

Pelletier, Benoît. 2008. "Point de presse de M. Benoît Pelletier, ministre responsable des Affaires intergouvernementales canadiennes, des Affaires autochtones, de la Francophonie canadienne, de la Réforme des institutions démocratiques et de l'Accès à l'information." *Assemblée nationale*, 4 novembre. http://www.assnat.qc.ca/fr/actualites-salle-presse/conferences-points-presse/ConferencePointPresse-3783.html.

Presse Canadienne. 2019. "Investissement Québec: plus de pouvoirs et de moyens pour le ministre Fitzgibbon." *Les Affaires*, June 13. https://www.lesaffaires.com/secteurs-d-activite/gouvernement/investissement-quebec-plus-de-pouvoirs-et-de-moyens-pour-le-ministre-fitzgibbon/610954.

Richer, Jocelyne. 2020. "Redéploiement en vue pour les délégations du Québec." *La Presse*, October 12. https://www.lapresse.ca/actualites/politique/2020-10-12/redeploiement-en-vue-pour-les-delegations-du-quebec.php.

Sharp, Mitchell. 1968. *Fédéralisme et conférences internationales sur l'éducation, Un supplément à Fédéralisme et relations internationales*, 9–13. Ottawa: Ministère des affaires extérieures.

St-Pierre Plamondon, Paul. 2020. "Pour en finir avec la pseudoscience du gouvernement Trudeau: Francois Legault doit reprendre le contrôle de nos aéroports et de nos frontières." *Le Journal de Montréal*, March 16. https://www.journaldequebec.com/2020/03/16/pour-en-finir-avec-la-pseudosci

ence-du-gouvernement-trudeau-francois-legault-doit-reprendre-le-controle-de-nos-aeroports-et-de-nos-frontieres.

Trudeau, Justin. 2020. "Allocution du Premier ministre pour annoncer le Fonds pour une rentrée scolaire sécuritaire." Cabinet du Premier ministre, August 26. https://pm.gc.ca/fr/nouvelles/discours/2020/08/26/allocution-du-premier-ministre-annoncer-fonds-rentree-scolaire.

TVA Nouvelles. 2020. "Frontières: le Bloc somme Trudeau d'agir." *Le Journal de Montréal*, March 15. https://www.journaldemontreal.com/2020/03/15/frontieres-le-bloc-somme-trudeau-dagir-1.

CHAPTER 5

Beneath the Skin: Canadian Global Health Policy in the Time of a Pandemic

Robert Huish

INTRODUCTION

Nations often export their domestic strength. Canada has been widely praised on the global stage for measures taken to "flatten the curve" of the COVID-19 pandemic (Karaivanov et al. 2020; Capano et al. 2020). In early 2020 while the country remained open for business with other nations that had known cases of COVID-19, by March 18, 2020, Ottawa started to close the borders, including the land border with the United States—a first in the country's history (Turnbull 2020). Reporting 12 cases of COVID-19 on March 5, Canada surpassed 100 cases on March 16, 2020, Prime Minister Justin Trudeau announced the closing of the border with the United States for all non-essential travel (Johns Hopkins Coronavirus Resource Centre 2020). Following this, provinces enacted lockdowns that closed most businesses, public spaces, and encouraged people to stay home for several weeks. The number of daily new cases in

R. Huish (✉)
Dalhousie University, Halifax, NS, Canada
e-mail: huish@Dal.Ca

D. Carment and R. Nimijean (eds.), *Political Turmoil in a Tumultuous World*, Canada and International Affairs, https://doi.org/10.1007/978-3-030-70686-9_5

Canada peaked on May 3, with 2,760 reported (Johns Hopkins Coronavirus Resource Centre 2020). Cases remained low and continued to decline until October 2020, when, as epidemiologists correctly predicted, the second wave emerged with close to 2,000 cases reported daily across the country (Coletta 2020). The second wave made quick work of public health ordinances, such as the Atlantic Bubble, a term given to the quarantine-free travel zone in Atlantic Canada and began to stress many provincial health systems.

Considering that many European nations were experiencing major upswings in cases, and that the United States was experiencing, and continues to endure, tens of thousands of cases daily, Canada stood out in the global community as an example of effective pandemic management. With strict social measures in place, a secured border, financial support for Canadians who were un- or under-employed, trust in public health officers, and access to universal health insurance, some initially turned to Canada as an example of effective pandemic management (Laupacis 2020), even though Tuite and Greer (2020), writing in the Canadian Medical Association Journal, claim that eliminating COVID-19 "may not be achievable in the Canadian context, but it is still a worthwhile goal." By November 2020, months before a promised vaccine rollout, Canada's public health efficacy seemed to be in trouble.

In as much as some important lessons can be taken away from Ottawa's handling of the COVID-19 pandemic, the measure of true grit comes at the provincial levels (Migone 2020). With some provinces and territories like Nova Scotia and Nunavut boasting almost no cases of COVID-19 during the summer of 2020 others, such as Ontario and Québec gave up on thorough contact tracing by early autumn of 2020 (Shingler and Leavitt 2020). Even amid the second wave, the provincial responses have varied greatly. Herein lies a greater challenge in approaching COVID-19 policy in Canada, and also in understanding how federalism, the organization of jurisdictions between provinces and Ottawa impacts Canadian global health management, both domestically and abroad (Bakvis and Skogstad 2020). The Canadian COVID-19 pandemic response is less about one approach to a global health crisis, but instead 13 interlocking responses to the crisis. Some of which proved successful and popular, while others fell short and exposed deep shortcomings in other areas of health care and social services. And to which each provincial jurisdiction tested, pressured, and challenged each other, especially along provincial borders. COVID-19 has, in many ways, exposed both the strengths and the shortcomings of federalism and health care within Canada. It has allowed for provinces to draw up plans based on their own local goals and capabilities, but it has also allowed for drastic inequalities to emerge between provinces (Godefroy and Lewis 2020). As Simpson (2020) writes, social isolation and quarantine measures are not inspired by "pure science" and are instead governed by political strategies that reinforce inequalities that shelter some from the virus and expose others to increased risk. What's more, the issue of COVID-19 within Indigenous communities brings about deep-seated structural inequalities rooted in "constitutional obscurities and legal fictions" (Craft et al. 2020: 50). These inequalities include the number of cases and rates of infection in each jurisdiction, but also the economic consequences for provinces that took on stricter measures than others, and feeling the need to enforce extended lockdowns as neighboring provinces opened up to more business opportunities but also to greater rates of infection.

The pandemic has brought on an era of intra-national borders and boundaries within the country that has never occurred before. The Atlantic Bubble, a regional plan for the provinces of New Brunswick, Nova Scotia, Prince Edward Island and Newfoundland and Labrador to allow for free movement within and between the provinces but enforces 14 days of self-isolation on anyone who enters the region, is an example of this (Mercer 2020). Conservation officers, now tasked as provincial border control agents, in the Atlantic Bubble could deny visitors entry, even from other provinces—a first for Canadian constitutionalism. While many thought that the Bubble would economically devastate the Atlantic region from a dearth of tourism, it has in fact been bolstered by a great deal of popular support and has even seen an uptick in various sectors of the economy, such as construction and real estate (Snan 2020; McEachern 2020). However, with the second wave taking Canada by storm in November 2020, the Atlantic Bubble burst, with each Atlantic province mandating 14 days strict self-isolation. The busted Bubble raises two important questions. First, how much does strict border enforcement matter about *who is let in*, compared to the performative behavior of society *within* the Bubble itself (Nash 2000)? Second, it raises the question as to whether or not Canada is a noteworthy example of effective pandemic management, or if it just looked good in contrast to the policies and actions of its neighbor to the South.

Considering the domestic challenges of COVID-19 within Canada, it raises the question as to what Canada's plan is when it comes to global efforts for pandemic planning, management, engagement, and recovery. While foreign relations are often handled by Ottawa, "health" is the business of provinces, which means that a total of 13 independent, but interlocking systems, provide health services to most Canadian citizens. It is why in the time of the COVID-19 pandemic there is no "Canada Plan." Instead there are 13 different policies, directed by 13 different provincial premiers, and 13 different provincial medical officers each tasked with responding to the COVID-19 pandemic in their own similar, but unique way. The one shared goal in each jurisdiction is to keep COVID-19 cases below the "hospital level," a measurement of health care capacity. Canada has long struggled with the pains and challenges of federalism, and yet often manages to be recognized globally as a land of stability in governance and progressiveness in terms of social health policy (Bakvis and Skogstad 2020). COVID-19 will strain federalism within the country as some provinces fare better than others and as the consequences of economic recovery are unequally shared across the provinces and territories (Béland et al. 2020; Mathen 2020). What's more, it may invite an opportunity for Ottawa to revisit discussions of the jurisdiction of provinces when it comes to health and well-being (see Michaud this volume).

Internal struggles aside, the nature of federalism in a pandemic may also bring about jurisdictional challenges when it comes to international travel, trade, and engagement. Nations worldwide closed down borders in order to prevent the spread of the virus, and with some 200,000 cases of COVID-19 in Canada as of October 2020, and with about 4,000 new active cases a day, many nations have good reason to keep their borders closed with Canada (Evans 2020). Such was the case on October 21, 2020, when the European union removed Canadians from the "white list" of countries, a "list of countries whose citizens would be allowed access for non-essential travel" (Evans 2020; CBC 2020). With thousands of new cases reported daily in Canada, the Atlantic Bubble and the territories reported none, or next to none for months on end during the pandemic. The temporary absence of COVID-19 in these provinces and territories is not just noteworthy; it is completely exceptional, as few national or provincial jurisdictions around the world could boast such low cases of COVID-19. Even New Zealand has more new cases, and only some Pacific Island Nations can boast zero COVID-19 cases (Google News 2020). Before the Atlantic Bubble burst, some raised the idea of making a "double Bubble" with international jurisdictions of similar

COVID-19 standing. Likewise, are there other provincial methods of contact tracing, social distancing, and self-isolation that align with other jurisdictions that could warrant double Bubbles?

I argue that COVID-19 will not be a passing hardship for Canada's place in the world. The pandemic will have long-term impacts on Canadian federalism in health care and in foreign affairs for years to come. It is unlikely that Canada will assume a leadership role in the pandemic response, but in order to remain open and competitive throughout the 2020s, exploring the capacity of provinces to pursue their own foreign relations, even on a temporary basis, may be an important step. COVID-19 has deeply impacted the business as usual foreign policy of every nation on earth. For Canada, the foreign policy challenge going forward will be one of keeping borders open for trade, while keeping provinces capable of handling health care capacity, all the while staying mindful of how the US structures its relationships and partnerships coming out of the pandemic. The Atlantic Bubble offers an opportunity to explore how border restrictions and Bubbles play a role during a pandemic, or if it is in fact the performative behavior within those spaces that matter more.

Canada's Place in the Global Health Landscape

In the past decade Canada, and other nations, have had opportunity to engage in Global Health Diplomacy, a concept that views the provision of health care, and investment in health care capacity, as a ground for bettering international relations (Adams et al. 2008). Health care is often viewed along stringent national boundaries. Single payer systems only provide care for compatriots, and health policy researchers often take comparative approaches between nations when discussing the difference in policy strategies and approaches. As Hoffman (2010) writes, "health" has been referred to as a national strategic interest and a global political priority. The long-standing belief is that good health can lead to improved peace, security, and economic prosperity. But in a time of a pandemic, does this approach still hold up? In previous global health emergencies such as SARS, H1N1, Ebola, and Zika, many nations have offered up funds and support to assist countries that were the most deeply impacted (Benton and Yi Dionne 2015). But for COVID-19, a moment to test global health diplomacy, many countries turned inward instead of outward. Borders were sealed, trade disrupted, and strict social measures such as shelter-in-place orders or social distancing were mandated around the world. Many of these orders were concerned less about "improving health globally, while bettering international relations," as would have been the principles of global health diplomacy (Adams et al. 2008). In fact, it was quite the opposite. International relationships around the world were shaken, and governments were not at all concerned with health globally, let alone the sustainable development goals. Instead, policies focused not on the "health of people" as much as "combatting the virus" by implementing social measures to keep severe cases below the crisis of capacity hospital levels.

Some countries, like Cuba, have invested deeply in structuring its foreign policy around health care cooperation and collaboration by sending medical teams to dozens of countries around the world (Ashton 2020; Reed 2020; Huish 2013). Other countries have taken on the role of major health donors, and more recently China has assumed a strong global position in constructing health infrastructure throughout the global South (Brautigam 2011). Canada's commitment to global health aid has steadily increased by 6% from $441 million in 2015 to $566 million in 2018, but it may be too little too late for strong global health diplomacy (Donor Tracker 2020). Canada is the 9th largest Official Development Assistant Donor Country, falling just behind Italy with 4.7 billion in disbursements, but placing 16th when looking at the total amount of aid as a percentage of Gross National Income (Donor Tracker 2020). The Trudeau administration's strategic priorities of Canada's Feminist International Assistance Policy champions gender equity, and within it a focus on sexual and reproductive health and rights, as well as maternal, newborn, and child health (Tiessen and Swan 2018). In 2018, some $556 million of ODA was earmarked under the category of health and population, which accounts for 16% of the country's ODA sector (Donor Tracker 2020).

Of Canada's $556 million ODA funds dedicated to global health, roughly, about $105 million, is categorized under "basic nutrition" through bilateral ODA. Investments in reproductive health, basic health care, personnel development for population and reproductive health, infectious disease control, and population policy and administrative management, all constitute between 8% and 12% of the budget. Of this bilateral aid, roughly 50% is earmarked for sub-Saharan Africa. What's more, Canada offered up its most generous commitment to multilateral health initiatives such as the Global Fund to Fight AIDS, Tuberculosis, and Malaria with some $699 million earmarked for 2020–2023 (Donor Tracker 2020).

On paper, Canada is showing an increased commitment to global health. But is it global health diplomacy, let alone global "health"? Simply put, Canada's ODA commitments to health do not fit well with the concepts of global health diplomacy, especially in the time of a pandemic. Health diplomacy, or medical internationalism as it has been called as well, refers to direct efforts to improve health outcomes (Hoffman 2010). This is best seen through the construction of medical facilities, the training of health workers, and improving access to medicines and vaccines in low-resource settings. So too, it involves comprehensive work on addressing vector-borne diseases in low resource areas. These sorts of downstream innovations have been widely praised in international circles, especially during natural disasters, and now with the pandemic, with only a handful of countries offering direct medical assistance to other nations. Canada's ODA in health is mostly looking at upstream determinants of health, such as food security, gender equity, and the improvement of living conditions that can have positive health benefits for maternal health.

The Canadian ODA budget for health is deeply committed to improvements in agriculture technology and food accessibility. Indeed, this can lead to positive health outcomes under the right conditions. However, these conditions are not always guaranteed and can be heavily influenced by social, economic, and political factors at the local level. Funds dedicated to improving nutrition through agriculture support, credit, or subsidies at the national level can overlook inequities at the regional and local level as well. As has been demonstrated in Ghana, even gender dynamics can have a serious impact on food security and nutrition levels (Shahadu 2017). Food security is about "access to" food, it is not in itself a process that guarantees positive health outcomes, and therefore can be problematic to include as a stand-alone health project. The upstream determinants of health, such as good nutrition, are incredibly important for improving health outcomes, but they cannot always be achieved let alone guaranteed through short-term development assistance programs.

One of the challenges then with Canadian global health diplomacy is that it does not always deal with "health," and this becomes notable during a pandemic. Medical textbooks and common dictionaries routinely define health as the absence of disease, illness, or injury. It is difficult to get a sense of concept from a definition of what it is not. The World

Health Organization's adopted 1947 definition of health considers it to be the "complete state of well-being, that achieves soundness in body and in mind" (World Health Organization 1947). This broad and comprehensive definition of health is widely praised, but poorly practiced both at the national and international level. All too often international health initiatives are routinely focused on eradicating diseases, rather than achieving a complete state of well-being among people. Campaigns to eradicate polio and malaria, and now the COVID-19 virus, are cases in point. Even at the national level, many health care systems with universal insurance are not designed around the values of achieving health in as much as they are about mitigating costs or creating economic stimulus. Britain's National Health Service was as much a post-war economic stimulus program as it was a system to ensure well-being. New Zealand's original insurance program only covered "accidents" in order to encourage farmers to access health resources. Canada's Medicare system is ultimately about preventing catastrophic cost to the patient, rather than working to achieve dedicated personal and population health outcomes. While Ottawa oversees the assurances of the Canada Health Act, it is up to each province to manage and finance the program to all of its residents.

For a country with a robust universal single payer health system, Canadian health diplomacy is very limited when it comes to health. Three reasons explain this. First, comprehensive downstream health care provision is not the business of Ottawa. The federal government has a role in ensuring safe food and in developing safe vaccines. The reflection is evident in foreign policy as the Canadian government has increased its ODA commitments in both areas. But in terms of improving health outcomes by bettering the complete well-being of individuals, Ottawa does not have a domestic toolkit to bring to the world stage.

Second, delivery of health care services remains a largely private enterprise in Canada to which 13 interlocking health systems provide insurance coverage to mitigate or eliminate costs to compatriots. While Ottawa has mobilized international health units through the military on many occasions, the capacity of the military to recruit and to retain medical professionals for international assistance remains limited (Mamuji 2012). Indeed, many health care providers seek international opportunities through multilateral organizations rather than through ODA from Ottawa.

Third, medical care is inherently nationalistic. The delivery of health care services and the provision of insurance to cover costs remain a point of pride of many countries, including Canada. To each country comes a unique design in terms of service delivery and finance. In almost every universal single payer system around the world, citizenship or permanent residency is required in order to access services. It is not a service for export, and it is not a service that is generously given out to noncompatriots. Funded through progressive taxation and transfer payments, Canada's 13 interlocking health care systems are meant to cover the costs of Canadians and not to adhere to the needs of foreigners. Beyond actual capacity for such outreach, there exists a ferociously nationalistic sentiment that Medicare only exists at great cost and commitment among Canadians and it should not be given away. Such sentiment reduces support for any programs that would see Canadian doctors serving abroad on taxpayer monies, or Canadian hospitals occupied with foreigners who may not have paid into the system. Canadians widely feel that their health care services could be vulnerable if overwhelmed by demand.

FEDERALISM OVER NATIONALISM

Little political appetite exists in Canada, or among many G7 nations, for practicing health care abroad or for investing in infrastructure commitments for foreign health care. This creates a void on the global stage that is actively filled by China, Russia, and even Cuba. China has built hospitals across the African continent, as well as in the Pacific and South America. Russia is now sending personal protective equipment to low-resource countries in the global South (Roth 2020). And Cuba has sent tens of thousands of medical professionals to countries across the world since 1960 (Huish 2013). During the COVID-19 pandemic, Cuba has sent hundreds of doctors to 38 countries, including hard hit nations in Europe like Italy and Andorra (Perez Riverol 2020). Indeed, the nationalistic tendencies of health care provision factor into a lack of medical internationalism by the G7 nations, but for Canada, so too does the nature of federalism.

Canadian federalism "evolved from an emphasis on divided jurisdictions to one of shared jurisdiction in practice" (Brown 2002). Brown's point is that domestically, the delivery of public services varies greatly between provincial jurisdictions, notably the delivery and structure of services in health care and education tend vary greatly, but now also in terms of alcohol and cannabis sales. Internationally, federalism requires policy to be an interdependent experience. Because provinces are so deeply involved with matters of trade and investment, it reduces Ottawa's ability to unilaterally implement policies or enter into international accords without provincial consultation. Likewise, the provinces do not have the legal power to enter into international accords. This makes Canadian federalism rather "busy" when it comes to international engagement. Ottawa must represent the country as a whole for international treaties and agreements, handle security and immigration matters (with some exceptions for Québec), and serve as the representative for multilateral agreements (Brown 2002). Federalism takes many shapes globally, and every jurisdiction has its own package of intergovernmental frameworks, such as Germany's Bundestag system, or Spain's *communidad autónoma*. What makes Canada unique is that it strictly adheres to domestic jurisdictions, while remaining open to changing dynamics of intergovernmental relations on the world stage.

Typically, this has involved a strong presence from the provinces when it comes to trade and investments. The "Team Canada" trade missions to China and parts of Asia speak to this (Potter 2004). So too do organized fact-finding missions on European health care that included provincial representatives traveling to Europe. Provinces have taken the lead on several trade initiatives with China, notably lobster exports from Nova Scotia, or fruit from British Columbia, or energy from Alberta. Investment and trade have been team Canada's goal, but little has been explored in terms of the value of broader international cooperation, assistance, or even global health diplomacy.

The COVID-19 pandemic and its aftermath may be the right opportunity to explore innovative foreign policy at the provincial level. The 2020 Trudeau government's Speech from the Throne made little mention of foreign policy beyond promising to maintain continued commitments to international climate change agreements. The speech included the following:

> The Government will invest more in international development while supporting developing countries on their economic recoveries and resilience. Canada will also support work to ensure that people around the world have access to a vaccine. We cannot eliminate this pandemic in Canada unless we end it everywhere. (Government of Canada 2020)

Three revealing messages are packed into this brief excerpt of the throne speech. First, is that official development assistance will remain "business as usual." Foreign assistance through debt relief, bilateral investments, and contributions to debt relief through the World Bank and the IMF is the likely means of executing this commitment.

Second, the emphasis on access to vaccines is an area well within Ottawa's wheelhouse, and one that aligns well with global commitments to finding a COVID-19 vaccine. Domestically, the oversight of vaccine development is a federal jurisdiction, and funding into multilateral alliances like COVAX is also something that the federal government can do without provincial buy in. Nevertheless, the lens of global health outreach through vaccine accessibility remains very narrow and limited in scope in terms of the values of global health diplomacy.

The third message of eliminating the pandemic in Canada by eradicating it abroad is a classic, albeit, tired approach to international disease management that has been heard over past decades from polio to smallpox (Kew et al. 2005). It is inherently inward-focused to protect the health of compatriots from foreign illness, rather than striving to achieve good by improving the health of all. Not just nuance, it reflects a very limited and lacking scope to global health outreach. Taken together, Ottawa's approach to foreign affairs during, and after, a pandemic brings very little new material to the table. In part, it reflects the nature of the limitations Ottawa has over health and health care portfolios beyond providing funds and overseeing vaccines. And yet, it also presents an important opportunity for innovation when looking at foreign affairs and federalism as a dynamic relationship of cooperation.

Double the Bubble

In as much as Canada has an interest in keeping borders closed to nations with high rates of COVID-19, so too do other countries have interests in keeping trade and travel limited with Canada during the pandemic. The October 2020 rates of increase in Ontario and Québec surpassed most American states. By the end of October 2020, Canada cleared 200,000 cases of COVID-19, which is roughly that of Belgium or Poland. The second wave of COVID-19 hit Québec particularly hard. Level 4 measures, or maximum alert measures, were enacted. Stay at home orders were put in place including the prohibition of visitors from other addresses. Masks became mandatory indoors, but not outdoors, as they were mandated in outbreak centers in New Brunswick. Some also suggested that grocery stores were not enforcing social distancing as much as their franchise associates were in other provinces. Grocery store manners and mask-wearing habits may be important areas for future research to explore in terms of the effectiveness of preventing COVID-19 transmission, as are policies that actually restrict movement in between jurisdictions. In Québec, residents of a Red Maximum Alert zone were prohibited from traveling to a yellow, orange, or green zone (Giroux 2020). Visitors from other Canadian provinces were not subjected to self-isolation or quarantine. Movement restrictions were placed on high-risk areas rather than isolated low-risk jurisdictions. People could enter high risk areas but could not leave, whereas in Atlantic Canada, the opposite was true.

The Atlantic Bubble was a 4-province free movement zone that allowed for residents to travel freely within it, but newcomers were required to self-isolate for 14 days. The Atlantic Bubble also shared strict lockdown policy measures regarding workspaces, schools, public gatherings, and mask wearing. Nova Scotia was very early to adapt a mandatory mask policy for all indoor spaces. Although the exact reason remains unclear, or if a combination of factors contributes to the region's low COVID-19 rates, the Atlantic Bubble had the lowest rates of COVID-19 of the Canadian provinces, and rivaled Canada's territories for low to non-existent levels. With 72 deaths and some 1,700 cases, the Atlantic Bubble has had roughly 1,200 cases per million people, whereas Canada as a whole has experienced 5,304 per million (Google News 2020). Most of these cases in the Bubble occurred in Nova Scotia after the initial lockdown period in March 2020. Between July and October 2020, cases remained low with daily infection rates rivaling that of isolated countries in the South Pacific.

The Atlantic Bubble was one of the few jurisdictions that have flat-lined COVID-19. Is it because of the policy measures put in place? Is it because of the limited borders and airports? Or is something else worth noting? The first two factors were likely supportive factors, but the idea of performative behavior, that is the expected public and social behavior within a place or space, may be noteworthy here. Mask laws, zero contact shopping, and staying indoors during the evening suggest that those within the Atlantic Bubble played by the rules. Why is another matter for further research. However, rule compliance may be the product of carefully thought-out public policy, fear of shaming from neighbors, good knowledge of public health protocols, adaptable work environments, or even the resultant collapse of tourist, leisure, and gig economies during the pandemic. Only as the rules were loosened, especially around extending hours and patronage in bars, did COVID-19 return, even though patrons were still following the rules set out by the province. The second wave uptick of some dozen cases a day in Nova Scotia, half a dozen in New Brunswick, and single-digit counts in Prince Edward Island, and Newfoundland and Labrador, still places Atlantic provinces as having the lowest numbers of COVID-19 within Canada. Even though the bubble burst, Atlantic Canada is the one region of North America with almost no COVID-19, placing it as one of the lowest risk jurisdictions anywhere it the world.

This impressive health achievement may provide an inimitable opportunity for the Atlantic provinces to take advantage of federalism and take the lead on global health diplomacy. Already, in some sectors the Atlantic Bubble is attracting trade and investment. The film industry has taken notice of low levels of COVID-19 in Atlantic Canada, as many production crews are redirecting toward the Maritimes (Mulligan 2020). Real estate is surging across the region as investors from Western Canada recognize the opportunity of remote work in a low-risk COVID-19 jurisdiction (McEachern 2020). Local breweries and manufacturers and trades have also enjoyed an uptick in business as dependence on foreign products becomes less desirable (Gorman 2020). Some businesses, such as those in the service industry, the airline industry, and the seafood export industry, have not fared well at all during the pandemic (Chisholm 2020). With enormous disruption to global trade and travel networks, and with an inimitable value of low COVID-19 numbers, could Atlantic provinces pursue innovative forms of global health diplomacy?

Traditionally, the provincial role in international affairs focused on trade and investment (Brown 2002). But could health, health care, and education find a new place in international collaboration and cooperation? Could Atlantic provinces "double the bubble" (if it returns) by finding other states, regions, or intra-national regions, with low COVID-19 rates and engage in bilateral cooperation? Certain physical limitations make this prospect challenging as jurisdictions with similar COVID-19 counts are in Asia and the middle of the Pacific. But the ideological challenges remain greater. Health care and education are deemed provincial public goods for compatriots. Their export potential or value as a platform for international cooperation and collaboration has not always been appreciated.

In some cases, in the Atlantic region universities did partner with foreign governments to offer a set block of reserved seats into medical school and residency programs in return for generous remuneration (Bradshaw 2011). Illuminating the tangible trade and investment opportunities in a double bubble may not be difficult to determine at first glance. But the purpose of double bubbles is to find a shared platform and experience during the pandemic. Singapore, a global hub for finance and commerce, has repeatedly sought out opportunities to develop a free movement zone with other countries or jurisdictions with a similar single-digit daily COVID-19 count, like Hong Kong (Yeung 2020). Taiwan is another example of a nation that can count daily COVID-19 cases on a single hand (Johns Hopkins Coronavirus Resource Centre 2020). Fiji and New Zealand are also part of this club (Johns Hopkins Coronavirus Resource Centre 2020). None of these countries would see loosening travel and trade restrictions with Canada to be a wise move. But connecting just with the Atlantic Bubble may be a different story.

Could jurisdictions with low COVID-19 cases form a new network of diplomacy and cooperation, to which trade and travel could follow? Or could low COVID-19 cases be a pre-requisite for engaging in new trade and partnerships? One Halifax travel agent suggests extending the Atlantic Bubble to select tourist hotels in Cuba. Nations in Western Africa with low COVID-19 numbers could also be included for travel, trade, and outreach (Stoodley 2020). The geographic distances between these jurisdictions are enormous, but not impossible. Could the power of Singapore or Taiwan's airlines connect to the Atlantic Bubble? Unfortunately, tourism would not get the go ahead easily with current Canadian Border Service Agency restrictions against any discretionary travel for foreigners entering Canada. Nevertheless, essential trade, research, and cooperation opportunities may yet exist. New Zealand is looking for agricultural export markets, as Nova Scotia is looking for new seafood markets. The ability for collaboration and cooperation on research into how these jurisdictions managed COVID-19 would be invaluable in itself. The first step in finding out would be to re-imagine the geographies of the pandemic to see the potential in the provinces themselves forming relationships and partnerships abroad.

CONCLUSION

It is not likely that Ottawa will show strong outward leadership during or after the pandemic. The economic and social cost of pandemic restrictions will be too high on the domestic front for Ottawa to worry about mending international relations. What's more, with a second wave underway in Ontario and in Québec, criticisms of early handling of the pandemic is growing. In July 2020, it was revealed that Canada's early pandemic warning system failed because it was silenced by Ottawa a year earlier. The early warning system titled Global Public Health Intelligence Network (GPHIN) was meant to gather "unofficial intelligence in cases where certain countries were inclined to hide outbreaks from the world" (Robertson 2020). However, government officials became suspicious of a unit mandated to collect "unofficial data," and instead relied on information vetted from the World Health Organization. Many argue that had GPHIN still been intact, Canada could have been ahead of the pandemic, like Singapore, South Korea, and New Zealand, countries that all relied on their own intelligence gathering to identify and respond to the pandemic. While still looking strong against the backdrop of the experience of COVID-19 in the United States, Canada is reeling from devastating consequences of delaying border closures, or by resisting the recommendation of the use of masks. It may well be up to the provinces to take the lead on foreign relations in terms of building new foundations of cooperation and collaboration.

It is why a global health diplomacy approach would be incredibly fitting. Connecting with other jurisdictions that had a similar COVID-19 experience can only work to foster deeper connections between regions, develop new trade and cooperation opportunities, and allow for important research on the subject itself. Canada has not been a leader in global health diplomacy as health has never really been Ottawa's business. But with a remarkable achievement in pandemic management in the Atlantic Bubble, and in a time when international trade and cooperation has been derailed, it may be an important opportunity to consider the place of provinces leading in diplomacy—notably health diplomacy. With a low-risk to COVID-19, what could Atlantic Canada attract from the world? What could Nova Scotia gain with deeper relations to major transport hubs in Asia? Could small island nations in the Pacific and could countries in Western Africa benefit from forms of development cooperation that was fostered in the Atlantic Bubble? As with all diplomacy, time will tell. The important factor is to bring the domestic, or in this case regional, strength to the world stage. And in this case, it would be for the Atlantic region flattening the COVID-19 curve and then keeping it low. However, before signing on to innovative intra-national trade and travel policies, what needs to be better understood is how and why the performative behavior of the Atlantic Bubble played a role in keeping COVID-19 so low within the region itself.

References

Adams, Vincanne, Thomas Novotny, and Hannah Leslie. 2008. "Global Health diplomacy." *Medical Anthropology* 27 (4): 315–323.

Ashton, John. 2020. "Shoe Leather Epidemiology in the Age of COVID: Lessons from Cuba." *Journal of the Royal Society of Medicine* 113 (7): 282–283.

Bakvis, Herman, and Grace Skogstad. 2020. *Canadian Federalism: Performance, Effectiveness, and Legitimacy.* Toronto: University of Toronto Press.

Béland, Daniel, André Lecours, Mireille Paquet, and Trevor Tombe. 2020. "A Critical Juncture in Fiscal Federalism? Canada's Response to COVID-19." *Canadian Journal of Political Science/Revue canadienne de science politique* 1–5.

Benton, Adia, and Kim Yi Dionne. 2015. "International Political Economy and the 2014 West African Ebola Outbreak." *African Studies Review* 58 (1): 223–236.

Bradshaw, James. 2011. "Dalhousie Medical School to Sell Saudis 10 Seats." *Globe and Mail*, March 17. https://www.theglobeandmail.com/news/national/dalhousie-medical-school-to-sell-saudis-10-seats/article573025/.

Brautigam, Deborah. 2011. *The Dragon's Gift: The Real Story of China in Africa.* Oxford: Oxford University Press.

Brown, Douglas. 2002. "Provinces Have a Role in Canadian Foreign Policy." *Federations. Special triple issue: Themes of international Conference on Federalism* 11–12.

Capano, Giliberto, Michael Howlett, Darryl SL Jarvis, M. Ramesh, and Nihit Goyal. 2020. "Mobilizing Policy (in) Capacity to Fight COVID-19: Understanding Variations in State Responses." *Policy and Society* 39 (3): 285–308.

CBC News. 2020. "EU Removes Canadians from List of Approved Travellers Because of COVID-19." *CBC News*, October 21. https://www.cbc.ca/news/business/eu-travel-canada-1.5770782.

Chisholm, Cassidy. 2020. "Cuts to WestJet Service 'a Major Blow' to Atlantic Airports as Region Still Isolated Due to COVID-19." *CBC News*,

October 14. https://www.cbc.ca/news/canada/nova-scotia/westjet-atlantic-canada-cuts-airports-1.5761873.

Coletta, Amanda. 2020. "Canada Celebrates Thanksgiving Amid Coronavirus Second Wave, Mixed Messages." *Washington Post*, October 11. https://www.washingtonpost.com/world/the_americas/canada-thanksgiving-coronavirus-trudeau/2020/10/09/59fc6c46-04d8-11eb-8879-7663b816bfa5_story.html.

Craft, Aimée, Deborah McGregor, and Jeffery Hewitt. 2020. "COVID-19 and First Nation's Responses." In *Vulnerable: The Law, Policy and Ethics of COVID-19*, edited by Colleen Flood, Vanessa MacDonnell, Jane Philpott, Sophie Thériault, and Sridhar Venkatapuram, 49–68. Ottawa: University of Ottawa Press.

Donor Tracker. 2020. "Canada—Global Health." https://donortracker.org/Canada/globalhealth.

Evans, Pete. 2020. "EU Removes Canadians from List of Approved Travellers Because of COVID-19." *CBC News*, October 21. https://www.cbc.ca/news/business/eu-travel-canada-1.5770782.

Giroux, Michelle. 2020. "Réflexions sur la mise en œuvre de la Loi sur la santé publique au Québec dans le contexte de la pandémie de COVID-19." In *Vulnerable: The Law, Policy and Ethics of COVID-19*, edited by Colleen Flood, Vanessa MacDonnell, Jane Philpott, Sophie Thériault, and Sridhar Venkatapuram, 69–78. Ottawa: University of Ottawa Press.

Godefroy, Raphael, and Joshua Lewis. 2020. "Estimates of COVID-19 Cases Across Four Canadian Provinces." *Journal of Epidemiology* 42 (4).

Google News. 2020. "COVID-19 Map." October 21. https://news.google.com/covid19/map?hl=en-CA&gl=CA&ceid=CA%3Aen.

Gorman, Michael. 2020. "N.S. Craft Breweries Turn to Online Sales, Home Deliveries to Keep Operating." *CBC News*, March 25. https://www.cbc.ca/news/canada/nova-scotia/covid-19-craft-brewing-beer-buy-local-1.5509054.

Government of Canada. 2020. "Speech from the Throne." September 23. https://www.canada.ca/en/privy-council/campaigns/speech-throne/2020/speech-from-the-throne.html.

Hoffman, Steven. 2010. "Strengthening Global Health Diplomacy in Canada's Foreign Policy Architecture: Literature Review and Key Informant Interviews." *Canadian Foreign Policy Journal* 16 (3): 17–41.

Huish, Robert. 2013. *Where No Doctor Has Gone Before: Cuba's Place in the Global Health Landscape*. Toronto: Wilfrid Laurier University Press.

Johns Hopkins Coronavirus Resource Centre. 2020. "COVID-19 Dashboard by the Center for Systems Science and Engineering at Johns Hopkins University." March 6. https://coronavirus.jhu.edu/map.html.

Karaivanov, Alexander, En Lu Shih, Hitoshi Shigeoka, Cong Chen, and Stephanie Pamplona. 2020. "Face Masks, Public Policies and Slowing the Spread of

COVID-19: Evidence from Canada" (No. w27891). National Bureau of Economic Research.

Kew, Olen, Sutter Roland, Esther de Gourville, Walter Dowdle, and Mark Pallansch. 2005. "Vaccine-Derived Polioviruses and the Endgame Strategy for Global Polio Eradication." *Annual Review of Microbiology* 59: 587–635.

Laupacis, Andreas. 2020. "Working Together to Contain and Manage COVID-19." *Canadian Medical Association Journal* 192 (13): E340–E341. https://www.cmaj.ca/content/192/13/E340.short.

Mamuji, Aaida. 2012. "Canadian Military Involvement in Humanitarian Assistance: Progress and Prudence in Natural Disaster Response." *Canadian Foreign Policy Journal* 18 (2): 208–224.

Mathen, Carissima. 2020. "Resisting the Siren's Call: Emergency Powers, Federalism and Public Policy." In *Vulnerable: The Law, Policy and Ethics of COVID-19*, edited by Colleen Flood, Vanessa MacDonnell, Jane Philpott, Sophie Thériault, and Sridhar Venkatapuram, 115–126. Ottawa: University of Ottawa Press.

McEachern, Terrance. 2020. "More Home Buyers Looking to Atlantic Bubble." *The Chronicle Herald*, October 15. https://www.thechronicleherald.ca/business/local-business/more-home-buyers-looking-to-atlantic-bubble-509929/.

Mercer, Greg. 2020. "The 'Atlantic Bubble' Has Largely Succeeded in Keeping Out COVID-19. But Can It Last?" *Globe and Mail*, October 2. https://www.theglobeandmail.com/canada/article-the-atlantic-bubble-has-largely-succeeded-in-keeping-out-covid-1/.

Migone, Andrea Riccardo. 2020. "Trust, but Customize: Federalism's Impact on the Canadian COVID-19 Response." *Policy and Society* 39 (3): 382–402.

Mulligan, Preston. 2020. "Lights, Camera, Action: Low COVID Numbers in N.S. Create Boom in Film Industry." *CBC News*, September 23. https://www.cbc.ca/news/canada/nova-scotia/covid-19-low-numbers-film-industry-boom-1.5733696.

Nash, Catherine. 2000. "Performativity in Practice: Some Recent Work in Cultural Geography." *Progress in human geography* 24 (4): 653–664.

Perez Riverol, Amilcar. 2020. "The Cuban Strategy for Combatting the COVID-19 Pandemic." *MEDICC Review* 22 (3).

Potter, Evan H. 2004. "Branding Canada: The Renaissance of Canada's Commercial Diplomacy." *International Studies Perspectives* 5 (1): 55–60.

Reed, Gail. 2020. "Mobilizing Primary Health Care: Cuba's Powerful Weapon Against COVID-19." *MEDICC Review* 22 (2): 54.

Robertson, Grant. 2020. "What Happened with Canada's Pandemic Alert System? The GPHIN Controversy Explained." *Globe and Mail*, October 5. https://www.theglobeandmail.com/canada/article-what-happened-with-canadas-pandemic-alert-system-the-gphin/.

Roth, Andrew. 2020. "Coronavirus: Russia Sends Plane Full of Medical Supplies to US." *The Guardian*, April 1. https://www.theguardian.com/world/2020/apr/01/coronavirus-russia-sends-plane-full-of-medical-supplies-to-us.

Shahadu, Somed. 2017. *Owning Food: The Impact of Living in Male-Headed Households on Women's Food Security—A Case Study of the Kumbungu District in Northern Ghana*. Halifax: Dalhousie University.

Shingler, Benjamin, and Sarah Leavitt. 2020. "Why Contact Tracing Remains a Hurdle for Québec in Containing COVID-19." *CBC News*, September 19. https://www.cbc.ca/news/canada/montreal/contact-tracing-hurdle-quebec-1.5730400.

Simpson, Michael. 2020. "For a Prefigurative Pandemic Politics: Disrupting the Racial Colonial Quarantine." *Political Geography* https://doi.org/10.1016/j.polgeo.2020.102274.

Snan, Nebal. 2020. "More Atlantic Canadians Are Against Bursting the Atlantic Bubble Despite Low COVID-19 Numbers." *The Chronicle Herald*, October 9. https://www.thechronicleherald.ca/news/local/more-atlantic-canadians-are-against-bursting-the-atlantic-bubble-despite-low-covid-19-numbers-507925/.

Stoodley, Chris. 2020. "Travel Agency Trying to Extend Atlantic Bubble to Caribbean." *Halifax Today*, October 11. https://www.halifaxtoday.ca/local-news/travel-agency-trying-to-extend-atlantic-bubble-to-caribbean-2784437.

Tiessen, Rebecca, and Emma Swan. 2018. "Canada's Feminist Foreign Policy Promises: An Ambitious Agenda for Gender Equality, Human Rights, Peace, and Security." In *Justin Trudeau and Canadian Foreign Policy*, edited by Norman Hillmer and Philippe Lasgassé, 187–205. Palgrave Macmillan.

Tuite, Ashleigh, and Amy Greer. 2020. "Shaping the Future of the COVID-19 Pandemic in Canada." *Canadian Medical Association Journal* 192 (37): E1074–E1075.

Turnbull, Sarah. 2020. "Canada-U.S. Border Now Closed to Non-essential Travel." *CTV News*, March 20. https://www.ctvnews.ca/health/coronavirus/canada-u-s-border-now-closed-to-non-essential-travel-1.4861409.

World Health Organization. 1947. *The Constitution of the World Health Organization*. Constitution, Geneva: WHO chronicle 1, 29.

Yeung, Jessie. 2020. "Hong Kong and Singapore to Set Up a 'Travel Bubble' as COVID Cases Fall." *CTV News*, October 15. https://www.ctvnews.ca/world/hong-kong-and-singapore-to-set-up-a-travel-bubble-as-covid-cases-fall-1.5146147.

CHAPTER 6

Geopolitics and Diplomacy in Canadian Arctic Relations

Kari Roberts

INTRODUCTION

The Arctic symbolizes Canada's northern identity, Indigeneity, and sovereignty and looms large in narratives about Canada's history, and also in visions of its future. There is tremendous emotional attachment to the Arctic, considered by some to be an essential component of "Canada's brand" (Paradis et al. 2018: 183). Prime Minister Stephen Harper reprioritized Arctic security and defence, in parallel with a warming climate, and rising global interest in investment, energy exploration, and commercial shipping opportunities in the region. Denmark and Canada's spirited flag planting antics on Hans Island, and Russia's positioning of its flag on the Arctic seabed, have catalysed what some have labelled the "race for the Arctic", prompting a reassertion of Canadian sovereignty in the region, as well as calls for collaboration among littoral states to avoid

K. Roberts (✉)
Mount Royal University, Calgary, AB, Canada
e-mail: kroberts@mtroyal.ca

© The Author(s), under exclusive license to Springer Nature
Switzerland AG 2021
D. Carment and R. Nimijean (eds.), *Political Turmoil in a Tumultuous World*, Canada and International Affairs,
https://doi.org/10.1007/978-3-030-70686-9_6

disrupting an otherwise cooperative neighbourhood. Canada's prioritization of Arctic cooperation is exemplified in its multiple regional commitments, including the Arctic Council, the 1992 Declaration of Friendship and Co-operation for the Arctic Region between Canada and Russia, and the 2008 Ilulissat Declaration.

As the polar ice melts and the world comes to the Arctic, Canada increasingly finds itself competing with three great powers there—the United States, Russia, and China—to harness the potential the Arctic holds, and to protect it from the potential geopolitical conflict this could bring. To complicate matters, Canada faces its own set of challenges with each of these nations, which necessitate striking a careful balance between asserting Canadian interests and sidestepping diplomatic landmines that have the potential to spill over into the Arctic. What is more, a host of other critical policy priorities converge for Canada in the Arctic (energy, climate change and the environment, and support for Indigenous communities) all of which generate considerable interprovincial discord. These challenges have prompted calls for a more robust and calculated Arctic strategy that allows Canada to support Indigenous communities, and to defend its economic, environmental, and security interests there. But, since 2015, while the Trudeau government has rhetorically acknowledged the importance of the Arctic, it seems to have adopted a "don't rock the boat" approach to the region. While this is not out of step with decades of Canadian Arctic policy, it does represent a shift from the Harper era. The COVID-19 pandemic further complicates inaction on this file, as it has forced many nations, including Canada, to scale back or even suspend key initiatives.

Canadian Arctic strategy is not made in a bubble: it does not operate outside the spectre of heightened tensions on the world stage, nor does it operate outside of Canada's domestic political turmoil. Both external geopolitical realities—notably relations with and between the great powers—and internal tensions within the federation are brought to bear on Canadian Arctic policy. As the superpowers jockey for position in the Arctic, there is potential for conflict right on Canada's doorstep. In addition to the unprecedented levels of acrimony among the major powers, Canada also faces tensions in its own bilateral relations with China, Russia, and the United States. These challenges are only exacerbated by interprovincial tensions that divide Canadians on key political issues of the day, many of which overlap with Arctic priorities. For example, in energy rich provinces, a robust pursuit of climate change miti- gation at the expense of the energy industry is politically fraught. In other places, a diluted response to the challenge of climate change is politi- cally unpopular. These stark differences are reflected in the rhetoric and policies of Canada's political parties, which have positioned themselves as profoundly and philosophically at loggerheads, and together comprise the political opposition in Trudeau's post-2019 minority government.

The Arctic is the backdrop for a multitude of competing issues, as well as the bitter domestic disagreements about how to address them. So while the region is affected by diverging interests in a dangerous world, it is also susceptible to irreconcilable differences within a divided country. What is more, it is becoming increasingly difficult to ascertain where domestic politics ends and international politics begins. Domestic antag- onisms towards Russia, and more recently towards China, and the United States (under Trump 2017–2020), restrict the Government of Canada's engagement with the world's superpowers, and this may further exacer- bate Canada's inaction on the Arctic file. Here the Trudeau government walks a delicate line between asserting Canadian interests, and avoiding conflict with the major powers, as well as managing internal conflicts that threaten national unity, and Trudeau's minority governing position. This chapter will consider the Trudeau government's approach to the Arctic in the context of its attempt to balance its complicated relations with the major powers and its national priorities in the region. The Arctic was already an inactive file prior to COVID-19, and now risks further neglect as public spending and diplomatic priorities are recalibrated. Canada cannot afford to deprioritize the Arctic and must find a way to strike a balance between these relationships and its national priorities.

HARPER'S ARCTIC REDISCOVERY: "USE IT OR LOSE IT"

There is no shortage of disagreement about the various threats and oppor- tunities for Canada in the Arctic. Some have warned of a coming conflict with Russia (Huebert 2009; Braun and Blank 2020), while others take the view that cooperation is the more likely scenario when it comes to competing sovereignty claims there (Lackenbauer and Lalonde 2019; Roberts 2015). Stephen Harper showed a keen personal interest in the Arctic, introducing a *Northern Strategy* for Canada that reflected a "use it or lose it strategy" in which Canada must assert its national sovereignty in the Arctic or risk losing its claim there altogether. In some ways, the

Arctic was part of Harper's political brand, which included the positioning of Canada as a global energy player, resisting NATO's involvement in regional defence, spending on icebreakers and power projection capabilities, and even funding the search for the ill-fated Franklin expedition.[1] Harper saw the Arctic in geopolitical terms, which informed his perception of both Russian and American presences there. When Russia annexed Crimea in 2014, this prompted a renewed push to view its Arctic activities through a *realpolitik* lens. Russia was seen as a hostile actor on the world stage and the Arctic was not immune to its malevolence. Harper believed that Canada should not rely on NATO to defend its interests in the Arctic, and consequently "increased the defence budget and initiated procurement projects, including stealth snowmobiles, Arctic drones, and controversial Arctic offshore patrol vessels", spending which continued to be prioritized until its curtailment following the financial crisis in 2008 when "several Arctic projects were put on hold or scaled back" (Østhagen et al. 2018: 7).

Harper's Arctic legacy is the promise of a more robust capacity for defending Canadian sovereignty; however, his tenure must also be acknowledged as one of neglect: Indigenous communities were not included in Harper's Northern development scenarios, an omission that US Secretary of State Hillary Clinton swiftly criticized (Ljunggren 2010). Canada's Arctic strategy was by no means resolved when Justin Trudeau took up the file in 2015.

Trudeau's Arctic Dilemma: Navigating Great Power Relations

Justin Trudeau's election victory was due, in part, to promises of addressing climate change, an area with significance for the North. Trudeau decried, "Canada is back", promising a return of Canadian leadership and cooperation in key areas such as climate change and peacekeeping. This suggested that, in addition to considering the Arctic from a defence and security perspective like his predecessor, Trudeau might view the Arctic as an element of a climate strategy. More than this, the Arctic connects with a number of Liberal priorities including

---

[1] The failed 1845 British expedition, led by John Franklin, sought to explore the Arctic and cross the Northwest Passage. In 2014 Canada led a successful effort to locate the wreckage of both ships, which are now considered National Historic Sites.

Indigenous communities, economic development, environmental security, and national sovereignty. In fact, *the Arctic and Northern Policy Framework* (2019) prioritizes environmental protection and reconciliation with Indigenous communities in the Canadian Arctic, while affirming the "importance of a comprehensive approach to Arctic defence and security" with an emphasis on the need to "deter would-be adversaries" and "develop capabilities to support unconventional security and safety missions in the Arctic" (Lackenbauer 2016: 14). *Strong, Secure, Engaged* acknowledges the importance of the Arctic for Canadian defence, underscores the importance of cooperation through the Arctic Council, and warns of the challenges of "increased commercial traffic, tourism, search and rescue, and natural or man-made disasters" (Government of Canada 2017: 51). It prioritizes joint intelligence and surveillance in the region with allies, a modernized North Warning System (NWS), expanded air defence of the Canadian Arctic Archipelago, the development of Arctic Offshore Patrol Ships, space-based surveillance assets such as the RADARSAT Constellation Mission, and enhanced ground surveillance and patrol capacity. Despite this document's focus on securitizing the North, there has not been much advancement on the Arctic file, due in part to some higher order calculations that seem to have intervened to relegate the Arctic—and the promise it holds in addressing a number of the government's key priorities—to the sidelines. Trudeau's promises are at times in direct conflict, and these have implications for the region. For example, domestically, Trudeau promised significant cuts to greenhouse gas emissions (by 2030) and a carbon tax, and then his government purchased the multibillion-dollar Trans Mountain pipeline expansion. For some, these actions are fundamentally at odds. On the other hand, Trudeau has been forced to strike a delicate balance between conflicting priorities that divide the country. In the Arctic, traditional and human security issues have been rhetorically prioritized. But in practice, for example, climate strategies are less robust than promised, leaving Northern communities questioning the government's commitment to environmental protection and reconciliation with Indigenous peoples. The assertion of Canadian sovereignty also faces a credibility problem as Canada carefully navigates challenging relations with the major powers, avoiding agitation in the Arctic. The following sections elaborate on how Canada's relations with the United States, Russia, and, to a lesser extent China are rife with complications that make tackling contentious issues in the Arctic risky.

CANADA-U.S. ARCTIC RELATIONS IN THE TRUMP ERA

With the United States, Trudeau had to carefully manage a delicate relationship with U.S. President Donald Trump who showed little interest in allegiances, sought zero sum trade relationships, and delivered on a promise to re-open the North American Free Trade Agreement (NAFTA). Moreover, the weak US response to the COVID-19 pandemic, and concerns about the premature opening of the US economy, raised concerns about the implications for Canada about the re-opening of the Canada-U.S. border. Managing border issues in the Trump era was challenging, as great care had to be taken not to raise the ire of a president sensitive to criticism or insinuations about the safety of people and goods coming from the United States. Addressing sovereignty disputes in the Arctic is challenging at the best of times but a combative Trump administration, under fire for a host of domestic missteps, was not an ideal broker for renewed assertions of Canada's sovereignty over the Northwest Passage (NWP). While the tone of Canada-U.S. relations is likely to warm under a Biden administration, the U.S. position on sovereignty in the NWP is not guaranteed to shift.

The 2016 US-Canada Joint Statement on Environment, Climate Change, and Arctic Leadership prioritized environmental security and conservation, sustainable energy development, and the inclusion of Indigenous and northern communities in addressing climate change—a priority that lined up with Canada's ratification of the United Nations Declaration on the Rights of Indigenous Peoples (UNDRIP) and reinforced Trudeau's "Canada is back" promise (Lackenbauer in Lackenbauer and Lalonde 2019: 20). This enabled Trudeau to prioritize "sociocultural and environmental priorities over the more hard security, resource development emphasis attributed to the Harper government" (Lackenbauer in Lackenbauer and Lalonde 2019: 24); however, it shared with Harper's approach the romanticism that has long been embedded in images of the Canadian North (Lackenbauer in Lackenbauer and Lalonde 2019: 24). But with Trump, Canada no longer had a partner on the sustainable energy and climate change files, nor could it expect a partner in leadership on northern issues.

When Trump came to power, he immediately rolled back Obama's climate initiatives, withdrew the United States from the Paris Climate Agreement, rejected climate science, and supported maximum American fossil fuel production, particularly coal (Boyd and Rabe 2019). Given that

"Canada is a net exporter of oil and gas, and virtually all energy exports go to US markets", Trudeau felt pressure to adjust Canada's climate policies to avoid placing "domestic industry at a competitive disadvantage relative to their American counterparts" (Boyd and Rabe 2019: 242). Trump's 2017 America First Offshore Energy Executive Order "reversed the Obama administration's ban on Arctic leases, immediately placing Canada's northern development policies at odds with both the Trump administration and the Russians" (Wallace 2019). This led to "offshore leases for Arctic oil and gas exploration with access to previously inaccessible acreages and overturned the indefinite drilling bans in much of the Arctic Ocean announced during the final days of the Obama administration" (Wallace 2019: 13). With respect to Arctic sovereignty, U.S. officials also reversed a previous willingness to agree to disagree on the NWP. Trump's Secretary of State, Mike Pompeo, resurrected the old disagreement about the Northwest Passage when he reminded the Arctic Council in 2019 that the United States considered the passage an international waterway. In 2018, Trump's Secretary of the Navy, Richard Spencer, advocated the United States send its warships through the NWP to reinforce its freedom of navigation.

The United States has long disputed Canada's claim to the NWP between Baffin Bay and the Beaufort Sea. Regulated by the United Nations Convention on the Law of the Sea (UNCLOS) and the Arctic Cooperation Agreement between the United States and Canada, the strait is a key shipping lane that connects the Arctic and Pacific Oceans, now a potential shipping alternative to the Suez and Panama Canals (Todorov 2017: 71). For decades the United States has flouted Canada's claim, exemplified by the infamous 1969 Manhattan voyage through the Passage, prompting the elder Prime Minister Trudeau to introduce the Arctic Waters Pollution Prevention Act (AWPPA) to regulate shipping in a 100-mile zone around the Arctic islands north of 60°, and in keeping with public pressure to assert Canadian sovereignty in the North (Elliot-Meisel 2009: 211). Canada bases its claim here on the grounds of ecological protection and the proximity of northern communities. While the disagreement persists, it has been mitigated by cooperation in other areas, notably the *Arctic Cooperation Agreement* enabling collaborative research and exploration, a key symbolic provision of which was a U.S. promise to seek Canada's consent when its icebreakers sought passage through waters believed by Canada to be sovereign (Todorov 2017: 73). This was not a legal recognition of Canadian sovereignty, but a relatively low-cost compromise to acknowledge Canada's belief in its sovereignty in the Passage (Charron 2005: 146). For decades, this was something both allies could live with; however, with increased ease of navigation in the NWP, opportunities now exist for commercial shipping (which the ACA did not address), and this prospect has reanimated U.S. repudiation of Canadian sovereignty claims here.

As traffic through the Arctic increases, the denial of Canadian sovereignty over the NWP is probably the greatest threat to Canada's Arctic sovereignty; however, it often takes a rhetorical backseat to warnings of Russian militarization in the region. Canada, the United States, and Russia are signatories to the 2008 Ilulissat Declaration, which commits them to the peaceful and orderly settlement of sovereignty disputes in the Arctic, the protection of marine life, and cooperation on scientific discovery and search and rescue. Unlike Canada and Russia, the United States is not a signatory of UNCLOS so its disregard of Canada's claims is consistent with its orientation towards such matters globally. The reality is that U.S. security may actually be heightened with Canada in control of the NWP, a region difficult to defend and which has not been a priority for the United States until more recently. The case could be made that, as Russia continues to assert itself on the world stage, and as China looks for shipping routes through the region, cooperation to secure surveillance and navigation oversight in the Passage benefits both allies. Nonetheless this approach has not been embraced by the Trudeau government, perhaps owing to the relatively low priority of the Arctic on the US agenda. Disputes over the NWP aside, the warming of the Arctic poses similar challenges for both the United States and Canada, and the U.S.' own Arctic strategy documents since 2016 focus mostly on the heightened security environment (Rodman 2020). This suggests that there is room for cooperation with Canada in the Arctic, especially after the U.S.' May 2020 announcement that it will exit the Open Skies Treaty. This will force Canada to decide if it shares U.S. concerns about Russia's flouting of the Treaty and to consider the wisdom of following the U.S.' lead to maintain continuity in the defence of North American airspace (Sevunts 2020b). With expanded shipping through the region, there is even potential for NORAD to take on enhanced marine security operations. Both Canada and the United States could benefit from expanded underwater infrastructure and cyber surveillance (Charron 2005). Proactive defence of the North is long overdue (Charron 2005: 87); however, this kind of cooperation, in the current climate, could be challenging.

Policy divergence in the Arctic may reflect negative trends in the wider Canada-US relationship, but the perils of allowing this relationship to drift further are stark. It is difficult to imagine a more dangerous time for the two allies to be divided. Given present geopolitical realities, rising conflict among superpowers, a surging pandemic, and the accompanying economic uncertainty and potential for conflict this brings, now is precisely the *wrong* time for the Canada-US relationship to become less unified. A glimmer of hope may be found in the U.S. unveiling in July 2020 of a new Arctic strategy, and the near simultaneous appointment of James DeHart as the new U.S. Arctic Coordinator, a position that had long been vacant (Sevunts 2020a). DeHart's strong security background signals U.S. recognition of the geopolitical importance of the Arctic region to U.S. interests, and of its desire to "catch up to Russia and China" in the Arctic, although DeHart was careful to indicate a desire to keep the region an area of low tension. While renewed Arctic interest from its ally may be good for Canada, this could also heighten vulnerabilities as the great powers vie for influence and resources on Canada's northern frontier. Increased engagement and coordination with Washington are going to be essential for Canada as this race for the Arctic intensifies. While the tone of relations is likely to improve under President Biden, at the time of writing, it is too soon to know precisely what impact this will have on Canada-U.S. Arctic relations.

In the age of Trump, cooperation seems unlikely due to the president's "zero-sum approach to conflicts, with allies and opponents alike seen through a lens of permanent competition" (Lajeunesse and Huebert 2019: 225). The Trump administration repudiates complicated or "nuanced or holistic understandings of problems", which were "jettisoned in favor of easily quantified results: either winning or losing. Within this new American approach to international relations, the dispute over the Northwest Passage could quickly shift from a longstanding but well-managed diplomatic irritant to political crisis" (Lajeunesse and Huebert 2019: 227). Moreover, even relations with Canada, its closest ally, were seen in transactional terms and suspicion persisted that Canada's "meek and mild" Prime Minister, often derided as "Justin", would "take advantage" and pursue "unfair" trade deals with the United States (Lajeunesse and Huebert 2019). Trump exhibited a "disregard" for the "special relationship" and tweeted that "Canada's steel industry is a potential security threat", and that he sought to destroy the Canadian automotive sector (Lajeunesse and Huebert 2019: 232). Trump's August 2020 executive order imposing a 10% tariff on Canadian aluminium imports was illustrative of the many irritants in the trade relationship.

The United States also disputes Russia's claim to the Northern Sea Route, seeing it as an international waterway in which the United States enjoys freedom of navigation. Both Canada and Russia assert that these are domestic shipping routes and therefore they fall under national laws. Unsurprisingly, Russia and Canada have been sympathetic to each other's claims and promote multilateral approaches to resolving these disputes. Cooperation in the Arctic has the potential to enable the Trudeau government to capitalize on its prioritization of multilateralism as well as its protection of northern communities; however, these have, by necessity, taken a backseat to avoiding tensions with Trump (Paradis et al. 2018). A decision to stay the course *vis-a-vis* U.S. Arctic relations may be understandable in the short term.

Relations with Russia in the Arctic

The chief area of disagreement between Canada and Russia in the Arctic is overlapping scientific claims regarding the extensions of their continental shelves, specifically the area between the Arctic Ocean's Lomonosov and Mendeleev Ridges. Each country has made a submission to the UN's Commission on the Limits of the Continental Shelf (CLCS), with a resolution likely years away. Both countries are committed to this process; however, Canadian officials have expressed concern about Russian militarization in the Arctic, in tandem with its growing adversarial relationship with NATO, prompting fears this could taint an otherwise cooperative relationship in the region. Canada responded to Russia's 2014 annexation of Crimea with swift sanctions, and tensions between the two nations escalated to record levels. The intervening years have seen Russia undertake opportunistic campaigns of disinformation meant to undermine democracy and Atlanticism, including recent allegations of disruptive efforts to fuel conspiracy theories about the COVID-19 virus (Thompson et al. 2020). 2020 saw the Canadian energy industry pummelled by an oil price war between Russia and Saudi Arabia, closely followed by the 2020 COVID-19 pandemic, both of which combined to hammer the global price of oil, and hit the sector hard. Once again, the Arctic has not been top of mind, likely because this is not an ideal environment in which to engage with Russia in the Arctic.

Nevertheless, economic turmoil and a global pandemic did not stop Russia from going ahead with May 2020 military exercises in the Russian Archipelago. The testing of new equipment by Russian paratroopers in the High Arctic reflects Russia's continued commitment to Arctic security and its history of demonstrating Russian military prowess, although whether it was a deliberately provocative warning to NATO is unclear. Like Canada, Russia's militarization in the region likely reflects its acknowledgement of the vulnerability of Arctic nations to melting ice and increased navigation in the region. Russia has the longest Arctic coastline and the largest Arctic population, and derives 11% of its GDP from its Arctic zone (Laruelle 2020), all of which render the Arctic critical to Russia's economy and security. Some see Russian activities in the Arctic—including reactivating old Cold War bases and modernizing air defence systems—as aggressive (Huebert in Brewster 2020). Others are careful to warn of the dangers of presuming Russian aggression and responding in kind, especially during a global pandemic when tensions are heightened, and opportunities for misunderstanding abound (Charron in Brewster 2020).

Russia views the Arctic as key to its resource economy and therefore its position as a regional power must be preserved. Since Crimea, Russia has experienced economic stagnation, capital outflows, decreased foreign investment and an overall decline in global energy prices, all devaluing the ruble. This has prompted a renewed interest in developing Arctic resources; however, because these are expensive to develop, and because funding this investment is challenging, activity has slowed. Nonetheless, Russia sees the Arctic as the future of its energy dominance and is unprepared to cede sovereignty there, or to leave this region vulnerable (Conley and Rohloff 2015: XII). It is important to acknowledge that Russia's activities in the region have not been aggressive: its leaders have prioritized sovereignty, but also cooperation in the Arctic through participation in bodies such as the Arctic Council, the Barents Euro-Arctic Council, and the UNCLOS, to name a few. Alongside these institutional commitments, Defence Minister Sergei Shoigu confirmed that Russia also considers it necessary to develop military infrastructure in the region, a priority reflected in the 2014 military doctrine which prioritizes the Arctic, specifically the modernization of the Russian navy and its northern fleet (Conley and Rohloff 2015: 1).

It bears noting that Russia shares many of the same security concerns raised by Canada and other Arctic nations, notably some of the so-called softer security issues such as environmental protection, climate change, and the impact of increased navigation in northern communities (Regehr 2017). Russia has also advocated collaboration to enable search and rescue, prevent smuggling, and to address environmental damage mitigation in the event of an oil spill, for example. Addressing all of these issues necessitates a build-up of naval bases along Russia's northern sea route and the "deployment of dual-use equipment and the performance of dual-purpose operations that involve search and rescue, monitoring civilian maritime and air traffic, navigation regulation, emergency response, and Arctic research" (Regehr 2017: 3). The 2008 *Foundations of Russian Federation Policy in the Arctic until 2020 and Beyond* identifies the Russian Arctic zone as a national strategic resource base, and prioritizes preserving the Arctic as a zone of peace and cooperation, protecting its unique ecological system, and developing the North Sea passage as a safe transportation conduit (Foundations of Russian Federation Policy in the Arctic to 2008). These are in step with Canadian objectives in the region; however, cooperative initiatives with Russia in the Arctic rarely make their way into the public consciousness. Instead, a different message seems to take hold that warns, "the Russians are coming!" (Lackenbauer and Lajeunesse 2016) and fails to appreciate the nuance in Russian foreign policy or its interests in the Arctic, and fails to consider that Russia, as an Arctic power, and a regional power more broadly, has interests that it intends to defend. For some, consideration of these interests, and a willingness to engage with Russia in the Arctic, are akin to legitimizing its bad behaviour elsewhere and this then impedes an ability to think creatively about engaging Russia.

After the Ukraine crisis, there was an understandable shift in relations with Russia in the Arctic. What was once an agenda of promoting innovative and collaborative thinking became a scramble to preserve existing levels of cooperation after a wave of post-Crimea sanctions (Conley and Rohloff 2015: v). There was a growing constituency in Canada that advocated a tougher stance with Russia following its annexation of Crimea, its key champion none other than Foreign Affairs Minister Chrystia Freeland. Known for backing Canada's Magnitsky Law,[2] Freeland took a firm approach to dealing with Russia, perhaps owing to her residency as a

---

[2] The 2017 *Justice for Victims of Corrupt Foreign Officials Act* (Bill S-226) enabled travel bans and sanctions on foreign nationals believed to be guilty of human rights violations or financial crimes (i.e. corruption and money laundering). Nicknamed the

journalist in Ukraine during the USSR's collapse, and/or the influential Ukrainian diaspora in Canada. It is possible that Freeland's reluctance to prioritize the Arctic may have been a tactic of avoidance; engaging in constructive dialogue with Russia at the Arctic Council at the time may have been undesirable.

While Crimea is not the Arctic, some have been quick to associate Russia's activities in its own backyard with its intentions in the Arctic (Huebert 2009; Braun and Blank 2020). Some warn that Russian efforts to cooperate in the Arctic reflect Russia's "charm offensive", designed to distract and fool NATO allies into letting their collective guards down in the Arctic (Braun and Blank 2020). However, there are a host of issues that lend themselves to Canadian and Russian cooperation in the region. As mentioned above, some of these issues are priorities of the Trudeau government, not the least of which is support for Indigenous communities, consistent with the 2016 decision to support the UNDRIP. Canada's strategy for northern development has included increasing the footprint and effectiveness of the Canadian Rangers as a key element of surveillance in the opening Arctic, as well as the development of a deep-water port in Nunavut, both part and parcel of both a northern sovereignty agenda, and the wider promise of economic development in the region. There is potential for convergence between Canada's decolonization priorities and the support for northern communities in Russia, which remain considerably underdeveloped (Russia is not a signatory to UNDRIP), as well as opportunities for joint financial and organizational support of the Inuit Circumpolar Council.

Turning a blind eye to collaborative opportunities such as these reflects a narrow view of the region in strictly defence and security terms; this view sees military solutions to existing problems. Canada faces many challenges in the Arctic, some of which involve the securitization of Canada's share of the region's resources and protecting its land and waters; however, none of this can be done in isolation. Many of the security challenges Canada faces are borderless, requiring joint action with Russia if any progress is to be made. Rather than assuming that conflict with Russia will spill over into the Arctic, the reverse may be possible. Michael Byers argues that a form of "complex and resilient interdependence" may be

Magnitsky Law, it was enacted in memory of Russian lawyer Sergei Magnitsky, who died in Russian custody after his wrongful imprisonment for exposing tax fraud.

possible, in which, as states cooperate in one region, they become accustomed to functioning cooperatively, enabling a breakdown of tensions in other areas (Byers 2019: 32). He writes, "a multiplicity of issues, actors, transnational channels of contact, and associated interdependencies made it possible for Russia and Western countries to treat their relations in the Arctic separately from the tensions and breakdowns elsewhere" (Byers 2019: 42). But after Crimea, military cooperation was suspended in the Arctic, sanctions and travel bans on Russia followed, and companies that might work with Russia in offshore oil and gas development were lobbied. Cooperation on search and rescue and the prevention of unregulated commercial fishing continued, undeterred by the tensions in Russia-West relations (Byers 2019: 34), although Trudeau's reversal on CF-18 replacement had implications for Arctic surveillance and defence.

Strong, Secure, Engaged, and the Trudeau government's stated intention to prioritize the defence and security of the Arctic, appear to leave room for drawing a distinction between militarization of the region and weaponization (Byers 2019), with the latter option presently off the table. The challenging environment of the Arctic makes monitoring other states' behaviour relatively easy, and Byers feels this diminishes any pressures of a security dilemma because surprises are highly unlikely (Byers 2019: 36). It is precisely because of the "cold, dark and dangerous" nature of the Arctic that Byers argues that the price of aggression in the region is raised, and this serves as a key disincentive for antagonizing other nations or escalating conflict in a region that is very difficult to defend. Burden sharing and cooperation are far more cost effective in this theatre (Byers 2019: 36). For these reasons, Canada's (and Russia's) commitment to the 1992 Open Skies Treaty, which fosters trust and transparency to help reduce the spectre of armed conflict, and which gives Canada (and its NATO allies) the ability to monitor Russian Arctic militarization, has been an essential tool of airspace defence in the Arctic. As the United States withdraws from the Treaty, Canada must now decide if it will follow the U.S.' lead, or remain committed to an imperfect, but essential mechanism for cooperation with Russia in the Arctic, in the spirit of the Ilulissat Declaration, which privileged peaceful dispute resolution (Bouffard and Lackenbauer 2020).

Canada-Russia relations are complicated—in the Arctic and beyond. It appears as though dual influences have been brought to bear on the Trudeau government's Arctic strategy since 2015: a reluctance to meaningfully engage with Russia in the region (due to distaste for Russian activities elsewhere), but also a desire to avoid full blown conflict as well, which together seem to have (intentionally or otherwise) shaped a "don't rock the boat" strategy in the region. The avoidance of conflict with the great powers—in the Arctic and beyond—appears to be priority number one for this government.

CANADA, CHINA, AND THE ARCTIC

China's efforts to build a "polar silk road", enabled by infrastructure and the development of sea lanes through the Arctic to open up opportunities for commercial shipping, are one that could present both opportunities and challenges for Canada. China's Arctic Policy contains four key priorities: resource development, shipping, scientific exploration, and regional governance, which suggest that China sees itself not as an interloper in the region, but as a key player (Lajeunesse 2018). China shares the U.S. position that the NWP is an international waterway, and not sovereign Canadian waters; however, it did seek Canada's permission as a courtesy prior to the 2017 crossing of the Chinese Snow Dragon icebreaker. China regularly flouts international law, specifically the UNCLOS, in the South China Sea (SCS) when it is empowered to do so, but it may feel less empowered in the Arctic, given the proximity and interests of other major powers in the region. Nonetheless, without Canada's key ally on board with its assertion of sovereignty in the NWP, securing China's long-term recognition of its sovereignty there may be challenging.

Some analysts have expressed concern that China's considerable investment in the region affords it a potentially worrisome coercive capacity (Lajeunesse 2018). Russia once shared similar concerns about a Chinese presence in the Arctic. While Chinese investment in energy development is welcome there—they have invested billions of dollars in oil and gas projects in Siberia and the Russian Arctic (Lajeunesse 2018)—Russia has been careful to exclude China from institutional representation on security matters. This has changed somewhat in recent years though as Western investment in Russia has dried up and Chinese investment is more lucrative. In fact, both China and Russia appear to be "taking advantage of their repetitive geopolitical tensions with the United States in order to intensify their cooperation" (Laruelle 2020), in the Arctic and beyond. This has critical implications for Canada as it navigates its own precarious relations among these powers.

Concerns about China's presence in the Arctic abound in Canada. Some see the promises in China's Arctic strategy that commit to ecological protection and the preservation and sustainability of northern communities as a ruse designed to convince Canadians (to whom these issues matter more) of the benign nature of its investment and presence in the region. Some fear this is the beginning of a plan to permanently insinuate itself into Arctic governance in the long term (Robinson 2013). After all, China views the Arctic passage as a lucrative and efficient transit corridor to Europe, and has actively pursued its mining interests in the region, notably in Greenland, both of which have implications for climate change. China envisions itself as a "near Arctic power", a position reflected in the July 2020 departure of the Chinese Polar Institute's icebreaker "Xue Long 2", for the Arctic, ostensibly on an ecological research mission (Staalesen 2020). China's investments in the region represent the northern tier of its lucrative Belt and Road initiative (Dolata 2018), a strategic economic development enterprise designed to facilitate China's influence in previously under developed, and under influenced, regions. Notwithstanding the pursuit of its interests in the region, China's efforts at confidence building in the Arctic appear to reflect an acknowledgement that it cannot operate there in isolation and that its peaceful use of Arctic shipping routes is going to require the cooperation of both Canada and Russia (Lajeunesse 2018).

Increased traffic through the NWP poses considerable risk to the environment, Indigenous communities, as well as Canadian sovereignty and the economic opportunity that Canadian sovereignty in the Arctic begets. Lajeunesse (2018: 6–7) notes that "enforcing Canadian jurisdiction and exercising control will largely be an exercise in soft power. Chinese resource companies will work with Canada on Ottawa's terms because there is no other immediate alternative" and that "compliance and respect for Canadian sovereignty and control will be driven by necessity and convenience". However, recent trade and diplomatic tensions between Canada and China are not conducive to cooperation. Canada's detention and possible extradition of Huawei's Meng Wanzhou prompted China to respond with charging two Canadians, Michael Kovrig and Michael Spavor, with spying, perceived by many to be a deliberate warning to Canada of the consequences of taking a hard line with China. Further Chinese retaliation has taken aim at Canada's agricultural producers, with trade restrictions introduced on Canadian canola and meat exports. Tensions have been further heightened following concerns about the potential source of the COVID-19 virus. Consequently, the Trudeau government faces few options with respect to its chilly relations with China and, like its relations with the United States and Russia, cannot afford to aggravate the relationship, or have these tensions spill over into the Arctic.

Discussion: COVID-19, Energy Wars, and Prioritizing the North in 2020 and Beyond

The Arctic is critical to Canada's security (broadly defined), economy, and socio-cultural well-being and is therefore a region that must not be ignored. Nonetheless, complicated relationships with the United States, Russia, and China challenge Canada's ability to pursue its interests aggressively in the region. Additionally, the North encompasses a host of other policy priorities for the Trudeau government, some of which have been impacted by the COVID-19 pandemic and the resulting consequences for Canada's energy industry and climate change agenda, both of which are sources of interprovincial discord. As the Arctic opens up and draws the attention of the world, and the presence of its major powers, Canada has little choice but to address pressing geopolitical and domestic priorities in the region. Nonetheless the obstacles to doing so are many, and three challenges have, perhaps understandably, intervened to relegate the region to the "too hard basket", at present, prompting criticism that the Trudeau government has not done enough to advance Canada's interests in the Arctic. Given these complications, it may be reasonable to expect that this approach becomes the norm in the short to medium term.

In addition to the domestic issues that converge in the Arctic (sustainability of Indigenous communities, environmental and human security, climate change, energy and resource development, maritime navigation, sovereignty and defence, to name a few), geopolitical concerns are also added into the mix, and sometimes even overlap with domestic considerations. The US' continued refusal to recognize Canadian sovereignty over the Northwest Passage, as well as its about face on climate change, its withdrawal from the Open Skies Treaty, its weak response to the COVID-19 epidemic raising concerns about the fluidity of the Canada-US border, and the intransigence of President Trump combined to make Canada-US relations the most challenging in recent memory. Overlapping sovereignty claims with Russia, its militarization of the Arctic, and the perception of its aggression towards the West, as well as heightened diplomatic tensions with China and concerns over its encroachment into the Arctic, are perpetual concerns.

Prime Minister Stephen Harper's Northern Strategy, brimming with assertive rhetoric, sought an increasingly militarized Arctic in which Canada should be prepared to assert its sovereignty or risk losing it altogether. But this was a different time in Canadian politics, and on the world stage. Trudeau has acknowledged the Arctic's importance, but seems to prefer a "don't rock the boat" approach to relations with the United States, Russia, and China there, perhaps in an effort to immunize the region from other irritants in these relationships. Trudeau promised harmony, which seems to come at the expense of a robust commitment to acting on difficult promises. Canada faces geopolitical tensions in the Arctic, a downturn in energy prices (partly due to the oil price war between Russia and Saudi Arabia, and COVID-19), interprovincial disputes about the scope and pace of climate change efforts against the backdrop of western bitterness over disputed pipeline development, and frustration within Indigenous communities over the federal government's failure to realize its promises of support. There is tremendous pressure on the government to act on contradictory files, and as these issues converge, and risk inflammation, the Arctic rests on the back burner.

The COVID-19 pandemic may have exacerbated an already weakened position for Canada in the global economy and geopolitical space. Relations with the United States, China, and Russia were in decline long before the pandemic, and now more than ever Canada must tread carefully in the Arctic and beyond given the high stakes. COVID-19 has underlined the importance of the Arctic because it reveals the vulnerability of Canada's energy sector, both to other producers and competitors, but also to global shocks that can have a tremendous economic impact. The Russia-Saudi spat has lowered oil prices and precipitated a market glut that has hurt Canada's energy sector; it has also caused Russia to reduce production in its Arctic wells (Kramer 2020). The pain in the Canadian energy sector has exacerbated bitter inter-provincial divisions across the country, as well as between energy producing provinces and Indigenous communities. COVID-19 has also had an impact upon Indigenous and northern communities, which have been targeted by the Trudeau government as priorities for federal relief. The North demands the government's attention, but so many of these files are complicated and contradictory. As the government grapples with national unity, it must also look for opportunities for cooperation with the great powers in the Arctic.

The Arctic has been "on ice" recently, but it may be time to warm it up, lest inaction becomes normalized. The government's priorities for economic development, fighting climate change, securing the environment, supporting Indigenous communities, addressing domestic discord over resource development, and defending Canadian sovereignty, are consistent with prioritizing the Arctic. These intersect with geopolitical considerations *vis-à-vis* the United States, Russia, and China—nations that share a number of Canada's priorities in the region. The Arctic has historically enjoyed relative immunity from global conflict. The challenge for Canada now is to prevent conflict in other theatres from obstructing cooperation in the Arctic. Asserting Canadian sovereignty in an increasingly accessible NWP, ensuring the safety of northern communities and the environment, prioritizing peaceful and orderly navigation through the region, and preventing geopolitical conflicts from infecting the Arctic are essential to Canada's national security, broadly defined, and therefore must be prioritized. This is a tall order, but Canada must not let disunity lead to paralysis in the Arctic.

REFERENCES

Bouffard, Troy, and P. Whitney Lackenbauer. 2020. "The U.S. Withdrawal from Open Skies: Implications for the Arctic, Quick Impact." *The North American and Arctic Defence and Security Network*, May 23.

Boulègue, Mathieu. 2019. "Russia's Military Posture in the Arctic: Managing Hard Power in a 'Low Tension' Environment." *London: Chatham House: Royal Institute of International Affairs.*

Boyd, Brenden, and Barry Rabe. 2019. "Whither Canadian Climate Policy in the Era of Trump?" In *Canada-US Relations: Sovereignty or Shared Institutions?*, edited by David Carment and Christopher Sands, 239–260. Springer International.

Braun, Aurel, and Stephen J Blank. 2020. "The Cold Reality Behind Russia's Charm Offensive: Why Canada Needs a Realistic Arctic Policy." *The MacDonald Laurier Institute.*

Brewster, Murray. 2020. "Russian Arctic Military Exercise Draws Awe and Concern." *CBC News*, May 11. https://www.cbc.ca/news/politics/russian-arctic-training-1.5563691. Accessed on May 19, 2020.

Byers, Michael. 2019. "Cold, Dark, and Dangerous: International Cooperation in the Arctic and Space." *Polar Record* 55: 32–47.

Charron, Andrea. 2005. "Canada, the United States, and the Northwest Passage: Sovereignty to the Side." *Polar Geography* 29 (2): 139–155.

Conley, Heather A., and Caroline Rohloff. 2015. *The New Ice Curtain: Russia's Strategic Reach to the Arctic, Center for Strategic and International Studies*. Lanham: Rowman and Littlefield.

Dolata, Petra. 2018. "A Global Arctic? Chinese Aspirations in the North." *Canadian Global Affairs Institute*, October.

Elliot-Meisel, Elizabeth, 2009. "Politics, Pride, and Precedent: The United States and Canada in the Northwest Passage." *Ocean Development & International Law* 40: 204–232.

"Foundations of Russian Federation Policy in the Arctic Until 2020 and Beyond." 2008. ARCTIS, September 18. http://www.arctis-search.com/Rus sian+Federation+Policy+for+the+Arctic+to+2020.

Government of Canada. 2017. "Strong, Secure, Engaged: Canada's Defence Policy." Department of National Defence. https://www.canada.ca/content/dam/dnd-mdn/documents/reports/2018/strong-secure-engaged/canada-defence-policy-report.pdf.

Huebert, Rob. 2009. "Canadian Arctic Sovereignty and Security in a Transforming Circumpolar World." *Foreign Policy for Canada's Tomorrow* 4, Canadian International Council.

Kramer, Andrew E. 2020. "Too Cold for an Oil Cut? Russia's Move Reveals a Long Running Bluff." *New York Times*, May 4. https://www.nytimes.com/2020/05/04/world/europe/russia-oil-cut.html?action=click&module=News&pgtype=Homepage. Accessed on May 19, 2020.

Lackenbauer, P. Whitney. 2016. "Canada's Northern Strategy: A Comprehensive Approach to Defence, Security and Safety." In *North of 60: Toward a Renewed Canadian Arctic Agenda*, edited by John Higginbotham and Jennifer Spence, 43–48. Centre for International Governance Innovation.

Lackenbauer, P. Whitney, and Lajeunesse, Adam. 2016. "Canadian Arctic Security: Russia's Not Coming." *Open Canada*, April 19. https://opencanada.org/canadian-arctic-security-russias-not-coming/.

Lackenbauer, P. Whitney, and Ryan Dean eds. 2016. "Canada's Northern Strategy Under Harper: Key Speeches, and Documents on Sovereignty, Security, and Governance 2006–2015." *Documents on Canadian Arctic Sovereignty and Security (DCASS)*.

Lackenbauer, P. Whitney, and Suzanne Lalonde, eds. 2019. *Breaking the Ice Curtain: Russia, Canada, and Arctic Security in a Changing Circumpolar World*. Canadian Global Affairs Institute.

Lajeunesse, Adam. 2018. "Finding Win-Win: China's Arctic Policy and What It Means for Canada." *Canadian Global Affairs Institute*.

Lajeunesse, Adam, and Rob Huebert. 2019. "Preparing for the Next Arctic Sovereignty Crisis: The Northwest Passage in the Age of Donald Trump." *International Journal* 74 (2): 225–239.

Laruelle, Marlene. 2020. "Russia's Arctic Policy: A Power Strategy and Its Limits." *Russie.Nie.Visions* 117 Ifri.

Ljunggren, David. 2010. "Clinton Rebuke Overshadows Canada's Arctic Meeting." *Reuters*, March 29. https://www.reuters.com/article/us-arctic-idUSTRE62S4ZP20100330.

Østhagen, Andreas, G. L. Sharp, and P. S. Hilde. 2018. "At Opposite Poles: Canada's and Norway's Approaches to Security in the Arctic." *The Polar Journal* 8 (1): 163–181.

Paradis, Mark, Richard D. Parker, and Patrick James. 2018. "Predicting the North: Sovereignty and the Canadian Brand in the Arctic." *Canadian Foreign Policy Journal* 24 (2): 182–201.

Regehr, Ernie. 2017. "Arctic Security and the Canadian Defence Policy Statement of 2017." *The Simons Foundation*. http://www.thesimonsfoundation.ca/highlights/arctic-security-and-canadian-defence-policy-statement-2017.

Roberts, Kari. 2015. "Why Russia Will Play by the Rules in the Arctic." *Canadian Foreign Policy Journal* 1 (2): 112–128.

Robinson, Roger. 2013. "China's 'Long Con' in the Arctic." *Macdonald-Laurier Institute Commentary*. https://www.macdonaldlaurier.ca/files/pdf/Inside%20Policy%20September%202013%20FINAL.pdf.

Rodman, Lyndsey. 2020. "The Pentagon's Arctic Strategies Reveal the Benefit of a North American Approach." *Canadian Global Affairs Institute*, May.

Sevunts, Levon. 2020a. "Appointment of U.S. Arctic Coordinator Signals More Muscular American Policy." *Radio Canada International*, July 30. https://www.rcinet.ca/en/2020/07/30/u-s-arctic-coordinator-jim-deh art-geopolitics/. Accessed on August 6, 2020.

Sevunts, Levon. 2020b. "U.S. Withdrawal from Open Skies Treaty Presents Canada with a 'Serious' Challenge, Says Expert." *CBC News*, May 26. https://www.cbc.ca/news/politics/open-skies-u-s-russia-canada-nuclear-war-1.5583696. Accessed on May 26, 2020.

Staalesen, Atle. 2020. "New Chinese Icebreaker Sets Course for Arctic." *The Barents Observer*, July 16. https://thebarentsobserver.com/en/arctic/2020/07/new-chinese-icebreaker-sets-course-arctic. Accessed on August 6, 2020.

"The Arctic and Northern Policy Framework." 2019. *Government of Canada*. https://www.rcaanc-cirnac.gc.ca/eng/1560523306861/1560523330587.

Thompson, Elizabeth, Katie Nicholson, and Jason Ho. 2020. "COVID-19 Disinformation Being Spread by Russia, China, SAY EXPERTS." *CBC News*, May 26. https://www.cbc.ca/news/politics/covid-coronavirus-russia-china-1.558 3961. Accessed on May 26, 2020.

Todorov, Andrey. 2017. "The Russia-USA Legal Dispute over the Straits of the Northern Sea Route and Similar Case of the Northwest Passage." *Arctic and North* 29: 62–75.

Wallace, Ron. 2019. "The Arctic Is Warming and Turning Red: Implications for Canada and Russia in an Evolving Polar Region." *Canadian Global Affairs Institute*. https://www.cgai.ca/the_arctic_is_warming_and_turning_red_implications_for_canada_and_russia_in_an_evolving_polar_region.

CHAPTER 7

A "Handyman's" Approach: Erin O'Toole and Canadian Foreign Policy

Paul Gecelovsky

INTRODUCTION

Leaders of political parties of all stripes hold an image of their state in mind. For many, this is the driving factor behind their candidacy: to mould the state according to their preferences. The self-perception or self-image (Boulding 1959; Holsti 1962) that leaders maintain shapes their decisions regarding what policies and behaviours a state will or will not undertake. Party leaders play an important role in determining the policies pursued and the image projected. This has been discussed in terms of a "nation brand" (Nimijean 2018; Olins 2005; Van Ham 2001, 2002) or, as Simon Anholt (2010, 2013) prefers, "competitive identity".

The image being crafted by Erin O'Toole (2020c) is the common "handyman", someone who is competent, professional, trustworthy and dependable but someone more comfortable with repair rather than construction or design. Contrastingly, Trudeau is depicted as a "poster

P. Gecelovsky (✉)
University of Windsor, Windsor, ON, Canada
e-mail: gecelov@uwindsor.ca

© The Author(s), under exclusive license to Springer Nature
Switzerland AG 2021
D. Carment and R. Nimijean (eds.), *Political Turmoil in a Tumultuous World*, Canada and International Affairs,
https://doi.org/10.1007/978-3-030-70686-9_7

boy" (O'Toole 2020c), a photogenic leader who is more worried about hashtags, tweets and likes than making hard decisions. O'Toole talks about returning Canada to what Campbell Clark (2020) has referred to as the "old normal", whereas Trudeau has positioned himself as a leader who champions change. O'Toole portrays his father as a labourer, a man who went to work every day for 30 years at the local GM plant, even though he was an executive with the company and, later, served as a member of provincial parliament from 1995 to 2014. The image of a labourer provides an obvious point of comparison to Trudeau's father who is well-known to all Canadians, positive or negative, as a former prime minister and, later, public intellectual. O'Toole comes from a small, bucolic town in Ontario where neighbours knew and cared for one another in times of need, providing food and solace, whereas Trudeau is an urbanite hailing from Ottawa and Montreal, large cities where neighbours are unknown and anonymous. O'Toole and Trudeau are presented less as two options, than as representing parallel Canadas: the conservative "heartland" and the progressive "hub" (Lind 2020), or, to adopt Stephen Harper's (2018) terminology, "somewheres" and "anywheres".

The purpose of this chapter is to examine the foreign policy platform outlined by Erin O'Toole and to determine where and how he plans to repair Canadian foreign policy. The first section of the chapter looks at how O'Toole was able to move from an initial position in the Conservative leadership contest of only 3% of party support to emerge as leader of the party. The divisions in the party and his position as a compromise candidate reduce somewhat his freedom to manoeuver. This is followed by a discussion of some of the changes to Canada's foreign policy that O'Toole has outlined in a various speeches and interviews, primarily since becoming the Conservative leader in late August 2020.

The Leadership Contest

The results of the 2019 general election were disappointing for the Conservatives, especially given the perceived vulnerability of the Liberal Party due to prime ministerial gaffes and ethical improprieties. There have been a number of missteps during Trudeau's time in office, such as his February 2018 trip to India where he donned traditional Indian garb (Nimijean 2018) and the September 2019 revelation that he wore blackface on a number of occasions in the past. More serious were the two separate reports from the Office of the Conflict of Interest and

Ethics Commissioner which concluded the prime minister had violated sections of the Conflict of Interest Act. In the first case, Trudeau and his family used a private aircraft owned by the Aga Khan to travel to his island resort on two separate occasions in 2016. In the second case, Trudeau attempted to exert influence over his Attorney-General, Jody Wilson-Raybould, to overturn a decision to prosecute SNC Lavalin on fraud charges in relation to its work in Libya in favour of negotiating a remediation agreement with the company. Not willing to accommodate Trudeau's request, Wilson-Raybould resigned from cabinet. Jane Philpott, President of the Treasury Board, also resigned from cabinet over the SNC Lavalin case. The gaffes and the resignation of two high-profile female ministers from a self-styled feminist prime minister's cabinet over the issue of prime ministerial interference and intimidation damaged both the prime minister's and the Liberal Party's image among Canadians. The belief among many Canadians was that the Trudeau government was vulnerable, and the Conservatives were well-positioned to defeat them and form a new government.

Looking closely at the overall election results in 2019, the CPC did not suffer the calamitous decline ascribed to it by some. The Conservatives increased their totals from the 2015 general election in all relevant categories, including number of votes (5,613,633–6,239,227), percentage of votes (29.3–35.8) and number of seats (99–121). They also won the popular vote—6,239,927 to 6,018,728—but the workings of the first-past-the-post electoral system failed to translate the popular vote victory into an electoral victory (Cairns 1968) wherein the Liberals captured 157 seats to the Conservatives 121 seats. Therefore, the 2019 general election was a success for the Conservatives by all metrics, except the only one that matters in the end: the number of seats captured in the House of Commons.

The blame for the failure of not winning more seats in the legislature was placed squarely on the inability of Andrew Scheer to move Canadians in key demographics and regions to vote Conservative. One commentator noted that Conservatives looked "unprincipled and grasping" and "weak and unconvincing" in outlining "a smorgasbord of boutique benefits" and "a near-Liberal agenda" (Brown 2020). Another described the Conservative platform as "random dreck" and "a dumb, pandering, unambitious mess that reeked of focus grouping" (Selley 2019). Peter MacKay directed his criticism at Scheer, commenting that the election failure was akin to having "a breakaway on an open net and missing the net" (Harris and

Thibedeau 2019). In an attempt to harness the increasing disenchant-ment among Conservatives regarding their leader, a number of party members, including some of whom were in the Harper government, formed an organization—Conservative Victory—whose sole purpose was to pressure Scheer to step down. Counted among the members of Conservative Victory were Kory Teneycke (director of communications for Harper), Sara MacIntyre (press secretary for Harper), John Reynolds (former Conservative MP) and Jeff Balingall (founder of Canada Proud and Ontario Proud, Conservative advocacy social media platforms). Given the growing rifts within the party in the aftermath of the 2019 general election, Andrew Scheer was not in a position to continue as leader and, so, on December 12, 2019, 53 days after the election, he resigned.

While the Conservative leadership race drew numerous candidates, only four qualified for the official process: Dr. Leslyn Lewis, lawyer and activist; Peter MacKay, former member of parliament (MP), leader of the Progressive Conservative Party of Canada, co-founder of the CPC and minister in the Harper Government; Erin O'Toole, MP and former minster in the Harper government; and, Derek Sloan, lawyer and MP for Hastings-Lennox and Addington. The leadership contest evolved into a two-person race between MacKay and O'Toole. Lewis and Sloan were regarded as minor candidates who would siphon off votes early in the process but would finish last and fall off the ballot. The questions were who would fall off first and to whom would those supporters migrate? In the competition between MacKay and O'Toole, the latter was able to position himself to the right ideologically of the former. This left O'Toole occupying the position most closely to that of former leader Stephen Harper.

To many members of the CPC, MacKay was still perceived as being a Progressive Conservative and, as such, leaning towards the left of the party, ideologically. MacKay was remembered by many as the former leader of the Progressive Conservatives who was outmanoeuvred by Stephen Harper in the 2003 merger of the Canadian Reform Conserva-tive Alliance and the Progressive Conservative parties to form the CPC. O'Toole played on MacKay's Progressive Conservative background in his campaign launch video released on January 27, 2020, where he stated that the party members had a choice between a "True Blue" conservative who would "take a principled conservative stand" (Clark 2020) on issues or a "Liberal-party lite" candidate (Platt 2020).

Another way in which MacKay's past worked against him concerned the general dislike of Progressive Conservatives in western Canada. In 1986, former Progressive Conservative prime minister, Brian Mulroney, awarded a $100 million aircraft maintenance contract for CF-18 Hornets to a Montreal firm even though a Winnipeg company had tendered a technically and financially superior bid (Campbell and Pal 1989). While the CF-18 contract was awarded over thirty years ago, the antipathy towards Mulroney and the PC party still festers in much of western Canada (Berdahl and Gibbins 2014), as it is part of the litany of wrongs perpetrated by Central Canadian politicians in the west that form the core grievances of the Wexit movement. Further, the failure of the PC and Liberal parties to reflect the interests of the west led to the creation of the Reform Party in 1987. Mackay's past as leader of the PCs meant that many in western Canada would not support his bid for the leadership of the Conservative Party. Finally, Jason Kenney, current Premier of Alberta and former minister in the Harper government, placed his considerable influence within the party, especially in the west, firmly behind O'Toole when, on March 5, 2020, Kenney bypassed MacKay and endorsed O'Toole as leader (Whittington 2020).

It was not just MacKay's roots in the PC party that harmed his leadership bid. Some wounds were self-inflicted. First, in October 2019, in the aftermath of the general election, MacKay stated, in a panel discussion in Washington, DC, that the issues of same-sex marriage and the reproductive rights of women "hung around Andrew Scheer's neck like a stinking albatross" (Harris and Thibedeau 2019). The comment was cited by Jason Kenney as one of the reasons he endorsed O'Toole: "No one will have their deeply held beliefs dismissed as 'stinking albatrosses' under Erin O'Toole's leadership" (Whittington 2020). Later, during the leadership campaign, MacKay told social conservatives to "park" their concerns (Levitz 2020). MacKay's comments worked to marginalize social conservative beliefs and the comments would move social conservatives to anyone-but-MacKay position in voting for a new leader.

Second, by late March 2020, the effects of the COVID-19 virus were beginning to be felt in all parts of Canada. Businesses and schools were being shut down in the midst of rising case numbers. The CPC leadership election campaign committee suspended the race on March 26, 2020 until a review in early May. MacKay criticized the move on both television and social media. He tweeted that "the leadership race must continue" and that this was "not a time to show weakness and push the pause button on our democratic process" (MacKay 2020). To press for the leadership race to continue in a growing health crisis when he was in the lead put MacKay offside with many Conservative Party members (Platt 2020).

In contrast to MacKay, O'Toole's campaign did not suffer from any substantive errors and proceeded from an initial position where he had only 3% of party support (to MacKay's 63%) to victory as leader of the party. Two groups within the Conservative membership played a particularly important role in O'Toole's victory. The first group was Conservatives in Québec. O'Toole's leadership team realized the significance that Québec would play in the contest. An electoral platform keying on protecting francophone culture was drafted specifically for Québec and O'Toole made numerous media appearances touting the platform, as well as demonstrating his growing facility in French (Platt 2020). Alupa Clark, O'Toole's campaign chair in the province, travelled extensively throughout Québec with and without the leadership candidate to firm up support for O'Toole. Social conservative voters formed a second bloc who were instrumental to O'Toole's victory. Unlike MacKay, who many social conservatives believed insulted or disregarded them, O'Toole worked cautiously to gain the support of social conservatives. While "not pretend[ing] he was a social conservative himself", O'Toole made it known that he "respected their place in the party" (Platt 2020). He pledged to allow free votes in parliament concerning abortion and conversion therapy. O'Toole also promised that, if he won an election and formed a government, he would provide "a seat at the table" (Whittington 2020) for pro-life advocates and pass legislation allowing healthcare professionals to cite conscience rights to deny services pertaining to abortions and medically-assisted dying.

After a number of delays caused by the onset of the coronavirus, the Conservative Party completed its leadership convention on August 23, 2020. The results of the first ballot surprised many as Leslyn Lewis (24.7%) and Derek Sloan (15.6%) obtained higher than anticipated vote totals and Peter MacKay (30.3%) achieved a lower than expected total. The vote and point totals for Lewis and Sloan combined surpassed those of MacKay and O'Toole thereby revealing the strength of the social conservative base in the party. After finishing last on the first ballot, Sloan was eliminated, and his support moved largely to Lewis on the second ballot. Lewis' strong performance on the second ballot startled some, as she increased her vote total by over 10% and captured the most votes (60,316) of any candidate. Both MacKay and O'Toole increased their vote totals by 1.3 and 3.9%, respectively. The workings of the point system used to determine the outcome of the leadership contest worked against Lewis, as she captured only 30% of the points and came in last place. This eliminated her from the race. On the third, and last, ballot the social conservatives who had supported Sloan and Lewis remembered the derisive comments made by MacKay and shifted their support largely to O'Toole. In the end, O'Toole captured 59% of the vote and 57% of the points to MacKay's 41% of the vote and 43% of the points thereby winning the leadership race, replacing Andrew Scheer, and becoming the third leader of the CPC.

In examining the leadership contest and its results, it is apparent that while Erin O'Toole won the leadership contest, for many Conservatives he is a compromise candidate. On the first ballot, O'Toole trailed MacKay by only 1593 votes and less than one per cent of the points (0.9); however, O'Toole prevailed in only two provinces—Alberta and Québec. What this means is that O'Toole had widespread support among Conservatives just not enough to allow him to capture more ridings. The results of the second ballot demonstrate a tepid level of support for O'Toole. Québec is the only province that he was able to capture after the second ballot, losing Alberta to Lewis. MacKay also lost British Columbia and Manitoba to Lewis. These movements reveal a party that is geographically divided with MacKay prevailing in the Maritimes, Ontario, and the Territories, Lewis in the west from Manitoba to British Columbia and O'Toole in Québec. It is only when Lewis is eliminated, and the choice is between MacKay and O'Toole does the west and Ontario move to support the latter. It is interesting to note that Ontario, O'Toole's home province, is won by MacKay on the first and second ballots and it is only the movement of a majority of the Lewis supporters to O'Toole on the third ballot that allows him to prevail there. For Lewis' supporters, the third ballot came down as much to a vote against MacKay as it was a vote for O'Toole. Going forward, O'Toole will need to build support within the party itself for his leadership, in addition to working to draw voters to support the Conservative Party.

The O'Toole Foreign Policy Platform

Within the party, O'Toole needs to maintain the support of the sizeable social conservative contingent while attempting to appeal to a wider range of Canadian voters. As noted above, the leader has committed to allowing social conservatives to voice their views on issues of importance to them, namely conversion therapy, medically-assisted dying and abortion. Unlike same-sex marriage which social conservatives seem to have accepted as a settled issue, abortion continues to divide the party, playing what Jeffrey Simpson (2015) once referred to as "a subterranean role in Conservative Party politics". The abortion issue is still relevant and unsettled for many Conservatives. Since O'Toole became leader of the party, over 20 epetitions concerning selective abortions have been filed on the Canadian government's epetition website by Conservative parliamentarians. In addition, an epetition seeking "full legal protection" for unborn children filed by Conservative MP Ted Falk, on October 5, 2020, has garnered over 35,000 Canadian signatures, a number only surpassed by an epetition concerning the firearms registry which amassed 58,870 signatures (Library of Parliament 2020). Finally, the Geneva Consensus Declaration put forward by the Trump Administration and supported by 33 other states was opened for signature in October 2020. The Declaration was put forward by the United States under the auspices of the World Health Assembly, the decision-making body of the World Health Organization. The Declaration reaffirms "the inherent dignity and worth of the human person", "the inherent right to life" of every person, there is "no international right to abortion, nor any international obligation on the part of States to finance or facilitate abortion" and that "in no case should abortion be promoted as a method of family planning". Also included in the Declaration is the recognition that "the family is the natural and fundamental group unit of society" (United States 2020) and should be protected by the state. This American-led initiative provides support for like-minded groups in Canada to press for the adoption of the Declaration. There is much in the Declaration, save those provisions concerning abortion, that O'Toole's comments lead one to believe that he would support, especially articles concerning the family. Additional pressure will mount in Canada if Roe v. Wade is weakened, or overturned, by a decision of the US Supreme Court. The Trudeau government's position is clear, as the prime minister has made it a condition for anyone wanting to run as a Liberal to support a woman's right to choose. The Conservative position is less clear, as both Andrew Scheer and Stephen Harper held pro-life views personally but vowed not to introduce any legislation related to the issue. While O'Toole has repeatedly stated his pro-choice position, he has pledged, as noted above, to allow pro-life proponents an opportunity to present their views and to hold free votes in parliament on abortion-related issues.

To provide some cover on the issue of abortion, O'Toole may adopt the Harper policy of not allowing funding for family planning and abortions outside of Canada. Harper's announcement of the Muskoka Initiative at the 2010 G8 meeting in Huntsville, Ontario committed Canada to provide $2.85 billion over five years to improve maternal, new born and child health and his 2011 commitment to the UN to address maternal health both carried the proviso that Canada's contribution would not be used to provide funding for services relating to abortions or contraception (Carrier and Tiessen 2013). The decision to not provide funding for abortions or contraception outside of Canada was explained by Harper as being necessary so as not to provoke dissension among Canadians but in reality the decision played to the social conservative base in the party and had more to do with domestic politics than foreign policy. A similar move by O'Toole would allow him to somewhat satisfy that same base within the party, while still preserving access to family planning and abortion services in Canada.

Many of the policy positions supported by O'Toole are similar to those of Andrew Scheer and Stephen Harper. In language like that used by Harper, O'Toole opined that "our values are not for sale" (O'Toole 2020d). He even went so far as to refer to himself as the "natural inheritor" (Vanderklippe 2020) of Harper's approach to policy. Scheer, during his tenure as leader, did not stray too far from the policy directives outlined by Harper. The one area in which Scheer veered away from Harper concerns international assistance. In the 2019 election campaign, Scheer pledged to reduce Canadian assistance by 25%, falsely claiming that a "significant chunk" of aid went to "middle- and upper-income" states, such as Argentina, Brazil, China, Italy and Mexico, among other, and "repressive regimes" like Iran, North Korea and Russia (Brown 2019; Gatehouse 2019).

Beyond international assistance, Scheer borrowed heavily from the Harper playbook concerning approaches to Iran, Israel, Russia, the United Nations (UN), and trade. There has been little change in these policy areas under the new leader, except in trade. O'Toole has advocated for a strong position against Iran and Russia and a similarly strong position in support of Israel. On Iran, he has maintained the Harper and Scheer approach labelling the state a "big disruptor", "destabilizer" and "threat to peace" (O'Toole 2018) throughout the Middle East and the world. The 2008 Russian invasion of Georgia and the May 2014 invasion of Crimea shifted Canada's Russia policy to a critical tone. Canada was quick to condemn the Russian actions announcing a series of measures going so far as to prohibit contact between Russian and Canadian diplomats in Ottawa. More recently, O'Toole has called for an extension of Magnitsky sanctions on a wider range of Russian officials to combat corruption and the growing assertiveness of Russian policy. O'Toole has expressed concerned over Russian incursions in the Arctic, especially in an attempt to remilitarize the far north. He sees the increased partnership between Russia and China in the Arctic region—Polar Silk Road—particularly worrisome and a direct threat to Canadian sovereignty and security (O'Toole 2018). Moving to Canada-Israel relations, O'Toole has reaffirmed the Harper and Scheer policy of unconditional support for Israel, confirming that it is "an important ally" (O'Toole 2018) for Canada. The Conservative positions on Iran and Israel will be supported by many in the Sunni Muslim, Jewish and Protestant Christian communities, while maintaining an aggressive approach towards Russia is a position that will garner the approval of Ukrainians (Carment and Landry 2016). Examining O'Toole's approach to Iran, Israel and Russia reveals a general tendency to perceive states in a Manichean manner. This is similar to the worldviews exhibited by Harper and Scheer whereby they interpreted the world through oppositional, bifurcated lenses of good-bad, right-wrong and friend-enemy.

The UN was the target of criticism by Harper and Scheer. While the exact phraseology differed, the usual terms of reproach included that Canada would "no longer just...go along and get along with everyone" (Harper 2011). O'Toole has continued this line of criticism stating that, unlike the Liberals who want "to outsource foreign policy to the UN", Canada, under his leadership, will take "strong positions" rather than "curry favour" with the UN and its member states (O'Toole 2018). The new leader also seeks to reform the institution following an "aspirational" and "principle-based approach" (O'Toole 2018), without providing any additional details.

Where O'Toole differs from Scheer, Harper, and every other Conservative leader going back to Diefenbaker is on the question of free trade (Hart 2002). The new leader has repeatedly eschewed a policy of what he perceives as unrestrained free trade in favour of a more balanced fair-trade approach where "countries follow the rules" (O'Toole 2020c). He has denounced the "bad trade" deals Canada has signed with the

US and China (O'Toole 2020b). While Canada does not have a bilateral trade deal with the People's Republic of China (PRC), O'Toole has been critical of the lax treatment accorded the Middle Kingdom within the World Trade Organization where China has not been made to "play by global rules" and has been allowed to "unfair access to our market" (O'Toole 2020d). These "bad trade" deals have led to "deindustrialization" (O'Toole 2020d) and the "killing of entire industries" (O'Toole 2020b) in Canada. In addition, O'Toole has been critical of the tepid response of the Trudeau government to the use of sanctions by both the US and China to signal their displeasure with Canadian policy.

The Conservative leader posits that the economy under Trudeau has focused too much attention on developing green technology and industries to the detriment of Canada's natural resources sector, including farming, fisheries, forestry, mining and oil and gas. He proposes to support a staples-based economy in resource-rich areas of Canada, especially rural Ontario and the prairies. O'Toole also avows to restore the "essential part of balance" (O'Toole 2020d) to the relationship between labour and management. Moving from past Conservative policy which favoured management's desire for economic efficiency, O'Toole (2020d) castigates the "financial and corporate elites who outsource jobs" in the quest for higher rates of return on investment and capital in the pursuit of enhanced shareholder value. "Organized labour helps build strong communities" and O'Toole is someone who "has their back" (O'Toole 2020c). In sum, a more balanced approach to economic growth is the central component of O'Toole's "Canada First" strategy, including balance between free and fair trade, green and staples industries, and management and labour.

In terms of bilateral relationships, the first, and overriding, priority for any Canadian political leader is the management of the Canada-US relationship. Over the last four years of the Trump presidency, the bilateral relationship has suffered, as many of the American relationships have, from the inconsistencies and sudden abrupt changes in the president's opinions and decisions. While the incoming president displays a more composed temperament and appears to base decisions on rational thinking, the Canada-US relationship will continue to have many areas in which the two states disagree. The exit of Trump and entrance of Biden will not erase the difficulties, small and large, from the bilateral relationship. The Biden presidency will provide both challenges and opportunities for Canada in general and the Conservatives in particular. Rebuilding the economies of both Canada and the US, including re-opening the border, in the period after the COVID-19 pandemic, will be the first priority for both governments. Beyond this, Biden's position on both climate change and Iran—the Americans will re-join both the Paris Climate Accord and the Iran Nuclear Agreement—is closer to Trudeau's than O'Toole's. However, the new American president has stated that his administration will take a harder line against Russia and China. Biden plans to re-join the Trans-Pacific Partnership as a means to counter China's growing presence throughout Asia via the Belt and Road Initiative. American changes in policy regarding Russia and China are similar to those advocated by O'Toole.

Second to the U.S. as a priority for any Canadian government is relations with the PRC. For O'Toole, "there is no greater geopolitical issue than dealing with the Communist Party of China's intentions to impose its own model of authoritarian governance on the world and erode a rules-based approach" (Glavin 2020). It is not only a security threat as its "chief economic exports" are "IT infringement, counterfeiting" and violations of "digital privacy" (O'Toole 2020c). Through strategic foreign direct investments, the Chinese have been able to acquire Canadian companies, such as Norsat and ITF. The latter of which the sale was blocked by the Harper government over security concerns but later overturned by the Trudeau government (Fife and Chase 2017). Moving to human rights, O'Toole asserted that China is engaging in the "ethnic cleansing" of Uyghurs in Xinjiang, creating a "police state" in Hong Kong, and "suppress[ing] Christian communities" (O'Toole 2020c) throughout the Middle Kingdom. Even after the Chinese had arrested Michael Kovrig and Michael Spavor in December 2018, in retaliation for the arrest of Meng Wanzhou in Vancouver, engaging in "hostage diplomacy" (O'Toole 2020d), Trudeau still sought to complete a trade deal. The above demonstrates what O'Toole (2020d) has characterized as a "cavalier and reckless" approach to the PRC by the Trudeau government, as it has not rebuked China forcefully for flouting international rules and norms because Trudeau was seeking to complete a bilateral free trade deal. It is interesting to note that the Trudeau government has assumed a somewhat harsher line towards China, since O'Toole became leader of the Conservative Party and Trudeau has been more vocal in his opposition to Chinese policies.

In response to increased Chinese aggression, O'Toole has outlined a series of retaliatory measure that he would implement. First, he would side with the other members of the Five Eyes—the US, Britain, Australia and New Zealand—and ban Huawei from Canada's 5G network. Second, he would increase scrutiny of Chinese foreign direct investment in Canada, especially in high-tech companies (Vanderklippe 2020). Third, Magnitsky sanctions would be imposed on those Communist Party of China officials involved in the arrest and detention of Michael Kovrig and Michael Spavor, as well as those implicated in the "re-education" camps for Uyghurs in Xinjiang (Glavin 2020). Fourth, O'Toole would crackdown on Communist Party of China activities in Canada and increase the "screening" (Vanderklippe 2020) of Chinese students and academics working in Canada. Finally, to reduce Canadian economic ties to the PRC, O'Toole would seek better relations with regional states, particularly India and Taiwan (O'Toole 2020c).

O'Toole's tough stance against China does enjoys the support of pro-Hong Kong Chinese groups in Canada (Glavin 2020) and some in the party believe that this approach will garner votes in the battleground ridings of the Greater Toronto Area and Metro Vancouver (Boutilier 2020). A note of caution must be sounded, however, as the Chinese diaspora is not monolithic and, since the late 1990s, the number of immigrants entering Canada from mainland China has far outnumber those from Hong Kong. There is a sizeable and active pro-PRC contingent in Canada. It was not that long ago that Harper also embraced a much stronger approach to China, only to alter course, in 2009, and adopt a more conciliatory approach downplaying human rights and democracy concerns in favour of increased commercial relations and broader support from the pro-PRC community in Canada (Mulroney 2015; Evans 2014). The "turn" (Nossal and Sarson 2014: 149) in Canada's China policy in 2009 moved it from being "a liability" and "a vote-losing factor" (Jiang 2011: 179) to a key component in Harper's majority government in 2011.

To help balance against China's expanding influence, regionally and globally, O'Toole discusses in numerous speeches and interviews (2018, 2020a, c, 2020d), the need for Canada to "grow our relationship" (2020c) with India. O'Toole wants to repair the Indo-Canadian relationship, one the Harper government worked to get "back on track" after "a long period of stasis" during previous Liberal governments, according to Harsh V. Pant and Ketan Mehta (Forthcoming), only to have the Trudeau government "struggle to make any noteworthy progress". Progress has been hampered due to a number of missteps by the prime minister, such as attending a Khalsa Day parade in Toronto in 2017 where he gave a speech and had his picture taken in front of the Khalistan flag, and including Jaspal Atwal, a member of a Khalistan separatist group, who was convicted of attempted murder of an Indian cabinet minister in 1986, as part of the Trudeau contingent at an official state dinner during the 2018 trip mentioned above where Trudeau wore traditional Indian clothing (Nimijean 2018). O'Toole appreciates the potential of India to be an economic and political counterweight to China in South Asia. He also recognizes the importance to his electoral success of capturing Indo-Canadian votes in the Greater Toronto Area and Metro Vancouver, a demographic which helped significantly in delivering Harper's 2011 majority government.

Finally, the Conservative leader is a firm proponent of creating a new plurilateral agreement allowing for "free markets, free trade, even free movement" (O'Toole 2020c) among Canada, Australia, New Zealand and the United Kingdom—CANZUK. As all are members of the World Trade Organization, their trade relations are already governed by the rules of that organization, including the reduction of any barriers to trade and the extension of most-favoured-nation status. The CANZUK states are also members of the Five Eyes, only the US is missing. From the perspective of the Five Eyes, CANZUK may be a way to further expand the agreement beyond an intelligence alliance, similar to the Canadian initiative in putting forward Article 2 in the North Atlantic Treaty, the purpose of which was to provide the basis for deepening relations among member states beyond the security realm to include political, cultural and economic ties (Keating 2013: 73). The purpose of CANZUK, then, may be an attempt to build upon the member states' history in the British Commonwealth to develop closer relations and common policies in a range of issue areas, to recreate a plurilateral anglosphere. This would appeal to the traditional Conservatives in the party, those who supported resuming the use of the word Royal to the air force and navy, restoring traditional British pips to officer uniforms (Ibbitson 2015: 9) and requiring photographs of Queen Elizabeth II to be displayed in Canadian embassies, as well as the Lester B. Pearson building in Ottawa (Delacourt 2013: 240).

Conclusion

The image of a handyman chosen by O'Toole is interesting, given that a handyman is someone who is called into repair something that is broken or needs fixing. It is someone who is adept at using tools to complete relatively simple tasks. You do not call a handyman to construct a house, let alone design it. In an assessment of another Conservative government, Denis Stairs (2001: 29) made the comparison between "architects" and "engineers" of policy, writing that architects are innovative and creative in establishing policies "afresh" to meet the challenges faced whereas engineers refer to policies "of standard design" to confront the problems faced. It seems that O'Toole has set his ambition below that of an engineer to be a "handyman" whose main task is simply to repair rather than create or construct. He is tinkering at the margins rather than seeking to rebuild or reorient Canada's foreign policy.

In vying for and winning the leadership of the Conservative Party, Erin O'Toole outlined an image and platform that members of the party found more acceptable than Peter MacKay, Leslyn Lewis and Derek Sloan. Conservative Party members preferred the O'Toole brand over the others. The challenge now is to draw more Canadians to vote for O'Toole and the Conservatives than for Trudeau and the Liberals. To this end, O'Toole has tried to provide contrast of both image and ideas between "the handyman" and "the poster boy" to the Canadian electorate. His success will be gauged by the results in the next election.

References

Anholt, Simon. 2010. *Place: Identity, Image and Reputation.* New York: Palgrave Macmillan.

Anholt, Simon. 2013. "Beyond the Nation Brand: The Role of Image and Identity in International Relations." *Exchange: The Journal of Public Diplomacy* 2 (1): 6–12.

Berdahl, Loleen, and Roger Gibbins. 2014. *Looking West: Regional Transformation and the Future of Canada.* Toronto: University of Toronto Press.

Boulding, Kenneth E. 1959. *The Image.* Ann Arbor: University of Michigan Press.

Boutilier, Alex. 2020. "Why Does Erin O'Toole Talk About China so Much?" *The Star*, September 29. https://www.thestar.com/politics/federal/2020/09/29/why-does-erin-otoole-talk-about-china-so-much.html. Accessed on November 10, 2020.

Bricker, Darrell, and John Ibbitson. 2013. *The Big Shift: The Seismic Change in Canadian Politics, Business, and Culture and What It Means for Our Future.* Toronto: HarperCollins.

Brown, Grant A. 2020. "Future of Conservatism Series, Part III: A New Ensemble for the Spring Leadership Season." C2C Journal, February 28. https://c2cjournal.ca/2020/02/future-of-conservatism-series-part-iii-a-new-ensemble-for-the-spring-leadership-season/. Accessed on May 15, 2020.

Brown, Stephen. 2019. "Foreign Aid on the Campaign Agenda." The McLeod Group, October 3. https://www.mcleodgroup.ca/2019/10/foreign-aid-on-the-campaign-agenda. Accessed on November 22, 2020.

Cairns, Alan C. 1968. "The Electoral System and the Party System in Canada: 1921–1965." Canadian Journal of Political Science 1 (1): 55–80.

Campbell, Robert, and Leslie A. Pal. 1989. The Real World of Canadian Politics: Cases in Process and Policy. Peterborough: Broadview Press.

Carment, David, and Joseph Landry. 2016. "Diaspora and Canadian Foreign Policy." In The Harper Era in Canadian Foreign Policy, edited by Adam Chapnick and Christopher Kukucha, 223–240. Vancouver: University of British Columbia Press.

Carrier, K., and R. Tiessen. 2013. "Woman and Children First: Maternal Health and the Silencing of Gender in Canadian Foreign Policy." In Canada in the World, edited by Heather A. Smith and C. Turenne Sjolander, 183–200. Toronto: Oxford University Press.

Clark, Campbell. 2020. "Behind Erin O'Toole's Old-School Image Lies a Thoroughly Modern Conservative Strategy." The Globe and Mail, October 22.

Delacourt, Susan. 2013. Shopping for Votes: How Politicians Choose Us and We Choose Them. Madeira Park, BC: Douglas & McIntyre.

Evans, Paul. 2014. Engaging China: Myth, Aspiration, and Strategy in Canadian Policy from Trudeau to Harper. Toronto: University of Toronto Press.

Fife, Robert, and Stephen Chase. 2017. "U.S. Rebukes Canada Over Chinese Takeover of Norsat." Globe and Mail, June 12.

Gatehouse, Jonathan. 2019. "Andrew Scheer's Claim About Foreign Aid Deemed False." CBC News, October 1. https://www.cbc.ca/news/politics/conservatives-foreign-aid-fact-check-1.5305045. Accessed on November 22, 2020.

Glavin, Terry. 2020. "O'Toole's Foreign Policy Giver Him an Edge Over Liberal-Left Timidity." Ottawa Citizen, August 26.

Harper, Stephen. 2018. Right Here Right Now: Politics and Leadership in the Age of Disruption. Toronto: Signal.

Harper, Stephen. 2011. "Prime Minister Stephen Harper's 2011 Convention Speech." Ottawa. 16 June. Available at: http://www.conservative.ca/?p=110. Accessed on February 4, 2014.

Harris, Kathleen, and Hannah Thibedeau. 2019. "Scheer's Conservatives Missed Scoring 'On an Open Net,' Says Peter MacKay as Leadership Talk Heats Up."

CBC News, October 31. https://www.cbc.ca/news/politics/mackay-scheer-conservative-leadership-1.5341633. Accessed on July 16, 2020.

Hart, Michael. 2002. *A Trading Nation: Canadian Trade Policy from Colonialism to Globalization*. Vancouver: University of British Columbia Press.

Holsti, Ole R. 1962. "The Belief System and National Images: A Case Study." *Journal of Conflict Resolution* 6: 244–252.

Ibbitson, John. 2015. *Stephen Harper*. Toronto: McClelland & Stewart.

Jiang, Wenran. 2011. "The Dragon Returns: Canada in China's Quest for Energy Security." In *Issues in Canada-China Relations*, edited by Pittman B. Potter with Thomas Adams, 165–197. Toronto: Canadian International Council. https://3mea0n49d5363860yn4ri4go-wpengine.netdna-ssl.com/wp-content/uploads/2017/04/CIC-Issues-in-Canada-China-Relations-2011.pdf.

Keating, Tom. 2013. *Canada and World Order: The Multilateralist Tradition in Canadian Foreign Policy*. Toronto: Oxford University Press.

Levitz, Stephanie. 2020. "Peter MacKay on Why He Lost Conservative Leadership and What It Means for the Party." *The Canadian Press*, September 16. https://www.cbc.ca/news/politics/peter-mackay-on-why-he-lost-1.5726524. Accessed on September 24, 2020.

Library of Parliament. 2020. "Petitions." https://petitions.ourcommons.ca/en/Petition/. Accessed on October 28, 2020.

Lind, Michael. 2020. *The New Class War: Saving Democracy from the Managerial Elite*. New York: Penguin.

MacKay, Peter. 2020. https://twitter.com/PeterMacKay/status/1243219981678063617.

Marland, Alex. 2016. *Brand Command: Canadian Politics and Democracy in the Age of Message Control*. Vancouver: University of British Columbia Press.

Mulroney, David. 2015. *Middle Power, Middle Kingdom*. Toronto: Allen Lane.

Nimijean, Richard. 2018. "Introduction: Is Canada Back?" *Canadian Foreign Policy Journal* 24 (2): 127–138.

Nossal, Kim Richard, and Leah Sarson. 2014. "About Face: Changes in Canada's China Policy, 2006–2012." *Canadian Foreign Policy Journal* 20 (2): 146–162.

Olins, Wally. 2005. "Making a National Brand." In *The New Public Diplomacy: Soft Power in International Relations*, edited by Jan Melissen, 169–179. New York: Palgrave Macmillan.

O'Toole, Erin. 2018. "Manning Networking Conference: Refreshing Canadian Foreign Policy." February 10. https://www.cpac.ca/en/programs/public-record/episodes/59365456/. Accessed on September 15, 2020.

O'Toole, Erin. 2020a. "The West Block: One on One With Erin O'Toole". *Global News*, August 30. https://globalnews.ca/video/7305344/the-west-block-one-on-one-with-erin-otoole. Accessed on September 12, 2020.

O'Toole, Erin. 2020b. "Do You Think It's Time for Economic Policy That Puts Canadian Workers First?" September 7. https://twitter.com/erinotoole/sta tus/1302991683072798721?lang=en. Accessed on October 15, 2020.

O'Toole. Erin. 2020c. "Hansard." *Our Commons*, September 30. https://www.ourcommons.ca/DocumentViewer/en/43-2/house/sitting-6/hansard. Accessed on October 15, 2020.

O'Toole, Erin. 2020d. "A New Conservative Vision". October 30. https://www.mediaevents.ca/canadianclub-20201030/. Accessed on November 5, 2020.

Pant, Harsh V., and Ketan Mehta. Forthcoming. "Canada-India Relations: Muddling Along?" In *The Palgrave Handbook in Canada in International Affairs*, edited by Robert W. Murray and Paul Gecelovsky. New York: Palgrave Macmillan.

Platt, Brian. 2020. The Rise of Erin O'Toole: Inside the Strategy That Took Him From Underdog to Victor in Conservative Leadership Race." *National Post*, September 4. https://nationalpost.com/news/politics/how-the-race-was-won-otooles-campaign-to-take-down-mackay-for-the-conservative-leader ship. Accessed on September 26.

Selley, Chris. 2019. "It's Not Scheer's Fault the Tories Lost. Blame the Dreck That Passed for His Platform." *National Post*, October 22. https://nationalpost.com/news/politics/election-2019/canadian-federal-election-2019-results-andrew-scheer-conservatives-justin-trudeau-liberals. Accessed on September 26, 2020.

Simpson, Jeffrey. 2015. "The Nepean Contest Wasn't About Substance." *Globe and Mail*, July 2. https://www.theglobeandmail.com/opinion/the-nepean-contest-wasnt-about-substance/article25217039/.

Stairs, Denis. 2001. "Architects or Engineers? The Conservatives and Foreign Policy." In *Diplomatic Departures: The Conservative Era in Canadian Foreign Policy, 1984–93*, edited by Nelson Michaud and Kim Richard Nossal, 25–42. Vancouver: University of British Columbia Press.

United States. 2020. "Geneva Consensus Declaration on Promoting Women's Health and Strengthening the Family." https://www.hhs.gov/about/age ncies/oga/global-health-diplomacy/protecting-life-global-health-policy/gen eva-declaration.html. Accessed on November 3, 2020.

Vanderklippe, Nathan. 2020. "In Selecting Erin O'Toole, Conservatives Elevate Hawkish Voice on China." *Globe and Mail*, August 24.

Van Ham, Peter. 2001. "The Rise of the Brand State: The Postmodern Politics of Image and Reputation." *Foreign Affairs* 80 (5): 2–6.

Van Ham, Peter. 2002. "Branding Territory: Inside the Wonderful World of PR and IR Theory." *Millennium* 31 (2): 249–269.

Whittington, Les. 2020. "Socons, Alienated Western Canadians Settle for O'Toole Rather Than MacKay." *The Hill Times*, August 26. https://www.hil ltimes.com/2020/08/26/socons-alienated-western-conservatives-settle-for-otoole-rather-than-mackay/261239. Accessed on September 16, 2020.

CHAPTER 8

Polarization, Populism, and the Pandemic: Implications for Canadian Outlook on the World

Frank Graves

INTRODUCTION

This chapter was originally intended to document the rise of what we call 'ordered', or what was originally called authoritarian, populism. In *Northern Populism: Causes and Consequences of the New Ordered Outlook* (2020) we argued that this force, which was so critical in explaining both Brexit and Trump, was very much evident in Canada. We were going to focus on the implications of ordered outlook for how Canadians see the external world and how this is sorting their preferences for the future.

The original purpose has been dramatically overtaken by the COVID-19 pandemic. This once in a lifetime collision of health and economic risk has wreaked the most dynamic shifts in public outlook and behaviour that

F. Graves (✉)
EKOS Research Associates, Ottawa, ON, Canada
e-mail: fgraves@ekos.com

© The Author(s), under exclusive license to Springer Nature
Switzerland AG 2021
D. Carment and R. Nimijean (eds.), *Political Turmoil in a Tumultuous World*, Canada and International Affairs,
https://doi.org/10.1007/978-3-030-70686-9_8

we have ever witnessed. The chapter instead looks at how the ordered-open axis relates to the outlook on the pandemic and for the coming contest for the post-pandemic future. In addition, the United States has just completed an election of historic proportions, which has major implications for this discussion.

Issues of Canada's place in the world have been dramatically reshaped and it appears that the pandemic may produce accelerated social change that would not have been possible without this great disruption. The future is highly uncertain, but most think we are on the cusp of a great transformation. At the very heart of this contest for the future is the open-ordered axis and issues of trade, borders, globalization, and immigration are central to this. There are mostly irreconcilable conflicts in this newly and starkly polarized Canada. There may also be some emerging opportunities for common ground and to learn from and evolve from the fault lines laid bare by the pandemic, such as the emergence of ordered or authoritarian populism. What are the global forces underpinning the authoritarian reflex and do these conditions exist in Canada?

ORDERED POPULISM

Let's begin with what we really mean by populism. Despite the intensity of interest in the topic, it really doesn't have a clear social scientific meaning. Populism is a much broader and vaguer concept than the more specific brand of populism that we are interested in here. Michael Cox (2018) does a good job of showing the common responses to what he calls the global rise of populism. The institutional order's response to this was twofold: surprise and distaste. Neither of these responses is particularly helpful. In *Money Week*, John Stepek (2017) notes that most expert opinion falls into two categories: sneering and patronizing. The view tends to be that populism itself is the problem, without an attempt to understand the forces which have led to its recent rise.

Some populist movements have had positive outcomes, such as those implemented by presidents Theodore and Franklin Roosevelt in the first half of the twentieth century. They produced the dramatic rise of the middle class and an unmatched era of shared prosperity. But this example, which some have labelled quasi-populist, is one of a very short list of historical success stories. On the other hand, the list of populist movements with disastrous culminations is long.

All of the key experts seem to agree that populism has two main ingredients: (1) the idea that there is a corrupt elite which invokes deep suspicion of the current establishment, and (2) a belief that power should be more properly restored to the people (who, more often than not, become 'my people', not 'others'). Other common features of populism, which some also describe as a strategy for governing or gaining power, are tendencies to nativism, scepticism toward established authorities such as the media and science, an aversion to foreigners, and in David Goodhart's (2017) terminology, an affinity to the local 'somewhere' rather than the global 'anywhere'. An ordered (authoritarian) outlook as three key components: (1) it emphasizes obedience, order and hostility to outgroups, (2) it is triggered under certain conditions, and (3) it produces a search for a strongman and a desire to turn back the clock and pull up the drawbridge.

In thinking about policy implications, the traditional left-right spectrum has morphed more into a debate about open-ordered. While there are some continuities in the open-ordered and left-right axes, there are also some profound differences, as evident in Table 8.1. This table gives a stylized summary of what we think are some of the key differences between the traditional left-right axis and the newer open-ordered axis. The exact lineage and evolution of left-right and open-ordered is unclear and demands further research.

The key conditions for the rise of authoritarian populism include: (1) declining middle class, wage stagnation and hyper-concentration of wealth at the very top of the system; (2) major value shifts which see more progressive values displacing traditional social conservative values which, in concert with (1), produce a cultural backlash by those seeing loss of identity and privilege; (3) a growing sense of external threat expressed in both a sharp long-term rise in the belief that the world has become overwhelmingly more dangerous and rising normative threat which sees the country and its public institutions moving in the wrong direction; and (4) declining trust and ideological polarization.

i. Declining Middle-Class Progress

Around a decade ago, we began to notice that some of the typical outlook on the economy and one's place in it was fundamentally different than it had been in the last century. The basic ideas of progress, shared

Table 8.1 Left-Right vs. Open-Ordered

Left-Right vs. Open-Ordered	
How is the new ordered outlook different from the traditional right?	
Left	**Right**
– Collectivism	– Individualism
– Active government	– Minimal government
– Social ills societally produced	– Individuals are authors of social problems
– Rehabilitation	– Punishment
Open	**Ordered**
– Cosmopolitan	– Parochial altruism (Haidt 2012)
– Anywhere	
– Pro-diversity and immigration	– Somewhere (Goodhart 2017)
– Optimistic about the future	– Deep reservations about diversity/anti-immigrant
– Reason and evidence	– Deeply pessimistic about future/public institutions
– Creativity	
	– Moral certainty
	– Good behaviour

prosperity and subscription to the middle-class dream all appeared to be unravelling (Graves 2016).

While those at the top are doing very well, there is a pervasive sense of stagnation and decline elsewhere. The basic middle-class bargain, which defined the period of shared prosperity in the last half of the twentieth century, is in tatters. For many, we have reached the end of progress. Only one in eight thinks they are better off than a year ago. Fears are highest when turned to the future; just 13% think the next generation will enjoy a better life.[1]

At the outset of the twenty-first century, in both Canada and the United States, between 60 and 70% of citizens identified as members of the middle class. In both countries, the incidence of self-defined middle-class membership has declined progressively to around 50%, as illustrated

---

[1] EKOS Research Associates, *"Through a Lens Darkly"*, October 10, 2017. Available online at: http://bit.ly/36zv8NS.

in Fig. 8.1. Self-defined middle class is strongly linked to income (0.7), but even more strongly linked to self-rated health (0.8) and quality of life (0.9). Clearly, such a profound hollowing of the middle class has registered dramatic impacts not only on economic outlook, but also on basic health and happiness in upper North America (Graves 2017).

ii. Major Value and Demographic Shifts

According to Norris and Inglehart (2019), the emergence of authoritarian populism is linked not only to long-term structural changes in living conditions and economic security, but also to a conservative backlash against what they called the silent revolution. This, which Inglehart had earlier described as the rhythms of post-materialism, saw a decline in deference (questioning authority) and a profound shift to new permissive and progressive values.

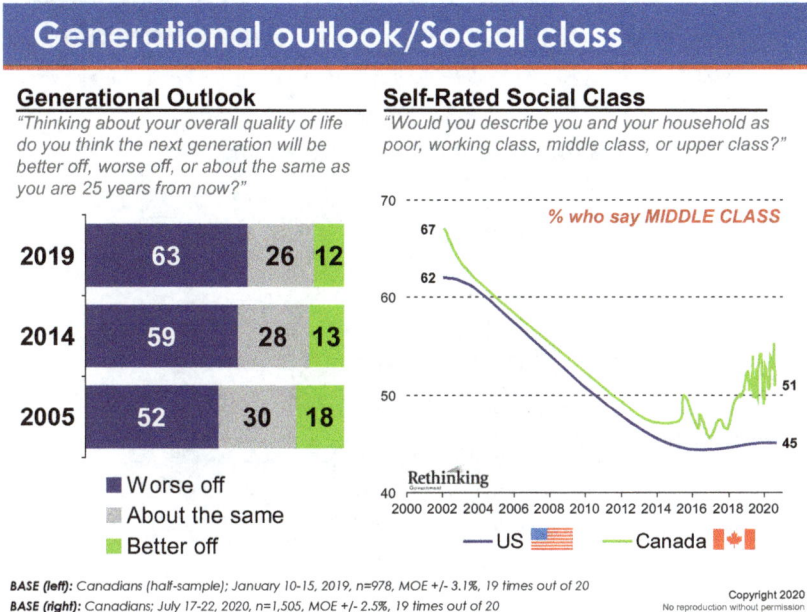

Generational outlook/Social class

Generational Outlook
"Thinking about your overall quality of life do you think the next generation will be better off, worse off, or about the same as you are 25 years from now?"

Year	Worse off	About the same	Better off
2019	63	26	12
2014	59	28	13
2005	52	30	18

■ Worse off
▨ About the same
■ Better off

Self-Rated Social Class
"Would you describe you and your household as poor, working class, middle class, or upper class?"

% who say MIDDLE CLASS

67
62
51
45

Rethinking

2000 2002 2004 2006 2008 2010 2012 2014 2016 2018 2020

— US   — Canada

Fig. 8.1 Generational outlook and self-rated social class

Of particular interest in Fig. 8.2 is the shift in the two values which declined most precipitously in Canada—respect for authority and traditional family values. These are very much critical ordered or authoritarian values. Along with economic stagnation and the fall from middle-class membership, these threatening value declines may have left the segment of society which continued to place high emphasis on them feeling angry and fearful about their loss (hence the appeal of making things 'great' again or taking back control).

This coalesces with dramatic demographic changes. At our centennial, our median age was 25 (Statistics Canada 2009); it is now 41 (Statistics Canada 2017). Visible minorities were a tiny fraction of the population; they are now 22% (Statistics Canada 2017). Religiosity has declined steeply in Canada and, particularly in Québec, Canada has de-Christianized during this same time period. These changes have all coalesced to produce this cultural backlash and authoritarian reflex.

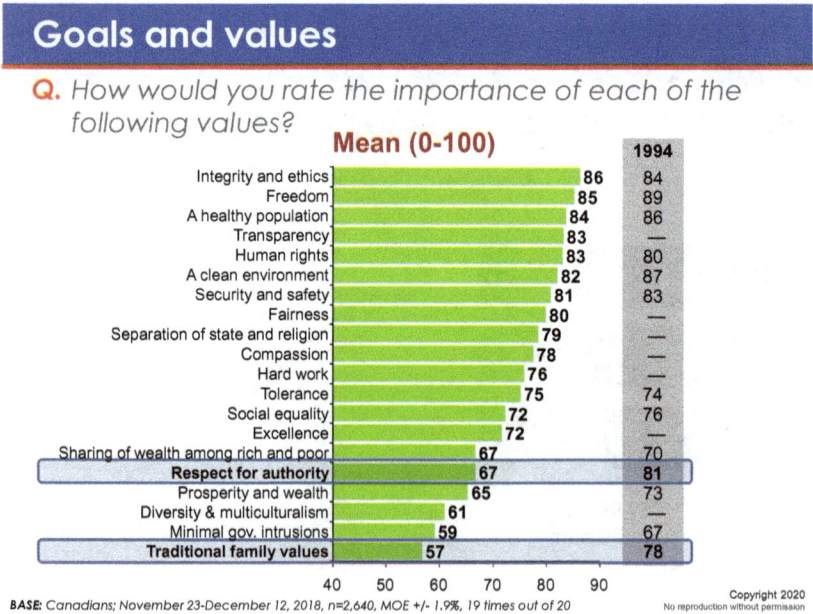

Goals and values

Q. How would you rate the importance of each of the following values?

Mean (0-100)

Value	Mean	1994
Integrity and ethics	86	84
Freedom	85	89
A healthy population	84	86
Transparency	83	—
Human rights	83	80
A clean environment	82	87
Security and safety	81	83
Fairness	80	—
Separation of state and religion	79	—
Compassion	78	—
Hard work	76	—
Tolerance	75	74
Social equality	72	76
Excellence	72	—
Sharing of wealth among rich and poor	67	70
Respect for authority	67	**81**
Prosperity and wealth	65	73
Diversity & multiculturalism	61	—
Minimal gov. intrusions	59	67
Traditional family values	57	**78**

BASE: Canadians; November 23-December 12, 2018, n=2,640, MOE +/- 1.9%, 19 times out of 20

Copyright 2020
No reproduction without permission

Fig. 8.2   Importance of select goals and values

iii. The Role of Threat

An equally prominent pre-condition for the emergence of ordered populism is the role of threat. We look at two indicators of threat, one focusing on a magnified sense of external threat and another which measures what Norris and Inglehart (2019) called 'normative threat' (a sense that the country is moving in a fundamentally wrong direction).

First, let's look at the sense of external threat. In Canada and the United States, there has been a greatly magnified sense that the world has become more dangerous since September 11, 2001. There is no evidence that this is dissipating and our tracking, displayed in Fig. 8.3, shows it is actually a stronger force in recent years. While most experts will say that the world is actually safer than it was 10 years ago, only three per cent agree with that assessment. The security ethic, which gripped upper North America in the aftermath of September 11, has not relaxed its

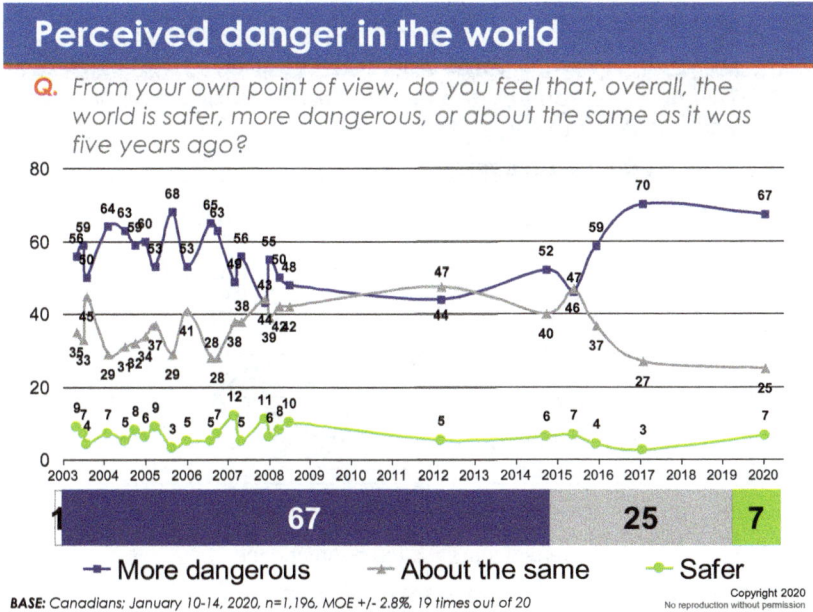

Fig. 8.3 Perceptions of trends in danger in the world

hold and continues to exert a corrosive influence on public confidence. Notably, our last update was taken a month before COVID-19 appeared in Canada. We expect that fears of a more dangerous world have not been eased by the global pandemic.

iv. Declining Trust

Some theorists associate declining trust in government and institutions as part of the cultural backlash evident in the rise of post-materialism. The long-term decline in trust is one of the factors underpinning the emergence of ordered outlook. Trust in government, institutions, scientific authority and elites is much lower among those with an ordered outlook. And as we can see in Fig. 8.4, in both Canada and the United States, trust in government has declined profoundly over the past 40 years. It is instructive that trust in government rose sharply in Canada after the

Tracking trust in government

Q. How much do you trust the government in Ottawa/Washington to do what is right?

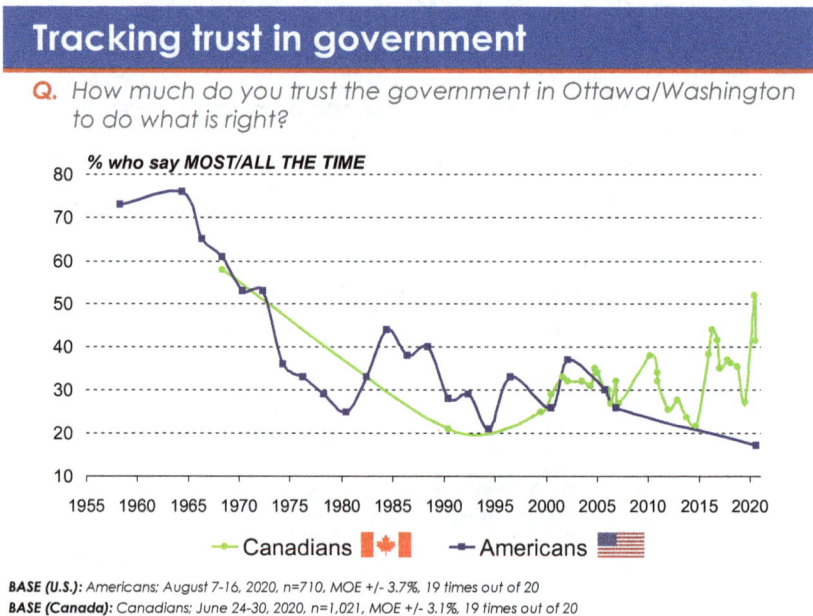

BASE (U.S.): Americans; August 7-16, 2020, n=710, MOE +/- 3.7%, 19 times out of 20
BASE (Canada): Canadians; June 24-30, 2020, n=1,021, MOE +/- 3.1%, 19 times out of 20

Fig. 8.4 Trust in federal governments (Canada vs. U.S.)

pandemic arrived. It reached its highest levels in 30 years and while it has receded recently, it is still at modern historic highs. We will show that this trust in government rebound is fairly unique to Canada. In Europe, the impacts were more modest and mixed and our poll result for the United States in August saw a 65-year low in trust in government.

Evidence of Polarization

Our research, along with international research suggests that Canada has become much more starkly polarized over the past few decades. Indeed, Boxell et al. (2020) found that Canada closely mirrors the United States in terms of the trajectory of polarization—or what they call *effective* polarization. Attitudes towards visible minority immigration are a good proxy for a broader authoritarian populism outlook. While aversion to visible minority immigration has been stable in most of Canada over the past several years, it has risen dramatically among the new Conservative base (see Fig. 8.5). This is strongly linked to an ordered outlook. Once again, we see the familiar pattern of widening polarization on a key indicator of ordered populism over the past several years. The Conservative base is now far more different (and polarized) on this issue than it was in recent years.

Immigration attitudes, and ordered outlook in general, are critical sorting variables explaining movements to the Conservative party since the last election. Comparing the incidence of ordered authoritarian outlook, we find that Liberal supporters who scored higher on ordered outlook have moved to the Conservatives (as have those 2015 Liberal supporters who were more opposed to visible minority immigration).

The Conservative base is over-represented in the self-identified working class and hugely over-represented in the non-university and male segments of the population. These differences have been progressively unfolding since 2013. The rising incidence of the working class in the conservative constituency (25% to 31% to 38%) mirrors changes in the Republican base in the United States and also mirrors a similar pattern of polarization on issues. A similar dramatic widening of differences on university-educated versus non-university-educated has also occurred in this period. This reflects the tendency for ordered populism to be more attractive to those in the less educated portions of society, who put less emphasis on reason and evidence and more emphasis on moral certainty

Attitudes to minorities by party support

Q. Forgetting about the overall number of immigrants coming to Canada, OF THOSE WHO COME would you say there are too few, too many or the right amount who are MEMBERS OF VISIBLE MINORITIES?

National

Year	Too many		About right	Too few
2019	6	40	43	12
2015	8	41	37	14
2013	9	38	42	11

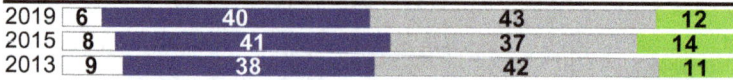

Liberal supporters

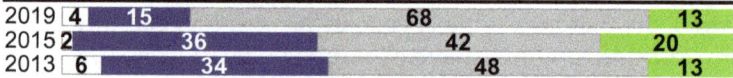

Year				
2019	4	15	68	13
2015	2	36	42	20
2013	6	34	48	13

Conservative supporters

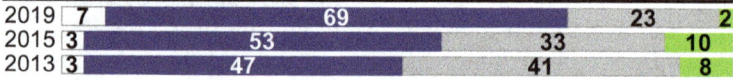

Year				
2019	7	69	23	2
2015	3	53	33	10
2013	3	47	41	8

☐ DK/NR   ■ Too many   ▨ About right   ■ Too few

BASE: Canadians (half-sample); April 3-11, 2019, n=507, MOE +/- 4.4%, 19 times out of 20

Fig. 8.5 Attitudes to visible minorities by federal party support

and order. Additionally, the Conservative base is dramatically more polarized on gender than it was in 2015. A five-point Liberal advantage with men in the 2015 election has turned into a 20-point disadvantage for a net 25-point shift of the male vote.

THE COVID-19 PANDEMIC

Among all the anxiety related to COVID-19, there are some positive benefits evident. We are seeing signs this crisis may be a segue to a better future which may not have been attainable without this tremendous shock to societies. Trust in professionals and institutions (and perhaps social cohesion) has risen fairly dramatically. Indeed, trust in government, politicians, and public servants has reached a 25-year high (see Fig. 8.4).

As we moved out of the initial phases of containment and hard lockdown, we moved into the uncharted waters of the pre-vaccine phase. Many of the fault lines which receded in the crisis phase are re-emerging.

In particular, divisions are emerging on the open-ordered fault line. Not only does this produce different responses to safe behaviour challenges, but it will also manifest itself in alternate versions of what post-COVID-19 Canada is going to look like.

An open question is whether we are on the cusp of grand transformation which is rooted in broad shifts going on for the past twenty or thirty years and perhaps redirected or accelerated by the pandemic. One of the critical areas of concern is how these forces might be altering how Canadians see our place in the world and how we are seen by the external world. We will focus on first part of this question and note that there have been some profound shifts in our outlook on the external world, which we linked to the rise of ordered populism (e.g. declining trust, rising and magnified sense of external threat). The impact of the ongoing COVID-19 crisis has had a further and more abrupt impact of global outlook and it is uncertain how this will ultimately reshape our outlook on the world and our foreign policy preferences. What is highly likely is that there will be major and lasting changes which are connected in part to the open-ordered contest for the future.

Let's consider the trajectory of public opinion, and its polarization, on some of the key aspects of this question. Let's first look at attitudes to globalization and how they have shifted since the beginning of the twenty-first century and further shifted since the onset of the pandemic (Fig. 8.6). At the close of the twentieth century, Canadians were enormously optimistic about globalization and trade. The world was now flat, history may have ended, and we would be floating on a cloud of prosperity fuelled by globalization trade and information technology. We can see from the earlier data (decline of middle class) that the end of history has been replaced with the apparent end of progress and shared prosperity. The buoyant views of globalization as a source of optimism (52% optimistic versus 17% pessimistic) in 1999 have been steadily trending downward. The pandemic seems to have pushed optimistic outlook to a new low of 22%. Similarly, our still-plurality-positive outlook on trade has been declining and the proportion of Canadians who believe free trade is a good thing has fallen from 52% to 41% (Fig. 8.7).

Turning to the issues of borders, and our relationship to the two superpowers, the changes have been even more dramatic. There is evidence of visceral anger at China, deep disillusionment with the United States (Fig. 8.8), and increased receptivity to stronger ties with Europe (Fig. 8.9). There is also some support for a more integrated North

Attitude to globalization

Q. When thinking about globalization which of the following terms best describes your attitude?

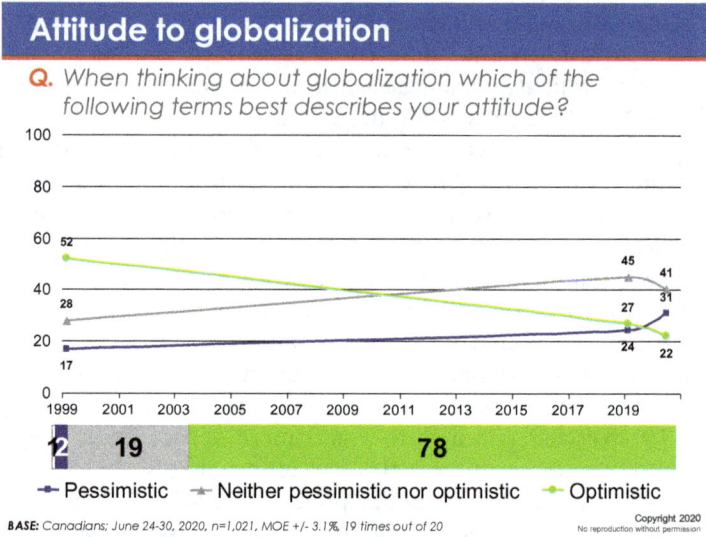

Fig. 8.6 Attitudes to globalization

Impact of free trade on Canada

Q. Is more free trade a good thing or a bad thing for Canada?

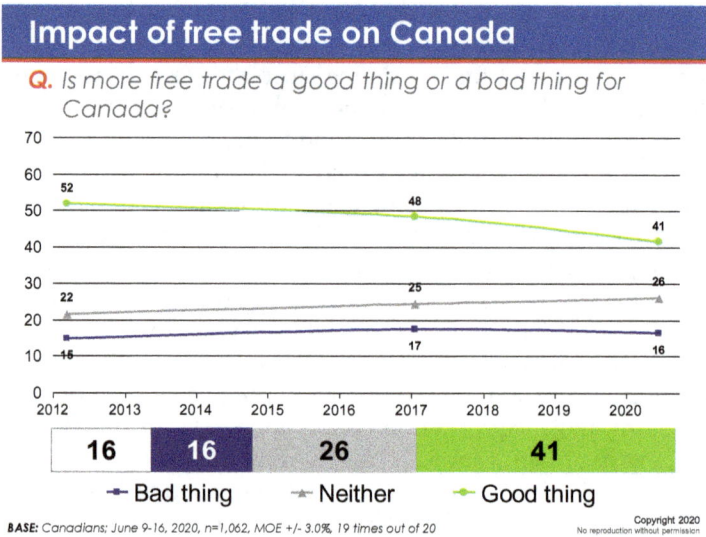

Fig. 8.7 Perceived impact of free trade on Canada

State of Canada-US Relations

Q. How would you currently describe relations between Canada and the U.S.?

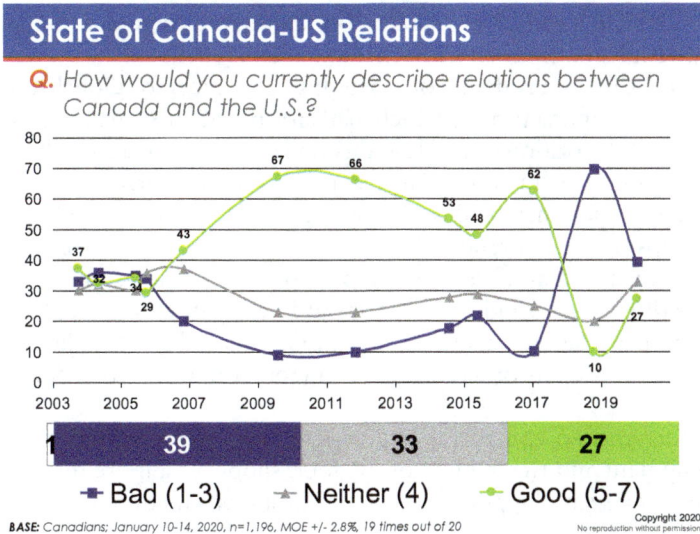

39	33	27

■ Bad (1-3)   ▲ Neither (4)   ● Good (5-7)

Fig. 8.8   State of Canada-US Relations

Preferred trading partner

Q. For much of the last century, Canada's economy has been closely tied to the United States. Over the last few decades, however, Canada has been opening up trade with other countries. Which of the following partners do you believe Canada should be trying to tie itself to more?

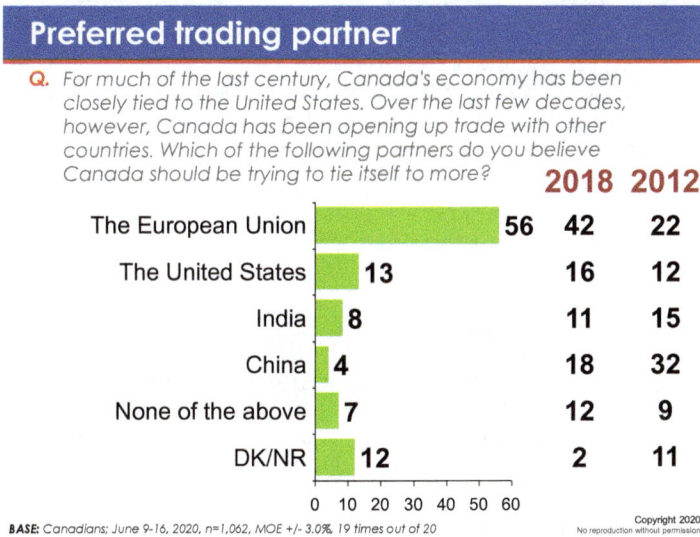

		2018	2012
The European Union	56	42	22
The United States	13	16	12
India	8	11	15
China	4	18	32
None of the above	7	12	9
DK/NR	12	2	11

Fig. 8.9   Preferred trading partner

America, which could be accelerated by the regime change in the United States and further tensions with China.

One of the by-products of changing attitudes to globalization is the issue of manufacturing, which had atrophied in Canada under the forces of globalization and de-industrialization. Our research reveals broad interest in a 'made-in-Canada' renewal of manufacturing capacity (Fig. 8.10), which may be linked to rising confidence in the public sector and perhaps point to a renewed case for national 'industrial policy'. Revitalizing Canada's manufacturing sector is seen as an appealing option for future as those increasingly worried about fragility of global supply chains. Renewing manufacturing and a made-in-Canada industrial policy appeals to both sides of open-ordered spectrum (something that very few things do).

Whether this an ephemeral response to shortages of personal protective equipment and the fragility of the food supply or a more durable shift remains to be seen. Support for more domestic production is dramatically

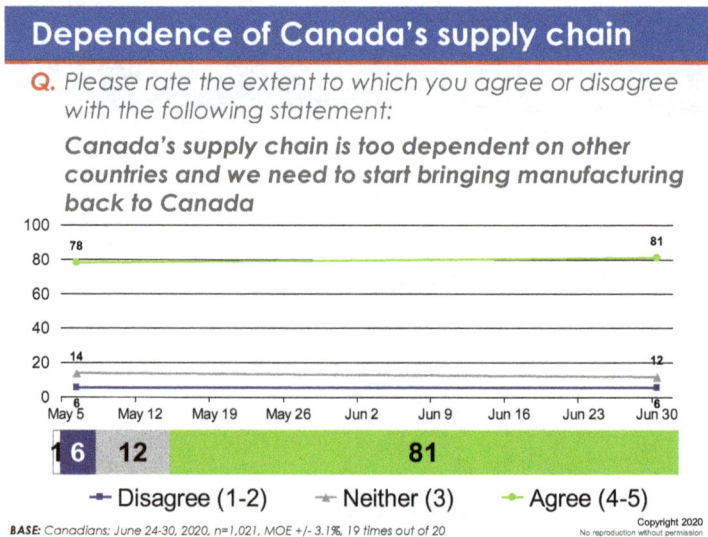

Dependence of Canada's supply chain

Q. Please rate the extent to which you agree or disagree with the following statement:

Canada's supply chain is too dependent on other countries and we need to start bringing manufacturing back to Canada

Disagree (1-2)   Neither (3)   Agree (4-5)

BASE: Canadians; June 24-30, 2020, n=1,021, MOE +/- 3.1%, 19 times out of 20

Copyright 2020
No reproduction without permission

Fig. 8.10 Perceived need for more domestic manufacturing

Demand for more domestic production

Q. *Please rate the extent to which you agree or disagree with the following statements:*

Businesses should be pushed to produce more medical supplies in Canada/the EU, even if it means higher prices

EUROPE*
% agree

| 2 | 9 | 22 | 67 | **41** |

Businesses should be pushed to produce more non-medical goods in Canada/the EU, even if it means higher prices

| 2 | 13 | 26 | 58 | **28** |

☐ DK/NR   ■ Disagree (1-2)   ▨ Neither (3)   ▨ Agree (4-5)

* *European figures drawn from "10 Takeaways from the COVID-19 Crisis", a study conducted for the European Council on Foreign Relations (July 2020)*

BASE: *Canadians; July 14-21, 2020, n=1,052, MOE +/- 3.0%, 19 times out of 20*

Fig. 8.11 Support for mandating more domestic production

higher in Canada than in the European Union (see Fig. 8.11). Canadians are also much more likely to say citizens should think twice about travelling abroad (see Fig. 8.12).

There is evidence that the importance Canadians place on social issues is on the rise. This covers a broad spectrum from health and climate change, to Indigenous issues, race, and inequality. The importance of reducing racial inequality is up 23 points from last year; Indigenous issues are up 19 points as illustrated in Fig. 8.13. Immigration has also risen in importance but not because of anti-immigrant sentiment. Views on immigration are overwhelmingly positive (see Fig. 8.14). Despite 'closing' attitudes on globalization, Canadians appear to embrace the ideal of multiculturalism.

THE TRUMP PARADOX

Finally, I would like to offer some insights into the recent U.S. election, arguably the most important election in modern history. When I polled across the border during the U.S. election, I found that

Views on travel abroad

Q. *To what extent do you agree or disagree with the following statements:*

Citizens should think twice before working, living, and travelling abroad

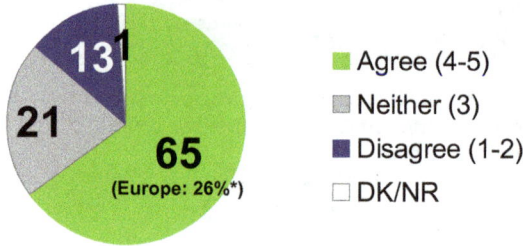

13 1
21
65
(Europe: 26%*)

■ Agree (4-5)
▨ Neither (3)
■ Disagree (1-2)
☐ DK/NR

* *European figures drawn from "10 Takeaways from the COVID-19 Crisis", a study conducted for the European Council on Foreign Relations (July 2020). European respondents prompted with "Once the coronavirus crisis is over".*
BASE: *Canadians; July 14-21, 2020, n=1,052, MOE +/- 3.0%, 19 times out of 20*

Fig. 8.12 Views on travel abroad

Reducing racial intolerance

Q. *Canada is facing a series of difficult challenges. Thinking not just of today but over the next five years, what priority should the federal government place on each of the following areas?* **Reducing racial intolerance in the country**

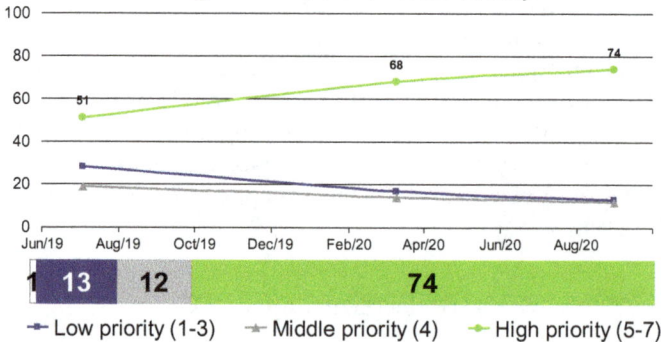

13   12   **74**

—■— Low priority (1-3)   —▲— Middle priority (4)   —●— High priority (5-7)

BASE: *Canadians (half-sample); August 11-31, 2020, n=794, MOE +/- 3.5%, 19 times out of 20*

Fig. 8.13 Public priorities: Reducing racial intolerance

Attitudes to immigration/visible minorities

Q. *In your opinion do you feel that there are too few, too many or about the right number of immigrants coming to Canada?*

Q. *Forgetting about the overall number of immigrants coming to Canada, OF THOSE WHO COME would you say there are too few, too many or the right amount who are MEMBERS OF VISIBLE MINORITIES?*

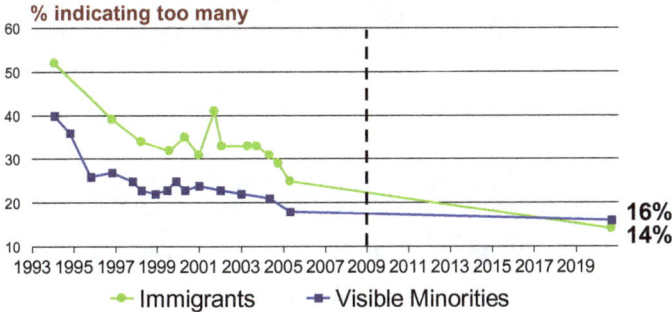

% indicating too many

16%
14%

1993 1995 1997 1999 2001 2003 2005 2007 2009 2011 2013 2015 2017 2019

— Immigrants   — Visible Minorities

BASE: *Canadians (half-sample each); August 11-31, 2020, n=787-812, MOE +/- 3.4-3.5%, 19 times out of 20*

Fig. 8.14 Attitudes to current immigration levels and number of visible minorities

Americans' trust in their federal government had reached a historical nadir; just 17% of Americans trust their government to do the right thing (by comparison, 41% of Canadians express a high degree of trust in their government). Furthermore, as illustrated in Fig. 8.15, just one in three say their government is headed in the right direction (compared to six in ten Canadians).

To make matters worse, it would seem the most advanced and powerful society on the planet has fumbled a massive health crisis. The U.S. government receives terrible marks on its handling of the COVID-19 crisis. Indeed, just 32% approve of how the U.S. government has handled the crisis, an approval rating that is barely half that of its Canadian counterpart (see Fig. 8.16).

The clamour south of the border has not gone unnoticed. Just one in five Canadians hold a favourable view of the United States, less than half what the Obama administration enjoyed (see Fig. 8.17). Eight in ten fear the United States is on the verge of chaos.

By Canadian standards, these marks are abysmal. If a Canadian government were rated so poorly by its populace, it would likely be looking at a meltdown similar to the Progressive Conservatives' two seats in the 1993

Direction of country/government

Q. *All things considered, would you say the country is moving in the right direction or the wrong direction?*

U.S. | 10 | 60 | 31

BASE: Americans (half-sample); August 7-16, 2020, n=369, MOE +/- 5.1%, 19 times out of 20

Canada | 5 | 32 | 63

BASE: Canadians (half-sample); July 15-16, 2020, n=356, MOE +/- 5.2%, 19 times out of 20

Q. *All things considered, would you say the U.S. federal government/Government of Canada is moving in the right direction or the wrong direction?*

U.S. | 6 | 59 | 35

BASE: Americans (half-sample); August 7-16, 2020, n=341, MOE +/- 5.3%, 19 times out of 20

Canada | 5 | 36 | 59

BASE: Canadians (half-sample); July 15-16, 2020, n=338, MOE +/- 5.3%, 19 times out of 20

□ DK/NR   ■ Wrong direction   ■ Right direction

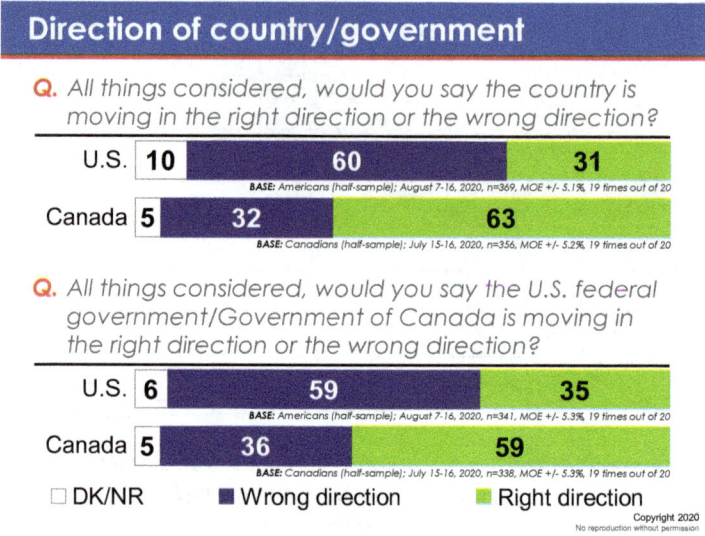

Fig. 8.15 Direction of country and federal government

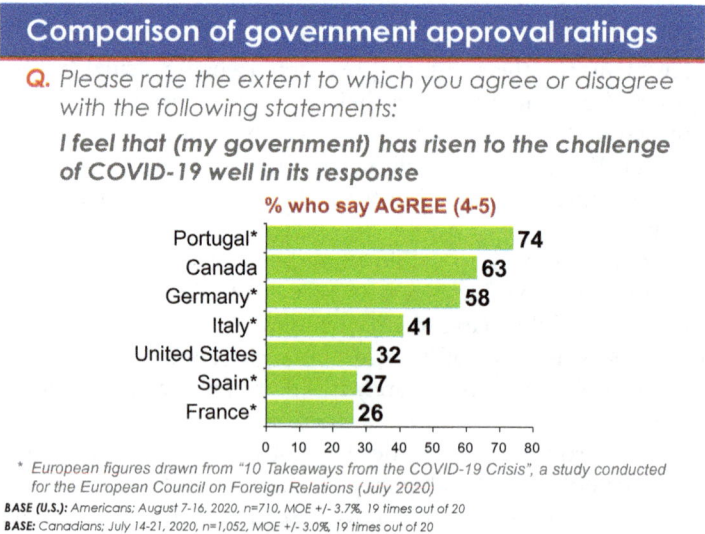

Comparison of government approval ratings

Q. *Please rate the extent to which you agree or disagree with the following statements:*

I feel that (my government) has risen to the challenge of COVID-19 well in its response

% who say AGREE (4-5)

Portugal* | 74
Canada | 63
Germany* | 58
Italy* | 41
United States | 32
Spain* | 27
France* | 26

0 10 20 30 40 50 60 70 80

* *European figures drawn from "10 Takeaways from the COVID-19 Crisis", a study conducted for the European Council on Foreign Relations (July 2020)*

BASE (U.S.): Americans; August 7-16, 2020, n=710, MOE +/- 3.7%, 19 times out of 20

BASE: Canadians; July 14-21, 2020, n=1,052, MOE +/- 3.0%, 19 times out of 20

Fig. 8.16 International comparison of government approval ratings

Reciprocal views

Q. *In general, would you describe your opinion of Canada/the United States as favorable or unfavorable?*

U.S. views on Canada

4	11	27	58

BASE: Americans; August 7-16, 2020, n=710, MOE +/- 3.7%, 19 times out of 20

Canadian views of the U.S.

0	68	10	22

BASE: Canadians; October 4-15, 2018, n=1,306, MOE +/- 2.7%, 19 times out of 20

□ DK/NR ■ Unfavourable (1-3) ▨ Neither (4) ■ Favourable (5-7)

Fig. 8.17   Canada and the U.S.: Reciprocal views

election. And yet, in what I refer to as the 'Trump Paradox', Donald Trump came within four percentage point of winning the popular vote. All of this begs the question: if America is so down, how is it that Donald Trump was so competitive?

There were two factors underlying Mr. Trump's paradoxically competitive position and the woeful outlook on the economy, the pandemic, and the country. First, voter fealty in the United States means that American voters are far more inelastic relative to other countries. Second and more importantly is the issue of authoritarian populism, which has created a heightened partisan polarization and is becoming an increasingly effective predictor of vote intention.

We created a nine-point index using four simple questions that ask nothing about politics, but rather about child rearing (questioning authority versus obedience, morality versus reason and evidence, creativity versus good behaviour, and order versus openness). This 'open-ordered' index tightly predicted support for the Conservative Party in the 2019 Canadian election and, similarly, there is a near-perfect linear correlation between ordered outlook and support for Donald Trump. At one end of the spectrum—the most 'ordered'—90% of respondents would vote for

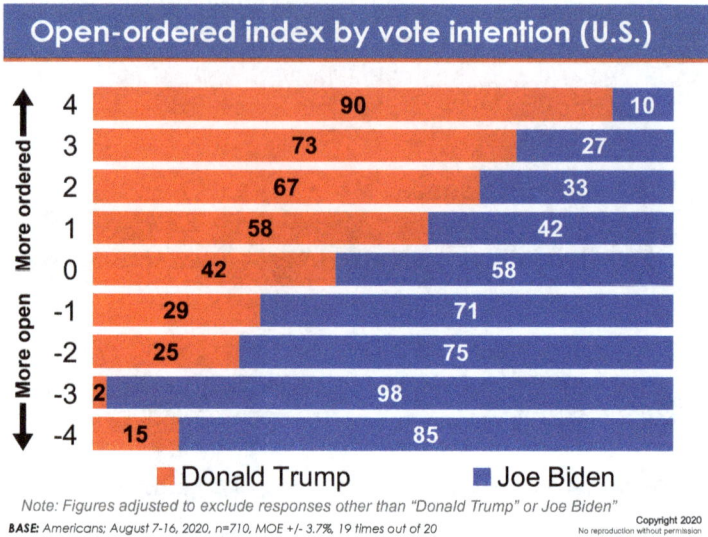

Fig. 8.18 Open-ordered outlook by presidential vote intention (U.S.)

Donald Trump. At the other end of the spectrum—the most 'open'—85% would vote for Joe Biden (see Fig. 8.18).

Our findings also suggest that this ordered outlook is becoming increasingly concentrated among the U.S. electorate. In 2016, 68% of those with an 'open' outlook were Clinton supporters. Today, 81% are Biden voters. The percentage of 'ordered' Americans who are Trump supporters is similarly up four points (Fig. 8.19). What is not clear, however, is whether this polarization favoured Trump or Biden.

CONCLUSIONS

We have argued that ordered (or authoritarian) populism is a critical force both in the world and in Canada. This expresses itself with a much-heightened level of polarization which sees the citizenry increasingly sorted into two largely irreconcilable groups. Our research coincides with international research (Boxell 2020) suggesting that Canada has become much more starkly polarized over the past few decades. This mimics the polarization that has occurred in the United States (and is not evident in other advanced western democracies in Europe).

Open-ordered: 2016 vs. 2020

2016 election

Q. *Which candidate did you vote for in the 2016 presidential election?*

	Donald Trump	Joe Biden/Hillary Clinton
Open	32	68
Ordered	69	31

2020 election

Q. *If the 2020 presidential election were held tomorrow, which candidate would you vote for?*

	Donald Trump	Joe Biden/Hillary Clinton
Open	19	81
Ordered	73	27

■ Donald Trump   ■ Joe Biden/Hillary Clinton

Note: *Figures adjusted to exclude responses other than "Donald Trump" or "Joe Biden"/ "Hillary Clinton"*

BASE: *Americans; August 7-16, 2020, n=710, MOE +/- 3.7%, 19 times out of 20*

Fig. 8.19 Open-ordered outlook by presidential vote intention (U.S.): 2020 vs. 2016

The recent U.S. election has seen the country split even more dramatically into two polarized camps which follow the open-ordered axis. For those thinking that this election has 'solved' some of the problems which have produced this polarization, we would argue it may well have just augmented them.

The forces which seem to produce what has been called the authoritarian reflex are complex and have been percolating for the past few decades. All of these forces, which include hyper-concentration of wealth, economic stagnation, cultural backlash by those experiencing economic dislocation, declining trust, a magnified sense of external threat, are present in Canada. An index measuring this outlook was a very strong predictor of voting in the last election and it predicts vote intentions in the United States even more tightly today than it did in 2016.

While the causes of this rising force are complex, it is our view that the prime mover which initiated this is the collapse of the middle-class bargain and shared prosperity. An angry and frightened portion of society have been left behind, which has provided fertile ground for authoritarian populism. This ordered outlook sees the external world very differently than the open portion of society. They are hostile to outgroups, want thicker borders, less immigration, and see globalization as a source of pessimism, not optimism.

Against this backdrop, COVID-19 arrived and produced a radical disruption in the lives of Canadians which was for most a once in a lifetime collision of economic and health risks. It has also had a dramatic, but rapidly evolving and uncertain impact on the forces noted above. Initially, much of the intense polarization which gripped Canada just before the pandemic relaxed its hold. Trust in government soared, while some of the intense regional and partisan polarization diminished.

Canadians' outlook on the external world has also been profoundly affected. Optimistic outlook on globalization, which was already in decline, plummeted to a new nadir. Canadians became much more wary of the two superpowers, China and the United States, which were seen as enormously negative influences on the pandemic crisis. Our desire to move freely in the world and to have others move freely to Canada sharply dropped. We wanted thicker borders and there is little evidence that this has changed as the horizon for the conclusion of the COVID-19 crisis has receded further and further into some uncertain future.

Linked to this, the fragility of global supply chains, particularly but not limited to personal protective equipment and vaccines, produced a dramatic shift in favour of restoring manufacturing in Canada. This sentiment appears to be ever stronger in Canada than in, for example, Europe.

Polarization seems to be creeping back into Canada and the ordered outlook is now underpinning some of the critical debates about safe behaviour, vaccine acceptance, and how rapidly we should 'open' the economy. All of this coalesces to produce an age of uncertainty, which is unprecedented in most Canadians' lifetimes.

As polarization and some of the strains of ordered populism re-emerge, there have been surprising and perhaps larger offsetting movements on the open side of the spectrum. Support for reshaping the economy to focus more on health, environment, quality of life, and social justice is at a historic high. Similarly, while some rising insularity is clearly evident, this has not had any impact on attitudes to immigration. If anything, support for immigration has risen to historic highs.

Most Canadians see us on the cusp of a major transformation (Fig. 8.20). There is broad receptivity to the idea that the crisis has laid bare some ugly truths that were more hidden before the crisis struck and

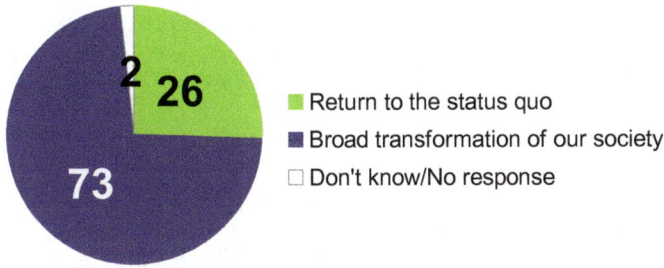

Outlook on post-COVID-19 world

Q. When the COVID-19 crisis ends, do you expect Canadian society to return to the status quo or do you expect a broad transformation of our society?

2   26

73

■ Return to the status quo
■ Broad transformation of our society
□ Don't know/No response

BASE: *Canadians; April 30-May 7, 2020, n=5,276, MOE +/- 1.4%, 19 times out of 20*

Fig. 8.20 Outlook on post-COVID-19 world

the public is now receptive to transformative changes that would not have been possible without this transformation.

However, different outlooks manifest themselves in alternate versions of what a post-COVID-19 world will look like. The open side stresses openness, health, education, environmental sustainability, and measures such as wealth taxes and a four-day workweek, with heavy emphasis on science and expertise. The ordered side stresses retreat from globalization, less porous borders, and a new emphasis on economic nationalism and security.

This contest for the future will come into sharper focus as the sense that the worst of the pandemic is behind us rises. A different American political regime, a highly uncertain economic outlook, and rising geopolitical tensions are all contributing to this era of uncertainty. The contest for which path post-pandemic Canada will follow is unclear but it will be staked out largely on the axis of the open-ordered divide. There are some opportunities for common ground on emerging areas such as the consensus to bolster a made-in-Canada manufacturing capacity.

Overall, it seems Canada is leaning significantly to the open side of this vision choice. Those who think that populism is now a spent force should consider the question of why a force driven ultimately by having a large portion of society left behind will stay dormant if those economic forces are not addressed.

References

Boxell, Levi, Matthew Gentzkow, and Jesse M Shapiro. 2020. "Cross-Country Trends in Affective Polarization." National Bureau of Economic Research. Working Paper 26669. January. Available at: http://www.nber.org/papers/w26669.

Cox, Michael. 2018. "Understanding the Global Rise of Populism." LSE IDEAS Strategic Update. February. Available at: http://bit.ly/302og8N.

Goodhart, David. 2017. *The Road to Somewhere: The Populist Revolt and the Future of Politics*. Oxford University Press.

Graves, Frank. 2016. "Understanding the New Public Outlook on the Economy and Middle-Class Decline: How FDI Attitudes are Caught in a Tentative Closing of the Canadian Mind." Paper delivered to the FDI Canada Forum 2015. School of Public Policy. University of Calgary. February. Available at: http://bit.ly/2T260vn.

Graves, Frank. 2017. "Understanding the Shifting Meaning of the Middle Class." Report Prepared for the Privy Council Office. March. Available at: http://bit.ly/2WtwBU5.

Graves, Frank, and Jeff Smith. 2020. "Northern Populism: Causes and Consequences of the New Ordered Outlook." The School of Public Policy Publications. Available at: https://ssrn.com/abstract=3641823.

Haidt, Jonathan. 2012. *The Righteous Mind: Why Good People are Divided by Politics and Religion*. New York: Pantheon Books.

Norris, Pippa, and Ronald F. Inglehart. 2019. *Cultural Backlash: Trump, Brexit, and Authoritarian Populism*. Cambridge: Cambridge University Press.

Statistics Canada. 2009. "Median Age in Canada, 1956 to 2006." Government of Canada. Available at: http://bit.ly/2YyhSon.

Statistics Canada. 2017. "Census Profile, 2016 Census." Statistics Canada Catalogue no. 98-316-X2016001. November 29. Available at: http://bit.ly/2HxkcoO.

Stepek, John. 2017. "What's Driving Populism, and Why it Matters to Investors." *MoneyWeek*, April 4. Available at: http://bit.ly/2ViHg4l.

PART III

Acting Abroad

CHAPTER 9

Canada's Strategic Engagement in the Middle East and North Africa

Chris Kilford

INTRODUCTION

This chapter broadly examines Canada's contemporary strategic engagement in the Middle East and North Africa (the MENA), which is
considered to include, for this purpose, the twenty-two states belonging
to the Arab League (less the Comoros, Djibouti, Mauritania, Somalia and
Sudan), plus Iran, Israel, and Turkey. This is not an easy task simply given
the vastness of the MENA and the diversity of states and peoples found
within it. It is also an area regarded as one of the least secure places in the
world, beset with brutal civil-wars, growing arsenals and frequent terrorist
activity.

Canada, it should be noted from the outset, is not a newcomer to the
MENA and Canadian soldiers fought and died throughout the region
in the First and Second World Wars. In the 1940s, Canada and Turkey
established diplomatic relations and during the 1950s and 1960s, Ottawa
followed suit with most other MENA countries (DeLong 2020). Canada

C. Kilford (✉)
Canadian International Council, Toronto, ON, Canada

© The Author(s), under exclusive license to Springer Nature
Switzerland AG 2021
D. Carment and R. Nimijean (eds.), *Political Turmoil
in a Tumultuous World*, Canada and International Affairs,
https://doi.org/10.1007/978-3-030-70686-9_9

also has a significant record of supporting past United Nations (UN) peacekeeping missions in the MENA and more recently, has proven to be a reliable partner in the fight against the so-called Islamic State (Daesh) and in the North Atlantic Treaty Organization's (NATO) efforts to help stabilize Iraq.

It has, however, never been in Canada's national interest to become deeply immersed in the region's volatile politics and when Canada has, the outcome has never been good. The decision, for example, by Stephen Harper's Conservative government to join the NATO-led campaign that ultimately led to the collapse of the Libyan government in 2011, was very much out of place with the helpful fixer image Canada has cultivated in the MENA for over half a century. The Harper government's decision to then pick sides and become deeply entangled in the Syrian civil war, without regard to the consequences, created yet another human and security tragedy that is far from over today. Helping to topple the Libyan government, and trying to do the same in Syria, was a stark reminder of what happens when Canadian governments actually do decide to "go along to get along" in concert with their closest allies (Roswell 2020).

Despite the Harper government's missteps in the MENA and the obligation that fell to the current government to try and put things back together again, Canada's associations with the people and most countries in the region continue to be close. But there is no question that the MENA, in general, is facing a period of marked instability brought on by several civil wars fuelled by regional backers, a struggle for influence between Iran, Saudi Arabia and Turkey, and weak economies further undermined by falling oil prices. With all this in mind, the question then becomes what should Canada's future strategic engagement in the region actually look like? Answering this question is the purpose of this chapter, which begins by examining Canada's past and current diplomatic, defence and development activities in the MENA, which is fundamental to understanding the challenges and opportunities that the region presents going forward. This examination is followed by a review of the important business and people-to-people ties that currently exist between Canada and the region. The chapter concludes with some broad policy options for Canadian policy makers to consider for a part of the world that will likely remain quite volatile for many years to come.

Canada's Diplomatic, Defence and Development Engagement in the MENA

When it comes to the MENA, in the past, Canada was often called upon by the international community, or its closest allies, to assist in defusing wars and other security challenges. It was a typical middle power role that Canadians, and generally politicians from every stripe, could agree on. Canada's first post-1945 foray into the region, for example, commenced in 1954 when a small group of officers deployed with the United Nations Truce Supervision Organization (UNTSO) to help enforce a ceasefire between Israel and its neighbours. The 1956 Suez Crisis, which created a major rift between the United States (US), Great Britain and France, was only de-escalated by the deployment of the world's first, multinational large-scale deployment of UN peacekeepers led by Canada. Tensions in Cyprus between the Greek and Turkish communities resulted in another significant deployment of Canadian peacekeepers in 1964.

There were also other circumstances that led Canada to become, often unexpectedly, entangled in the region. When the Shah of Iran's regime was near collapse in 1979, Ken Taylor, Canada's Ambassador in Tehran, managed to evacuate 850 Canadians and in 1980, hid six US Embassy diplomats for almost a year, until they were able to escape (Government of Canada [hereafter Canada] 2019g). In July 2006, fighting between Israel and Hezbollah inside Lebanon caused the Canadian government to evacuate almost 15,000 Canadians and other nationalities by sea and air (Canada 2018f).

In 1991, Canada joined the international U.S.-led military coalition to drive out Iraq following its invasion of Kuwait the year before. In 2003, and although Canada did not take part in Operation IRAQI FREEDOM directly, over thirty Canadian exchange officers were allowed to remain with their U.S. and British units who did deploy, while other Canadian military assets indirectly assisted the US-led campaign (Canadian Broadcasting Corporation 2003). While the Canadian government under Liberal Prime Minister Jean Chretien was opposed to direct military action in the MENA in 2003, the same was not true for Conservative Prime Minister Stephen Harper's government, which came into office in 2006.

In 2011, for example and with the Arab Spring underway, Canada played a leading role in the ouster of Libyan dictator Moammar Gadhafi.

The 2011 decision by NATO to essentially remove the Gadhafi government led to a country-wide institutional collapse and disrupted the immediate region. With Gadhafi gone, John Baird, Canada's then foreign minister, turned his attention to Iran, telling the UN General Assembly in 2012 that in Canada's view, Iran was "the most significant threat to global peace and security". Syrian President Bashar al-Assad, he added, also had to go and Canada threw its entire weight behind the Syrian opposition (National Post 2012). At around the same time, the U.S. decision to simultaneously reduce its troop numbers in Iraq and support the Syrian opposition led to a security vacuum in both countries that Daesh quickly filled, until it was largely defeated in late 2018. However, the end result was a Syrian refugee tidal wave that swamped the region and flooded Europe, the expansion of Iranian and Russian political and military influence, and continuing uncertainty exemplified by the US drone strike that killed Iranian Major General Qassem Soleimani and Iraqi Shia militia leader Abu Mahdi al-Muhandis on January 3, 2020 (Clark 2020).

Defeating Daesh became a major pre-occupation for Canada, leading Ottawa to join the Global Coalition "to degrade and ultimately defeat Daesh in Iraq and Syria" in September 2014 (Canada 2018e). In Kuwait, Canada's Operational Support Detachment, which had transitioned to a general-purpose Operational Support Hub in May 2014, became a major support base for the anti-Daesh effort (Canada 2020f). Over a short period, Canada increased its operational footprint in the region in conjunction with its allies and in support of Iraqi and Kurdish forces. By December 2017, Daesh had lost ninety-five per cent of its territory, including Mosul, Iraq's second largest city, and the Syrian city of Raqqa, its nominal capital.

With Daesh in full retreat, Prime Minister Justin Trudeau revealed in July 2018 that Canada would assume command of a new NATO training mission in Iraq (Canada 2018c). In addition, in April 2019, Canada announced that it would renew its contribution and send fifty-five military personnel to Operation CALUMET, the Multinational Force and Observers (MFO) in the Sinai Peninsula overseeing the implementation of the Egyptian-Israeli Treaty of Peace, until March 31, 2022 (Canada 2019c). Contrastingly, when it came to UN peacekeeping contributions, Canada only had four military personnel deployed in the MENA in June 2020 (United Nations 2020a).

In 2016, the Canadian government also began expanding its development assistance with Iraq, Jordan and Lebanon, announcing that up to

$3.5 billion would be invested over five years to improve security and provide humanitarian assistance. In Jordan's case, Canada's humanitarian assistance programme focused on helping some 660,000 registered Syrian refugees living there. The government also stated its priorities in the Middle East would include combatting terrorism, preventing the spread of weapons of mass destruction, and encouraging regional democratic and economic reforms that would allow for increased two-way investment and trade (Canada 2019a).

In Iraq, Canada focused on stabilization efforts primarily through Operation IMPACT, the Canadian Armed Forces contribution to the Global Coalition against Daesh, and leading NATO Mission Iraq, until at least March 31, 2021. In practice, these missions are designed to provide training and advice to Iraqi defence and security officials and their respective supporting institutions from top to bottom. With authority to deploy up to 850 military personnel in support of this effort, capacity-building activities with the Iraqi, Jordanian and Lebanese Armed Forces, are now central to Canada's strategic involvement in the Middle East (Canada 2019d). However, the COVID-19 pandemic caused the Iraqi Security Forces to suspend training in April 2020, and for now the deployed Canadian contingent remains at approximately 100 personnel with no clear date as to when full operations might resume (Canada 2020h). In addition to military support, Global Affairs' Counter-Terrorism Capacity Building Program (CTCBP) provides training to law enforcement officials in Iraq, Jordan and Lebanon (Canada 2019d). From September 2019 to September 2021, Canada and Morocco are also co-chairing the Global Counterterrorism Forum (GCTF), an international body composed of twenty-nine countries and the European Union whose aim is to combat terrorism and prosecute those responsible for terrorist acts (GCTF 2020).

Previously, on the diplomatic front, the Canada–Gulf Cooperation Council (GCC) Strategic Dialogue was announced in 2013 with a view to promoting mutual economic prosperity as well as security in the Gulf region. A ministerial meeting of the Canada-GCC Strategic Dialogue was subsequently held in Saudi Arabia in 2016, but the 2017 meeting was cancelled due to tensions within the GCC itself and in particular after Saudi Arabia blockaded Qatar on June 5, 2017 (Canada 2018b). Relations between Canada and Saudi Arabia then faltered when former Canadian Foreign Minister Chrystia Freeland tweeted on August 3, 2018 that Canada was gravely concerned about the arrests of civil society and women's rights activists in the Kingdom. The Saudi response was swift.

Canada's ambassador to Saudi Arabia was expelled, its ambassador was recalled, Saudi students studying in Canada were ordered home, and Canadian grain shipments destined for the Kingdom cancelled.

In the light of Saudi Arabia's poor human rights record and their ongoing involvement in Yemen's civil war, media and public focus then shifted to Canada's $14 billion deal to sell approximately 700 light armoured vehicles (LAV) to Riyadh (Brewster 2019). In 2014, then-Prime Minister Stephen Harper agreed to sell the London, Ontario produced armoured vehicles to Saudi Arabia. Then came the 2015 Saudi-led intervention in Yemen, whose actions there only served to remind the international community of Saudi Arabia's own dismal human rights record including executions, arbitrary arrests, political and media suppression and discrimination against women.

Saudi Arabia's international standing took another significant blow in October 2018, when Jamal Khashoggi, a Saudi journalist and *Washington Post* columnist, was brutally murdered by a government hit team after he entered the Saudi consulate in Istanbul, Turkey. Against this backdrop, an Angus-Reid poll held between October 24 and 29, 2018 resulted in ninety per cent of respondents saying that Canada should not sell arms to Saudi Arabia in the future, and forty-six per cent indicating that the current LAV deal should be cancelled (Angus Reid 2018). Despite opposition to the deal over numerous human rights concerns and the war in Yemen, the Trudeau government refused to cancel the agreement, no doubt with Canadian jobs, their future election prospects, and the billions of dollars of penalties that would have been incurred well in mind.

As for Canada's relations with Iran, prior to 1955, the British Embassy in Tehran looked after Canada's interests, but this changed in 1956 with the establishment of an Iranian mission in Ottawa, followed by a Canadian mission in Tehran in 1959. In January 1961, Canada appointed its first Ambassador to Iran and the mission was raised to embassy status the following month. From that point on, relations ebbed and flowed until the Iranian Revolution caused the embassy to close its doors on January 27, 1980. During the 1980–1988 Iran-Iraq war, Canada and Iran did maintain diplomatic relations but for the majority of this period, Denmark provided on-the-ground consular services. In the summer of 1988, normal diplomatic relations between Canada and Iran resumed and in 1990, ambassadors were exchanged (DeLong 2020).

Relations, however, drastically deteriorated in June 2003 after Iranian-Canadian freelance photographer Zahra Kazemi was arrested while photographing the families of detainees waiting outside Tehran's Evin prison. Three weeks later she was dead, having been tortured, raped and murdered by Iranian authorities while in custody. The nature of her death, and the resulting failure of the Iranian government to prosecute those involved, attracted widespread international attention and in November 2003, Canada officially tabled a resolution in the UN General Assembly condemning Iran's human rights record. It would be the first of many such Canadian-sponsored resolutions directed at Iran (Canada 2005).

When the Conservative Party came to power in 2006, it soon re-oriented Canadian foreign policy in the Middle East, tilting closer to Israel while continuing to criticize Tehran for its human rights abuses, its nuclear programme, its destabilizing role in the region, and opposition to Israel (Juneau 2019). In early September 2012, Canada finally cut diplomatic ties and also announced the establishment of the *State Immunity Act—An Order Establishing a List of Foreign State Supporters of Terrorism.* Given that there were reasonable grounds to believe that "Iran and Syria have supported or continue to support terrorist entities", both countries, the government announced, would be placed on the list (Canada 2012).

Previously, in March 2012, the government had also introduced the *Justice for Victims of Terrorism Act* (JVTA), which allowed victims of terrorism to seek redress for terrorist acts committed in or outside Canada from January 1, 1985 onwards. Perpetrators of terrorism and those that supported them, including listed foreign states, were now liable for their actions under the Canadian Criminal Code and non-immune property and financial assets in Canada could be seized to settle claims (Canada 2012, 2015). When it comes to terrorist groups or entities that "have knowingly carried out, attempted to carry out, participated in or facilitated a terrorist activity", the Canadian government keeps a detailed list, which includes sixty terrorist groups or entities, of which almost fifty per cent are connected with the MENA (Canada 2018a). In 2019, the Iranian sponsored Al-Ashtar Brigades, the Fatemiyoun Division and Harakat al-Sabireen, were also added (Canada 2019e).

During the 2015 Canadian election campaign, the opposition Liberals pledged that if elected they would re-establish diplomatic relations with Iran and following their election win, two diplomatic missions were despatched to Tehran in May and October 2017 to discuss restoring diplomatic ties. From the government's perspective, the main argument to re-open lines of communication between Ottawa and Tehran was to address human rights issues and defend unjustly imprisoned Canadians in Iran. "How can Canada possibly defend our people", the government argued, "when we have no one in the country to do it on our behalf, no one who knows the lay of the land, the right officials to approach, and so on?" (Canada 2018d). Nevertheless, and despite a lengthy parliamentary debate, in June 2018, Conservative and Liberal parliamentarians joined forces to support a Conservative non-binding motion calling on the government to abandon all negotiations with Iran. Approved by a 248-to-45 vote, the Liberal government suspended its efforts (Canada 2018d).

Many factors explain why the effort to re-open the Canadian embassy in Tehran failed. One major obstacle, noted University of Ottawa professor Thomas Juneau (2019), was the JVTA that made Iran liable for damages due to acts of terrorism. In addition, Concordia University academic Dr. Homa Hoodfar, a dual Canadian-Iranian citizen, had been arrested in Iran in June 2016 and held for 112 days in the notorious Evin prison before her release. Then, on January 24, 2018, Canadian-Iranian dual citizen Dr. Kavous Seyed-Emami, a professor of sociology at Imam Sadiq University in Tehran, was arrested on charges of espionage and spying and also held in Evin prison. Two weeks later he was dead, supposedly having committed suicide. As Amnesty International noted, his case was like many others in Iran where the authorities engage in orchestrated campaigns to cover up evidence of torture "and unlawful deaths while publicly defaming the deceased" (Amnesty International 2018).

Canada's Business and People-to-People Connections in the MENA

Despite the absence of diplomatic relations with Iran and Syria, in the rest of the MENA, Canada's relations are anchored by a robust network of country-to-country business and civil society connections. Indeed, keeping track of where Canadians are in the MENA at any one time is not easy. For example, 131,445 Canadians visited Turkey in 2019 (Republic of Turkey 2020). Elsewhere, more than 9000 Canadians live in Qatar, and 6000 reside in Kuwait (Canada 2020f, g). Some 35,000 Canadian citizens also live in Israel while the Canadian-Lebanese community constitutes the largest ethnic Arab group in Canada (Canada 2020b, c).

A plethora of regional and bilateral business councils and other organizational links also exist. From a business-to-business perspective, since

1983, the Canada-Arab Business Council has focused exclusively on promoting trade and investment between Canada and Arab countries in the MENA region (Canada-Arab Business Council 2020). More recently, country-to-country business associations that also promote bilateral relations in the MENA have followed such as the Canadian-Turkish Business Council, the Canada-Israel Chamber of Commerce, the Canada-Egypt Business Council, the Council for Development Canada-Algeria, and the Iraq-Canada Business Council, just to name a few.

Bilateral trade between Canada and the MENA was $14.1 billion in 2015, rising to $18.5 billion in 2019 and equating to 1.56% of Canada's international trade (Canada 2020a). As Table 9.1 shows, in general, trade levels have increased, but a substantial portion of this increase did result from the previously mentioned $14 billion light-armoured vehicle contract with Saudi Arabia (Brewster 2020). Indeed, seventy per cent of

Table 9.1 Canada's Bilateral Merchandise Trade in the MENA (plus Iran and Turkey) in millions of dollars 2015–2019 (Canada 2020a)

Country	2015	2016	2017	2018	2019	Exports and Imports 2019: %
Algeria	1550.40	2375.50	1533.80	778.3	738.3	0.062
Bahrain	89.1	66.8	116.6	334.4	247.4	0.021
Egypt	1169.10	1364.90	1281.80	1306.50	1793.60	0.15
Iran	126	182.3	220.4	215.4	357	0.03
Iraq	180.5	128.8	143.7	199.7	147.1	0.012
Israel	1550.80	1716.70	1737.50	1901.50	1673.00	0.14
Jordan	166.9	173.1	174.9	179.2	228.8	0.019
Lebanon	142.1	179.1	157.8	150.5	156.6	0.013
Libya	43.2	25.1	28.6	120.6	177.9	0.015
Morocco	717.1	766.1	819.8	910	916.2	0.077
Oman	205.7	176.2	126.8	208.5	152	0.013
Qatar	227.1	211.4	174.1	246.4	331.7	0.028
Saudi Arabia	3167.20	2966.50	4115.40	5694.40	6113.70	0.512
Tunisia	212.4	196.7	154.5	171.5	238.9	0.02
Turkey	2420.20	2520.30	3051.00	3666.70	3582.00	0.3
UAE	2166.30	1918.50	1791.70	1672.60	1712.00	0.143
Total	14,134.10	14,968.00	15,628.40	17,756.20	18,566.20	1.56

Syria and Yemen are not included in the table because Canada's bi-lateral trade is limited to non-existent as both countries are engaged in civil wars.

Canada's non-US international arms exports head to the MENA, and Saudi Arabia is Canada's main customer (Canada 2020i). Turkey is also a major importer of Canadian military goods and technology. However, in October 2019, Ottawa placed an arms embargo on future sales to Ankara because of Turkish military activities in Syria. In April 2020, the arms embargo was extended indefinitely (Brewster 2020).

A contributing factor as to why bilateral trade is somewhat limited between Canada and the MENA is simply to do with the challenges that doing business in this region presents. In January 2020, Transparency International noted that the MENA had an average score of 39/100 in their 2019 *Perceptions of Corruption Index*. The United Arab Emirates (UAE) had the best score of 71/100, followed by Qatar at 62/100. However, countries such as Egypt and Turkey scored 35/100 and 39/100, respectively. For comparison purposes, Canada ranked 77/100 (Transparency International 2020). The World Bank's 2019 *Ease of Doing Business Index* is also telling in this regard, with only the UAE listed in the top 25 countries worldwide for doing business (World Bank 2019).

Another important factor limiting Canadian engagement, business and otherwise, is the state of basic human rights and media freedom in the MENA. Freedom House's (2019) *2019 Global Freedom Index* only reported Israel and Tunisia as "Free" and Jordan, Kuwait, Lebanon and Morocco as "Partly Free". Every other country in the MENA was labelled "Not Free". Nevertheless, Canada does have a Free Trade Agreement (FTA) with Jordan and Foreign Investment Promotion and Protection Agreements with Egypt, Jordan, Kuwait, and Lebanon (Canada 2020e). The right for Israel to live in peace and security with its neighbours, which has been at the core of Canada's Middle East policy since 1948, has also continued to underpin Canada's Middle Eastern presence. The 1997 Canada-Israel FTA, updated in 2019, was Canada's first FTA outside of North America (Canada 2020b).

Another important aspect helping to bolster closer ties with the MENA is Canadian remittances. Carleton University's *Canadian International Development Platform*, for example, notes that in 2018, the top five MENA countries receiving remittance money from Canada were Lebanon ($820 million), Egypt ($412 million), Morocco ($150 million), Iran ($94 million) and Israel ($72 million). For those countries in the MENA not directly affected by the Syrian refugee crisis, Canadian foreign aid when compared to remittances is very limited. In 2018, Morocco received $11.1 million and Egypt just $7.3 million (Carleton University 2020).

On the educational front, a small number of Canada-accredited schools operate in the MENA offering Kindergarten to Grade 12 programmes and also accredited university degrees. In 2004, for example, the Canadian International College in Cairo partnered with Cape Breton University and began offering fully accredited Canadian degrees (Cape Breton University 2020). The University of Calgary followed suit in 2007, establishing a campus in Qatar providing Bachelor and Master's degrees in Nursing (University of Calgary 2020). For over thirty years, the Canadian Bureau for International Education (CBIE) has also managed the Government of Libya's North American Scholarship Programme, which brings post-secondary students to Canada from Libya (CBIE 2020). On the other hand, Ottawa-based Algonquin College's campus, which opened in Jazan, Saudi Arabia in 2013, encountered numerous challenges and operations were transferred to a British company in 2017 (Canadian Broadcasting Corporation 2017).

As Table 9.2 demonstrates, the MENA is also a source of immigrants, political refugees and students, with Iran coming first in all three categories. And while few Turks immigrate to Canada, since the July 2016 failed military coup attempt, which the Turkish government blamed on followers of Turkish Islamic cleric Fetullah Gülen, matters have changed dramatically. Between 2017–2019, for example, 4697 Turkish citizens were granted refugee status by Canada, the highest number of accepted claims from any country. Not every Turkish refugee accepted by Canada was a member of the Gülen movement, but the assumption made by the Canadian government was that most were and would be at risk if they returned to Turkey (Canada 2019h).

Canada's Policy Options in the MENA

Given what has been discussed in this chapter, it is evident that a single strategic engagement policy for the MENA is not advisable simply because the region is so incredibly diverse. On the ground, no single supranational NATO or EU-like organization is present for Canada to link-in with. Nor do any overarching regional trade mechanisms exist, such as the Asia Pacific Trans-Pacific Partnership. Some regional bodies, such as the Arab League and the Organization of Islamic Cooperation are present, but Canada does not have observer status in either. Moreover, in quite a few instances, members in both organizations have very significant political differences with each other and almost all have issues surrounding

Table 9.2 Immigrants, Political Refugees and Students coming to Canada from the MENA plus Iran, Israel and Turkey (Canada 2019b, f, i)

Country	Immigrants (2011–2016 data)	Granted political asylum (2019 data)	Students (2019 data)
Algeria	17,180	68	2660
Bahrain	450	6	0
Egypt	16,155	1032	1575
Iran	42,070	2744	9975
Iraq	20,665	484	175
Israel	4740	68	30
Jordan	3985	113	925
Lebanon	9375	207	575
Libya	1915	334	525
Morocco	15,105	8	3080
Oman	335	0	85
Palestinian Authority	–	370	175
Qatar	765	1	20
Saudi Arabia	5465	282	1190
Syria	29,945	719	280
Tunisia	6700	21	1515
Turkey	4260	2043	3285
UAE	6130	4	40
Yemen	845	707	250

their lack of human rights, the rule of law and media freedom just to name a few. On the other hand, multi-lateral organizations such as La Francophonie do help promote ties between Canada and many member and associate member countries in the MENA, and former Governor General of Canada, Michaëlle Jean led La Francophonie from 2014–2018.

The spread of COVID-19 has also unsettled the world and the MENA is no exception. Indeed, well-before COVID-19 came along, the MENA was faced with numerous challenges including weak governance, rampant corruption, economic inequality, and growing numbers of unemployed youth. Iran has reported very high COVID-19 case numbers and an already fragile economy could easily fail. On the energy front, the shift to renewable sources was already taking the wind out of international oils sales well before the collapse of oil prices. With its oil revenues sliding downward, Saudi Arabia is at great risk of financial setback. Certainly, the de facto ruler of Saudi Arabia, Muhammad bin Salman and his 2016

"Vision 2030" plan to rapidly reform and modernize the country has been set-back. Instead, simple economic survival has moved to the forefront with the recent suspension of cost-of-living allowances for state workers, higher gas prices and a sales tax that leapt from five to fifteen per cent (Al Arabiya 2020).

Kurds in Iran, Iraq, Syria and Turkey are also increasingly restless. Despite recent setbacks, such as the ill-timed 2017 independence referendum in Iraq's Kurdish region, and the US near-abandonment of Syria's Kurds in 2019, it is only a matter of time before Kurds throughout the region seek a greater voice. The largely Kurdish-based HDP party, that won enough votes to gain entry into the Turkish parliament in 2015, is an excellent case. Elsewhere, civil wars in Libya, Syria, Yemen and civil unrest in Egypt, Lebanon and Iraq, also threaten regional security, and to some extent Canada, especially when terrorist organizations find safe places to operate.

Once Canada and the world exits the COVID-19 pandemic, a government-led examination of its overall foreign policy is definitely in order. This should include a review of bilateral relations with every country in the MENA simply because the people-to-people and business-to-business ties are increasing. Trade with Libya is a good example. If the civil war ends, and stability and security returns, Canadian companies could play an important role in helping to rebuild Libya and surpassing pre-Arab Spring bilateral trade levels that stood at $270.8 million in 2010 (Canada 2020d). Canada will also need to be mindful of China's growing presence in the MENA. Beijing has become the region's largest trading partner with two-way trade reaching $294.4 billion in 2019 and Saudi Arabia is now China's main supplier of crude oil (Chaziza 2020).

There is also a need to continue aiding global and coalition-led efforts to contain and ideally end the constant state of conflict that exists throughout the MENA. To this end, Operation IMPACT, and continuing troop contributions to the UN and MFO will remain very important. In future, Canada could also look to expand bilateral relations with MENA countries through NATO mechanisms such as the 2004 Istanbul Cooperation Initiative (members are Bahrain, Qatar, Kuwait and the UAE) and the Mediterranean Dialogue (members are Algeria, Egypt, Israel, Jordan, Mauritania, Morocco and Tunisia). To some extent, this is already happening through Canada's Military Training and Cooperation Programme, which is building capacity and bilateral ties in the MENA through defence diplomacy efforts in Jordan, Kuwait, Morocco, Oman and Tunisia (Canada 2020j).

In addition to military efforts, diplomacy is also key. The most sensitive diplomatic sticking point in the MENA is whether or not to re-establish diplomatic relations with Iran. It is quite apparent from the political debate in Canada that this will not happen unless there is a fundamental political change in Tehran. The general argument is that Iran's poor human rights record and regional meddling is the major roadblock in this issue. However, many countries in the MENA have similar records and that has not led Canada to suspend diplomatic relations. Simply put, Iran is an important regional country and Canadian-Iranian people-to-people ties are increasing. There are, as a result, good reasons to re-open the debate about diplomatic relations, even if re-opening embassies remains a decision for another day.

A growing number of Syrians are also living in Canada and between November 2015 and April 2019, 63,938 Syrian refugees were admitted to Canada (Canadian Broadcasting Corporation 2019a). Moving forward, the absence of diplomatic relations with Syria will also impact people-to-people relationships and to a lesser extent, business opportunities. Practically, however, the JVTA stands in the way of re-establishing full diplomatic ties with both Iran and Syria, although something in between could be considered if there is no desire to rescind the JVTA for now. Elsewhere in the MENA, Canada does have a robust footprint with embassies in Algeria, Egypt, Iraq, Israel, Jordan, Kuwait, Lebanon, Libya (the embassy is currently located in Tunisia), Morocco, Qatar, Saudi Arabia (with cross-accreditation to Bahrain, Oman and Yemen), Tunisia, Turkey and the UAE. In addition, and in recognition of trade opportunities, a trade office operates in Erbil, Iraq in the Kurdish Regional Government (KRG) region. The establishment of a trade office in the KRG is an example of a sound forward-leaning policy as the Kurdish population throughout the MENA is increasing as is their economic and political influence.

From a development perspective, the Canadian government has worked hard to alleviate the human suffering brought on by the Syrian civil war and the rise and fall of Daesh. Canada's Middle East Strategy, for example, has committed up to $1.4 billion over five years (2016–2021) to provide governance and community support in Iraq, Jordan, Lebanon and Syria (Canada 2019d). In Yemen, and since 2015, Canada has also provided almost $180 million in humanitarian assistance (Canadian Broadcasting Corporation 2019b). The irony is that Canadian arms exports also go to countries in the MENA who are engaged in various regional proxy wars that have subsequently resulted in the call for increased humanitarian assistance. Nevertheless, when it is in Canada's interests, there is no apparent appetite in Ottawa to end such sales, even to countries with the most appalling human rights records. This is an area where future Canadian governments will need to weigh up the moral implications of providing a region of the world already awash with weapons with even more.

From a Canadian government perspective, the obvious conclusion is to continue treading carefully in the MENA. In the immediate future, the aim should be to extract Canada, militarily, from Iraq, but in good order and having left behind Iraqi security services than can largely function on their own. Canada must also remain mindful that Canadian citizens and businesses are becoming more and more engaged in the MENA while immigrants, political refugees and students flow in the other direction seeking new opportunities here. The January 2019 downing of Ukraine International Airlines Flight 752 in Iran, with fifty-five Canadian citizens and thirty permanent residents aboard, was also a very stark reminder that Canadians do come from, live and also work throughout the MENA. It was also a blunt reminder that not having formal diplomatic relations, as is the case with Iran, often leaves one looking from the outside in.

References

Al Arabiya. 2020. "Coronavirus: Saudi Arabia's $26 bln Spending Cuts Scale Back Vision 2030, Triples VAT." May 11. https://english.alarabiya.net/en/coronavirus/2020/05/11/Coronavirus-Saudi-Arabia-reduces-expenditures-by-100-bln-riyals-to-triple-VAT. Accessed on August 8, 2020.

Amnesty International. 2018. "You Can Now See Your Husband, But There Is Just One Thing—He Is Dead." May 2. https://www.amnesty.ca/blog/%E2%80%9Cyou-can-now-see-your-husband-there-just-one-thing-%E2%80%93he-dead%E2%80%9D. Accessed on April 11, 2020.

Angus Reid. 2018. "Nine-in-Ten Canadians Say 'no' to Future Arms Deals with Saudi Arabia; Divided over Cancelling Current One." November 6. http://angusreid.org/saudi-arabia-canada-khashoggi/. Accessed on August 8, 2020.

Brewster, Murray. 2019. "Canada Risked Losing More Than $7B in Investment over Saudi Spat, Documents Show." *CBC News*, March 15. https://www.cbc.

ca/news/politics/saudi-arabia-canada-direct-investment-1.5057144. Accessed on March 6, 2020.

Brewster, Murray. 2020. "Canada Extends Ban on Arms Sales to NATO Ally Turkey." *CBC News*, April 22. https://www.cbc.ca/news/politics/turkey-can ada-arms-sales-nato-1.5541714. Accessed on April 24, 2020.

Canada-Arab Business Council. 2020. "About Us." https://c-abc.ca/about/. Accessed on March 7, 2020.

Canadian Broadcasting Corporation. 2003. "PM Says 'It's Possible" Canadian Soldiers in Iraq." April 4. https://www.cbc.ca/news/canada/pm-says-it-s-pos sible-canadian-soldiers-in-iraq-1.367559. Accessed on February 21, 2020.

Canadian Broadcasting Corporation. 2017. "Final Tally for Failed Algonquin College Campus Hits $9M." December 12. https://www.cbc.ca/news/canada/ottawa/final-tally-for-failed-algonquin-college-campus-hits-9m-1.444 4412. Accessed on March 7, 2020.

Canadian Broadcasting Corporation 2019a. "Canadians May Not Be as 'Obsessed' over Immigration This Election, But It Remains a Key Issue for Parties." October 7. https://www.cbc.ca/news/canada/british-columbia/ref ugees-2019-election-1.5310154. Accessed on July 2, 2020.

Canadian Broadcasting Corporation. 2019b. "Canada Pledges $47M in Aid at Conference on Yemen." February 26. https://www.cbc.ca/news/world/yemen-aid-pledges-canada-1.5033836. Accessed on April 21, 2020.

Canadian Bureau of International Education. 2020. "The Libyan-North American Scholarship Program." n.d. https://cbie.ca/what-we-do/current-pro grams/libyan-north-american-scholarship/. Accessed on April 27, 2020.

Cape Breton University. 2020. "CIC Cairo." https://www.cbu.ca/future-stu dents/student-services/international-student-services/cic-cairo/. Accessed on July 7, 2020.

Carleton University. 2020. "Canadian International Development Platform—Canada's Foreign Aid, 2019." http://cidpnsi.ca/#analyses. Accessed on July 7, 2020.

Chaziza, Mordechai. 2020. "China's New Silk Road Strategy and the Middle East." *The Begin-Sadat Centre for Strategic Studies*, March 24. https://besace nter.org/perspectives-papers/china-silk-road-middle-east/. Accessed on April 14, 2020.

Clark, Campbell. 2020. "What Does Canada Want in the Middle East? A Hard Month of Diplomacy Has Forced Trudeau to Find Out." *Globe and Mail*, February 1. https://www.theglobeandmail.com/world/article-what-does-canada-want-in-the-middle-east-a-hard-month-of-diplomacy/. Accessed on February 28, 2020.

DeLong, Linwood. 2020. "A Guide to Canadian Diplomatic Relations 1925–2019." *Canadian Global Affairs Institute*, January. https://www.cgai.ca/a_g

uide_to_canadian_diplomatic_relations_1925_2019#Canadian. Accessed on July 2, 2020.

Freedom House. 2019. "Global Freedom Index." https://freedomhouse.org/. Accessed on March 20, 2020.

Global Counterterrorism Forum. 2020. "Structure." https://www.thegctf.org/About-us/Structure. Accessed on July 2, 2020.

Government of Canada. 2005. "Kazemi Case: Minister Pettigrew Makes Chronology of Events Public." June 15. https://www.canada.ca/en/news/archive/2005/06/kazemi-case-minister-pettigrew-makes-chronology-events-public.html. Accessed on April 11, 2020.

Government of Canada. 2012. "Order Establishing a List of Foreign State Supporters of Terrorism, State Immunity Act." September 7. http://www.gazette.gc.ca/rp-pr/p2/2012/2012-09-26/html/sor-dors170-eng.html. Accessed on February 26, 2020.

Government of Canada. 2015. "Justice for Victims of Terrorism." December 2. https://www.publicsafety.gc.ca/cnt/ntnl-scrt/cntr-trrrsm/jstc-vctms-trrrsm-en.aspx. Accessed on February 26, 2020.

Government of Canada. 2018a. "About the Listing Process." February 15. https://www.publicsafety.gc.ca/cnt/ntnl-scrt/cntr-trrrsm/lstd-ntts/bt-lstng-prcss-en.aspx. Accessed on February 27, 2020.

Government of Canada. 2018b. "Canada–Gulf Cooperation Council (GCC) Strategic Dialogue." March 1. https://www.international.gc.ca/world-monde/international_relations-relations_internationales/mena-moan/gcc-can ada-ccg.aspx?lang=eng. Accessed on March 1, 2020.

Government of Canada. 2018c. "Canada to Assume Command of New NATO Training Mission in Iraq." July 11. https://pm.gc.ca/en/news/news-rel eases/2018/07/11/canada-assume-command-new-nato-training-mission-iraq. Accessed on February 21, 2020.

Government of Canada. 2018d. "House of Commons Debates. 42nd Parliament, 1st Session, Edited Hansard Number 312." June 11. https://www.ourcom mons.ca/DocumentViewer/en/42-1/house/sitting-312/hansard. Accessed on July 2, 2020.

Government of Canada. 2018e. "Operation Impact." October 12. https://www.canada.ca/en/department-national-defence/services/operations/military-ope rations/current-operations/operation-impact.html. Accessed on February 21, 2020.

Government of Canada. 2018f. "Operation Lion." December 11. https://www.canada.ca/en/department-national-defence/services/military-history/his tory-heritage/past-operations/middle-east/lion.html. Accessed on February 21, 2020.

Government of Canada. 2019a. "Canada and the Middle East and North Africa." July 25. https://www.international.gc.ca/world-monde/internati

onal_relations-relations_internationales/mena-moan/index.aspx?lang=eng. Accessed on February 29, 2019.

Government of Canada. 2019b. "Canada—Study Permit Holders by Country of Citizenship and Year in Which Permit(s) Became Effective." December. https://open.canada.ca/data/en/dataset/90115b00-f9b8-49e8-afa3-b4cff8facaee. Accessed on February 29, 2020.

Government of Canada. 2019c. "Canada Renews Its Military Contribution to the Multinational Force and Observers in the Sinai Peninsula." April 25. https://www.canada.ca/en/department-national-defence/news/2019/04/canada-renews-its-military-contribution-to-the-multinational-force-and-obs ervers-in-the-sinai-peninsula.html. Accessed on April 13, 2020.

Government of Canada. 2019d. "Canada's Middle East Engagement Strategy." August 22. https://www.international.gc.ca/world-monde/international_r elations-relations_internationales/mena-moan/strategy-strategie.aspx?lang= eng#a1. Accessed on March 1, 2020.

Government of Canada. 2019e. "Currently Listed Entities." June 21. https://www.publicsafety.gc.ca/cnt/ntnl-scrt/cntr-trrrsm/lstd-ntts/crrnt-lstd-ntts-en.aspx. Accessed on February 23, 2020.

Government of Canada. 2019f. "Immigration and Ethnocultural Diversity Highlight Tables." February 20. https://www12.statcan.gc.ca/census-rec ensement/2016/dp-pd/hlt-fst/imm/Table.cfm?Lang=E&T=21&Geo=01& SO=10D. Accessed on March 25, 2020.

Government of Canada. 2019g. "Ken Taylor and the Canadian Caper." June 21. https://www.international.gc.ca/gac-amc/history-histoire/ken-tay lor.aspx?lang=eng. Accessed on February 21, 2020.

Government of Canada. 2019h. "Refugee Claims Statistics." May 22. https://irb-cisr.gc.ca/en/statistics/protection/Pages/index.aspx. Accessed on June 10, 2020.

Government of Canada. 2019i. "Refugee Protection Claims (New System) by Country of Alleged Persecution—2019." February 20. https://www.irb-cisr.gc.ca/en/statistics/protection/Pages/RPDStat2019.aspx. Accessed on March 25, 2020.

Government of Canada. 2020a. "Annual Merchandise Trade." February 25. https://www.international.gc.ca/economist-economiste/statistics-statistiq ues/annual_merchandise_trade-commerce_des_marchandises_annuel.aspx?lan g=eng. Accessed on March 20, 2020.

Government of Canada. 2020b. "Canada-Israel Relations." February 12. https://www.canadainternational.gc.ca/israel/bilateral_relations_bilaterales/index.aspx?lang=eng. Accessed on February 22, 2020.

Government of Canada. 2020c. "Canada-Lebanon Relations." December 27. https://www.international.gc.ca/country-pays/lebanon-liban/relations. aspx?lang=eng#a1. Accessed on February 22, 2020.

Government of Canada. 2020d. "Canada-Libya Relations." March 26. https://www.canadainternational.gc.ca/libya-libye/bilateral_relations_bilaterales/can ada-libya-libye_bu.aspx?lang=eng. Accessed on April 27, 2020.

Government of Canada. 2020e. "Canada-Jordan Relations." January 22. https://www.international.gc.ca/country-pays/jordan-jordanie/relations. aspx?lang=eng#a1. Accessed on February 22, 2020.

Government of Canada. 2020f. "Canada-Kuwait Relations." February 4. https://www.canadainternational.gc.ca/kuwait-koweit/bilateral_relations_ bilaterales/canada-kuwait.aspx?lang=eng. Accessed on February 22, 2020.

Government of Canada. 2020g. "Canada-Qatar Relations." March 12. https://www.canadainternational.gc.ca/qatar/bilateral_relations_bilaterales/index. aspx?lang=eng. Accessed on March 25, 2020.

Government of Canada. 2020h. "Operation IMPACT." https://www.can ada.ca/en/department-national-defence/services/operations/military-operat ions/current-operations/operation-impact.html. Accessed on May 20, 2020.

Government of Canada. 2020i. "Report on Exports of Military Goods from Canada – 2018." February 13. https://www.international.gc.ca/trade-com merce/controls-controles/reports-rapports/military_goods-2018-marchandi ses_militaires.aspx?lang=eng#a6_3. Accessed on April 15, 2020.

Government of Canada. 2020j. "What Is DMTC/MTCP?" February 4. https://www.canada.ca/en/department-national-defence/programs/mil itary-training-cooperation-program/directorate-military-training-cooper ation/what-is-dmtc-mtcp.html. Accessed on April 27, 2020.

Juneau, Thomas. 2019. "A Story of Failed Re-engagement: Canada and Iran, 2015–2018." *Canadian Foreign Policy Journal* 25 (1). https://www.tandfo nline.com/doi/full/10.1080/11926422.2018.1564683.

National Post. 2012. "Foreign Minister John Baird Delivers Scathing Attack on UN Inaction in Syria." October 1. https://nationalpost.com/news/canada/ foreign-minister-john-baird-delivers-scathing-attack-on-un-inaction-in-syria. Accessed on February 21, 2020.

Republic of Turkey. 2020. "Relations Between Turkey and Canada." http://www.mfa.gov.tr/relations-between-turkey-and-canada.en.mfa. Accessed on June 10, 2020.

Roswell, Ben. 2020. "Populist Unilateralism and the Threat to Canadian Power." *Canadian Foreign Policy Journal* 26 (2) March 26, 2020. https://www.tandfonline.com/doi/pdf/10.1080/11926422.2020.1730210?needAc cess=true.

Transparency International. 2020. "2019 Perceptions of Corruption Index." January. https://www.transparency.org/cpi2019?/news/feature/cpi-2019. Accessed on March 20, 2020.

The Global Counterterrorism Forum (GCTF). 2020. "About Us." https://www.thegctf.org/. Accessed on February 26, 2020.

The World Bank. 2019. "Ease of Doing Business Index." https://data.worldb
ank.org/indicator/IC.BUS.EASE.XQ. Accessed on March 20, 2020.
United Nations. 2020. "Troop and Police Contributors." https://peacekeeping.
un.org/en/troop-and-police-contributors. Accessed on July 2, 2020.
University of Calgary in Qatar. 2020. "About Us." https://www.ucalgary.edu.
qa/about-us. Accessed on March 7, 2020.

CHAPTER 10

Justin Trudeau and Institutional Informality: Canada's Response to the COVID-19 Crisis

Michael W. Manulak

INTRODUCTION

The government of Prime Minister Justin Trudeau came into office in 2015 seeking to renew Canada's role on the world stage. At the centre of this commitment was reengagement within multilateral institutions and vocal support for the rules-based international order. The government campaigned for a non-permanent seat on the United Nations (UN) Security Council, recommitted to peace operations, and altered the tone of its participation within international organizations. Its 2017 defence policy review, *Strong, Secure, Engaged*, committed to equipping the Canadian Armed Forces for such a global role (DND 2017) and its feminist international assistance policy provided a point of focus for its international development policies (GAC 2019).

M. W. Manulak (✉)
Norman Paterson School of International Affairs, Carleton University, Ottawa, ON, Canada
e-mail: michael.manulak@carleton.ca

© The Author(s), under exclusive license to Springer Nature Switzerland AG 2021
D. Carment and R. Nimijean (eds.), *Political Turmoil in a Tumultuous World*, Canada and International Affairs,
https://doi.org/10.1007/978-3-030-70686-9_10

211

This approach was challenged fundamentally by the election of U.S. President Donald Trump in 2016. The president's "America First" approach to the world shook the assumptions upon which the Trudeau government's foreign policy was based. Deepening U.S. geopolitical rivalry with China and ongoing tensions with Russia produced a global landscape that was defined increasingly by great power competition. A more assertive China and a revanchist Russia further complicated Canada's multilateral equation. This competition manifested itself within many of the institutions that Canada prioritized in its multilateral engagements. The rapidly changing global context triggered a rethink about the means available to realizing its commitment to foster international cooperation.

Geopolitical shifts led the government—more than any preceding it—to embrace informal international institutions as a means of addressing key global challenges and reinforcing the broader international order. In global crises, less formal institutional arrangements offer numerous comparative advantages relative to formal intergovernmental organizations, including flexibility and a capacity for rapid policy coordination. The government's embrace of such institutions was on full display in Canada's diplomatic response to the COVID-19 pandemic in late 2019 and early 2020. The use of informal mechanisms, such as the Ministerial Coordination Group on COVID-19, highlights this distinctive aspect of the government's foreign policy.

This chapter explains the increased Canadian use of informal international institutions in the current global context. After introducing the subject, I provide background on the international crisis sparked by COVID-19, examining the cooperative challenge posed by the pandemic and the difficulties that many international institutions faced in tackling them. Focusing on their flexibility, I discuss the reasons why informal modes of cooperation emerged as an instrument of choice in dealing with the pandemic. I conclude with a discussion of implications for Canada's international policies.

INFORMAL INSTITUTIONS AND CANADIAN FOREIGN POLICY

Informal international institutions are defined by the non-binding nature of commitments undertaken within them and by the absence of formal organizational structures, such as secretariats and headquarters. While they date back at least to the Congress of Vienna, informal international institutions have grown in prevalence since the 1990s. The number of these bodies has more than quadrupled since that time, all while the number of formal intergovernmental organizations has plateaued—or even declined—in the new millennium (Abbott et al. 2018; Berridge 2015: 181; Vabulas and Snidal 2013). In addition to their prevalence, these institutions have grown in prominence, with formats such as the G20 and the BRICS serving as highly-visible centres of global governance.

Lowered start-up costs for international association and technological improvements have enabled a form of *multilateralism à la carte*, whereby coalitions of relevant actors come together to address specific cooperative challenges in well-defined issue areas (Patrick 2015). This dynamic has given rise to new strategic multilateral dynamics, where focal institutions can be bypassed for more appealing alternatives. In some cases, regime shifting or competitive regime creation results (Morse and Keohane 2014). Leading states may also engage in competitive multilateralism as a means of disciplining allies and partners (Belo and Carment 2020). Such strategies may also be used to overcome or circumvent domestic opposition (Kaye 2013).

In addition to the G20 and the well-established G7, the Canadian government has been an active participant in dozens of informal fora. In the non-proliferation space alone, Canada participates in, among others, the Proliferation Security Initiative, the Global Initiative to Combat Nuclear Terrorism, and the Global Partnership Against the Spread of Weapons and Materials of Mass Destruction. These institutions supplement Canada's heavy participation in the export control regimes, including the Nuclear Suppliers Group and Australia Group. Informal cooperation occurs at a high political level, such as within Informal Intergovernmental Organizations (Vabulas and Snidal 2013), at lower, more technical levels, through Trans-Governmental Networks (Raustiala 2002; Slaughter 2004), and through other, less conventional forms of collaboration, such as international public-private partnerships and consortia.

The Trudeau government has embraced informal modes of cooperation more aggressively than past governments, playing a prominent convening role within such institutions. In 2017, the government helped to catalyse the creation of the Lima Group to tackle the political and economic crisis in Venezuela. The Group brought twelve countries together to produce the Lima Declaration, furthering hemispheric policy cooperation in support of a peaceful exit to the Venezuelan crisis.[1] In early 2020, the government spearheaded a five-country International Coordination and Response Group to push for a full and transparent investigation into the causes of the Flight PS752 tragedy. In that context, Prime Minister Trudeau announced the Safer Skies Strategy to establish a common set of practices to protect passengers flying in or near conflict zones. Canada has been an active participant within the recently launched Alliance for Multilateralism. In addition, the Trudeau government has heightened its engagement within existing informal fora, including the aforementioned Proliferation Security Initiative, where it spearheaded an institutional modernization effort from 2015 to 2017 (Manulak, forthcoming).

Commitments made within these institutional settings are political in nature, typically taking the form of declarations or joint statements. While these commitments do not have the force of international law, they are taken seriously by participating states and result in broad-based coordination of national policies. Institutions can be tailored to particular global challenges and, given their light organizational footprint, can entail fewer costs. The prevalence of such institutions is explained also by vast improvements in Information, Communication, and Transportation Technologies (Manulak and Snidal 2021). In the case of the Trudeau government, the embrace of institutional informality is explained by the comparative advantages of such mechanisms, as well as a need to adapt to changed geopolitical realities.

PANDEMIC POLITICS AND THE LAW OF THE JUNGLE

As the pandemic caused by the novel coronavirus reached Canada in early 2020, states restricted international travel and hardened borders. Many countries came to recognize the limits of their emergency preparedness, including insufficient stockpiles of personal protective equipment and the vulnerability entailed in their reliance on global supply chains. As a result, many governments introduced unilateral measures to limit

---

[1] In the case of the Lima Group, the effort was supported by the United States. While the United States has not participated in several informal institutions, it has been a heavy participant in many such efforts. The United States, for example, is a leading player in all of the informal counter-proliferation bodies described in this chapter.

the export of critical supplies. The nationalist reflex was reinforced by growing talk of the need to restrict trade and investment as a means of reducing vulnerability to "foreign" contagions and threats.

Leading commentators reflected on how the crisis would accelerate the shift to "globalization 2.0," where world political and economic integration would be highly fragmented, or generate outright "de-globalization" (Kaplan 2020; Haass 2020). In this world, pockets of economic and military integration might emerge, where allies collaborate closely and exclude rival blocs. States would rebuild predominantly *national* economies, not globally-integrated ones (Wright 2020). In this environment, the state apparatus would re-emerge as the principal vehicle for securing national welfare, even if this would result in a world that is "less open, less prosperous, less free" (Walt 2020). In Canada, prominent observers questioned the wisdom of multi-country supply chains and advocated measures to increase national self-sufficiency (Burney 2020; MacKay 2020).

The uncooperative international reflex was reinforced and exacerbated by a thoroughly "America first" response to the crisis in Washington. In closing its borders to European travellers, for instance, the United States did not consult its allies beforehand. Rumours also circulated early in the crisis that the Trump administration sought to leverage the American ties of a German vaccine-developer to secure first access to any vaccine. The implications of the American response were made salient in Ottawa when the Trump administration acted to disrupt the export to Canada of urgently-needed N95 medical masks in early April 2020, a measure that was preceded by talk of stationing American troops along the Canada-U.S. border. These steps were coupled with a U.S. national response that was widely panned as slow and inadequate. Such U.S. actions led some to call for a reassessment of the Canada-U.S. relationship (Nimijean and Carment 2020).[2] Talks also emerged within the North Atlantic Treaty Organization and the Five Eyes intelligence community on the need to enhance economic security through reduced reliance on Chinese trade and investment.

U.S. diplomatic engagement was no more cooperative. The main thrust of U.S. diplomacy through the first half of 2020 was the attribution

---

[2] For a further analysis of the Canada-U.S. relations in the era of Donald Trump, see Hillmer and Lagaassé (2018) and Nimijean (2019).

of blame for the pandemic on Chinese mismanagement and the suggestion that the virus originated at a Chinese lab. Progress on a UN Security Council resolution and a G7 statement was obstructed by U.S. insistence that the resulting texts refer to a "China virus" or a "Wuhan virus." The administration engaged in increasingly divisive rhetoric vis-à-vis China and sought to accelerate Sino-American economic "de-coupling." The Chinese response also left much to be desired. After attempting to cover up the initial outbreak, Chinese government officials suggested that the virus originated from a U.S. military visit to China in fall 2019. Numerous Chinese diplomats indulged in a nationalist brand of "wolf warrior" diplomacy, using Beijing's economic leverage to bully and intimidate those who criticized China's response to the crisis. Touting itself as a leader in the global response, the government exported medical equipment internationally and clumsily insisted on significant fanfare when the supply shipments were received.

A lack of leadership among the world's two leading powers manifested itself in competition within international organizations, with unfortunate results for the global response to the pandemic. Within the World Health Organization (WHO), the most critical vehicle for generating cooperative global action on the pandemic, China flexed its political muscle to secure a deferential response from global health officials. The visibility and extent of Chinese influence led some observers to dub the UN agency the "Chinese Health Organization." In April 2020, President Trump called for the suspension of funding to the WHO until an inquiry had been conducted into its reaction to the crisis and, a month later, announced his intention to withdraw the United States from the organization altogether. At least politically, this great power tussle overshadowed the organization's activities and deprived the agency of funding when those funds were most needed.

Canada's Global Interests

The overwhelmingly nationalist response to the crisis within many countries threatened Canada's global interests. The pandemic presented policymakers with a classic interdependence problem. Any effective response would need to be a global one. The pandemic could not be contained within national borders, no matter how thick. In this respect, the spread of COVID-19 was not dissimilar to other transnational problems, such as climate change or internet governance. Even if Canadians were vaccinated, the country would be threatened by the persistence of the virus in any corner of the globe. In addition to the health consequences, the breakdown of global supply chains for critical health materials limited the efforts of many governments to contain the virus' spread. Such a self-defeating possibility undermined global action.

The pandemic also badly hurt the Canadian economy, particularly due to the effects of nationally-mandated social distancing and the shutdown of businesses. Unemployment soared and government expenditures to keep the economy afloat escalated rapidly. The national debt ballooned. The impulse among some countries to de-globalize their economies, furthermore, threatened the country's longer-term economic recovery. This was especially so in the context of a sustained assault in the years preceding the pandemic by the Trump administration on the World Trade Organization (WTO) and global trading norms. The ongoing and future prosperity of Canadians relied on the international community's ability to re-constitute the global trading system after the pandemic. Canada had an interest in ensuring that economic measures instituted in response to the pandemic—particularly in the United States—were temporary, proportionate, non-discriminatory, and absolutely necessary. Canada's economic security was, the government maintained, enhanced when its trading relations were integrated into an international framework of rules, norms, and institutions.

As the virus spread through the Global South, where the capacity of public authorities and health systems was more limited, the potential social and political implications were even more far-reaching. In fragile states, a public health emergency had the potential to fuel instability. Political upheaval and conflict could further sap government capacity and undermine efforts to contain the virus. Export restrictions, the virtual shutdown of global tourism, and a freefall in commodity prices led to economic hardship and the depletion of scarce foreign currency reserves. Menacingly, certain governments also seized on the pandemic as a reason to enhance surveillance and monitoring systems over their own populations and to curtail rights of public assembly. The weakening of liberal democratic norms and institutions was a significant Canadian concern. In Canada and throughout the world, the pandemic contributed to increases in gender-based violence and had a substantial, differentiated impact on racialized communities.

Canada's extensive global interests led it to favour a concerted multilateral response. Yet the international bodies that could facilitate such a response faced significant hurdles to action. Sino-American rivalry in the context of the G20 and the UN Security Council, in particular, rendered cooperation in those crucial fora underwhelming or altogether absent. The activities of the WHO in tackling the crisis, already constrained by resource limitations, were politicized by the great power competition. In addition to suspending its funding and announcing its intention to withdraw from the organization, the United States insisted on a review of the WHO's response to the pandemic at the height of the crisis. This action, many argued, diverted attention from the organization's activities at a moment when a singular focus was most necessary. Owing to shifting power configurations, it became clear that many existing international institutions would face great difficulty in responding to the pandemic.

Even in the absence of institutional dysfunction, the cooperation problem facing states was considerable. This was an incredibly fast-moving crisis, involving a novel virus that was highly contagious. Within weeks of confirmed human-to-human transmission, the virus had spread internationally causing a public health emergency in dozens of countries. Individual governments responded rapidly and in a largely uncoordinated fashion in an attempt to protect their populations. The nature of the problem, therefore, demanded rapid intergovernmental policy coordination that would have been a challenge, even for well-functioning institutions.

Flexibility was also at a premium, particularly in terms of institutional participation, scope, and decision-making. The fast-moving pandemic created a need for cooperation that engaged a broad array of states in collective efforts to tackle the problem. It also necessitated the exclusion of prominent spoiler states that had prevented action in other fora. Flexibility in terms of institutional scope was necessary, given the unique and constantly-evolving social, political, and economic dimensions of the issue. Fruitful collaboration needed to occur to facilitate the repatriation of citizens abroad, the re-establishment of global supply chains, the exchange of public health best practices, and the need to support less-developed countries. Institutional mechanisms to tackle such a broad-ranging cooperative challenge, therefore, needed to accommodate multiple salient dimensions of the issue as they emerged. Established, formal organizations with their legally-entrenched mandates and decision-rules provided less flexibility in such a dynamic and uncertain environment. High uncertainty also made flexibility in decision-making procedures crucial.

EMBRACING INFORMALITY: THE MINISTERIAL COORDINATION GROUP ON COVID-19 AND OTHER INFORMAL ACTIVITIES

In the wake of the crisis, with borders closing and global supply chains breaking down, governments faced immediate difficulties repatriating their citizens abroad and securing the necessary medical equipment to protect their populations. No institutional machinery existed that might bring key states together to tackle multiple dimensions of the fast-moving crisis, especially with the G20 route obstructed by Chinese-American muscle-flexing. Other institutions did not have a broad enough scope to address effectively the set of issues posed by the pandemic.

To counter this cooperative challenge, Canada emerged as a leader in convening what came to be known as the Ministerial Coordination Group on COVID-19 (MCGC). The institution grew out of a series of bilateral telephone discussions that Canada's foreign minister, François-Philippe Champagne, held primarily to facilitate the repatriation of citizens abroad. On 15 March, Champagne expanded the format to include the foreign ministers of Australia, Brazil, Germany, Italy, and South Korea (GAC 2020f). Two further discussions were held within a week of that first call, expanding participation to include Morocco, Peru, Turkey, and the United Kingdom, as well as representatives from the European Union (GAC 2020d, e). Early discussions focused principally on the sharing of best practices in crisis response and on coordination of complex repatriation cases. The Canadian-convened forum gathered momentum leading to the expansion of institutional scope to include more far-reaching dialogue on the growing threat to global supply chains.

As discussion became more structured, working-level calls were added to the MCGC format to complement those occurring at the ministerial level. Michael Grant, Assistant Deputy Minister for the Americas at Global Affairs Canada, served as the lead on the Canadian side. In the first days of April, working-level conversations produced draft principles focused on the maintenance of effective global links. On 17 April, fourteen ministers approved the principles, committing to policy coordination in an effort to keep transportation ties and supply chains open (GAC 2020b). The principles were made more impactful by the continued expansion of the MCGC's membership to include states that housed critical shipping and transportation hubs, including France, Indonesia, Singapore, and South Africa. Combined with existing hub states, including Italy, South Korea, and the United Kingdom, the MCGC membership now featured vital links within global transportation and supply chains. The MCGC's remit expanded to include strong statements on the need to support vulnerable countries, including those in Africa, as well as small island developing states. While there were some differences in the degree of confidence governments were willing to express in the WHO, the declaration voiced support for multilateral institutions.

A chief virtue of the MCGC format was the flexibility that derived from its institutional informality. The capacity to expand participation as the mechanism matured, encompassing a regionally-representative and globally-influential set of states, helped to enhance the efficacy and influence of the MCGC. In addition, as the problems facing participating states evolved, the scope of discussion broadened. The ability to add issues and players to the work of the Group advanced shared interests. In an institutional setting so rife with uncertainty, flexibility was highly important. In addition, the capacity to move swiftly to facilitate coordination was vital. Within a month of launching the MCGC, deliberations had produced a set of principles that articulated shared objectives to guide intergovernmental action as well as more than a dozen ministerial meetings. In the world of high-level diplomacy, this is a significant achievement.

The membership of the MCGC is notable, also, for the absence of U.S. participation. Indeed, the MCGC discussions emerged following G7 and G20 meetings that failed to result in agreement on joint actions. Given the lack of alignment between MCGC states and U.S. policy, this is perhaps unsurprising. Senior U.S. policymakers viewed the crisis as an accelerant for U.S. efforts, already underway, to bring manufacturing jobs "back" to America and de-couple the U.S. and Chinese economies (Lighthizer 2020). Such an approach is, in key respects, the antithesis of the MCGC's policy thrust. While U.S. Secretary of State Mike Pompeo was invited to participate in the teleconferences, U.S. involvement was not seen as a precondition for proceeding with the initiative and may have even been regarded as an obstacle to productive discussions. In any event, Pompeo showed little interest in joining.

Another notable feature of the MCGC story is the role of Information and Communications Technologies in fostering effective and rapid coordination among international actors. Although many ministers had pre-existing ties, participants initially coordinated their efforts and discussions via a series of text messages sent by the Canadian foreign minister. This "SMS diplomacy," as it was dubbed by Champagne, is reflective of the pervasive role of new technology in modern statecraft. An institutional forum came into being without governments ever coming physically together. Put into the context of international relations history, this is a remarkable—and perhaps unprecedented—development. Such an informal mode of interactions, moreover, stripped intergovernmental relations of the formality that normally accompanies discussions at a high political level.[3] By disintermediating these interactions, minimizing the role of bureaucratic players and formal protocols, agreements could be made with greater speed and adaptability.

The MCGC was not the only informal institutional effort in which Canada was involved. The Alliance for Multilateralism, originally spearheaded by France and Germany alongside the UN General Assembly in September 2019, promotes multilateral cooperation and reinforces the rules-based international order. Canada has played a leadership role within the Alliance, serving as one of seven "co-hosts" of the 66-country effort. The Alliance held a virtual meeting in May 2020 and 54 participating states endorsed a joint declaration on COVID-19 (AA 2020). The declaration underlined the need for governments to support the multilateral order in responding to the crisis, making particular reference to the need to back the WHO and other UN agencies during the pandemic. While the principles endorsed through the MCGC and the Alliance for Multilateralism had some overlap, particularly regarding the need to ensure that measures disrupting global supply chains were temporary, proportionate, and non-discriminatory, they were complementary in key respects. The MCGC principles were of a more pragmatic quality, focused on concrete ways of keeping key global transportation and trade hubs open during the crisis. The Alliance declaration was of a more political character, parrying attacks on key multilateral norms and institutions.

---

[3] Bilateral discussions, even relatively brief ones via telephone, will often entail the preparation of a briefing binder with background information and points to register. When Foreign Ministers interact on an almost impromptu basis, these types of preparations are impossible.

Throughout the crisis, Canadian officials also continued their participation in trans-governmental networks. International networks of medical regulators were particularly active during the crisis. The International Coalition of Medicines Regulatory Authorities (ICMRA), an executive-level network comprised of 29 national regulatory agencies, engaged via teleconference to further regulatory standards related to clinical trials for COVID-19 treatments and vaccines. To further this effort, the ICMRA agreed on a joint statement outlining a series of regulatory recommendations and joint actions (IMCRA 2020). In addition, Canadian health regulators engaged heavily on emerging scientific and health regulatory issues within the Australia-Canada-Singapore-Switzerland consortium and through multilateral "cluster" meetings with international partners, including the U.S. Food and Drug Administration and the European Medicines Agency. Experts connected through their work on Action Packages as a part of the Global Health Security Agenda (GHSA), a multinational initiative, collaborated in the sharing of best practices related to laboratories, quarantine, supplies, contract-tracing, and vital research (GHSA 2020). Canada occupied a rotating seat on the Steering Group for the GHSA in 2019–2020.

Canada also gave significant emphasis to informal collaborations involving private and non-governmental players. Canada committed $40 million in support of the Coalition for Epidemic Preparedness Innovations (CEPI), an informal international initiative emerging from the World Economic Forum, in support of research on a vaccine (GAC 2020a). On 12 May, Canada committed $600 million towards a third replenishment of Global Alliance for Vaccines and Immunization (GAVI) (GAC 2020c). GAVI, a public-private global health partnership touted for being less bureaucratic than traditional intergovernmental organizations, played a central role in mobilizing vaccine research and in distributing information concerning the pandemic. In September 2020, the government committed $220 million to the COVAX facility, helping to support global vaccine development and distribution (PMO 2020). These substantial financial commitments, made in a coordinated fashion with Canada's international partners, aimed to accelerate health research addressing the pandemic.

Although Canada engaged heavily in informal international institutions, this does not suggest that it was less committed to cooperation within formal intergovernmental organizations. Indeed, the government was a vocal and active supporter of these organizations. Canada backed the UN Secretary-General's call for a global ceasefire amid the pandemic (GAC 2020g). The government announced substantial funding commitments for the humanitarian activities of UN agencies, including the WHO, the World Food Programme, and the UN High Commissioner for Refugees (GAC 2020a). The government also worked extensively to reinforce politically the position of the WTO, challenged by the introduction of discriminatory trade measures in response to the pandemic. A substantial portion of this support was given expression through informal groupings and coalitions, including the MCGC and the Alliance for Multilateralism. Efforts to back the UN Secretary-General's call for a global ceasefire were coordinated through the informal Group of Friends of Children and Armed Conflict and the Group of Friends of the Protection of Civilians (GAC 2020h). Similarly, Canada co-chaired the United Nations Group of Friends of the Sustainable Development Goals financing. Canada also spearheaded the informal, 12-country "Ottawa Group" to strengthen and modernize the WTO.

DISCUSSION

In a fast-moving and uncertain global environment, impacted heavily by great power competition, the government of Justin Trudeau has embraced institutional informality as a means of advancing its interests in international cooperation. This approach was on full display following the outbreak of COVID-19 pandemic, when the government used informal international institutions as a means of reinforcing a global order under strain. While the Trudeau government has employed informal institutions more than its predecessors, international relations scholars note that the prevalence and prominence of these institutions have been a longer-term trend in world politics. Employing new communication technologies, states choose informal mechanisms because of their flexibility and adaptability relative to formal intergovernmental bodies.

This trend is likely to be accelerated by two large-scale, system-level changes currently afoot. First, geopolitical competition between the United States and China will make the prospects for productive cooperation within many established formal international organizations less certain and more political than in the recent past. This dynamic was seen during the COVID-19 pandemic when the world's two leading states clashed in the context of the WHO, affecting the organization's capacity for action. Even with a more cooperative administration in the

White House, this type of institutional dysfunction is likely to become a persistent feature of the international environment in the medium to longer term. As a consequence, coalitions of states will have an interest in banding together in informal groupings to fill governance gaps. Cooperation in the "post-American world" could thus become more varied and less universal than the modes of governance preceding it.[4]

Second, in the post-COVID-19 world, where states have been forced to make unprecedented use of online tools to achieve policy coordination at a distance, it is probable that less-centralized modes of cooperation will become more prevalent. Formal intergovernmental bodies, with their heavy emphasis on in-person meetings of permanent missions based at geographic hubs, may be slower to adapt to this changed reality than informal institutions with their less-centralized institutional logic and cooperative architecture. The rise of informal institutions in recent years has, to a considerable extent, relied on the availability of new information, communication, and transportation technologies to facilitate a mode of cooperation predicated heavily on the capacity of national government officials based in capitals to interact in a decentralized fashion. Thus, the ethos of informal institutions may be better-suited to the post-COVID-19 forms of international organization.

While informal institutions are likely to continue their growing role in world politics, it is important to note that formal organizations will nevertheless continue to occupy a central place in the international landscape. In contexts where an international legal foundation and enforcement mechanisms are important to enabling cooperation; for example, informal institutions offer fewer comparative advantages. Indeed, a significant proportion of the Trudeau government's embrace of institutional informality has been oriented towards supporting formal organizations, such as the WTO and those of the UN system. Thus, rather than being competitive with formal mechanisms, informal cooperation can complement and orchestrate the work of more formal venues. Synergies can emerge. Key to comprehending the shifting mode of cooperation, therefore, is understanding the interplay between these two institutional forms.

The increasing informal design of international institutions and the interplay of these institutions with established intergovernmental organizations have important implications for Canadian diplomacy. The mode

---

[4] Peter Boehm (2020) has noted that the pandemic has demonstrated the viability of virtual modes of diplomacy that may continue following the pandemic.

of intergovernmental interaction in these settings is distinct from that seen within more formal bodies. Informal forms of cooperation tend to be less centralized and hierarchical than formal ones. Absent an organizational headquarters and the centralizing role played by secretariats and permanent missions interacting in close physical proximity, relations within informal institutions are conducted primarily among dispersed officials based in national capitals using modern communication technologies.[5] Despite significant advances, online platforms and video-teleconferencing remain unwieldy and difficult to manage as the number of participants increases. Indeed, within the MCGC, Canada excluded certain states from the initiative in view of the need to keep calls manageable and productive. Thus, the impulse to include actors is weighed constantly against the necessity of limiting participation as a matter of practicality. Even in the context of a multilateral institution, therefore, these decentralized interactions frequently take on a bilateral or plurilateral character.

The mode of cooperation within informal institutions thus has a networked quality, with officials engaged in an ongoing and more free-flowing set of interactions. A large proportion of these discussions include only subsets of international actors, meaning that decisions surrounding exclusion/inclusion regularly shape states' capacity for influence. Those that are influential are positioned at the centre of intergovernmental networks, by virtue of the number of direct connections they enjoy or their capacity to broker subsections of the institutional population. Actors at the centre of intergovernmental networks exercise influence by virtue of their position within the wider social structure. For example, they may enjoy asymmetries of information, benefit from superior go-it-alone power, or are positioned to gatekeep (Manulak 2019).

Canada's use of institutional informality is illustrative of these dynamics. In convening the MCGC, Canada positioned itself at the centre of a consequential intergovernmental network in responding to a significant global threat facing the international community. Canada's foreign minister served as the chief point of connection between a diverse

---

[5] This does not suggest that informal institutions do not feature in-person meetings. Most hold in-person meetings at regular intervals (often, on an annual basis) to exchange information and take decisions. At the same time, a large proportion of "intersessional" interactions are conducted via email and telephone from national capitals. Relative to formal international organizations with permanent missions based in close physical proximity to each other and to intergovernmental bodies, the proportion of in-person interactions is lower.

and influential subset of international actors. The Canadian initiative was preceded and complemented by a series of bilateral telephone discussions at the foreign minister level. Canada appears to have exercised a high degree of what social network analysts call network centrality, positioning itself as a point of connection among a set of international actors that were less well-connected. Given the multi-dimensional nature of the COVID-19 issue, furthermore, Canada was positioned as a point of connection between multiple issue networks, including those related to global trade, support for the wider multilateral system, and those concerned with border policies.

Canada's role at the hub of the MCGC process positioned it to exercise greater influence on intergovernmental relations. Having interacted with dozens of states, both via telephone and text messaging in the early stages of the pandemic, the minister had good information on the attitudes and positions of key states within the international system. In establishing the MCGC, Canada was able to decide which states would be invited to participate in the process and which would not receive an invitation. Both increased the likelihood of productive conversations by including states with compatible views and excluding potential spoilers. The latter group may have included Canada's southern neighbour. By virtue of the need to keep calls manageable and productive, Canada excluded other states from the process as well. In addition, as the MCGC gained momentum, Canada was positioned to agenda-set. As convenor of the calls, Canada set the agenda, determining which issues would be discussed. In doing so, the government was able to ensure that the forum aligned well with Canada's crisis management priorities.

Network position can, however, constrain as much as it empowers (Kahler 2009: 5). While Canada has amplified its influence and advanced its interests through its engagement in informal—as well as formal—institutions, it is also restrained somewhat by these ties. Canada's deep links with the United States, for example, influence Sino-Canadian relations. As Dani Belo and David Carment (2020) show, moreover, the United States may use multilateral alliances to discipline potential defectors and extract relative gains. In this way, prior relational choices can have persistent effects.

The longer-term impact of the MCGC process and Canada's embrace of institutional informality are more difficult to discern. The diplomatic outputs of the effort, measured in terms of the number of meetings and joint statements, furthering policy coordination, are evident. More complicated is assessing the impact of such coordination in shaping the behaviour of international actors outside of the MCGC circle. Did agreement among 14 states influence the policies and attitudes of a wider subsection of the international population in a manner that furthered Canada's global interests, for example? Did the agreement among a coalition of states featuring important international shipping and transportation hubs play an important part in reinforcing global links and quickly re-establishing supply chains? Were these activities constrained in any major way by existing relations, including close Canada-U.S. ties? Did these efforts have a normative impact, de-legitimizing protectionist and xenophobic national responses in other countries? It is similarly difficult to determine the precise impact of these efforts on Canada's main international priorities, such as its unsuccessful campaign for a non-permanent seat on the UN Security Council and its efforts to modernize the WTO. Notwithstanding these open questions, which can only be better answered with the passage of time, it is clear that—by virtue of its position within intergovernmental networks—Canada was able to exercise influence over the international response to COVID-19 pandemic.

CONCLUSION

As a response to a complex and uncertain international environment, the government of Justin Trudeau embraced informal institutionalism. Perhaps more than any preceding it, the Trudeau government capitalized on the flexibility and speed enabled by informal institutions to fill governance gaps created in large part by an unpredictable and uncooperative U.S. administration. These efforts aimed not just at furthering policy coordination, but sought to advance Canada's global interests by reinforcing key norms, rules, and institutions. Notwithstanding greater U.S. diplomatic support for key formal international organizations, institutional informality is likely to continue under the new administration of president-elect Joe Biden. Indeed, growth of informal international institutions was a prominent feature throughout Biden's term as vice-president from 2009 to 2017.

This approach was evident in Canada's response to the COVID-19 pandemic, where the government engaged actively in informal international institutions as a means of addressing a fast-moving and dangerous global crisis. The government played a catalytic role in the creation of the Ministerial Coordination Group on COVID-19, supported the efforts of the Alliance for Multilateralism, and participated in numerous transgovernmental networks of medical regulators. The MCGC effort, in particular, helped to mobilize an international coalition of states representing key global hubs for shipping and transportation. Canada's foray into "designer multilateralism" furthered its efforts to prevent a breakdown of global supply chains, so critical both to the immediate response to the crisis and to the country's longer-term economic recovery. Rather than competing with the activities of formal intergovernmental organizations, moreover, a large proportion of these efforts sought to support work underway within these bodies.

This chapter has further argued that the increasingly informal design of international institutions is likely to be a continuing feature of the international environment. Sino-American competition and advancements in the use of Information and Communications Technologies, two phenomena that have been accelerated by the pandemic, are likely to increase the role of informal institutions in world politics going forward. The implications of these developments for foreign policymaking and diplomacy are considerable. Given the free-flowing and decentralized nature of cooperation in informal institutional contexts, states seeking to exercise international influence aim to position themselves at the centre of intergovernmental networks. The forms of influence conferred by network centrality can be seen in Canada's MCGC diplomacy, where it was positioned to control access to this forum and exercise agenda-setting power.

Acknowledgements I am grateful to David Carment and Richard Nimijean for their excellent work in editing this volume and their constructive comments on this chapter, as well as to Kaia Counter for terrific research assistance throughout. I'd also like to thank the public servants that contributed confidential insights to help inform the research contained in this chapter.

References

Abbott, Kenneth W., Céline Kauffmann, and Jeong-Rim Lee. 2018. "The Contribution of Trans-Governmental Networks to International Regulatory Co-operation." OECD Regulatory Policy Working Papers, No. 10.

Belo, Dani, and David Carment. 2020. "Unilateralism and Competitive Multilateralism in Gray-zone Conflict: A Comparison of Russia and the United States." Air University, August 3. https://www.airuniversity.af.edu/Wild-Blue-Yonder/Article-Display/Article/2292990/unilateralism-and-com petitive-multilateralism-in-gray-zone-conflict-a-compariso/. Accessed on October 17, 2020.

Berridge, G.R. 2015. *Diplomacy: Theory and Practice*. London: Palgrave Macmillan.

Boehm, Peter M. 2020. "Is Zoom Diplomacy the New Normal? COVID-19 and the End of the Air Kiss." *Policy*, May 21. https://policymagazine.ca/is-zoom-diplomacy-the-new-normal-covid-19-and-the-end-of-the-air-kiss/. Accessed on July 17, 2020.

Burney, Derek H. 2020. "Derek H. Burney: Greater self-reliance will be an absolute necessity post-COVID-19." National Post. 16 April. https://nation alpost.com/opinion/derek-h-burney-greater-self-reliance-will-be-an-absolute-necessity-post-covid-19.

Department of National Defence (DND). "Strong, Secure, Engaged." Government of Canada. 2017. http://dgpaapp.forces.gc.ca/en/canada-defence-pol icy/docs/canada-defence-policy-report.pdf.

German Federal Foreign Office (AA). 2020. "We Need Strong Global Cooperation and Solidarity to Fight COVID-19, Joint Declaration of the Alliance for Multilateralism." https://www.auswaertiges-amt.de/en/newsroom/news/all iance-multilateralism-covid19/2333394. Accessed on May 26, 2020.

Global Affairs Canada (GAC). 2019. *Canada's Feminist International Assistance Policy*. Ottawa: Global Affairs Canada.

GAC. 2020a. "Backgrounder- Canada Provides Funding to Address COVID-19 Pandemic." Government of Canada, April 5. https://www.canada.ca/en/glo bal-affairs/news/2020/04/backgrounder---canada-provides-funding-to-add ress-covid-19-pandemic.html.

GAC. 2020b. "Declaration of the Ministerial Coordination Group on COVID-19 on Maintaining Essential Global Link." Government of Canada, April 17. https://www.canada.ca/en/global-affairs/news/2020/04/declaration-of-the-ministerial-coordination-group-on-covid19covid19-on-maintaining-ess ential-global-links.html.

GAC. 2020c. "Minister Gould Announces Funding for Global Vaccinations." Government of Canada, May 12. https://www.canada.ca/en/global-affairs/news/2020/05/minister-gould-announces-funding-for-global-vaccinations.html.

GAC. 2020d. "Readout: Minister of Foreign Affairs Continues Dialogue with International Partners on Respective Situations and Responses to COVID-19." Government of Canada, March 19. https://www.canada.ca/en/glo bal-affairs/news/2020/03/readout-minister-of-foreign-affairs-continues-dia logue-with-international-partners-on-respective-situations-and-responses-to-covid-19.html.

GAC. 2020e. "Readout: Minister of Foreign Affairs Continues to Coordinate with International Partners on Respective Situations and Responses to

COVID-19." Government of Canada, March 21. https://www.canada.ca/
en/global-affairs/news/2020/03/readout-minister-of-foreign-affairs-contin
ues-to-coordinate-with-international-partners-on-respective-situations-and-res
ponses-to-covid-190.html.

GAC. 2020f. "Readout: Minister of Foreign Affairs Speaks with Counterparts
from COVID-19-Affected Countries." Government of Canada, March 15.
https://www.canada.ca/en/global-affairs/news/2020/03/readout-minister-
of-foreign-affairs-speaks-with-counterparts-from-covid-19-affected-countries.
html.

GAC. 2020g. "Statement in Support of Global Ceasefire." Government of
Canada, April 10. https://www.canada.ca/en/global-affairs/news/2020/
04/statement-in-support-of-global-ceasefire.html.

GAC. 2020h. "Statement on Behalf of 59 Countries in Their National Capacity
and as Members of the Group of Friends of Women, Peace and Security,
the Group of Friends of Children and Armed Conflict and/or the Group of
Friends of the Protection of Civilians – Amended." Government of Canada,
March 30. https://www.international.gc.ca/world-monde/international_rela
tions-relations_internationales/un-onu/statements-declarations/2020-03-30-
53-countries-pays.aspx?lang=eng.

Global Health Security Agenda. 2020. "Chair's Statement," March 17. https://
ghsagenda.org/2020/03/17/covid-19-chairs-statement-what-is-the-role-of-
ghsa2024-in-this-pandemic/. Accessed on May 26, 2020.

Haass, Richard N. 2020. "Deglobalization and its Discontents." *Project
Syndicate*. 12 May. https://www.project-syndicate.org/commentary/deglob
alizaton-discontents-by-richard-n-haass-2020-05?barrier=accesspaylog.

Hillmer, Norman, and Philippe Lagassé. 2018. "The Age of Trump and
Trudeau." In *Justin Trudeau and Canadian Foreign Policy*, edited by Norman
Hillmer and Philippe Lagassé, 1–16. Cham: Palgrave-Macmillan.

International Coalition of Medicines Regulatory Authorities. 2020. "ICMRA
Statement on COVID-19," April 28. http://www.icmra.info/drupal/news/
statement_on_COVID-19. Accessed on May 26, 2020.

Kahler, Miles, ed. 2009. *Networked Politics: Agency, Power, and Governance*.
Ithaca: Cornell University Press.

Kaplan, Robert D. 2020. "Coronavirus Ushers in the Globalization We Were
Afraid Of." 20 March. Bloomberg. https://www.bloomberg.com/opinion/
articles/2020-03-20/coronavirus-ushers-in-the-globalization-we-were-afr
aid-of.

Kaye, David. 2013. "Stealth Multilateralism: U.S. Foreign Policy without
Treaties—Or the Senate." *Foreign Affairs* 92 (5).

Lighthizer, Robert E. 2020. "The Era of Offshoring U.S. Jobs Is Over." *New
York Times*, May 11. https://www.nytimes.com/2020/05/11/opinion/cor
onavirus-jobs-offshoring.html.

MacKay, Peter. 2020. "Peter MacKay: Defending Canadian sovereignty on the international stage." National Post. 23 April.

Manulak, Michael W. 2019. "Why and How to Succeed at Network Diplomacy." *The Washington Quarterly* 42 (1).

Manulak, Michael W. Forthcoming. "The Networked Diplomacy of Informal International Institutions: The Case of the Proliferation Security Initiative." *Global Governance*.

Manulak Michael W., and Duncan Snidal. 2021. "The Supply of Informal International Governance: Hierarchy plus Networks in Global Governance." In *Global Governance in a World of Change*, edited by Michael Barnett, Jon Pevehouse, and Kal Raustiala. Cambridge: Cambridge University Press.

Morse, Julia C., and Robert O. Keohane. 2014. "Contested Multilateralism." *Review of International Organization* 9 (2): 385–412.

Nimijean, Richard. 2019. "Where Is the Relationship Going? The View from Canada." In *Canada-U.S. Relations: Sovereignty or Shared Institutions*, edited by David Carment and Christopher Sands. Cham: Palgrave-Macmillan.

Nimijean, Richard, and David Carment. 2020. "Rethinking the Canada-US Relationship After the Pandemic." *Policy Option*, May 7. https://policyopt ions.irpp.org/magazines/may-2020/rethinking-the-canada-us-relationship-after-the-pandemic/. Accessed on October 17, 2020.

Patrick, Stewart. 2015. "Multilateralism à la Carte: The New World of Global Governance." Valdai Papers (22).

Prime Minister's Office (PMO). 2020. "New Agreements to Secure Additional Vaccine Candidates for COVID-19." Government of Canada, September 25. https://pm.gc.ca/en/news/news-releases/2020/09/25/new-agreements-secure-additional-vaccine-candidates-covid-19.

Raustiala, Kal. 2002. "The Architecture of International Cooperation: Transgovernmental Networks and the Future of International Law." *Virginia Journal of International Law* 43: 1–92.

Slaughter, Anne-Marie. 2004. *A New World Order.* Princeton: Princeton University Press.

Vabulas, Felicity, and Duncan Snidal. 2013. "Organization without Delegation: Informal Intergovernmental Organizations and the Spectrum of Intergovernmental Arrangements." *Review of International Organizations* 8 (2).

Walt, Stephen. 2020. Quoted in: Allen, John R. et al. "How the World Will Look After the Coronavirus Pandemic." *Foreign Policy.* 20 March. https://foreignpolicy.com/2020/03/20/world-order-after-coroanvirus-pandemic/.

Wright, Thomas. 2020. "Stretching the international order to its breaking point." Brookings, 6 April. https://www.brookings.edu/blog/order-from-chaos/2020/04/06/stretching-the-international-order-to-its-breaking-point/.

CHAPTER 11

Situating Canada's Feminist Foreign Policy Priorities in the Context of the COVID-19 Pandemic and a Rapidly Changing Global Context

Rebecca Tiessen

INTRODUCTION

Feminist foreign policies are growing in popularity around the world. Since 2014, several countries including Canada have adopted feminist foreign policies. Canada's first official foray into feminist foreign policy was the 2017 launch of Canada's Feminist International Assistance Policy. In February 2020, Canada's Minister of International Affairs, François-Philippe Champagne, announced Canada's plans to expand its feminist foreign policy commitments by working with civil society to devise a Feminist White Paper (Government of Canada 2020a). Other

R. Tiessen (✉)
School of International Development and Global Studies, University of Ottawa, Ottawa, ON, Canada
e-mail: Rebecca.Tiessen@uottawa.ca

© The Author(s), under exclusive license to Springer Nature
Switzerland AG 2021
D. Carment and R. Nimijean (eds.), *Political Turmoil in a Tumultuous World*, Canada and International Affairs,
https://doi.org/10.1007/978-3-030-70686-9_11

233

Canadian commitments that comprise Canada's feminist foreign policy include *Canada's National Action Plan on Women, Peace and Security*; *Strong, Secure, Engaged: Canada's Defence Policy*; and Canada's 2018 Trade Policy. This chapter examines the global context in which feminist foreign policy is becoming increasingly popular; the current state of Canada's feminist foreign policy; and considerations for Canada's next steps in the creation of an expanded vision of a feminist foreign policy in the light of the COVID-19 pandemic and a rapidly changing global context. Through these analyses, this chapter considers the implications for Canada as a leader among nations in terms of maximizing opportunities, addressing weaknesses and committing resources for enacting a feminist foreign policy, with attention to the broad global challenges we are facing and the specific implications brought on by the COVID-19 pandemic.

Governments around the world are adopting feminist foreign policies and/or enhanced feminist commitments. Canada's commitments to feminist foreign policy reaffirm Canada's history of global leadership on gender equality (Tiessen 2016), alongside a handful of other countries engaged in feminist foreign policymaking. Several "next steps" and future priorities will determine Canada's leadership role; namely, efforts to mitigate the global impacts of COVID-19, an ability to respond to some of the emerging critiques of Canada's current feminist policy priorities, and broader commitments to policy coherence through an explicit feminist foreign policy document that might emerge from the forthcoming "White Paper" on feminist foreign policy. Canada must also confront some of the challenges and limitations of its feminist commitments to date including failures to "walk the talk" on feminism whether through contradictory trade practices, record-low foreign aid spending, missed opportunities or partial prioritization of feminist actions at home and abroad, and slow progress in finalizing a national action plan on missing and murdered Indigenous women (MMIW).

While many countries including Canada have officially declared that their foreign policy is feminist, there remains some ambiguity among many about this term and its implications for foreign policy. A feminist foreign policy, as defined by the Centre for Feminist Foreign Policy (CFFP) (2020), is "a framework which elevates the everyday lived experience of marginalized communities to the forefront and provides a broader and deeper analysis of global issues". The definition continues to explain how a feminist foreign policy can be distinguished from traditional foreign policy thinking by moving beyond a "focus on military force, violence and domination by offering an alternate and intersectional rethinking of security from the viewpoint of the most marginalised". A feminist foreign policy is therefore, "a powerful lens through which we can interrogate the hierarchical and global systems of power that have left millions of people in a perpetual state of vulnerability" (CFFP 2020). Key principles of a feminist foreign policy include its increased emphasis on democratic processes; structural changes to the status quo, patterns of oppression and forms of discrimination; and commitments to a more just process of international interactions (CFFP 2020). Feminist foreign policy "must be steered by the fundamental feminist principle of 'the personal is political'" and "move away from understanding feminism as a 'project' or an intervention. Feminism is, and always has been, about redressing power imbalances" (Swan 2020: 15).

A feminist foreign policy is also able to adapt to changing global realities. In light of the COVID-19 pandemic, a feminist foreign policy must address the growing inequality and marginalization that arise from new circumstances. The COVID-19 pandemic has exacerbated gender inequalities and resulted in a disproportionate impact on women, their rights and their labour (Morse and Anderson 2020). Several vulnerabilities emerge or are exacerbated by the COVID-19 pandemic stemming from increased food insecurity, limited access to health care and sexual and reproductive health and rights (SRHR), education, water and sanitation, economic opportunities, and lack of democratic participation (CFFP 2020). The pandemic is unravelling the significant gains made over the past 25 years in gender equality work, often requiring women to leave their jobs to expand their care roles at home and increasing social and economic vulnerabilities of women and girls (Morse and Anderson 2020; Harvey-Wong 2020). Now, more than ever, a feminist foreign policy is needed for addressing growing gender inequalities and for ensuring our foreign policy priorities are responsive and pro-active by tackling systemic discrimination observed through racism, sexism and ableism; and to the health and economic crisis resulting from the COVID-19 pandemic. New visions for addressing global issues can be found around the world through the design and implementation of feminist foreign policies.

FEMINIST FOREIGN POLICIES AROUND THE WORLD

Sweden's feminist foreign policy, introduced in 2014, is considered the first official feminist foreign policy. Since its inception, Sweden's feminist foreign policy has also undergone review and revision. The Swedish feminist foreign policy is comprised of three pillars (rights, representation and resources). Over time, research on the impact of Sweden's feminist foreign policy has highlighted both successes and failures of translating policy into practice. Nonetheless, feminist foreign policy in Sweden is linked to the creation of norm changes and challenges gendered practices and structures in global politics. Sweden's feminist foreign policy has expanded beyond promises and rhetoric to "reality checks and research" (Aggestam and Annika 2019). The emphasis on feminist research as well as feminist monitoring and evaluation marks an important expansion of feminist foreign policy commitments.

Canada followed Sweden's lead and in 2017 released its first of four feminist policies that comprise Canada's unofficial feminist foreign policy: the Feminist International Assistance Policy. The other three policy documents include: *Strong Secure Engaged: Canada's National Defence Policy*; *Canada's National Action Plan on Women Peace and Security*; and Canada's 2018 Trade Policy. With this new policy, Canada joined Sweden with an official feminist policy commitment, echoing the prioritization of gender equality shared by countries such as Australia, Norway and the United Kingdom.

At the end of the G7 meetings in 2019, France advanced its priorities of gender equality and feminist foreign policy. Specific gender-focussed activities of the G7 meeting included "official meetings of ministers of gender equality (or relevant high-ranking officials), a high-level council of advisors … and a large gathering of civil society advocates from G7 and other countries together known as the Women 7" (Thompson 2019). Since the initial meeting of the Women 7 (W7) in Germany in 2015, W7 meetings have remained a prominent parallel event alongside subsequent G7 meetings. One strategy France has committed to in its efforts to stay focussed on gender equality is to nominate France's ambassador to Canada—Kareen Rispal—to the high-profile feminist leaders advisory council (Thompson 2019).

At the time of writing, Mexico is considered the most recent country to commit to a feminist foreign policy—what has been deemed as an emerging "global gold standard" in foreign policy design (Thompson

2020). Mexico's feminist foreign policy includes five principles to guide its foreign-policy activities:

> Conducting all aspects of foreign policy with the intent to advance gender equality and a feminist agenda; achieving gender parity at all levels of staff in the foreign ministry; combatting all forms of gender-based violence, including within the ministry; making equality visible; and practicing intersectional feminism, which is to say, an approach that values not only women's rights but also other intersecting social, economic, and environmental justice issues. (Thompson 2020)

The last principle is significant given some of the critiques of previous feminist foreign policies for offering little guidance in the way of commitments to transgender people or LGBTQ (Mason 2019). In addition to advancing women's rights, Mexico has been explicit about protecting the rights for gay, bisexual and transgender people as well as advancing a "broader social and economic justice initiatives" (Thompson 2020). Mexico's commitments include actions and timelines to ensure the roll-out of this policy leads to significant changes to social inequality. The activities include developing "trainings, working groups and manuals". The goals highlight commitments to "equal pay, employment parity", and "the application of a gender lens to every foreign-policy position, resolution, and mandate" (Thompson 2020).

Evidence of emerging feminist foreign policies can be found in other countries. The coalition agreement reached by the government of Luxembourg, for example, committed to a feminist foreign policy. In a 43-page policy statement delivered by the Minister of Foreign and European Affairs the feminist foreign policy is addressed in greater detail, pointing to Luxembourg's way forward on gender equality priorities. The Minister defined Luxembourg's vision for a feminist foreign policy as an acknowledgement of women's rights as human rights and commitments to defending the fundamental political and economic rights of women and girls and sexual-determination rights for all. The commitments highlighted in this statement include strengthening the participation of women at all levels in diplomacy, co-operation, defence and civilian missions abroad. Among Luxembourg's reasons for celebration in addressing gender equality, the Ministry of Foreign Affairs noted that they had achieved a 50/50 quota in its recruitment over the past few years and the development of a National Action Plan on Women, Peace and Security (Government of Luxembourg 2019).

Feminist commitments and gender equality priorities can be found in many government policies around the world. This global context provides a framework within which to consider Canada's explicit efforts to introduce and implement a feminist foreign policy. Beyond the fanfare and glossy announcements, feminist foreign policies require careful scrutiny and critical analysis to ensure that governments are "walking the talk". While feminist foreign policies may have become a global gold standard for policy rhetoric, it is imperative that these commitments are also examined carefully in relation to their impacts. With new issues emerging as a result of the COVID-19 global pandemic, we must consider the strengths and weaknesses of feminist foreign policies and the opportunities to expand our commitments to ensure feminist principles translate into a comprehensive approach to the pressing issues we are facing. After three years of rhetorical commitments to feminist foreign policy, and with Canada's "White Paper" on Feminist Foreign Policy on the horizon, a critical examination of successes and persistent challenges is crucial for moving forward and for considering Canada's potential leadership role in its efforts to prioritize a feminist foreign policy vision.

Canada's Feminist International Assistance Policy: The First of Several Feminist Foreign Policy Priorities

In 2017 Canada introduced a new aid policy—the Feminist International Assistance Policy (FIAP). The FIAP strives for international leadership on gender equality and ensures targeted funding in support of the empowerment of women and girls to the amount of 15% of Canada's $2.6 billion bilateral development assistance. As part of this initiative, the Government of Canada will allocate $150 million over five years to respond to the needs of local women's organizations in developing countries that are working to advance the rights of women and girls and promote gender equality (GAC 2017). The policy commits the government to apply a "human-rights approach" to six focus areas: (1) Gender Equality and the empowerment of women and girls; (2) Human dignity; (3) Growth that works for everyone; (4) Environment and climate action; (5) Inclusive

governance; and (6) Peace and security (GAC 2017). The FIAP character-
izes programming for gender equality and the empowerment of women
and girls as central to its feminist strategy—a strategy that leads to "a
more peaceful, more inclusive and more prosperous world" (GAC 2017).
Specific interventions planned as part of Canada's FIAP include investments targeted at particular groups and programme outcomes, increased
and improved partnerships, and strategies to promote innovation—all
commitments that are believed to reduce gender inequality and increase
opportunities for everyone's success. While other countries have similar
commitments to gender equality and feminist foreign policies, Canada's
FIAP is a demonstration of deliberate commitments specific to international development. The FIAP is an important discursive shift for Canada
and has been the subject of much attention in scholarly and non-academic
analyses.

   In addition to the launch of the FIAP, under the Trudeau government, Canada has demonstrated a commitment to feminist priorities in
its targeted funding to programmes that advance women's rights and
support locally based women's organizations. Resources provided to the
Equality Fund, for example, are ear-marked for investing in women's
organizations and movements around the world (GAC 2018). In doing
so, Canada is demonstrating a commitment to the feminist principle of
supporting the everyday lived experiences of marginalized communities.

CRITICAL EXAMINATION OF THE FEMINIST INTERNATIONAL ASSISTANCE POLICY

A review of the first few years of the FIAP has shed light on many
opportunities for expanding Canada's feminist foreign policy vision as
well as some of the inherent weaknesses including conceptual ambiguity, instrumentalist rhetoric and limited and insufficient attention to
intersectionality.

   The lack of clear definition of feminism within Canada's public
speeches and in its policy statements, including the FIAP, has meant
a lack of clarity about what a feminist foreign policy means and what
kind of feminism is employed in these statements. Feminist ideas range
from instrumentalist (emphasis on individual action to effect change)
to transformative (focus on systemic changes to address the underlying
causes of inequality, discrimination and oppression). The FIAP makes
references to both instrumentalist and transformative change processes

needed, though greater focus is on the former including, for example, "Action area 5: Inclusive governance" addresses increasing the number of women in leadership roles and politics.

The ambiguous, and sometimes narrow, feminist approach emphasizing specifically women's and girls' rights employed in the FIAP reduces the gender transformative focus by avoiding explicit attention to structural and systemic inequalities and gender norms and practices that reproduce inequality. Addressing oppression, discrimination, marginalization and inequality through a feminist lens requires changes to the structures and institutions where inequality dwells. The use of "fuzz words" (Cornwall 2007) broadens the appeal of policy documents to diverse audience. Buzzwords that are not defined are employed without concrete referents and are interpreted freely by different users. Furthermore, the conflation of gender with "women and girls" limits a feminist approach to individualism and reduces the FIAP to an instrumentalist guide to addressing inequality. In making this case, Cadesky (2020) argues that the FIAP perpetuates simplistic solutions to these deep structural challenges, noting the weaknesses of this "magic bullet" approach.

The explicit emphasis on women and girls limits discussions of gender to a binary one, neglecting broader gender inequalities that may be experienced by individuals who identify as LGBTQ and non-binary individuals (Tiessen 2019; Aylward and Brown 2020). The FIAP does mention intersectionality through an overarching commitment to its inclusive approach. This statement is provided at the start of the policy document as a guidepost. However, insufficient attention to how intersectionality can be incorporated into Canada's commitments is made throughout the document. The FIAP is criticized as a missed opportunity to identify the specific vulnerabilities of diverse groups including LGBTQ (Mason 2019). The FIAP's references to marginalized groups are therefore "vague" and it is silent on the vulnerabilities of certain groups such as trans individuals (Aylward and Brown 2020). The incoherent and weak framing of intersectionality in the FIAP is removed from the origins of feminist change and activism (Mason 2019). The FIAP similarly excludes men and masculinities in its feminist vision and gender programming, thereby avoiding the important analyses of gender norms and structural and institutional power relations (Nacyte 2018). All of these challenges noted here provide insight into how to move forward in Canada's next steps in formalizing a feminist foreign policy more broadly and in relation to the preparation of the White Paper on Feminist Foreign Policy in particular.

CANADA'S FUTURE LEADERSHIP POTENTIAL

The critical insights and lessons learned from Canada's FIAP offer rich examples for Canada to review and expand its feminist foreign policy priorities within and across departments. Among the lessons learned through the analysis of Canada's FIAP is the need for a progressive and transformative feminist foreign policy that is comprehensive and coherent. Second, Canada's feminist foreign policy must strive to reduce hypocrisy. Third, an important test of commitment to a feminist foreign policy is in the outcomes, resource commitments and sustained practice. An important indicator of feminist foreign policy impact will come from partner organizations engaged in its implementation. Therefore, partner country perspectives on Canada's feminist foreign policy are essential. Studies documenting partner countries' perceptions of Canada's FIAP (see Rao and Tiessen 2020) shed light on the need for understanding feminism through a transnational lens—one that reflects different cultural realities and priorities and how those cultural practices shape the way that feminism is understood and enacted. These reflections from partner countries shed light on the dialogical nature of foreign policy and the significance of an audience for foreign values and priorities. Similarly, efforts to develop Canada's feminist foreign policy must be more than a branding exercise. They must lead to a sound "product" and concrete action (Tiessen and Black 2019). Beyond the branding exercise is a clear set of commitments to feminist principles and to delivery on these principles (Tiessen and Black 2019).

Canada's feminist commitments can also reshape existing commitments in a more explicitly feminist way. As Brown and Swiss (2018) argue, commitments to sexual and reproductive health and rights are an example of deepening previous commitments to maternal and newborn health programming. After three years of feminist foreign policy priorities in Canada, it is a crucial time for reflection on remaining gaps and challenges in the light of contemporary issues, beginning with some thoughts on delayed actions on a range of issues not highlighted as part of Canada's feminist commitments. Among those is Canada's promise to address MMIW and to prepare a national action plan based on findings from the inquiry. The government of Canada received the inquiry's report in June 2019 along with the 231 calls for justice that comprise the report. At the time of writing, the national action plan to address the inquiry's findings has not been completed. While the COVID-19 pandemic has certainly created new priorities, it has also revealed the clear need for a national action plan to prevent violence against women. The national crisis of violence against Indigenous women is both a domestic and global challenge that must be addressed in light of Canada's commitments to the Sustainable Development Goals, particularly Goal 5 on Gender Equality and Empowerment of all Women and Girls. It also constitutes an important inter-nation challenge within Canada to address historical and contemporary institutionalized practices that have marginalized and impoverished communities within the country. There are no good terms to encapsulate the nature of the inequality and systemic oppression experienced by Indigenous communities but these analogies to "other world" poverty within Canada are important to highlight (Smith 2017).

Oxfam Canada's Feminist Scorecard for the year 2019 reinforces this missed opportunity for a self-proclaimed feminist government to address this pressing issue faced by Indigenous women (Oxfam Canada 2019). The Oxfam Feminist Scorecard 2020 also highlights gaps in Canada's work to address work and pay equity between men and women; weak to moderate set of commitments to address discrepancies in work on gender-based violence and sexual and reproductive health; the need for a national care child care system; and the importance of addressing conflict and crisis. In this assessment, Oxfam Canada points to Canada's back-tracking on policies to support refugees and continuing to sell arms to Saudi Arabia (Oxfam Canada 2020a).

Canada's weak performance and missed opportunities on key indicators that link to commitments to the Sustainable Development Goals, as noted above, may well explain some of the challenges Canada experienced in securing a seat in the Security Council. The challenges noted here reinforce criticisms that Canada's rhetoric on feminist priorities is strong but their action on these priorities remains weak. Since 2017, the Government of Canada has made several announcements of funding commitments directly linked to feminist priorities and gender equality, including increased funding for sexual and reproductive health and rights (GAC 2020) and funding for local women's rights organizations, women's economic empowerment and skills training (GAC 2018).

However, these funding announcements have demonstrated a reorientation of some funding towards feminist programmes, in line with the commitments set out in the FIAP, but without an increase in foreign aid allocations in recent years, with a smaller percentage of Canadian funding going towards official development assistance between 2015 and 2019—less than the allocation under the Harper governments (Brown 2020).

The 2020 global COVID-19 pandemic has only served to heighten our need for a feminist foreign policy by exposing the depth of inequality that a global health crisis produces and the distinct gender impacts it has. Examples of that inequality include increased violence against women and gender-based violence and fewer opportunities to leave abusive relationships, lack of access to routine health care including sexual and reproductive health care, unequal work burdens resulting from lack of childcare and increased household and reproductive labour including caring for sick members of the family, etc.

The COVID-19 pandemic makes the interconnections across issues and the interdependence between nations all the more apparent, driving home the need for strong policy coherence across sectors from economic development and trade to security within and between countries. This health crisis provides an opportunity for countries to use their feminist foreign policy commitments to demonstrate their leadership by translating policy and rhetoric into practice.

As of June 11, 2020, Canada's federal government had committed over $1 billion to support efforts to deal with the COVID-19 pandemic at home and abroad including efforts to protect Canadians and ensure their safe return home for those abroad, supporting collaborative efforts with diverse leaders (including Indigenous leaders) across the country, supporting international initiatives and multilateral commitments, and "flexible arrangements" for businesses striving to meet Canada Revenue Agency requirements (Government of Canada 2020b). A few months later, on September 29, 2020, Canada announced an additional $400 million in international development funding ear-marked for "trusted partners on the ground fighting COVID-19" to address issues arising from the pandemic. This funding is part of a larger set of commitments that show that Canada's total international COVID-19 response now stands at approximately $1.142 billion (Bhushan et al. 2020). The announcement specifies that the funding will be used to ensure women and girls who are most "disproportionately impacted by the consequences of COVID-19, benefit from this new funding" (Government of Canada 2020c). Canada's international COVID-19 response, according to a report published in the Canadian International Development Platform, represents "some of the largest one time additions to the IAE [international aid envelope] Canada has ever undertaken" (Bhushan et al. 2020).

Additional funding that has been deemed by leaders in Canada's NGO community as central to Canada's feminist leadership includes the investment of $8.9 million in support to programmes that offer sexual and reproductive health, including abortions (National Post 2020). Additional funding of $2 million is going to the United Nations trust fund to support programming that ends violence against women and combats gender-based violence internationally (Wright 2020). Additional commitments to international efforts that will demonstrate feminist leadership on the part of Canada include broadening and redefining our commitments to security. Canada's plans to double its sales to military weaponry to Saudi Arabia (known for its human rights abuses) are a clear contradiction to those feminist values (Cecco 2020). Other countries and states have demonstrated feminist principles in their efforts to address the COVID-19 pandemic. For example, the state of Hawaii has called for a feminist economic recovery plan, noting the need for cultural changes that are substantive and for efforts that prioritize "the care economy and the health and well-being of the most marginalized: Indigenous women, women of color, incarcerated people, aging women, domestic violence survivors and LGBTQIA + people" (Thompson and Kripke 2020). Other examples of the rationale for a feminist foreign policy in the face of a global health crisis include the nature of commitments that have had significant positive impacts, particularly examples from New Zealand and Prime Minister Ardern's commitments to "empathy and putting people first" (Thompson and Kripke 2020). Other critics are calling for much greater investments within Canada and in Canada's international support to recognize unpaid care work. According to research by Oxfam Canada, the COVID-19 pandemic has had a disproportionately negative impact on women, particularly Indigenous women and black women. To address this, "Canada can take action by supporting activities that recognize, reduce and redistribute care work from women to men and from household to state—this means investment in child care, essential care workers and shifting the gender norms that perpetuate inequality" (Oxfam Canada 2020b).

The potential longevity of a feminist foreign policy is an additional consideration given divisions within the country on the priority to be given to feminist policies. During the 2019 election campaign, the Conservative Party leader ran a campaign that included further cuts to foreign aid by 25%—cuts that would have significantly affected Canada's ability to deliver high quality, comprehensive development programming (see Brown this volume). There is little discussion among other party leaders about sustaining a feminist foreign policy in future governments. However, the association of feminist foreign policy with the Liberal government raises concerns of its potential enduring role if another party wins the next election. Opportunities for international leadership through a feminist foreign policy abound. Canada is not alone in its commitment to feminist priorities as several other countries including Sweden, France and Mexico adopt feminist foreign policies, and a growing number of countries are heading in this direction. However, global leadership in feminist foreign policy requires a consistent, comprehensive and whole-of-government approach. Feminist leadership must simultaneously reflect domestic priorities, particularly in addressing violence against women and MMIW as a demonstration of Canada's commitments to meeting the priorities of the SDGs, and international priorities through its foreign policies. A consolidation of feminist foreign policy commitments across countries will also reinforce a strong leadership commitment and amplify the lessons learned through cross-national insights and analyses. The Canadian government, along with other countries committed to a feminist foreign policy, must therefore mobilize multilateral efforts (Tiessen and Swan 2018).

Conclusion

A growing number of countries are adopting feminist foreign policies and feminist principles in their efforts to address a wide range of issues, not the least of which are the challenges arising as a result of the COVID-19 pandemic. These efforts often include a particular emphasis on the disproportionate impact of political and economic policies on women and girls. However, the feminist policies and principles are increasingly addressing broader societal and systemic issues that require alternative approaches and strategies. The COVID-19 pandemic, and the resulting inequality of impacts resulting from economic insecurity, increased unpaid care work, higher rates of domestic violence, and a growing gap in access to sexual and reproductive health and rights has exposed the need for a new set of priorities and commitments that can more effectively demonstrate innovative strategies both domestically and internationally for Canada. While Canada is among the earliest countries to adopt a feminist foreign policy, its leadership among nations will depend on its ability to translate this commitment to a comprehensive, whole-of-government strategy, with sustained action and sufficient resources. Canada's forthcoming White Paper on Feminist Foreign Policy will provide one such guiding document for Canada to consider its evolving role in relation to other leading feminist nations. The nature of Canada's leadership, in the light of its failed bid to join the Security Council in 2020, will hinge on concerted efforts to drive the feminist foreign policy agenda forward, to learn from the advancements of feminist peer nations and government agencies and to redirect its efforts nationally and internationally in line with the innovations that a feminist foreign policy can bring.

References

Aggestam, Karin, and Rosamond B. Annika. 2019. "Feminist Foreign Policy 3.0: Advancing Ethics and Gender Equality in Global Politics." *The SAIS Review of International Affairs* 39 (1): 37–48. http://dx.doi.org.proxy.bib.uottawa.ca/10.1353/sais.2019.0003.

Aylward, Erin, and Stephen Brown. 2020. "Sexual Orientation and Gender Identity in Canada's "Feminist" International Assistance." *International Journal.* Online first. https://journals.sagepub.com/doi/full/10.1177/0020702020953425. Accessed on October 7, 2020.

Bhushan, Aniket, Bridget Steele, and Lance Hadley. 2020. "Throne Speech: Opportunity to Stimulate Canada's Support for Development." Canadian International Development Platform, October 1. http://cidpnsi.ca/throne-speech-opportunity-to-stimulate-canadas-support-for-development/. Accessed on October 7, 2020.

Brown, Stephen. 2020. "Foreign Aid Flows: The Canadian Government Is Still Not Stepping Up to the Plate." Centre for International Policy Studies, April 20. https://www.cipscepi.ca/2020/04/20/foreign-aid-flows-the-canadian-government-is-still-not-stepping-up-to-the-plate/.

Brown, Stephen, and Liam Swiss. 2018. "Canada's Feminist International Assistance Policy: Bold Statement or Feminist Fig Leaf?" In *How Ottawa Spends, 2017-2018*, edited by Katherine A.H. Graham and Allan M. Maslove,

117–131. Ottawa: School of Public Policy and Administration, Carleton University.

Cadesky, Jessica. 2020. "Built on Shaky Ground: Situating Canada's Feminist International Assistance Policy within the Literature." *International Journal*. Online First. September 20, 2020. https://journals.sagepub.com/doi/full/10.1177/0020702020953424.

Cecco, Leyland. 2020. "Canada Doubles Weapons Sales to Saudi Arabia Despite Moritorium." *The Guardian*, June 9 https://www.theguardian.com/world/2020/jun/09/canada-doubles-weapons-sales-to-saudi-arabia-despite-morato rium. Accessed on March 24, 2021.

Centre for Feminist Foreign Policy. 2020. "Feminist Foreign Policy." https://centreforfeministforeignpolicy.org/feminist-foreign-policy. Accessed on July 27, 2020.

Cornwall, Andrea. 2007. "Buzzwords and Fuzzwords: Deconstructing Development Discourse." *Development in Practice* 17 (4–5): 471–484. https://doi.org/10.1080/09614520701469302.

Global Affairs Canada. 2017. "Canada Launches New Feminist International Assistance Policy." Government of Canada, June 9. https://www.canada.ca/en/global-affairs/news/2017/06/canada_launches_newfeministinternational assistancepolicy.html.

Global Affairs Canada. 2018. "Partnership to Fund Gender Equality and the Empowerment of Women and Girls in Canada and Abroad." Government of Canada. Last modified January 7, 2020. https://www.international.gc.ca/gac-amc/campaign-campagne/gender_equality-egalite_des_genres/index.aspx?lang=eng.

Global Affairs Canada. 2020. "Sexual and Reproductive Health and Rights: Canada's approach." Government of Canada. Last modified January 10, 2020. https://www.international.gc.ca/world-monde/issues_development-enjeux_developpement/global_health-sante_mondiale/reproductive-reprod uctifs.aspx?lang=eng.

Government of Canada. 2020a. "Address by Minister of Foreign Affairs to the Montreal Council on Foreign Relations." Last modified February 2, 2020. https://www.canada.ca/en/global-affairs/news/2020/02/address-by-min ister-of-foreign-affairs-to-the-montreal-council-on-foreign-relations.html.

Government of Canada. 2020b. "Government of Canada Takes Action on COVID-19." Last modified June 11, 2020. https://www.canada.ca/en/pub lic-health/services/diseases/2019-novel-coronavirus-infection/canadas-rep onse/government-canada-takes-action-covid-19.html.

Government of Canada. 2020c. "Prime Minister Co-chairs High-Level Meeting to Address Economic Devastation Caused by COVID-19 an Announce New Funding to Fight the Pandemic". https://pm.gc.ca/en/news/news-rel

eases/2020/09/29/prime-minister-co-chairs-high-level-meeting-address-eco
nomic. Accessed on October 7, 2020.

Government of Luxembourg. 2019. "Foreign Policy Address." https://maee.
gouvernement.lu/content/dam/gouv_maee/ministère/déclarations-de-pol
itique-étrangère/2019/EN-Declaration-de-politique-etrangere-2019.pdf.
Accessed on January 27, 2020.

Harvey-Wong, Vivien. 2020. "Corona Virus – A Backwards Step for Gender
Equality." *United Nations Children's Fund News and Insights*, July 8. https://
www.unicef.org.au/blog/news-and-insights/may-2020/coronavirus-gender.

Mason, Corinne. 2019. "Buzzwords and Fuzzwords: Flattening Intersectionality in Canadian Aid." *Canadian Foreign Policy Journal* 25 (2): 203–219.
https://doi.org/10.1080/11926422.2019.1592002.

Morse, Michelle M., and Grace Anderson. 2020. "The Shadow Pandemic: How
the COVID-19 Crisis is Exacerbating Gender Inequality." *United Nations
Foundation Blog*, April 14. https://unfoundation.org/blog/post/shadow-
pandemic-how-covid19-crisis-exacerbating-gender-inequality/.

Nacyte, Laura. 2018. "Canada's Feminist International Assistance Policy: Security for Whom?" *LSE Engenderings*, January 2. http://blogs.lse.ac.uk/gen
der/2018/01/22/canadas-feminist-international-assistance-policy-security-
for-whom/.

Oxfam Canada. 2019. "Feminist Scorecard 2019: Turning Feminist Promises
into Progress." https://www.oxfam.ca/feminist-policy-scorecard-2019/.
Accessed on July 27, 2020.

Oxfam Canada. 2020a. "Feminist Scorecard 2020: Is Canada Living up to Its
Feminist Foreign Policy Promises?" https://www.oxfam.ca/feminist-policy-
scorecard-2020/#care_work. Accessed on July 27, 2020.

Oxfam Canada. 2020b. "71 per cent of Canadian Women Feeling More Anxious,
Depressed, Isolated, Overworked or Ill Because of Increased Unpaid Care
Work Caused By COVID-19: Oxfam Survey." Last modified June 18, 2020.
https://www.oxfam.ca/news/71-per-cent-of-canadian-women-feeling-more-
anxious-depressed-isolated-overworked-or-ill-because-of-increased-unpaid-
care-work-caused-by-covid-19-oxfam-survey/.

Rao, Sheila, and Rebecca Tiessen. 2020. "Whose Feminism (s)? Overseas Partner
Organization's Perceptions of Canada's Feminist International Assistance
Policy (FIAP)." *International Journal*. Online first. https://journals.sagepub.
com/doi/full/10.1177/0020702020960120. Accessed on October 7, 2020.

Smith, Heather. 2017. "Not High on Our Radar: The Harper Government and
the Missing and Murdered Aboriginal Women in Canada." In *Obligations
and Omissions: Canada's Ambiguous Actions on Gender Equality*, edited by
Rebecca Tiessen and Stephen Baranyi, 261–283. Montreal: McGill-Queen's
University Press.

Swan, Emma. 2020. "'The Personal Is Political!': Exploring the Limits of Canada's Feminist International Assistance Policy Under Occupation and Blockade." *Canadian Foreign Policy Journal.* Online first. https://www.tandfonline.com/doi/abs/10.1080/11926422.2020.1805340. Accessed on October 7, 2020.

Thompson, Lyric. 2019. "A French Feminist Foreign Policy." *Foreign Policy*, May 20. https://foreignpolicy.com/2019/05/20/g7-france-feminist-foreign-policy/.

Thompson, Lyric. 2020. "Mexican Diplomacy Has Gone Feminist." *Foreign Policy*, January 14. https://foreignpolicy.com/2020/01/14/mexican-diplomacy-feminist-foreign-policy/.

Thompson, Lyric, and Gawain Kripke. 2020. "Women Leaders Successfully Fighting Coronavirus Show Why We Need a Feminist Foreign Policy." *NBC News*, May 21. https://www.nbcnews.com/think/opinion/women-leaders-successfully-fighting-coronavirus-show-why-we-need-feminist-ncna1212131.

Tiessen, Rebecca. 2016. "Gender Equality and the "Two CIDAs": Successes and Setbacks, 1976-2015." In *Rethinking Canadian Aid, Second Edition*, edited by Stephen Brown, Molly D. Heyer, and David R. Black, 195–207. Ottawa: University of Ottawa Press.

Tiessen, Rebecca. 2019. "What's New About Canada's Feminist International Assistance Policy and Why 'More of the Same' Matters." *The School of Public Policy Publications* 12 (44): 1–15. https://doaj.org/article/692dbce3111a4bf9b0f4a356e4b933f3.

Tiessen, Rebecca, and Emma Swan. 2018. "Canada's Feminist Foreign Policy Promises: An Ambitious Agenda for Gender Equality, Human Rights, Peace and Security." In *Justin Trudeau and Canadian Foreign Policy*, edited by Norman Hillmer and Phillpe Lagassé, 187–205. London, UK: Palgrave Macmillan.

Tiessen, Rebecca, and David Black. 2019. "Canada's Feminist International Assistance Policy: To Whom Is Canada Back?" In *Canada, Nation Branding and Domestic Politics*, edited by Richard Nimijean and David Carment, Chapter 4. London, UK: Routledge Press.

Wright, Teresa. 2020. "Feds Commit $8.9 M in Foreign Aid for Reproductive Health Services Amid COVID-19." *National Post*, June 9. https://nationalpost.com/pmn/news-pmn/canada-news-pmn/feds-commit-8-9m-in-foreign-aid-for-reproductive-health-services-amid-covid-19.

CHAPTER 12

Going Viral: Development Assistance Under the Trudeau Minority Government

Stephen Brown

INTRODUCTION

The October 2019 federal election had the potential of throwing a gigantic wrench in Canada's foreign aid program. In a provocative move, the Conservative Party had promised to cut international assistance by 25%. Although the Conservatives won the most votes, the Liberals, led by Justin Trudeau, won the most seats and formed a minority government. Given the negligible attention that the Liberals paid to foreign aid in the campaign and the lack of influence of other parties in setting the policy agenda even under minority government, there was no reason to expect the Liberals to make any significant changes. Rather, they seemed likely to show continuity with their first mandate and focus on the implementation of the Feminist International Assistance Policy, which they had adopted in 2017. Then, the COVID-19 pandemic hit, causing political turmoil in Canada and tumult around the world.

S. Brown (✉)
University of Ottawa, Ottawa, ON, Canada
e-mail: brown@uottawa.ca

D. Carment and R. Nimijean (eds.), *Political Turmoil in a Tumultuous World*, Canada and International Affairs, https://doi.org/10.1007/978-3-030-70686-9_12

251

This chapter traces the evolution of Canadian aid in the first year of the Trudeau minority government within those sudden, unexpected, and far-reaching changes in national and international circumstances. It begins with an examination of the electoral context and its immediate aftermath, which suggest continuity in Canada's aid program. It then analyzes the consequences of COVID-19 for the Canadian aid program on: (1) the total amount of aid, (2) priority sectors and preferred aid modalities, and (3) the fundamental rationale for aid. It argues that the aid budget is unlikely to increase significantly, meaning that new pandemic-related spending in health, food/agriculture, and humanitarian assistance will come mainly at the expense of other sectors and divert resources within those sectors as well. Canada's growing focus on short-term welfare (as opposed to long-term growth), the increasingly multilateral approach to aid delivery, and the greater reliance on local staff and organizations in the Global South—all of which resulted from the COVID-19 crisis—may not last in the post-pandemic aid landscape. Similarly, the shift in rhetoric toward more enlightened self-interest, which emphasizes the alignment of Canadian and international interests, may be reversed once the world emerges from the coronavirus-induced crisis. The chapter concludes, first, by highlighting the Liberals and Conservatives shared lack of interest in changing Canada's current level of engagement with international development. Second, it suggests that the pandemic's potential to impel lasting changes to the Canadian aid program and to defend its global relevance will depend primarily on the political will to resist post-pandemic pressure to cut the aid budget significantly and realign aid with narrowly defined self-interest.

Foreign Aid, the 2019 Elections and Inter-party Dynamics

The 2019 federal elections had the potential to reshape Canadian development assistance. As is usually the case in Canada, foreign policy more generally and foreign aid in particular were not important campaign issues—until the Conservatives decided to use aid to grab headlines. On October 1, three weeks before the vote, Conservative Party leader Andrew Scheer held a press conference at which he announced that, if victorious, his party would cut international assistance by 25%. He used wildly inaccurate claims about Canadian aid to justify this significant policy change, apparently seeking to whip up populist outrage against wasteful spending and support to dictators (Gatehouse 2019; Wright 2019). Regardless of the rationale, the promise to slash aid constituted a significant departure from past Conservative policies, which had historically been at least as favorable to aid spending as the Liberals. For instance, the Liberal governments of Jean Chrétien and Paul Martin (1994–2005) and the Conservative government of Stephen Harper (2006–2015) spent on average the same proportion of gross national income on official development assistance, whereas Justin Trudeau's first government (2015–2019) spent a bit less (Brown 2018: 147).

The Liberals could have seized upon this campaign surprise as an opportunity to distinguish itself from its "stingy" rivals and burnish its claims to internationalism. However, at a press conference, Trudeau repeatedly ignored questions on foreign aid (Dzsurdzsa 2019). His reluctance to say anything reflected the Liberal electoral platform's vagueness about the party's intentions regarding international assistance: After offering some self-congratulatory bromides about Canada's place in the world, the platform commits only to "continuing to increase Canada's international development assistance every year"—which, phrased thus, could fail to even match the inflation rate—and "spending no less than 10% of our international development assistance budget on education" (Liberal Party of Canada 2019).

The election of a minority Liberal government at the October 21 general election was the plausible scenario with the greatest potential for boosting foreign aid. Both the New Democratic Party (NDP) and the Greens had long-standing commitments to increase aid to meet the UN target of 0.7% of gross national income, which would require increasing Canadian aid expenditure by a factor of about 2.5, but otherwise their respective platforms said very little about development assistance, and the Bloc Québécois' election manifesto did not mention it at all (Brown 2019). An important precedent existed: In 2005, Paul Martin's Liberal minority government obtained NDP support for the federal budget in exchange for an immediate injection of $500 million into the aid envelope, among other measures (CBC 2005). However, the NDP did not in any case include in 2019 any foreign policy issues on its list of six "urgent priorities" upon which any form of alliance or coalition with a minority Liberal government would be conditional (Tunney 2019)—and, after the election, no multipronged deal was negotiated between the Trudeau Liberals and any other party.

INITIAL EXPECTATIONS AND BUSINESS AS USUAL

Given the above, there was no reason to expect any significant changes to Canadian foreign aid after the Trudeau minority government was sworn in. All signs pointed toward only very modest budget increases. New programming would continue to be framed by the Liberals' Feminist International Assistance Policy (FIAP), launched in 2017 (see Tiessen this volume). The only sign of a new priority was the mention of education in the Liberal election platform, repeated in the mandate letter of the new Minister of International Development, Karina Gould (Trudeau 2019), whereas the FIAP document frequently mentions education, but never singles it out as a sector that would be assigned a minimum of 10% of total aid spending. The only FIAP spending targets relate to the proportion of projects that either specifically target or integrate the crosscutting "action area" of gender equality or the empowerment of women and girls, set to reach 95% by 2021–2022 (Government of Canada 2017: 71).[1] The mandate letter contained no real surprises, but noticeably did not mention the promotion of the rights of lesbian, gay, bisexual, transgender, and intersex (LGBTI) people in developing countries, despite it being a prominent issue under Justin Trudeau's first government. However, it is unclear whether that omission signaled a loss of interest or was merely an oversight (Aylward and Brown 2020).

The appointment of Gould as the new development minister suggested a certain degree of continuity, notably because she had previously been the Parliamentary Secretary to that position for a year before being promoted to Cabinet in early 2017. At a conference on liberal internationalism and the legacy of Pierre Trudeau's foreign policy, she staked out a strong case for a rules-based international order. Contrasting her government's position with that of the Conservative Party under Stephen Harper and Andrew Scheer, and referring to herself as "a Liberal [liberal?] internationalist and a feminist," Gould argued that Canada's "own self-interest lies in a more peaceful, stable, equitable world" and extolled the merits of FIAP (quoted in Wells 2020). In so doing, she linked policies of the Trudeau *fils* government to the legacy of Trudeau *père* and reinforced liberal/Liberal internationalism as the brand of both her party and her government's aid program, promoting both to the Liberal's electoral base (Brown 2018).

---

[1] See discussion in Brown and Swiss (2017).

During this period, the Canadian government ramped up its campaign for a non-permanent seat on the United Nations Security Council, using its aid program and internationalist posture to try to win votes from developing countries. In January 2020, Gould made an official trip to vote-rich Africa, as did Minister of Foreign Affairs François-Philippe Champagne and his Parliamentary Secretary, MP Rob Oliphant, followed by Trudeau himself in February, accompanied by Somalia-born Minister of Families, Children and Social Development Ahmed Hussen. The sudden attention paid to the continent contrasted sharply with the apparent disinterest under the Trudeau Liberals' previous government—Chrystia Freeland never set foot on the continent during her three-year tenure as Foreign Minister—and its motivation was quite transparent.

Other than that public charm offensive in Africa and a de facto increased interest in agriculture and food security, it otherwise seemed to be business as usual at Global Affairs Canada. The appearance and subsequent spread of a novel coronavirus in China and then Iran and Italy just strengthened the case that we live in an interconnected world and cannot afford to cut ourselves off from what happens elsewhere. But then the outbreak turned into a global pandemic, with far-reaching consequences on well-being around the world. COVID-19's irruption onto the global scene raises several key questions for Canadian foreign aid and development cooperation more generally: will governments provide more aid? What impact will the pandemic have on priority sectors and preferred aid modalities? How does it affect aid's fundamental rationale? The next section explores each of these issues in turn for the case of Canada.[2]

WILL SUPPLY FOLLOW DEMAND?

By mid-March 2020, it became clear that COVID-19 could not be contained and its effects would be profoundly felt across the world. The disease itself quickly infected millions and preventive measures (such as lockdowns and curfews) disproportionately affected the most vulnerable people in the Global South, especially women, workers in the informal sector, refugees, migrant workers, and LGBTI people (Al-Ali 2020). Poor people often lack the ability to wash their hands frequently and also live in conditions under which it is not possible to maintain physical distancing.

---

[2] A more in-depth examination of global trends, including variations on some of this chapter's analysis, can be found in Brown (2021).

Moreover, they usually have very limited access to quality health care as well as broader social safety nets, making them extremely vulnerable in case of disease or other causes of lost income. One study cautioned that 400–500 million people could be pushed below the poverty line as a result of the coronavirus pandemic (Sumner et al. 2020). David Beasley, the head of the World Food Programme, warned of "the worst humanitarian crisis since World War Two" and the possibility of "multiple famines of biblical proportions" (quoted in UN News 2020), while one international NGO referred to COVID-19 as "the hunger virus" (Oxfam 2020a). Years and perhaps a decade or more of development progress could be undone (Economist 2020; Gates Foundation 2020).

While the pandemic caused the need for assistance to mushroom, it also triggered a dramatic drop in sources of development financing, including domestic revenues in developing countries, foreign investment, trade, and remittances from abroad. According to the Organisation for Economic Co-operation and Development (OECD), the Global South's external private financing could drop by 45% between 2019 and 2020, representing a reduction of US$700 billion (OECD 2020c). Clearly, the need for international assistance was suddenly much greater. To what extent would Canada provide more aid?

Before the pandemic hit, Canada was already less generous than the average of its fellow members of the OECD's Development Assistance Committee, the main club of Western aid donors. In 2019, Norway, Sweden, Denmark, the United Kingdom, Germany, and the Netherlands all provided between two and four times more development assistance than Canada, relative to the size of their economy (OECD 2020a: 7). These unfavorable comparisons had little influence on the Canadian government, which, as mentioned above, had shown little interest in making any significant increases.

The pandemic had an immediate impact on the Canadian aid program, which reacted by repatriating many of its international staff and announcing a series of new measures. Within weeks, the Canadian government committed $52 million to the World Health Organization and other partners, soon followed by an additional $110 million to be disbursed mainly through United Nations agencies, and $40 million for vaccine development. Although described as "increasing" international aid and as "new money," it was not clear that these funds actually constituted supplements to Canada's aid budget (Blanchfield 2020b). Analysts from the Canadian Council for International Co-operation, the umbrella group of development NGOs, stated that they actually came from "previously unallocated pools in [the government's] international assistance envelope" and highlighted that Canada and other donors needed to "Up the ambition and acknowledge that existing aid resources will not be enough" (Charles and Kindornay 2020).

Indeed, these announcements represented a small proportion of Canada's annual aid budget of $6 billion and could be considered a rounding error in the growing hundreds of billions of dollars that the government was spending domestically to offset the deleterious impact of the pandemic on Canadian citizens and businesses. Neither the modesty of the amounts (though Gould promised more to come) nor the urgency and importance of the cause prevented Opposition Critic for Foreign Affairs Erin O'Toole, who was running for the Conservative Party leadership, from tweeting his objections in early April: "Foreign aid can wait. Right now, the Trudeau government should prioritize Canadians" (quoted in von Scheel 2020). The tenor of those comments, however, did not seem to elicit much support from Canadians or within the Conservative Party, whose other officials did not echo the criticism. Mike Lake, the Conservative foreign aid critic, disavowed O'Toole's position and expressed his support for pandemic-related international assistance, as long as the funding was "taken only from the existing foreign aid budget" (von Scheel 2020).

In the run-up to the UN vote on Security Council temporary membership, Canada's Prime Minister and Foreign Minister tried to woo foreign governments by positioning Canada as a leader in the global fight against COVID-19. They made official calls to numerous leaders of small countries in sub-Saharan Africa, the Caribbean, and the Pacific whose importance was temporarily amplified by the UN General Assembly's one-country-one-vote principle. Although the purpose of the calls was officially to discuss the global response to the pandemic, the Prime Minister's Office admitted at the time that "the Security Council campaign has come up in some conversations" (Carbert 2020). Trudeau also cohosted a virtual UN meeting on COVID-19 a few weeks before the UN vote, at which Canada did not pledge any new contributions. Still, strong efforts—and stronger track records—from rivals Norway and Ireland contrasted with "too little, too late" from Canada (which was probably also too transparently instrumentalist), resulted in the latter being defeated in the first round of voting in June 2020.

Over time, the Canadian government made additional pandemic-related aid announcements. For instance, in late June, it committed $180 million "to address the immediate humanitarian and developmental impacts of the pandemic" and $120 million "to accelerate the development, production and equitable distribution of new COVID-19 diagnostics, therapeutics and vaccines" (Blanchfield 2020a). In September, Trudeau announced an "extra" $400 million in development and humanitarian assistance, mainly to support responses to the pandemic (Blanchfield 2020c), though again it was not clear that these funds represented an increase in planned spending, rather than a routine allocation of resources from the existing envelope. Overall, with a few exceptions, the prominence that the government gave to the global dimension of the pandemic dropped after Canada lost the Security Council vote.

As of the end of September 2020, the government has not yet made available any total of expected aid expenditures related to the global pandemic, nor has it given any clear indication of what its intentions are regarding the overall aid budget. The September 2020 Throne Speech merely promised to "invest more in international development" (Governor General 2020: 30). A few days later, in his speech to the UN General Assembly, Trudeau (2020b) stated that Canada "will keep increasing our international assistance budget every year," repeating almost word for word the vague commitment cited above that can be found in the 2019 Liberal election platform.

Pressure for any important change in the international assistance envelope remains weak, be it from opposition parties or voters more generally. A few Canadian development NGOs have argued that Canadian spending on fighting COVID-19 abroad should represent at least 1% of its spending on the pandemic domestically, which would require an extra $2 billion in foreign aid as of September 2020, an amount that will grow as the Canadian government continues to announce more spending on its domestic response. Still, there is no sign of sustained pressure on this point or of broader resonance, though some have stated the obvious point, which bears repeating, that "existing resources will simply not be enough" (Charles and Kindornay 2020). By way of contrast, Germany increased its aid budget by 30% or €3 billion (about Cdn$4.5 billion) for 2020 and 2021 in response to the pandemic (Johnson et al. 2020).

After his populist tweet failed to gain any traction, O'Toole—who replaced Scheer as Conservative leader and Leader of the Opposition in August 2020—dropped the "Canada first" approach to foreign aid.

His party leadership platform heavily criticized the UN and the multi-lateral system, but did not suggest cutting the aid budget, nor did his main rival Peter MacKay. Rather, O'Toole promised to "allocate funding to pro-pluralism education and development initiatives through organizations with proven track records of effectiveness" (O'Toole 2020), which does not sound very different from something the Liberals could have written, especially given the latter's recent emphasis on the education sector. The main difference is that the Conservatives suggest that they would spend aid more effectively, notably by doing so through more trustworthy partners, tracing some continuity with Scheer's critique of development assistance under the Trudeau government and harkening back to the Harper government's frequent invocation of greater aid effectiveness (Brown 2015).

Notwithstanding Scheer's grandstanding before the 2019 elections on his plan to cut aid by 25%, a consensus seems to exist within both the Liberal and Conservative parties that Canada's aid should remain around its current level. Although, as mentioned above, the New Democrats and Greens both advocate more than doubling aid to meet Canada's international commitments of 0.7% of gross national income (Brown 2019), the issue does not attract much attention from most Canadians, other than the staff of development NGOs and a few academics (e.g., Brown 2020). It is therefore unlikely that Canada will make any important increases to its aid budget, regardless of the COVID-19 crisis.

In fact, aid spending might go down in 2020, despite the unforeseen cost of repatriating Canadian staff in March/April 2020, because the pandemic has delayed many project activities. Lapsed funds are normally returned to the Treasury Board, rather than rolled over to the next year. However, the Canadian government could avoid the loss of funds by making "one-off" contributions to multilateral organizations, including to the UN agencies' emergency appeals, before the end of the fiscal year, or by prepaying their annual contributions to multilateral agencies, as it has done on many occasions over the decades. Alternatively, the Canadian government might be content to see aid spending fall, as long as its share of Canada's shrinking gross national income remains constant or even increases, allowing it to claim in the latter case greater generosity according to that metric.

Canada is not alone in not opening its purse. While OECD donor countries made a collective—albeit cautiously phrased—promise to "strive to protect ODA budgets" (OECD 2020b: 2), their aid commitments in

January-May 2020 dropped by one third—US$7 billion—compared to the same period in 2019 (Breed and Sternberg 2020: 2, 8). The United Kingdom actually announced a cut of £2.9 billion to its 2020 aid expenditures (BBC 2020), a sum equivalent to about Cdn$5 billion, close to Canada's total annual aid disbursements. Notwithstanding Germany's aid budget increase mentioned above, an OECD survey found few indications in April 2020 that donors were planning to increase overall spending abroad in response to the pandemic (Ahmad et al. 2020), though this could change over time. If total Canadian and other bilateral donors' assistance will increase at best only marginally, any pandemic-related activities will require the reallocation of aid program resources that would otherwise be spent on other areas.

What Impact on Priorities and Modalities?

Over the course of decades, the aid pendulum swings back and forth between a prioritization of welfare spending to meet needs quickly and emphasis on long-term growth, which will theoretically do more to reduce poverty in the long run. In 2000, with the adoption of the Millennium Development Goals, donors' emphasis had returned to social spending, but after the 2008 global financial crisis it swung strongly back toward the promotion of growth and the private sector and, relatedly, donor self-interest (Mawdsley 2018).

Canada is no exception to that trend. Under the Harper government, Canadian aid was increasingly instrumentalized and in particular "recommercialized" (Brown 2016b, c; see also Gecelovsky 2019). Though its successor, the Trudeau government, distinguished its international role from its predecessor at the rhetorical level and branded its aid program very differently, its aid shows "remarkable continuity" with the previous government's practices (Brown 2018: 159). Despite espousing a feminist approach and women's empowerment, FIAP retains an "unwavering focus on economic growth as the path to poverty alleviation" (Parisi 2020: 173).

The catastrophic impact of COVID-19 on the Global South dictates a reorientation of development assistance away from long-term growth objectives toward more immediate needs. Access to food and health services is particularly urgent (Cardwell and Ghazalian 2020; Okoi and Bwawa 2020) and could fall under the rubric of humanitarian assistance. But where will the funds come from, if the overall budget does not significantly increase, and at what cost? As aid analysts have noted, "As donors shift priorities towards COVID-19, a 'zero-sum' funding competition between individual sectors is likely and will be fierce" (Johnson et al. 2020). Similarly, Cardwell and Ghazalian (2020: 2) recognize that "increased humanitarian spending may come at the expense of other forms of ODA [official development assistance]." Canada's Minister of International Development Karina Gould seems well aware of this problem, stating that "What keeps me up at night is not just the immediate needs of the pandemic, but the collateral damage if we turn our attention away from our core activities" (quoted in Blanchfield 2020a), but she lacks the power to set Canada's aid budget.

Without an overall budget increase, new funding to the health sector, for instance, means that fewer resources will be available for education, legal reform, or supporting women's entrepreneurship. Even within a sector, new priorities imply a concurrent deprioritization of others. Spending any proportion of the health sector allocations on COVID-19 will require sacrificing funding for other areas, such as HIV/AIDS, tuberculosis and malaria, or children's standard vaccinations. Such cutbacks are particularly ill-timed, as the pandemic already makes it harder for people to access treatments and other health services. As a result, COVID-19 will negatively affect the health even of people who do not get the virus, just as recent Ebola outbreaks indirectly led to higher prevalence of measles and maternal mortality in Western and Central Africa (Gigova 2019; Gould 2020; OECD 2020c: 11).

The impact has two important short-term effects on aid modalities as well, which could translate into a longer-term change. First, the urgency of the need to act prompted the Canadian government to channel much of its initial pandemic-related spending via multilateral institutions and funds. Indeed, in addition to the required speed, the basic importance of a joint response impelled the prioritization of collaborative efforts. Joint measures are especially relevant in instances of not only humanitarian assistance but also global public goods, in this case best illustrated by coordinated efforts to develop and make globally available effective treatments and a vaccine for COVID-19 (Nickerson and Herder 2020). COVID-19 could therefore be an impetus for moving away from "branded" bilateral initiatives that promote donor visibility at the expense of effectiveness (Brown 2018; Vollmer 2014) toward more multilateralism and pooled funds.

Second, the pandemic has erected barriers to the deployment of international staff in developing countries. As noted above, one of Canada's first responses to the COVID-19 was to repatriate many of its aid workers stationed abroad. As a result, aid projects must increasingly rely on local staff—something that Southern-based development actors have been advocating for years, if not decades. Localization, as the phenomenon is known, does not just imply counting more on country nationals for labor; it also involves "transferring power and decision-making into the hands of local people, and organisations" (Roche and Tarpey 2020), which is something the Canadian government has always been reluctant to do. Even locally based Canadian aid officials have very little decision-making authority compared to other donors (den Heyer 2012).

It remains to be seen, however, if increased multilateralism and localization are temporary or lasting effects of the pandemic. The fate of trends will depend in part on how effective the modalities prove to be. Also key in both instances will be the political will in Canada and other donor countries to relinquish both control and the ability to claim direct credit for positive outcomes.

The Rationale for Aid: Global vs. National Perspectives

Debates on the overarching motive for aid are unending and unresolvable. Actors will never agree on the fundamental purposes of aid—nor do they need to, as enlightened forms of self-interest are compatible with altruistic perspectives (Black 2016). The COVID-19 pandemic, however, highlights the underlying tensions. Should Canada provide assistance because of the sheer scale of human suffering caused or exacerbated by the coronavirus? Or should it act because a "virus reservoir" anywhere in the world could affect Canada's economy and the health of Canadians, even if Canada has the disease under control within its own borders?

Whereas O'Toole's outdated tweet suggested the need for a "Canada first" approach (or maybe even "Canada only"), it seems quite uncontroversial for the government to take a position that straddles altruism and enlightened self-interest. For instance, weeks before the Security Council vote, Trudeau combined the two perspectives when addressing Canada's response to the global economic crisis caused by COVID-19, emphasizing Canadian economic interests:

Canadian jobs and businesses depend on stable and productive economies in other countries – so it matters to us how everyone weathers this storm. We cannot forget those who are most vulnerable, whether they are living in remote regions or in the Caribbean. For so many, this pandemic is devastating. More than 300 million people around the world will be out of work. And more than 30 million people will be pushed into extreme poverty. We can't wait for others to act. It's not in our self-interest, and it's just not who we are. (Trudeau 2020a)

Gould, as noted above, had already made the case for altruism as self-interest before the pandemic was declared. Since then, whereas Trudeau emphasized Canadian economic interests, she places greater emphasis on Canadians' health and safety. For example, she argued that "we will only be safe until [sic] everyone, everywhere on the planet is safe" and "Our health here depends on the health of the other 'over there'" (Gould 2020). In other examples of intertwined national and international interests, she stated that "Our global response is part of our domestic response: we will not be safe from COVID-19 in Canada until everyone, everywhere is" (quoted in GAC 2020) and "We strongly believe that supporting other countries in their fight against COVID-19 is crucial to protect Canadians at home" (quoted in PMO 2020).

Despite these statements, domestic and international interests do not always dovetail so neatly. They can sometimes be in direct competition. Notably, a tension—if not an outright contradiction—developed between the government's principled support for universal access to vaccination on the one hand and "vaccine nationalism" on the other hand, including the imperative of meeting popular expectations that the government would secure a sufficient supply to meet the needs of its citizens (e.g., Attaran 2020). For instance, as mentioned above, Trudeau announced $120 million in June 2020 for an initiative that would help ensure that treatments and vaccines would be made available to the poor and middle-income countries. On that occasion, he stated, "We're also committed to working with countries around the world on how we can pool procurement efforts to make sure all countries have access to the vaccine" (quoted in Blanchfield 2020a).

Despite Trudeau's commitment to pooled procurement and Gould's support for "fair, and equitable access to COVID-19 vaccines" (quoted in PMO 2020), the government sought "Canada first" access by signing bilateral contracts with numerous pharmaceutical companies for early access to several as-yet-unapproved vaccines for the country's population. In August, Procurement Minister Anita Anand said that her government wanted to ensure that "Canadians are at the front of the line when a vaccine becomes available" (quoted in Jones and Harris 2020). However, by elbowing its way to the front, Canada pushes lower-income countries to the back of the line and delays their access to vaccines. Because it is a zero-sum game, prioritizing the wealthy over the most vulnerable actually reduces the total number of lives saved by vaccines (Gates Foundation 2020: 16; Labonte et al. 2020).

In an apparent attempt to mitigate criticism of the government's vaccine nationalism, Trudeau announced in September 2020, alongside the government's sixth bilateral vaccine procurement agreement, a $220 million contribution to the COVAX Facility, a global procurement mechanism, in order to help make vaccines available in low- and middle-income countries (PMO 2020). By then, Canada and other high-income countries, representing 13% of the world's population, had already secured more than half of the potential supply of five of the most promising vaccine candidates (Oxfam 2020b).

Conclusion: Canadian Aid in a Post-pandemic World?

In late 2019, the newly re-elected Liberal government seemed prepared for business as usual for its foreign aid program. Its main focus was to continue to implement the Feminist International Assistance Policy, still barely two years old. At most, there would be some minor tweaks, such as additional official attention to education and, unofficially, food security and agriculture, but no significant changes in direction or levels of funding. The government's minority status was not a significant variable, just as it had not been under the Harper Conservatives minorities between 2006 and 2011 (Brown 2016a). During its first few months of its new mandate, the Liberal government ramped up its liberal/Liberal internationalist rhetoric aimed at the domestic audience, while also seeking greater visibility internationally as part of its unsuccessful campaign for a seat on the UN Security Council.

Like for any external shock, it is tempting to declare, "This changes everything!" The pandemic did force some rapid reorientations in how governments and international agencies deliver aid. The Canadian government rapidly brought expatriate staff back to Canada, necessitating greater reliance on local staff; announced a series of COVID-related contributions, mainly to multilateral organizations and international initiatives, often in support of global public goods; and prompted an increase of resources to the health, food, and humanitarian sectors, at the expense of other areas. The government also responded by shifting how it justifies foreign aid, increasingly presenting it as being in Canada's interest, be it economic (as argued by Trudeau) or for Canadians' health and security (as emphasized by Gould). COVID-19 initially led to greater involvement in the aid file by the Prime Minister and the Minister of Foreign Affairs, who had already become more visible before the pandemic hit. Discussing the pandemic response was a pretext to engage with their counterparts in Africa, the Caribbean, and the Pacific, presumably through an electoral calculus related to the June 2020 vote on Security Council membership. The charm offensive, however, tapered off after Canada's bid failed.

It is uncertain how enduring the new de facto aid priorities and modalities will be. The pandemic presents Canada and development actors as a whole with an important opportunity to do things differently and "build back better." The results of this forced experiment will influence whether aid returns essentially to business as usual, but even more important will be the will of political leaders to take the required steps, even if they involve less visibility and control on the part of the Canadian and other donor governments.

The pull of the status quo is strong in Canadian development assistance. Given the Trudeau Liberals' much ballyhooed internationalist rhetoric, including the now cliché declaration of Canada being "back," one could have expected commensurately greater emphasis on foreign aid. However, only nominal increases in aid spending have followed and the government has focused on the feminist rebranding of its aid and niche thematic programming, rather than seeking broader changes (Black 2020: 232). The relatively modest level of financial resources that the Canadian government is currently willing to allocate to foreign aid is already the "Achilles Heel" of FIAP and the credibility of the government's oft-repeated claims to global leadership in development cooperation (Brown and Swiss 2017: 118). Meanwhile, the Conservatives have abandoned their populist proposal to significantly cut aid, at least for now, and have not articulated any proposals that differ much from what is currently in place. As in the past, despite partisan differences in rhetoric, the Liberals' and Conservatives' approach to Canada's aid program varies quite little in concrete terms (Brown 2018).

The Trudeau government will no doubt continue to express its commitment to internationalism and to alleviating suffering around the world, especially among women and girls. However, an important indicator of its actual commitment to international development in the post-pandemic world will be the medium-term evolution of the Canadian aid budget. Although needs in the Global South have dramatically increased because of COVID-19 and the pandemic will have a lasting negative impact, there is a significant risk of post-pandemic budget cuts to Canadian aid. The government will be under tremendous pressure to cut spending to try to get the ballooning deficit under control. Balancing budgets is commonly done on the backs of the world's poor, as they do not play much of a role in the Canadian electoral calculations. If the Conservative Party comes back to power, the risk will be multiplied—although drastic aid cuts might be avoided if the Conservatives want to avoid seeming too mean-spirited, a factor that appears to have contributed to their defeat in 2015.

Moreover, as the pandemic threat fades, the recent rise of justifications based on enlightened self-interest could give way once again to more narrowly defined short-term interests, which in turn could divert attention from poverty reduction and the welfare of the world's most vulnerable people. Ultimately, if that scenario comes to pass, Canada's role as a global development actor would become even more marginal than it is today, and it could take a decade or more to rebuild once the pendulum starts to swing back in the opposite direction.

Acknowledgements The author is grateful to David Carment, Richard Nimijean, Morgane Rosier, and Liam Swiss for helpful suggestions and to the Social Sciences and Humanities Research Council of Canada for financial support.

REFERENCES

Ahmad, Yasmin, Emily Bosch, Eleanor Carey, and Ida Mc Donnell. 2020. "Six Decades of ODA: Insights and Outlook in the COVID-19 Crisis." *OECD Development Co-operation Profiles*. Paris: OECD. https://doi.org/10.1787/2dcf1367-en.

Al-Ali, Nadje. 2020. "Covid-19 and Feminism in the Global South: Challenges, Initiatives and Dilemmas." *European Journal of Women's Studies* 27 (4): 333–347. https://doi.org/10.1177/1350506820943617.

Attaran, Amir. 2020. "How the Liberals Are Bungling the Vaccine Endgame." *Maclean's*, August 24. https://www.macleans.ca/opinion/how-the-liberals-are-bungling-the-vaccine-endgame/. Accessed on August 29, 2020.

Aylward, Erin, and Stephen Brown. 2020. "Sexual Orientation and Gender Identity in Canada's 'Feminist' International Assistance." *International Journal* 75 (3): 313–328. https://doi.org/10.1177/0020702020953425.

BBC. 2020. "Coronavirus: UK Foreign Aid Spending Cut by £2.9bn Amid Economic Downturn." *BBC News*, July 23. https://www.bbc.com/news/uk-politics-53508933. Accessed on September 27, 2020.

Black, David R. 2016. "Humane Internationalism and the Malaise of Canadian Aid Policy." In *Rethinking Canadian Aid*, 2nd ed., edited by Stephen Brown, Molly den Heyer, and David R. Black, 17–35. Ottawa: University of Ottawa Press.

Black, David R. 2020. "Canada and the Changing Landscape of Global Development Cooperation." *Canadian Foreign Policy Journal* 26 (2): 228–234. https://doi.org/10.1080/11926422.2019.1682019.

Blanchfield, Mike. 2020a. "Canada Pledges $300 Million to Address Humanitarian Concerns of COVID-19 Abroad." *CBC News*, June 27. https://www.cbc.ca/news/politics/global-citizen-covid-19-fundraiser-1.5629974. Accessed on August 26, 2020.

Blanchfield, Mike. 2020b. "Gould, Aid Groups Discuss Helping World's Poorest with $100 M Funding Boost." *National Post*, April 6. https://nationalpost.com/pmn/news-pmn/canada-news-pmn/gould-aid-groups-discuss-helping-worlds-poorest-with-100m-funding-boost. Accessed on August 26, 2020.

Blanchfield, Mike. 2020c. "Trudeau Pledges Extra $400 Million in Humanitarian Aid to Fight COVID-19." *CTV News*, September 29. https://www.ctvnews.ca/politics/trudeau-pledges-extra-400-million-in-humanitarian-aid-to-fight-covid-1.5124537. Accessed on September 30, 2020.

Breed, Dean, and Lewis Sternberg. 2020. "How Are Aid Budgets Changing Due to the Covid-19 Crisis?" Development Initiatives, July 22. https://devinit.org/resources/how-are-aid-budgets-changing-due-covid-19-crisis/. Accessed on August 29, 2020.

Brown, Stephen. 2015. "Aid Effectiveness and the Framing of New Canadian Aid Initiatives." In *Readings in Canadian Foreign Policy: Classic Debates and New Ideas*, 3rd ed., edited by Duane Bratt and Christopher J. Kukucha, 467–481. Don Mills, ON: Oxford University Press.

Brown, Stephen. 2016a. "Canadian Aid Policy During the Harper Years." In *The Harper Era in Canadian Foreign Policy: Parliament, Politics, and Canada's*

Global Posture, edited by Adam Chapnick and Christopher J. Kukucha, 167–180. Vancouver: UBC Press.

Brown, Stephen. 2016b. "The Instrumentalization of Foreign Aid under the Harper Government." *Studies in Political Economy* 97 (1): 18–36. https://doi.org/10.1080/07078552.2016.1174461.

Brown, Stephen. 2016c. "Undermining Foreign Aid: The Extractive Sector and the Recommercialization of Canadian Development Assistance." In *Rethinking Canadian Aid*, 2nd ed., edited by Stephen Brown, Molly den Heyer, and David R. Black, 273–94. Ottawa: University of Ottawa Press.

Brown, Stephen. 2018. "All About That Base? Branding and the Domestic Politics of Canadian Foreign Aid." *Canadian Foreign Policy Journal* 24 (2): 145–164. https://doi.org/10.1080/11926422.2018.1461666.

Brown, Stephen. 2019. "Foreign Aid on the Campaign Agenda." Blog Entry, McLeod Group, October 3. https://www.mcleodgroup.ca/2019/10/foreign-aid-on-the-campaign-agenda/. Accessed August 26, 2020.

Brown, Stephen. 2020. "Foreign Aid Flows: The Canadian Government Is Still Not Stepping Up to the Plate." Blog Entry, McLeod Group, April 16. https://www.mcleodgroup.ca/2020/04/foreign-aid-flows-the-canadian-government-is-still-not-stepping-up-to-the-plate/. Accessed on August 26, 2020.

Brown, Stephen. 2021. "The Impact of COVID-19 on Development Assistance." *International Journal* 76 (1). https://doi.org/10.1177/0020702020986888.

Brown, Stephen, and Liam Swiss. 2017. "Canada's Feminist International Assistance Policy: Game Changer or Fig Leaf?" In *How Ottawa Spends, 2017–2018*, edited by Katherine A.H. Graham and Allan M. Maslove, 117–131. Ottawa: Carleton University.

Carbert, Michelle. 2020. "Trudeau to Co-host United Nations Meeting as Vote for Security Council Seat Nears." *Globe and Mail*, May 26. https://www.theglobeandmail.com/politics/article-trudeau-to-co-host-united-nations-meeting-as-vote-for-security-council/. Accessed on August 28, 2020.

Cardwell, Ryan, and Pascal L. Ghazalian. 2020. "COVID-19 and International Food Assistance: Policy Proposals to Keep Food Flowing." *World Development* 135 (105059): 1–4. https://doi.org/10.1016/j.worlddev.2020.105059.

CBC. 2005. "PM Shells Out $4.6B for NDP's Support." *CBC News*, April 26. https://www.cbc.ca/news/canada/pm-shells-out-4-6b-for-ndp-s-support-1.541632. Accessed on August 26, 2020.

Charles, Gavin, and Shannon Kindornay. 2020. "Canada Should Pursue More Ambitious International Aid Plan." *Policy Options*, May 8. https://policyoptions.irpp.org/magazines/may-2020/canada-should-pursue-more-ambitious-international-aid-plan/. Accessed on August 26, 2020.

den Heyer, Molly. 2012. "Untangling Canadian Aid Policy: International Agreements, CIDA'S Policies, and Micro-Policy Negotiations in Tanzania." In *Struggling for Effectiveness: CIDA and Canadian Foreign Aid*, edited by Stephen Brown, 186–216. Montreal and Kingston: McGill-Queen's University Press.

Dzsurdzsa, Cosmin. 2019. "Justin Trudeau Resorts to Completely Ignoring Reporter's Questions." *The Post Millennial*, October 1. https://thepostmille nnial.com/watch-justin-trudeau-resorts-to-completely-ignoring-reporters-que stions/. Accessed on August 23, 2020.

Economist. 2020. "From Plague to Penury: The Pandemic Is Plunging Millions Back into Extreme Poverty." *The Economist*, September 26. https://www.eco nomist.com/international/2020/09/26/the-pandemic-is-plunging-millions-back-into-extreme-poverty/. Accessed on September 26, 2020.

GAC. 2020. "Canada Announces Support for Equitable Access to New COVID-19 Medical Solutions." News Release, June 27. https://www.canada.ca/en/ global-affairs/news/2020/06/canada-announces-support-for-equitable-acc ess-to-new-covid-19-medical-solutions.html. Accessed on August 29, 2020.

Gatehouse, Jonathon. 2019. "Andrew Scheer's Claim About Foreign Aid Deemed False." *CBC News*, October 1. https://www.cbc.ca/news/pol itics/conservatives-foreign-aid-fact-check-1.5305045. Accessed on August 23, 2020.

Gates Foundation. 2020. *COVID-19, A Global Perspective: 2020 Goalkeepers Report*. Bill and Melinda Gates Foundation.

Gecelovsky, Paul. 2019. "From Humane to Responsible: Stephen Harper, Narrative and Canadian Foreign Policy." *Canadian Foreign Policy Journal* 26 (3): 239–256. https://doi.org/10.1080/11926422.2019.1684962.

Gigova, Radina. 2019. "Measles Has Claimed More Than Twice as Many Lives as Ebola in DRC." *CNN*, November 28. https://www.cnn.com/2019/11/ 28/africa/measles-ebola-drc/index.html. Accessed on August 28, 2020.

Gould, Karina. 2020. "Rebuilding a More Resilient Planet." *Thomson Reuters Foundation News*, May 1. http://news.trust.org/item/20200501102506-sxegy/. Accessed on August 29, 2020.

Government of Canada. 2017. *Canada's Feminist International Assistance Policy*. Ottawa: Global Affairs Canada. https://www.international.gc.ca/ world-monde/issues_development-enjeux_developpement/priorities-priori tes/policy-politique.aspx?lang=eng. Accessed on August 26, 2020.

Governor General. 2020. "A Stronger and More Resilient Canada: Speech from the Throne to Open the Second Session of the Forty-Third Parliament of Canada." Government of Canada, September 23. https://www.canada.ca/ en/privy-council/campaigns/speech-throne/2020/speech-from-the-throne. html. Accessed on September 26, 2020.

Johnson, Zoe, Isabela Vera, and Raimund Zühr. 2020. "How Are Donor Countries Responding to COVID-19? Early Analyses and Trends to Watch." May 13. https://donortracker.org/insights/how-are-donor-countries-responding-covid-19-early-analyses-and-trends-watch. Accessed on August 28, 2020.

Jones, Ryan Patrick, and Kathleen Harris. 2020. "Feds Sign Agreements with Pfizer, Moderna for Millions of Doses of COVID-19 Vaccines." *CBC News*, August 5. https://www.cbc.ca/news/politics/vaccine-procurement-anand-bains-1.5674820. Accessed on September 26, 2020.

Labonte, Ronald, Katrina Plamondon, Mira Johri, and Srinivas Murthy. 2020. "Canada's 'me first' COVID-19 Vaccine Strategy May Come at the Cost of Global Health." *The Conversation*, September 27. https://theconversation.com/canadas-me-first-covid-19-vaccine-strategy-may-come-at-the-cost-of-global-health-146908. Accessed on September 28, 2020.

Liberal Party of Canada. 2019. "Help for the World's Most Vulnerable People." https://liberal.ca/our-platform/help-for-the-worlds-most-vulnerable-people/. Accessed on August 23, 2020.

Mawdsley, Emma. 2018. "The 'Southernisation' of Development?" *Asia Pacific Viewpoint* 59 (2): 173–185. https://doi.org/10.1111/apv.12192.

Nickerson, Jason W., and Matthew Herder. 2020. "COVID-19 Vaccines as Global Public Goods." In *Vulnerable: The Law, Policy and Ethics of COVID-19*, edited by Colleen M. Flood, Vanessa MacDonnell, Jane Philpott, Sophie Thériault, and Sridhar Venkatapuram, 591–600. Ottawa: University of Ottawa Press.

OECD. 2020a. "Aid by DAC Members Increases in 2019 with More Aid to the Poorest Countries," April 16. Paris: Organisation for Economic Co-operation and Development. https://www.oecd.org/dac/financing-sustainable-development/development-finance-data/ODA-2019-detailed-summary.pdf. Accessed on August 26, 2020.

OECD. 2020b. "COVID-19 Global Pandemic: Joint Statement by the Development Assistance Committee (DAC) of the Organisation for Economic Co-operation and Development (OECD)," April 9. https://www.oecd.org/dac/development-assistance-committee/DAC-Joint-Statement-COVID-19.pdf. Accessed on August 29, 2020.

OECD. 2020c. "The Impact of the Coronavirus (COVID-19) Crisis on Development Finance." Paris: OECD. https://www.oecd.org/coronavirus/policy-responses/the-impact-of-the-coronavirus-covid-19-crisis-on-development-finance-9de00b3b/. Accessed on August 28, 2020.

Okoi, Obasesam, and Tatenda Bwawa. 2020. "How Health Inequality Affect [sic] Responses to the COVID-19 Pandemic in Sub-Saharan Africa." *World Development* 135 (105067): 1–4. https://doi.org/10.1016/j.worlddev.2020.105067.

O'Toole, Erin. 2020. "Foreign Policy." https://erinotoole.ca/platform/foreign-policy/. Accessed on August 26, 2020.

Oxfam. 2020a. "The Hunger Virus: How COVID-19 Is Fuelling Hunger in a Hungry World." Media Briefing, July 9. https://www.oxfam.org/en/research/hunger-virus-how-covid-19-fuelling-hunger-hungry-world. Accessed on August 29, 2020.

Oxfam. 2020b. "Small Group of Rich Nations Have Bought Up More Than Half the Future Supply of Leading COVID-19 Vaccine Contenders." Press release, September 15. https://www.oxfam.org/en/press-releases/small-group-rich-nations-have-bought-more-half-future-supply-leading-covid-19. Accessed on September 27, 2020.

Parisi, Laura. 2020. "Canada's New Feminist International Assistance Policy: Business as Usual?" *Foreign Policy Analysis* 16 (2): 163–180. https://doi.org/10.1093/fpa/orz027.

PMO. 2020. "New Agreements to Secure Additional Vaccine Candidates for COVID-19." Prime Minister's Office, September 25. https://pm.gc.ca/en/news/news-releases/2020/09/25/new-agreements-secure-additional-vaccine-candidates-covid-19. Accessed on September 27, 2020.

Roche, Chris, and Fiona Tarpey. 2020. "COVID-19, Localisation and Locally Led Development: A Critical Juncture." Devpolicy Blog, March 23. https://devpolicy.org/covid-19-localisation-and-locally-led-development-a-critical-juncture-20200323/. Accessed on August 29, 2020.

Sumner, Andy, Eduardo Ortiz-Juarez, and Chris Hoy. 2020. "Precarity and the Pandemic: COVID-19 and Poverty Incidence, Intensity, and Severity in Developing Countries." WIDER Working Paper 2020/77. Helsinki: UNU-WIDER. https://doi.org/10.35188/UNU-WIDER/2020/834-4.

Trudeau, Justin. 2019. "Minister of International Development Mandate Letter." Prime Minister's Office, December 13. https://pm.gc.ca/en/mandate-letters/2019/12/13/minister-international-development-mandate-letter. Accessed on August 23, 2020.

Trudeau, Justin. 2020a. "Prime Minister's Remarks on Keeping Canadians Safe and Working with Other Countries to Fight COVID-19." Prime Minister's Office, May 26. https://pm.gc.ca/en/news/speeches/2020/05/26/prime-ministers-remarks-keeping-canadians-safe-and-working-other-countries. Accessed on August 29, 2020.

Trudeau, Justin. 2020b. "Remarks for the United Nations General Assembly Plenary Meeting." YouTube video, 8:25. Posted by "Justin Trudeau – Prime Minister of Canada," September 25. https://www.youtube.com/watch?v=xVxZ2HeMn9o. Accessed on September 30, 2020.

Tunney, Catherine. 2019. "NDP Leader Jagmeet Singh Begins to Lay Out Minority Scenario Priorities." *CBC News*, October 10. https://www.cbc.ca/

news/politics/ndp-singh-priorities-minority-1.5315981. Accessed on August 23, 2020.

UN News. 2020. "As Famines of 'Biblical Proportion' Loom, Security Council Urged to 'Act Fast'." *UN News*, April 21. https://news.un.org/en/story/2020/04/1062272. Accessed on August 28, 2020.

Vollmer, Frank. 2014. "Debating 'Visibility' and Its Effects on the Effective Delivery of Official Development Assistance – Diagnosis, Justification and Possibilities." *Information Development* 30 (4): 298–312. https://doi.org/10.1177/0266666913491955.

von Scheel, Elise. 2020. "Canada's Plan for COVID-19 International Aid Just Beginning, Minister Says." *CBC News*, April 8. https://www.cbc.ca/news/politics/covid-pandemic-coronavirus-foreign-aid-1.5525508. Accessed on August 26, 2020.

Wells, Paul. 2020. "Karina Gould on Pierre Trudeau's Legacy." *Maclean's*, January 10. https://www.macleans.ca/politics/ottawa/karina-gould-on-pie rre-trudeaus-legacy/. Accessed on August 26, 2020.

Wright, Teresa. 2019. "Baloney Meter: Andrew Scheer Says Canada Sends Foreign Aid to Rich Countries." *National Post*, October 2. https://nation alpost.com/pmn/news-pmn/canada-news-pmn/baloney-meter-andrew-sch eer-says-canada-sends-foreign-aid-to-rich-countries. Accessed on August 23, 2020.

CHAPTER 13

Stuck in the Middle with You: Canada–China Relations in the Era of U.S.–China Clashes

Duane Bratt

INTRODUCTION

COVID-19 has fundamentally changed the relationship between Canada, China, and the United States. It has led to rising anti-China sentiment, calls for re-shoring essential products, and pledges to hold China "accountable" for the pandemic in both the United States and Canada. However, relations between China and Canada/United States were problematic before COVID-19. Canada, for historical and economic reasons, had largely desired greater relations with China. Although there was a segment of Canadian society that was wary of China. This debate between optimists and pessimists regarding China has been exacerbated by growing clashes between the United States and China. Canada has been stuck in the middle between two superpowers. The COVID-19 pandemic took a bad situation and made it much worse. Possibly irreversibly so.

D. Bratt (✉)
Mount Royal University, Calgary, AB, Canada
e-mail: dbratt@mtroyal.ca

273

Canada recognized the People's Republic of China (PRC) in 1970. From Pierre Trudeau, through Brian Mulroney, Jean Chrétien, and Paul Martin, there was a realization in Ottawa about the importance of the Chinese market and the need to cultivate it. As Paul Evans wrote several years ago, "[w]ith the exception of Canada's relations with the United States, no other relationship is as complex, pressing, and diverse at the levels of policy and management as the one with China" (Evans 2014: 8). The economic relationship still matters. After all, for decades, a goal of Canadian policy has been to diversify its trade dependence upon the United States. During the 1970s, there were efforts at increasing trade with Japan and Europe. Today the efforts involve increasing trade with China. This is because China is now the world's second largest economy and estimates are that by 2030 it will have surpassed the United States in GDP. There have been substantial increases in bilateral trade with China over the decades. China has become Canada's second largest trade partner (although at 7% it is still dwarfed by U.S. trade's 65%) and has maintained a large bilateral trade surplus. Nevertheless, there remain great opportunities for enhanced trade in sectors such as energy, agriculture, and financial services. In addition, despite the size of the two economies, overall bilateral investment remains relatively low. Chinese foreign direct investment (FDI) is only 2% of total FDI in Canada. Beyond the economics, is the flow of people. There are almost two million Canadian citizens of Chinese ancestry, and China represents the largest source of foreign students (125,000) and tourists (500,000) to Canada. While these monetary and human connections are important, they are matched by clashes over democracy, human rights, environment, espionage, and China's growing military and diplomatic assertiveness around the world (Burton 2015). This has been the dilemma facing recent Canadian governments and greatly exacerbated by the U.S.–China relationship and COVID-19.

The divide between Canadian optimists and pessimists regarding China can be largely broken down into partisanship, values, geography, and views of continentalism. In general, Liberals (like both Trudeaus and Jean Chrétien) have been more optimistic towards China than the Conservatives (such as Stephen Harper and Erin O'Toole). The old Progressive Conservatives were generally more optimistic towards China. Even a cold warrior such as John Diefenbaker negotiated wheat sales to China in the early 1960s. Brian Mulroney's government was also relatively restrained in its response to the Tiananmen Square massacre (Gecelovsky and Keenleyside 1995). However, under the new Conservative Party of Canada

(CPC), there is a combination of a pro-China and an anti-China wing that compete for control. In some periods, such as 2006–2009 or 2020, the anti-China wing dominates, and in other periods, such as 2010–2015, the pro-China wing ascends. British Columbia, because of its location on the Pacific Ocean and a large Chinese diaspora, has generally been more pro-China than the rest of the country. However, it must be said that those from Hong Kong are much more anti-China, especially over the last two years. Canadians who emphasize economic prosperity are more pro-China than those who emphasize values such as democracy, human rights, and the rule of law. Canadians who want to diversify their economy from dependence on the United States tend to be more pro-China, those who see their politics and economics through the American lens are more anti-China. As the United States has itself become more anti-China under the Trump administration, the pro-US/anti-China faction within Canada has become louder. In some cases, these factors may cause internal contradictions, but in other cases, they are reinforcing themselves. This clash between optimists and pessimists plays itself out through this chapter, especially in the final section on future options for Canadian-Chinese relations.

This chapter examines Canada's economic, diplomatic, and security relations with China in the context of a series of clashes between the United States and China. It is divided into five parts. Part one contrasts Stephen Harper's approach to China with the early years of Justin Trudeau's approach. Part two describes U.S.–China relations in the Trump era. Part three focuses on the arrest of Meng Wanzhou on a US extradition request and the subsequent retaliation by China. Part four shows how the deteriorating relationship between Canada and China has become even worse because of the COVID-19 outbreak. The final part is a conclusion and a look at the possible future Canada–China relationship.

Stephen Harper and Justin Trudeau and China: 2006–December 2018

In many respects, there had been a largely bipartisan consensus in Canadian foreign policy since World War II between the Liberal and Progressive Conservative governments. This changed with the appearance of the Conservative Party of Canada in 2003. The CPC was the result of a merger between the Reform/Canadian Alliance and Progressive Conservative parties after over a decade of intracene fighting among

Canadian conservatives. When the CPC came to power in 2006, it chose to revise Canada's foreign policy towards the UN, Arctic, the Middle East, development assistance, climate change, and, for our purposes here, China (Chapnick and Kukucha 2016). Harper, reflecting the Chinese pessimistic wing of the CPC, wanted to shift Canada's Asian focus from "totalitarian China" to "democratic India." Harper, and many other key members of his government and party, described China as a "godless, totalitarian country with nuclear weapons aimed at Canada" (Evans 2014: 62). In the initial years of his government's mandate, Harper publicly criticized China's human rights record, allowed several members of the Conservative caucus to visit Taiwan (also known as the Republic of China—the statehood of which is disputed by China), awarded honorary Canadian citizenship to the Dalai Lama (who advocates Tibetan independence from China), declined to attend the opening ceremony of the 2008 Olympics in the Chinese capital of Beijing, and refused to visit China until 2009 (Nossal and Sarson 2014). In a memorable quote during his first year as Prime Minister, Harper, discussing his criticism of China's human rights record, said "I think Canadians want us to promote our trade relations worldwide, and we do that, but I don't think Canadians want us to sell out important Canadian values. They don't want us to sell that out to the almighty dollar" (CBC 2006).

However, the Harper government soon realized that it was not advisable to isolate or antagonize China, and there was consequently a slight rapprochement towards China (Nossal and Sarson 2014). In 2009, both the Minister of Foreign Affairs Lawrence Cannon and the Minister of International Trade Stockwell Day made official visits to China. Later in the year, in December, Prime Minister Harper himself finally went to China—a trip marked by Chinese Premier Wen Jiabao's telling Harper that by waiting "too long" to visit, he had created serious "problems of mutual trust" (Lui 2013: 101). In June 2010, Chinese President Hu Jintao reciprocated Harper's visit through a state visit of his own.

There were two high-profile decisions that reflected the eventual improvement in Sino-Canadian relations during the Harper era. The first, in December 2013, was Industry Canada's approval of the purchase of the Canadian hydrocarbons company Nexen by China National Offshore Oil Corporation (CNOOC) at a cost of $15.1 billion. The Nexen case illustrated the tensions between the Chinese optimists and pessimists within the CPC. The pessimists argued that CNOOC was a Chinese state-owned enterprise, and there were fears that this would give Nexen, as a wholly-owned subsidiary of CNOOC, a competitive advantage over privately-owned companies owing to its lower capital costs through state subsidies and access to cheap loans. There were also concerns that Nexen would now operate as an arm of the Chinese government, and that there would be a lack of reciprocity for Canadian firms. Nevertheless, the optimists pointed to the economic benefits of the deal, especially that CNOOC significantly overpaid for Nexen, and the importance of liberalizing international investment rules. Ultimately, the optimists held sway and guided the Harper government's decision to approve it (Bratt 2015: 440–444).

The second decision occurred in September 2014 when the Canadian government ratified a Foreign Investment Promotion and Protection Agreement (FIPPA) with China (Smythe 2015: 427–428). The FIPPA protects Canadian and Chinese investors from discriminatory practices by mandating national treatment—this means that neither country is able to take action on behalf of, or against, a company based on ownership. At the time, Canada had FIPPAs with around two dozen countries, but none of them generated as much controversy as the one with China. That was because, while the FIPPA appeared to guarantee national treatment, there remained questions about whether Canadian firms would have fair access to the Chinese market and whether the processes were sufficiently transparent in the event of a potential dispute between a Canadian investor and the Chinese state (Smythe 2015: 427–428).

In 2015, after a decade of CPC rule, Justin Trudeau and the Liberals formed a majority government. In his first international visit after being elected, the November 2015 UN-sponsored climate change summit in Paris, Trudeau proclaimed that "Canada is Back!" (Fitz-Morris 2015). Since that time, Trudeau and the rest of his government have used the phrase as their foreign policy slogan. It is evident from Trudeau's quote, as well as the subsequent actions from his government, that he sought to bring back Canada's traditional foreign policy and reverse the transformation that was attempted by the Harper government (Blanchfield 2017; Hillmer and Lagassé 2018).

In particular, Trudeau came to office hoping to improve relations with China for several reasons (Calvert 2018; Lim 2020). First, it was a reaction to the previous Harper government that, as mentioned above, had been noticeably chilly towards China. Second, it was also a return to an optimistic view of China that had been expressed by previous Liberal governments. In particular, Chrétien's 1994 Team Canada trade summit when the Prime Minister, other cabinet ministers, provincial premiers, and business leaders all arrived at once to meet their Chinese counterparts. This resulted in billions of dollars' worth of bilateral economic activity. Third, the legacy of his father Pierre Trudeau. The elder Trudeau had been well respected in China because of things such as visiting China in 1960 (Trudeau and Hébert 1961) and becoming one of the first Western countries to diplomatically recognize China in 1970. Fourth, there is a large number of Chinese-Canadians, especially in the seat-rich greater Vancouver area, who are generally optimistic towards China and were seeking better relations. Trudeau's primary objective was to negotiate a comprehensive free trade agreement with China.

To help persuade the Chinese that Canada was serious about free trade negotiations, Trudeau took a number of steps to differentiate his approach to China from the Harper government. Canada quickly joined the Chinese-created Asia Infrastructure Investment Bank. In March 2017, Trudeau appointed John McCallum as Canada's Ambassador to China. As a political appointment, instead of coming from Canada's diplomatic corps, it was a signal that China was a priority country. Typically, Canada only dispatched political appointees to the United States, United Kingdom, France, and Israel. McCallum's appointment was initially seen as a stroke of genius because he had been a senior cabinet minister in previous Liberal governments, had an economics background (at both McGill University and Royal Bank of Canada), came from a riding (Markham-Thornhill) with a large number of Chinese-Canadians, and spoke Mandarin (due to his marriage to a Chinese-Canadian). Ottawa also approved two controversial Chinese foreign investments. It overturned the Harper government's decision to block Hong Kong-based O-Net Communications from acquiring ITF Technologies (a fibre-optic company). Then, it approved Hytera's purchase of Norsat, a satellite technology firm with military contracts in the United States and Taiwan (Lim 2020: 29).

Chinese Premier Li Keqiang met with Trudeau in Ottawa in September 2016 and signed a joint statement to "launch exploratory discussions for a possible Canada-China Free Trade Agreement" (PM 2016). After a series of other high-level meetings, Trudeau visited China in December 2017, but was unable to advance the trade talks beyond the exploratory stage into formal negotiations. China objected to Canada's progressive trade agenda, as it had been outlined in August 2017 (Freeland 2017).

It was unwilling to discuss the entrenchment of labour, gender, environment, and governance issues in the negotiating framework of the free trade talks. This shows how the tension between the Chinese optimists (economic benefits of free trade with China) and Chinese pessimists (pursuing human rights in China) can play itself out even within the same Canadian government wrestling with one issue. The decision of the Trudeau government in May 2018 to quash the foreign takeover of Aecorn by the state-owned China Communications Construction Co. Ltd (CCCC) also contributed to keeping the free trade talks on hold.

Trade negotiations with China have been controversial at home. This is because while there are great economic possibilities, Canadians are concerned about the anti-democratic nature of China, its human rights abuses, and allegations of Chinese security agencies spying on Canada. Since the mid-1990s, the Canadian Security and Intelligence Service (CSIS) has been warning about extensive Chinese political, commercial, and societal spying. However, this did not truly reach the public consciousness until a bombshell speech by CSIS head Richard Fadden in 2010. Speaking to the Royal Canadian Military Institute in Toronto, Fadden claimed, "there are several municipal politicians in British Columbia and in at least two provinces there are ministers of the Crown who we think are under at least the general influence of a foreign government" (CBC 2010). Fadden did not specify the foreign government, but he was clearly referring to China. Jonathan Manthorpe's (2019) bestseller, *Claws of the Panda,* also extensively documented Chinese activity in Canada.

> Since before it came to power in 1949, the Chinese Communist Party has been establishing links through which it can influence Canadian political, commercial, media, and academic discourse to its own advantage. The construction of that network has grown and spread dramatically since diplomatic relations were established in 1970. The CCP now has the capacity to ensure its interests are voiced, and can often dominate, when matters of concern to Beijing are raised in Canada's Parliament, its provincial legislatures and municipal council halls, its media, and its lecture theatres. (Manthorpe 2019: 6)

In August 2018, concerns about China's human rights record dramatically increased with revelations about its treatment of its Uyghur minority. The United Nations reported that one million ethnic Uyghurs and other

Muslim minorities were being held in internment camps in the far western province of Xinjiang (United Nations 2018). There was some criticism of China by McCallum and other Canadian officials. However, the overall response from Ottawa was muted—there was no sustained rebuke from Trudeau or Foreign Ministers Chrystia Freeland and François-Philippe Champagne—nor sanctions of any kind.

Security issues can now be added to the list of Chinese espionage and human rights abuses. Recent events in Hong Kong have further complicated Canada's relations with China. Throughout most of 2019 and 2020, there have been constant anti-government protests. The origin of the protests was a proposed extradition treaty between Hong Kong and China. However, the shelving of the extradition treaty legislation did not end the protests. Instead, the protestors moved towards advocating for enhanced democracy in Hong Kong and criticizing the Chinese communist government. The response occurred a year later when the Hong Kong government, on orders from Beijing, brought in a controversial national security law. The law was aimed at curtailing the pro-democracy protests, but is so vague that it could be interpreted in ways that would affect all of Hong Kongers' day-to-day lives (Davidson 2020). This was a clear attack on the approach that governed Hong Kong for the last two decades. When Britain negotiated the handover of Hong Kong back to China in 1997, the formula was "one country, two systems." This would ensure Chinese sovereignty over Hong Kong while maintaining Hong Kong's economic and political autonomy. There remain real fears that if protests continue, they will be quashed with force either by the Hong Kong police or, in echoes of the 1989 Tiananmen Square massacre, by the Chinese People's Liberation Army. Because there are almost 300,000 Canadian passport holders in Hong Kong, Canada has a stake in ensuring that the protests are not met with force. However, the Canadian response has not been as critical because of its own ongoing difficulties in dealing with Beijing. It did join with the United States, Britain, and Australia in issuing a statement that said "direct imposition of national security legislation on Hong Kong by the Beijing authorities, rather than through Hong Kong's own institutions...would curtail the Hong Kong people's liberties, and in doing so, dramatically erode the autonomy and the system that made it so prosperous" (Chase and Fife 2020a). Nevertheless, unlike Britain, Canada has not yet committed to allowing immigration from Hong Kong, nor has it said what it would do to protect the Canadian citizens living in Hong Kong. Recently, Canada started to accept some

Hong Kong pro-democracy activists as refugees, so it is possible that this could eventually lead to greater flows of Hong Kongers to Canada (Chase and Fife 2020c).

U.S.–CHINA RELATIONS IN THE TRUMP ERA: 2017–2020

An even bigger complication in Canada's deteriorating bilateral relationship with China is the United States. This is because there are ongoing security and trade issues between China and the United States, and Canada is stuck in the middle between the world's most dominant country and the world's rising power. Graham Allison documented 16 cases over 500 years in which a dominant power was confronted by a rising power. In 12 cases, a major war resulted and in only 4 was there a peaceful resolution (Allison 2017). Avoiding the Thucydides's Trap will be *the* geopolitical challenge of the twenty-first century. Not just for the United States and China, but for the rest of the world including Canada.

There had been growing economic and security tensions between the United States and China over the last two decades. Responding to a rising China's behaviour was a bipartisan concern across the entire US government (Doran 2018). For example, the Obama administration frequently threatened to brand China a currency manipulator; whereby China took steps to artificially, and in violation of international trade agreements, keep the yuan low. However, these pre-existing tensions really escalated with the election of US President Donald Trump. Trump came to power promising to end or revise existing trade agreements. His focus was to prevent trade deficits and negotiate bilateral, as opposed to multilateral, agreements. Soon after his inauguration, Trump pulled the United States out of the Trans-Pacific Partnership (TPP) that had been negotiated by his predecessor Barack Obama with Japan, Canada, and nine other countries (ironically one of the goals of the TPP was to balance growing Chinese economic power in the Asia-Pacific region). The remaining eleven countries renegotiated a new deal, now called the Comprehensive and Progressive Agreement for Trans-Pacific Partnership (CPTPP). The CPTPP came into force on December 30, 2018. In addition, Trump, after threatening to withdraw unilaterally from the North American Free Trade Agreement (NAFTA), instead launched renegotiations with Canada and Mexico. The renegotiated NAFTA, now called the United States-Mexico-Canada Agreement (USMCA), came into force on July 1, 2020. The Trump administration has also been critical of the

World Trade Organization (WTO). While they have not withdrawn from the organization, they have used their clout to prevent the appointment of judges to the WTO's appellate body, which has damaged its dispute settlement mechanism (Johnson 2019).

Trump's trade agenda was also fixated on China. Trump had promised during the 2016 election campaign to fix China's "longtime abuse of the broken international system and unfair practices." Given his fixation on ending trade deficits, the fact that, in 2016, the United States had a $346 billion trade deficit in goods with China made it a logical target (Census 2020). Trump later appointed China-hawk Peter Navarro as his White House National Trade Council Director. Navarro would join Robert Lighthizer (US Trade Representative), Steve Mnuchin (Treasury Secretary), and Wilbur Ross (Commerce Secretary) as the team that would lead the trade fight against China.

In his first year in office, Trump seemed to weaken his rhetoric against China, due to a mutual charm offensive with Chinese President Xi Jinping. He tweeted: "I don't blame China, I blame the incompetence of past Admins for allowing China to take advantage of the U.S. on trade leading up to a point where the U.S. is losing $100's of billions. How can you blame China for taking advantage of people that had no clue? I would've done same!" (Trump 2017).

However, the temporary truce ended in January 2018 when Trump issued his first set of tariffs—aimed at Chinese solar panels and washing machines. In March 2018, Trump applied tariffs on an additional US$50–60 billion worth of Chinese goods. Over 1300 categories of Chinese imports were listed for tariffs, including aircraft parts, batteries, flat-panel televisions, medical devices, satellites, and various weapons. China responded on April 2 by imposing tariffs on 128 products it imports from America, including aluminium, airplanes, cars, pork, soybeans, fruit, nuts, and steel piping. In total, there were hundreds of billions of dollars of tariffs on almost every product that is traded between the United States and China. On October 11, 2019, Trump announced that China and the United States had reached a tentative agreement for the "first phase" of a trade deal. China agreeing to buy up to $50 billion in American farm products and to accept more American financial services in their market, with the United States agreeing to suspend new tariffs scheduled for October 15 (BBC 2020). Trump has succeeded in reducing America's trade deficit with China. At the end of May 2020, it had dropped to $103 billion. However, this was due to a combination of the tariff impacts and the economic recession caused by COVID-19. In 2016, U.S.–China trade was $48 billion a month, but in 2020 it had dropped to $36 billion a month (Census 2020).

THE ARREST OF MENG WANZHOU AND THE AFTERMATH: DECEMBER 2018–2020

Trudeau's hope for improved relations with China had been dashed with the collapse of free trade talks before they ever really got started. However, there was nothing inherently wrong with maintaining the status quo, but by the end of 2018 Sino-Canadian relations were about to get a lot worse. The consequence was, as Preston Lim has written, that "Trudeau's approach to China has, like Harper's, waxed 'hot and cold,' even if the respective sequencing of engagement, has differed" (Lim 2020: 26). The biggest strain on Sino-Canadian relations since the Korean War began in December 2018, when the chief financial officer and deputy chair (as well as being the daughter of the founder) of Huawei, the large Chinese telecommunications firm, Meng Wanzhou was arrested at the Vancouver Airport. Meng's arrest was due to an extradition request by U.S. authorities on suspicion of violating U.S. sanctions against Iran. Although Canada argued that it was bound by its extradition treaty and could not politically interfere with Meng's arrest, the Chinese quickly retaliated against Canada. Within days, two Canadians (former diplomat Michael Kovrig and businessman Michael Spavor) were detained by Chinese authorities where they remain in a small cell in a Chinese jail. Former Canadian ambassador to China Guy Saint-Jacques has suggested that the Chinese "know they cannot kick them [the U.S.] so they turned around and kicked us" (Alini 2018).

Trump made the situation even worse when he suggested that Meng could be released as part of the negotiations for improved U.S. trade relations with China. "If I think it's good for what will be certainly the largest trade ever made – which is a very important thing – what's good for national security – I would certainly intervene if I thought it was necessary" (Canadian Press 2018). John Bolton, who was U.S. National Security Advisor at the time of Meng's arrest, has maintained that "it was not politically motivated at all." However, Bolton also acknowledged that Trump saw Meng—Trump compared Meng (the daughter of Huawei's founder) with his own daughter Ivanka Trump—as a bargaining chip in his wider trade war with China (CBC 2020).

This left Canada in an awkward position. In response, then-Foreign Minister Chrystia Freeland asserted that "Canada understands the rule of law and extradition ought not ever to be politicized or used as tools to resolve other issues" (MacDonald and Kapelos 2018). Trudeau echoed his minister when he said that "the escalating trade war between them [China and the U.S.] is going to have all sorts of unintended consequences on Canada, potentially on the entire global economy. We're very worried about that" (Blanchfield 2018).

Sino-Canadian relations deteriorated further when Canada's Ambassador to China John McCallum told the press "[f]rom Canada's point of view, if [the U.S.] drops the extradition request, that would be great for Canada" (Canadian Press 2019). This led to McCallum being fired on January 26, 2019. It would be months before a replacement would be found, meaning that Canada had no ambassador to China as their relations tumbled. It was not until September 2019 that a new ambassador—Dominic Barton—was appointed. Tensions further escalated in March 2019 when China banned Canadian canola claiming that it was contaminated. Canola is one of Canada's largest exports to China with $2.8 billion in sales in 2018. Then, in June 2019, China also banned Canadian pork and beef exports for similar reasons. Canada sells China $500 million a year worth of pork and another $100 million in beef. In November 2019, the ban on pork and beef was lifted, but canola restrictions remain (Flanagan and O'Brien 2019). The Canada-China Business Council, an organization made up of Canadian corporations who operate in China, has also reported that business was down 43% in 2019 leading to a loss of around $4.5 billion in exports (Vanderklippe and Chase 2020).

It is not insignificant that Meng was a senior executive with Huawei. This is because Huawei is another issue creating conflict between the United States, Canada, and China. The United States has banned Huawei from operating in their country because they believe it has the potential for Chinese spying. The United States has also been pressuring its "Five Eyes" intelligence partners (United States, United Kingdom, Canada, Australia, and New Zealand) to do likewise or, at the very least, prevent them from contributing to their advanced super-fast 5G telecommunications networks. Canada remains the only Five Eyes country that has not either banned or greatly restricted Huawei from their 5G network and remains undecided on the future role of Huawei. CSIS has strenuously recommended that Huawei be banned from Canada's 5G network because it could be used for Chinese espionage or to cripple Canada's infrastructure during an international crisis. On the other hand, the Communications Security Establishment has maintained that there are technological ways of mitigating this type of risk. Canada is also challenged by the fact that two of its three major telecommunications firms—Telus and Bell—have already invested several billion dollars in incorporating Huawei gear in earlier generations of their networks. In addition, Huawei has established research partnerships with about two dozen Canadian universities bringing in millions of dollars of funding for Canadian researchers and institutions.

On May 27, 2020, the B.C. Supreme Court upheld Meng's arrest and extradition to the United States. China's embassy in Ottawa blamed political collusion between Canada and the United States: "the purpose of the United States is to bring down Huawei and other Chinese high-tech companies, and Canada has been acting in the process as an accomplice of the United States....the whole case is entirely a grave political incident" (Fife et al. 2020). Several weeks later, in obvious retaliation for the court's decision, China charged the two Michaels with espionage (Vanderklippe 2020). In contrast, Foreign Minister Champagne said, "the Canadian judiciary operates independently, and today's decision…was an independent decision of the Supreme Court of British Columbia" (Fife et al. 2020).

Some prominent Canadians have advocated a swap of Meng for the two Michaels. A public letter was signed by 19 individuals, among others, former Liberal Cabinet Ministers John Manley, Lloyd Axworthy, and Allan Rock; Derek Burney (former Chief of Staff to Prime Minister Mulroney); and former NDP leader Ed Broadbent. This group, who are clearly Chinese optimists, wrote, "the two Michaels will remain in their Chinese prison cells until Meng is free to return to China." They also made the point that such a trade would help Canada "redefine its strategic approach to China" (A Letter to the Prime Minister of Canada 2020). Chinese officials have concurred. Zhao Lijian, a spokesman for China's Ministry of Foreign Affairs, stated that "such options are within the rule of law and could open up space for resolution to the situation of the two Canadians" (Chase and Fife 2020b). However, the Trudeau government has rejected "hostage diplomacy" saying "going against the independence of our justice system would endanger the millions of Canadians who live and travel overseas every single year" (Chase and Fife

2020b). The Trudeau government's position reflects widespread Canadian public opinion as well, despite the letter signatories' credentials, as the majority of the scholarly and expert opinion.

COVID-19: 2020

Canada's arrest of Meng and China's subsequent retaliation appeared to be the nadir of Sino-Canadian relations, at least since the 1970 recognition. The ongoing trade war and security and intelligence challenges between the United States and China have greatly contributed to the problems Canada is facing with China. However, the spread from China of COVID-19—creating a global health pandemic—took a bad situation and made it much worse. As of writing (October 2020), over 9000 Canadians have died of COVID-19, over 200,000 Americans, and over 1 million around the world (CSSE 2020). In early October 2020, Trump and his wife, senior presidential staffers, and several Republican Senators all tested positive for COVID-19. This highlighted COVID-19 for the 2020 U.S. election campaign. While the United States and Canada have been dealing with the COVID-19 pandemic (with various degrees of success and failure), both countries (and many others too) have also focused the blame for the pandemic on China. For example, Trump has repeatedly called COVID-19 the "Wuhan virus" or "China virus." He also withdrew the United States from the World Health Organization (WHO) claiming that the international body had been corrupted by China in its inadequate response to COVID-19. In addition, Australia has requested that the WHO conduct an investigation into the origins of COVID-19 in China. Canada's official response to China's role in spreading COVID-19 has been slightly more restrained. In June, Trudeau simply said that "I think there are many questions that need to be asked about the World Health Organization, about China and other countries' behaviours through this" (Connolly 2020). This difference in tone was recognized by China. China's Ambassador to Canada Cong Peiwu stated that he appreciated Canada's "cool-headed" response to COVID-19 as opposed to the United States that he felt was "smearing" China (Blanchfield 2020).

The opposition CPC has been much more aggressive in their anti-China rhetoric reflecting the almost unanimous dominance of the Chinese pessimists within the party. Newly elected CPC leader Erin O'Toole has been very critical of China and the Trudeau government's handling of

China. During the CPC leadership race, O'Toole compared the COVID-19 outbreak with Igor Gouzenko's December 1945 defection to Canada. He wrote that Gouzenko's revelations of Soviet spying led to the cold war and China's negligent response to COVID-19 will likely lead to another cold war (O'Toole 2020a). After becoming leader in August 2020, O'Toole continued his criticism, writing "for decades, many Canadian corporate and financial insiders were espousing deeper and closer ties with China at all costs. They were willing to look past the Chinese government's numerous human rights abuses, flagrant trade abuses and security issues because the potential to sell into the massive Chinese market was so lucrative" (O'Toole 2020b). O'Toole promised that if he became Prime Minister he would work with Canada's allies (Five Eyes partners, Japan, and India) to hold China to account, ban Huawei from participating in Canada's 5G network, develop new markets, and "repatriate some critical manufacturing" from China (O'Toole 2020b).

Even some Canadian premiers have gotten involved. Alberta Premier Jason Kenney is a former senior cabinet minister in the Harper government, a prominent Chinese pessimist, and arguably the most powerful conservative politician in Canada. Kenney gave a remarkable speech in Washington, warning that China "will soon face a 'great reckoning' for its efforts to play down, obfuscate, and cover up the dangers posed by the novel coronavirus when it first emerged in the Chinese city of Wuhan" (McCarten 2020). This speech led to a public condemnation from the Chinese consulate in Calgary (Bresge 2020).

It is not just politicians; public opinion in Canada towards China has dramatically plummeted. According to Angus Reid in May 2020, only 14% of Canadians surveyed had a positive view of China compared to 48% in 2017. It is clear that COVID-19 is primarily responsible for the decline. 85% of respondents disagreed with the statement "the Chinese government has been transparent and honest about the COVID-19 situation in that country" with over half (53%) strongly disagreeing. 78% of respondents want Huawei banned from participating in the building of Canada's 5G network. Finally, only 11% felt Canada should focus its trade efforts on China (down from 40% in 2015) and 76% of respondents said Canada should prioritize human rights and the rule of law over economic opportunity (Angus Reid Institute 2020). Nanos Research confirmed many of these findings with a poll in July 2020. 90% of respondents had a negative or somewhat negative view of the Chinese government (there has been a steady decline since Nanos started tracking it in 2016) and 69% had a negative or somewhat negative impression of Huawei. Yet, demonstrating the economic importance of China as well as the unpredictability of the Trump administration, 43% of respondents still felt that Canada should pursue a new free trade agreement with China (Nanos 2020).

CONCLUSION

Despite obvious differences in size, political systems, and values, there has been a desire in Canada among the Chinese optimists to have strong economic relations with China. This has included negotiating a FIPPA and pursuing a free trade agreement. However, the last several years have seen enormous friction in the bilateral relationship between Canada and China. This was sparked by two key events: the arrest of Meng and the subsequent Chinese retaliation, and the role of China in spreading COVID-19. These events have led to the ascendency in Canada of the Chinese pessimists. In addition, in both events, we can clearly see the role of the United States has been an unescapable variable in Canada–China relations.

In the future, Canada has several options for managing relations with China. One option is for Canada to work with its allies to create both a security and trade buffer against China. On the security side, there are indications of coordination against a perceived Chinese threat. For example, the joint response from the United States, United Kingdom, Australia, and Canada over China's security law in Hong Kong. In addition, Canada could join the rest of the Five Eyes community in banning Huawei from its 5G network. Defence investments in surface ships and submarines and joint operations with allies such as Japan and Australia would help counter Chinese military activity in Asia-Pacific and the Arctic (Robertson 2020: 8–9). On the trade side, the CPTPP was an attempt to balance Chinese economic might in the Asia-Pacific. The change in the US presidency could create an opportunity for the United States to rejoin the trade pact. This reflects the other challenge that Canada has with regard to China, and that has been the unpredictable nature of the Trump administration. Canada would need to work with the United States to balance China, but that coordination has become a lot more difficult since Trump became President. This can be seen in unilateral tariffs against Canadian steel and aluminium, the renegotiation of NAFTA, and the mixed messages around Meng's extradition request. President Joe Biden is likely to continue the pressure on China. However, in contrast to

Trump, Biden would also more likely to work with Canada in pressuring China, as opposed to trying to bully Canada (see Nimijean, Carment, and Stewart this volume).

Another option is for Canada to "decouple" its economy from China. This would involve not only greatly restricting trade and investment, but severing existing supply chains. Already there are serious discussions in the United States around a "decoupling" of its economy from China. A "decoupling" could be across the board, or in certain key sectors. Many countries have become dependent upon China for rare earth minerals, industrial products, and electronics. For example, 87% of laptop components and 78% of cell phones come from China (Fife and Chase 2020). Already Canadian officials are emphasizing the potential for mining rare earth minerals (i.e., cobalt required for lithium-ion batteries) in Canada (Lilly 2020). There are cost challenges for mining rare earth minerals in Canada due to high labour costs and environmental regulations, but lessening dependence on China adds a new positive variable (Lilly 2020).

However, the decoupling option would have consequences for Canada. It would make Canada even more dependent upon the American market. In particular, the agriculture and oil and gas sectors, concentrated in Western Canada, would resist losing the Chinese market. This exacerbates the national unity challenge facing the Liberal government since the October 2019 election that reduced their majority government to a minority, and left them with no seats between Winnipeg and Vancouver. For example, a major goal for expanding the Trans Mountain Pipeline (which goes from the Alberta oil sands to the B.C. coast), the scene of one of the biggest domestic political battles in recent years, is to diversify away from the U.S. market and get a world price for Canadian crude (Bratt 2015). It is ironic that one of Canada's most noted Chinese pessimists—Alberta Premier Jason Kenney—is simultaneously one of the biggest proponents of the Trans Mountain Pipeline.

There is a variation on the "decoupling" option. That would be "ensur[ing] supply chain resiliency and redundancy" may be a better response (Robertson 2020: 8). Identifying critical supplies and Canadian suppliers will need to be part of this option. At a minimum, COVID-19 has revealed a dependency that Canada has on medical equipment, drugs, and vitamins. It is likely that, in the future, there will be a return to Canada for the manufacturing of important medical products.

Another option is for Canada to try and take a middle route between the United States and China (Carment and Nimijean 2020). This argument is part of a larger Canadian foreign policy literature on how Canada is too dependent upon the United States (Clarkson 2015; Bow and Lennox 2015). However, this ignores the geographical, cultural, economic, security, and values that have tied Canada and the United States for a century. Even under the severe stress of the Trump administration, those ties have remained. This option also does not take into account Canadian public opinion that, as a response to the Meng arrest and Chinese retaliation as well as COVID-19, has swung sharply against China. This does not mean that, at moments, Canada can take a different foreign policy from the United States, as it did at times during the cold war with the Soviet Union but doing it on the China file would be fraught with extreme difficulties.

This is just a partial list of possible options in addressing the Sino-Canadian relations moving forward. However, as the brief discussion revealed, there is no simple answer as each option has both upsides and downsides. Nevertheless, Canada needs to reconsider the entire relationship because it cannot go back to the period prior to December 2018.

REFERENCES

"A Letter to the Prime Minister of Canada." 2020. June 23. https://assets.doc umentcloud.org/documents/6956527/Letter-to-Prime-Minister.pdf.

Alini, Erica. 2018. "Huawei Saga will Freeze Trade Talks, Hurt Canadian Investment in China: Experts." *Global News*, December 13.

Allison, Graham. 2017. *Destined for War: Can America and China Escape Thucydides's Trap?* Boston: Houghton, Mifflin, Harcourt.

Angus Reid Institute. 2020. "Canadian Opinions of China Reach New Low." May 13. http://angusreid.org/covid19-china/.

Blanchfield, Mike. 2017. *Swingback: Getting Along in the World with Harper and Trudeau.* Montréal, QC and Kingston, ON: McGill-Queen's University Press.

Blanchfield, Mike. 2018. "'Unintended Consequences on Canada:' Trudeau Fears Economic Fallout from U.S.–China Spat." *National Post*, December 14. https://nationalpost.com/news/politics/canada-will-shortly-see-spavor-second-detained-canadian-in-china-trudeau.

Blanchfield, Mike. 2020. "China Likes Canada's 'Cool-Head' Amid U.S. 'Smears' Over COVID-19: Envoy." *Victoria Times-Colonist*, May 1.

Bow, Brian and Patrick Lennox. 2015. "The 'Independence' Debates, Then and Now: False Choices and Real Challenges." In *Readings in Canadian Foreign Policy: Classic Debates and New Ideas*, 3rd ed., edited by Duane Bratt and Christopher Kukucha, 109–112. Don Mills, ON: Oxford University Press.

Bratt, Duane. 2015. "The Energy Triangle: Canada, the United States, and China." In *Readings in Canadian Foreign Policy: Classic Debates and New Ideas*, 3rd ed., edited by Duane Bratt and Christopher Kukucha, 434–449. Don Mills, ON: Oxford University Press.

Bresge, Adina. 2020. "Chinese Consulate Blasts Alberta Premier Jason Kenney for COVID-19 Criticism." *Globe and Mail*, May 17. https://www.theglobea ndmail.com/canada/article-chinese-consulate-blasts-alberta-premier-jason-kenney-for-covid-1-2/.

British Broadcasting Corporation. 2020. "A Quick Guide to the U.S.–China Trade War." *BBC News*, January 16. https://www.bbc.com/news/business-45899310.

Burton, Charles. 2015. "The Dynamic of Relations Between Canada and China." In *Readings in Canadian Foreign Policy: Classic Debates and New Ideas*, 3rd ed., edited by Duane Bratt and Christopher Kukucha, 171–185. Don Mills, ON: Oxford University Press.

Calvert, Phillip. 2018. "Justin Trudeau's China Challenges." In *Justin Trudeau and Canadian Foreign Policy: Canada Among Nations 2017*, edited by Norman Hillmer and Philip Lagassé, 145–164. Toronto: Palgrave Macmillan.

Canadian Broadcasting Corporation. 2006. "Won't Sell Out Human Rights Despite China Snub: PM." *CBC News*, November 15. https://www.cbc.ca/news/world/won-t-sell-out-on-rights-despite-china-snub-pm-1.570708.

Canadian Broadcasting Corporation. 2010. "Some Politicians Under Foreign Sway: CSIS." *CBC News*, June 22. https://www.cbc.ca/news/politics/some-politicians-under-foreign-sway-csis-1.909345.

Canadian Broadcasting Corporation. 2020. "Trump Had Superficial, Transactional View of Meng Extradition Case, Bolton Tells CBC Radio." *CBC Radio: The Current*, June 26. https://www.cbc.ca/radio/thecurrent/bolton-interv iew-trump-current-1.5628262.

Canadian Press. 2018. "Trump Willingness to 'Intervene' on Huawei Case Leaves Canada in a Tough Spot Over Ex-diplomat's Arrest." *Global News*, December 12. https://globalnews.ca/news/4754297/trump-huawei-canada-arrest/.

Canadian Press. 2019. "McCallum Says Dropping Meng Extradition Would Be 'Great' for Canada: Report." *CTV News*. January 25. https://www.ctv news.ca/politics/mccallum-says-dropping-meng-extradition-would-be-great-for-canada-report-1.4269945.

Carment, David and Richard Nimijean. 2020. "Canada's China–U.S. Conundrum." *The Hill Times,* February 24. https://www.hilltimes.com/2020/02/24/canadas-china-u-s-conundrum/235047.

Center for Systems Science and Engineering, Johns Hopkins University. 2020. *Mapping COVID-19.* https://gisanddata.maps.arcgis.com/apps/opsdashbo ard/index.html#/bda7594740fd40299423467b48e9ecf6.

Chapnick, Andrew, and Christopher Kukucha (eds.). 2016. *The Harper Era in Canadian Foreign Policy: Parliament, Politics, and Canada's Global Posture.* Vancouver: University of British Columbia Press.

Chase, Steven and Robert Fife. 2020a. "Canada and Its Allies Condemn China's Hong Kong Crackdown as Tool for Political Persecution." *Globe and Mail,* May 29. https://www.theglobeandmail.com/politics/article-can ada-and-allies-say-chinas-hong-kong-crackdown-conflicts-with/.

Chase, Steven and Robert Fife. 2020b. "Trudeau Rejects Calls to Free Meng." *Globe and Mail,* June 26. https://www.theglobeandmail.com/politics/article-trading-meng-for-kovrig-and-spavor-would-put-more-canadians-at-ris k-of/.

Chase, Steven and Robert Fife. 2020c. "Canada Starts Accepting Hong Kong Activists as Refugees." *Globe and Mail,* October 7.

Clarkson, Stephen. 2015. "The Choice to Be Made." In *Readings in Canadian Foreign Policy: Classic Debates and New Ideas,* 3rd ed., edited by Duane Bratt and Christopher Kukucha, 92–108. Don Mills, ON: Oxford University Press.

Connolly, Amanda. 2020. "'Many Questions' After Report That WHO Praised China to Get COVID-19 Data: Trudeau." *Global News,* June 2. https://glo balnews.ca/news/7016947/coronavirus-justin-trudeau-who-china-report/.

Davidson, Helen. 2020. "Hong Kong Police Given Sweeping Powers Under New Security Law." *The Guardian,* July 7. https://www.theguardian.com/world/2020/jul/07/hong-kong-police-given-sweeping-powers-under-new-security-law.

Dobson, Wendy. 2019. *Living with China: A Middle Power Finds Its Way.* Toronto: University of Toronto Press.

Doran, Charles F. 2019. "The United States and Canada: In Search of Partnership." In *Canada–US Relations: Sovereignty or Shared Institutions. Canada Among Nations 2018,* edited by David Carment and Christopher Sands, 17–38. Toronto: Palgrave Macmillan.

Evans, Paul. 2014. *Engaging China: Myth, Aspiration, and Strategy in Canadian Policy from Trudeau to Harper.* Toronto: University of Toronto Press.

Fife, Robert, Steven Chase, Andrea Woo, and Mike Hager. 2020. "Canada Braces for Economic Retaliation from China Following Meng Wanzhou Court Ruling." *The Globe and Mail,* May 28. https://www.theglobeandm ail.com/canada/article-bc-judge-denies-early-attempt-by-meng-wanzhou-to-gain-her-freedom/.

Fife, Robert and Steven Chase. 2020. "Five Eyes Allies Urged to Lessen Dependence on China." *The Globe and Mail*, May 21. https://www.theglo beandmail.com/politics/article-fives-eyes-allies-urged-to-lessen-dependence-on-china/.

Fitz-Morris, James. 2015. "Justin Trudeau Tells Paris Climate Summit Canada Ready to Do More." *CBC News*, November 30. https://www.cbc.ca/news/politics/trudeau-address-climate-change-paris-1.3343394.

Flanagan, Ryan and Cillian O'Brien. 2019. "China to Resume Importing Beef and Pork from Canada." *CTV News*, November 5. https://www.ctvnews.ca/politics/china-to-resume-importing-beef-and-pork-from-canada-1.4671186.

Freeland, Chrystia. 2017. "Address by Foreign Affairs Minister on the Modernization of the North American Free Trade Agreement (NAFTA)." *Government of Canada*, August 14. http://www.canada.ca/en/global-aff airs/news/2017/08/address_by_foreignaffairsministeronthemodernization ofthenorthame.html.

Gecelovsky, Paul and T.A. Keenleyside. 1995. "Canada's International Human Rights Policy in Practice: Tiananmen Square." *International Journal* 50 (3) (Summer): 564–593.

Hillmer, Norman, and Philip Lagassé (eds.). 2018. *Justin Trudeau and Canadian Foreign Policy: Canada Among Nations 2017*. Toronto: Palgrave Macmillan.

Johnson, Keith. 2019. "How Trump May Finally Kill the WTO." *Foreign Policy*. December 9. https://foreignpolicy.com/2019/12/09/trump-may-kill-wto-finally-appellate-body-world-trade-organization/.

Lilly, Meredith B. 2020. "Hewers of Wood and Drawers of Water 2.0: How American and Chinese Economic Nationalism Influence Canadian Trade Policy in the Twenty-First Century." *Canadian Foreign Policy Journal* 26 (2): 167–181.

Lim, Preston. 2020. "Sino-Canadian Relations in the Age of Justin Trudeau." *Canadian Foreign Policy Journal* 26 (1): 25–40.

Lui, Andrew. 2013. "Sleeping with the Dragon: The Harper Government, China, and How Not to Do Human Rights." In *Canada in the World: Internationalism in Canadian Foreign Policy*, edited by Heather A. Smith and Claire Turenne Sjolander, 90–107. Don Mills, ON: Oxford University Press.

MacDonald, Brennan and Vassy Kapelos. 2018. "Donald Trump Undermined Canada on Huawei Arrest, Says Former U.S. Ambassador." *CBC News*, December 19. https://www.cbc.ca/news/politics/trump-undermined-canada-huawei-arrest-1.4951409.

Manthorpe, Jonathan. 2019. *Claws of the Panda: Beijing's Campaign of Influence and Intimidation in Canada*. Toronto: Cormorant Books.

McCarten, James. 2020. "Kenney Slams China's Handling of COVID-19, Calls for a 'Great Reckoning' for Country's Role." *Global News,* May 13. https://globalnews.ca/news/6940836/jason-kenney-china-covid-19-coronavirus/.

Nanos, Nik. 2020. "Canada Is Stuck Between Its Former Rock and an Increasingly Hard Place." *Globe and Mail,* July 18.

Nossal, Kim Richard and Leah Sarson. 2014. "About Face: Explaining Changes in Canada's China Policy, 2006–2012." *Canadian Foreign Policy Journal* 20 (2): 146–162.

O'Toole, Erin. 2020a. "Erin O'Toole on COVID-19: We Are on the Brink of a New Cold War with China." *National Post,* April 23. https://nationalpost.com/opinion/erin-otoole-on-covid-19-we-on-the-brink-of-a-new-cold-war-with-china.

O'Toole, Erin. 2020b. "Erin O'Toole: As Prime Minister, I Will Stand Up to China." *National Post,* September 1. https://nationalpost.com/opinion/erin-otoole-as-prime-minister-i-will-stand-up-to-china.

Prime Minister of Canada. 2016. *Joint Statement Between Canada and the People's Republic of China.* September 23. https:pm.gc.ca/eng/news/2016/09/23/joint-statement-between-canada-and-peoples-republic-china.

Robertson, Colin. 2020. *What to Do About China: A Menu of Options.* Ottawa: Canadian Global Affairs Institute, June.

Smythe, Elizabeth. 2015. "Canada and the Negotiation of Investment Rules: Open for Whose Business?" In *Readings in Canadian Foreign Policy: Classic Debates and New Ideas,* 3rd ed., edited by Duane Bratt and Christopher Kukucha, 415–433. Don Mills, ON: Oxford University Press.

Trudeau, Pierre, and Jacques Hébert. 1961. *Two Innocents in Red China.* Vancouver: Douglas & McIntyre.

Trump, Donald. Twitter Post. November 9, 2017, 6:39 pm. https://twitter.com/realDonaldTrump/status/928769154345324544?s=20.

United Nations, Committee on the Elimination of Racial Discrimination. 2018. *Concluding Observations on the Combined Fourteenth to Seventeenth Periodic Reports of China (Including Hong Kong, China and Macao, China).* CERD/C/CHN/CO/14-17. August 30.

United States Census Bureau. 2020. "Foreign Trade: Trade in Goods with China." https://www.census.gov/foreign-trade/balance/c5700.html#2016.

Vanderklippe, Nathan. 2020. "China Charges Kovrig and Spavor with Espionage." *Globe and Mail.* June 20.

Vanderklippe, Nathan and Steven Chase. 2020. "Barton Takes Harder Line on China." *Globe and Mail,* May 13.

CHAPTER 14

The Impact of Ukraine's Informal Economy on Women: Mobilizing Canada's Diaspora for Growth and Opportunity During Crisis

Milana Nikolko, Samuel MacIsaac, and David Carment

INTRODUCTION

The purpose of this chapter is to advance an understanding of the limitations and strengths of Canada's diaspora support to improving gender dynamics in situations of state fragility. The Canadian government has frequently cited the correlation between gender empowerment and

The authors would like to thank SSHRCC for its support in this research.

M. Nikolko (✉) · S. MacIsaac · D. Carment
Carleton University, Ottawa, ON, Canada
e-mail: MilanaNikolko@cunet.carleton.ca

S. MacIsaac
e-mail: samuelmacisaac@cmail.carleton.ca

D. Carment
e-mail: DavidCarment@cunet.carleton.ca

295

stability using, for example, the UNDP's Gender Empowerment index. Getting more women involved in economic and political processes, it is argued, can only build social cohesiveness through enhanced inclusivity. Beyond this, having women contribute to a country's formal economy can generate wealth that brings real and immediate benefits at the local level, potentially reducing social divides and tensions. Informal self-employment is of particular concern as these activities, such as in the most egregious cases of selling flowers in street markets, and cigarettes outside stations, become a part of sexual exploitation. They all carry some risk, limited job security and most importantly, do little to enhance Ukraine's overall economic and human development record.

With a 30% increase in unemployment coupled with a large informal economy, Ukraine poses a number of challenges to Canada's gender-based policies. On the one hand, Ukraine has a sizeable and increasing male migration to EU states. With a concomitant expansion of the predominantly male military, Ukrainian women have become a crucial part of the informal economy, dependent on remittances but also increasingly present in a variety of informal activities. Unfortunately, household surveys rarely, if at all, incorporate measurements of women's contributions at home as part of the country's overall GDP. On the other hand, the 2014 Russian intervention in Ukraine demonstrated the need for a more comprehensive approach to engage those fragile and conflict affected states such as Ukraine to prevent polarization, support durable solutions to complex disputes and help move states out of their macroeconomic malaise (Carment et al. 2019). As a multicultural immigrant nation, Canada has a pivotal role to play in meeting all of these challenges (Nimijean 2017).

For Canada, the intertwined dynamics of a growing Ukrainian informal sector and employment-related gender inequities have the potential to negatively impact its international programming priorities. For example, private sector development is a key concern for Canada's ODA initiatives in Ukraine. However, in the absence of a full understanding of how gender equality is impacted through long-term social, human capital, and physical investment, Ukraine's (and by extension Canada's) development goals may not be met; or worse, be undermined. At the same time, gender equality is a cross-cutting theme integrated into all of Canada's development programming. Thus, there is a need to conduct even more research into the relationship between the informal sector and gender equality in Ukraine.

First, women from Ukraine's agricultural sector are destined to remain householders as their employment choices remain relatively limited. Those women having professional accreditation in the agricultural sector who lose their jobs have few options available to them and are often reduced to generally unrecognized household work. The net impact is a loss of human capital investments and limited opportunities for upward mobility that hamper economic and broader social development.

Second, diaspora connections between Canada and Ukraine, both directly and indirectly, influence gender dynamics, economics, and household consumption. We argue that women's work in informal activities plays a vital role in sustaining Ukrainian households and limiting economic hardship despite being largely ignored in Canada's aggregate statistics used to formulate policy on Ukraine. Despite a dependency trap problem coupled with under and unpaid work, sex trafficking, and informal services activities, women play an essential role in sustaining households during the crisis.

Third, despite a drop in female informal employment according to official figures, a number of Ukrainian women resort to informal household work that is mostly unaccounted. Significant changes in the economy have, on the one hand, helped offset hardship at the community and household levels, but have not addressed the longer-term fragility of the country, nor helped women overcome poverty. We surmise that in the long run, diaspora remittances from Canada to Ukraine may be more effective when they are invested in social, human, and physical capital, rather than subsistence consumption that perpetuates an ongoing dependency trap.

These linkages are nested within a broader set of diaspora cooperative strategies connecting home and host states. Where much has been written about the negative impacts of diaspora on state fragility and contested sovereignty, the absence of research on diaspora cooperation is partly related to a lack of theorizing and partly to limited policy development in host states (Carment and Sadjed 2017; Carment and Landry 2017). The lack of host-state policy is particularly evident in the Canadian context where there is no formal federal government policy on diaspora, especially in contrast to the United States and the European Union, which have formalized and institutionalized structures addressing diaspora issues (Prasad and Savatic 2018).

This point is important for a couple of reasons. First, as the international system undergoes a diminution in effectiveness and capacity, as a result of COVID-19 the importance of diaspora activities has risen commensurately (Carment and Sadjed 2017; Nikolko 2016).[1] For example, globally, foreign direct investment (FDI) has dropped off precipitously over the last year since the pandemic struck meaning there is more room for diaspora related investment and financial flows. Second, despite their growing importance, Canadian policymakers have mostly taken diaspora as a given in existing policies (such as immigration, foreign aid, labour, investment, peacebuilding and banking), rather than as an actor that might require or benefit from more precise and specific rules to unleash their full potential—both for host and home state interests.

Indeed, conventional Canadian foreign policy perspectives examine international affairs as conducted by formal organizations in which non-state actors are viewed as a challenge to governance and cooperation rather than a positive contributor (Young and Henders 2012). But, as diaspora become prominent players in the Canadian context, they have the potential to diffuse power and authority, adding additional layers of complexity to governance structures and obscuring accountability (Carment et al. 2020).

There is a great deal of ambiguity about how Canada's diaspora policies might be developed given the private and often personal nature that diasporic connections entail. Consider a diaspora sending country and the informal mechanisms of cooperation at the household level that work to support its moral economy (Carment and Sadjed 2017). In this case, we have diaspora as facilitators, if not agents of change, who adapt to the changing circumstances around them to support the homeland economy. Diaspora are also key drivers of development, through remittances and direct investment the transfer of human and social capital, and through direct support for democracy processes and peacebuilding in fragile states. However, scholarly work on the causal connections to these outcomes remains limited (Carment and Calleja 2018).

In this chapter, drawing on the Canada–Ukraine experience we examine both opportunities and challenges through which host states such as Canada should engage its sizeable diaspora to address international development in a divided world. In the Ukrainian case, the

---

[1] A recent survey shows that gender vulnerability in both formal and informal sectors of the Ukrainian economy has worsened since the beginning of the pandemic. For a rapid gender assessment of the situation and needs of women in the context of COVID-19 in Ukraine, see: https://reliefweb.int/report/ukraine/rapid-gender-assessment-situation-and-needs-women-context-covid-19-ukraine-enuk.

2014 crisis highlighted long-term fragility and a cycle of dependency on foreign work and subsistence aimed inflows of remittances from diaspora members. Furthermore, the subsistence perpetuated by dependency on foreign flows compounds the existing subsistence and traditional reproductive roles of Ukrainian women, further entrenching patriarchal gender dynamics. An expanded interpretation of the informal economy, that includes the foreign activities of labour migrants, remittance flows, household work and other labour roles, including traditionally unpaid or self-employed work performed by women sheds light on diasporic mobilization patterns.

The relationship between Ukraine's diaspora and Canada is conditioned by both homeland institutions and structures, as well as by the host-state's integration regime. This integration is reflected in institutional arrangements, such as political representational structures, associations and multicultural policies (Kymlicka and Banting 2006; Nikolko 2016). In essence, Canada is institutionally open to supporting Ukrainian sovereignty through multiple, formally mandated state-driven channels, including aid, trade and military assistance (Carment and Calleja 2018). At the same time, there are transnational channels that include remittances, representation in international organizations, and investment flows, among others.

Thus, Ukraine's Canadian diaspora enjoys strong positionality (Nikolko 2016, Carment et al. 2020). In theory, Canada's Ukrainian diaspora efforts should be wide-ranging and comprehensive: political (e.g. lobbying), economic (remittances, investment or brain circulation), social (such as the promotion of human and other rights of the transnational groups within divided societies) and cultural (media production, the creation of subcultures) (Carment and Calleja 2018) and even legal (transitional justice and work of memories) (Nikolko 2019). However, as we argue below, the crisis of 2014 proved to be a litmus test for these assumptions.

Despite the fact its migration policy is very stringent, Canada has been one of the major destinations for Ukrainians who decide to take the risk and change their country of living. Around 90% of all new migrants coming to Canada go through a competitive process of selection. Today, flows from Ukraine to Canada are diminishing. Ukraine is not among the top ten of those nations that send immigrants to Canada. Nevertheless, Ukrainian-Canadians, spread out over several waves of migration, constitute almost 4% of Canada's total population of 37 million. Of the more than 1,360,000 who identify themselves as Ukrainian in Canada, around 69,000 were born in Ukraine (8%) and only 144,260 (or 11.5% of the total) speak the Ukrainian language.

For more than a hundred years of Ukrainian emigration history, successive waves of settlement created a unique emigrant landscape in Canada. There have been four "waves of migration", each a mixture of labour migrants and political refugees. The first wave, which took place roughly between 1880 and 1914, consisted mainly of labour migrants attempting to escape inadequate economic conditions. The second wave occurred between 1920 and 1930 and consisted of a combination of labour migrants and political refugees. The third wave occurred between 1940 and 1954 and consisted mainly of political refugees. Between 1945 and 1955, 250,000 eastern and western Ukrainians emigrated to North and South America, Australia and various parts of Europe. The fourth wave began in the late 1980s and continues to this day. The majority of fourth-wave emigrants are labour migrants, although some refugees can also be found within this wave.

The 2014 Crisis and Its Impact on Women

Amid ongoing political and military conflict, the effects of the 2014 crisis had severe impacts on its economy and the Ukrainian people. The hostile political environment, in addition to hot conflict in the Donbas region, hampered Ukrainian growth and profoundly impacted households' economic security. According to the World Bank, Ukrainian GDP plummeted from 143.1 billion constant 2010 USD in 2013 to 121.2 billion in 2015 while employment for those 15 years and over dropped from 60.2 to 56.6% from 2013 to 2014.[2]

The 2014 crisis also precipitated increased outward migration flows, mainly from the affected Eastern regions. These flows constituted a reversal of the pre-2014 trend that Western regions supplied next to all migrant outflows. Asylum seekers passage into the EU went from fewer than 1000 to almost 15,000 in 2014 and over 20,000 in 2015. Moreover, FDI outflows increased, triggering capital flight fears. The ensuing inflationary pressure did little to alleviate households' efforts to get by, with

---

[2] The World Bank. Ukraine. Economic Overview. http://pubdocs.worldbank.org/pubdocs/publicdoc/2016/4/542921459504749981/Ukraine-Macroeconomic-Update-April-2016-UKR.pdf.

year-over-year inflation nearing the 50% mark in 2015 according to the World Bank. Although of limited scope, remittances received in Ukraine immensely helped maintain consumption needs, despite dropping from 9.7 billion USD in 2013 to 7.4 billion USD in 2014 and hit a record high of 12 billion in 2019 (World Bank 2019).

Aggravating pre-existing difficulties of a post-crisis IMF mandate to downsize the public sector and other austerity measures, 63% of households live below the minimum wage in Ukraine. In rural areas, this percentage increased to 72%. Given that 44% of the rural population are adult women and 38% are men, poverty in rural communities affects women disproportionately and "cements" structural inequalities.

In 2016, the number of households living below the poverty line was 48% for both urban and rural households (Dutchak 2018). The crisis affected the country's overall gender balance as well. According to the World Economic Forum in 2016, Ukraine was ranked 69th out of 144 countries in the World Economic Forum's Global Gender Gap report, having dropped from 48th place a decade earlier.

Estimates on the size and impact of Ukraine's informal economy vary significantly, but most reports suggest that it plays a crucial role especially given the decline of the agricultural and industrial sectors in some parts of Ukraine. Over the last year alone, Ukraine's formal economy has declined significantly in the face of global economic collapse. Informal activities are one way of cushioning the impact of economic hardship on Ukrainian households.

Although women constitute 42% of those employed in the informal sector according to the State Statistics Service of Ukraine (SSSU), a broader interpretation of the informal economy, that includes the foreign activities of labour migrants, remittance flows, household work and other labour roles, including traditionally unpaid or self-employed work, is dominated by women (Strelnyk 2017). They are more engaged in the informal economy in micro, small and medium-sized enterprises (MSMEs), without the rights and benefits commensurate with legalized occupations.

At the same time, employers in both the public and private sectors regularly specify gender when advertising vacancies and use information from interviews regarding family circumstances to deny women employment. Women are also pushed away from entrepreneurship due to reduced access to capital and gendered social norms that supersede formal sector labour regulations (Aidis et al. 2007). As a result, women are increasingly pushed into seeking primary or secondary employment in the unregulated informal sector, despite evidence that women traditionally have more limited informal networks than their male counterparts due to fewer contacts dating back to Soviet times (Smallbone and Welter 2001). The result is reduced benefits, punishing work terms and health and security issues, that undermine Ukraine's development goals.

Thus, over the last 25 years, women have played a less active role in the formal economy and have, as a result, received fewer economic benefits. One of the main indicators of this shift is the difference in payrolls between men and women. Between 2000 and 2016, the paid labour wage gap fluctuated between 31% in 2003/2004 and 22.2% in 2010 (UNDP: 43). Despite a previous steady decrease in this gap since 2004, it has grown significantly since the 2014 crisis. Besides, horizontal and vertical stratification of the Ukrainian market labour is increasingly evident. Women work in lower-paid sectors of the economy and hold lower positions on average. For instance, after 1991, the ratio of women employed in well-paid industries dropped to 22% (against 28% for men) and increased in low wage sectors to 65% (compared to 54% for men). Vertical segregation is equally pervasive. Traditional "female dominant sectors", such as the public sector boast high employment rates (76%) for women, yet 81% of civil servants holding a "first category" position (e.g. top managers) are men (SSSU 2015).[3]

The disproportionate engagement of women in reproductive labour keeps many of them from entering "productive" economic activity. Among economically inactive women, approximately 29% are housewives, whereas the same figure for inactive men is closer to 10%. In 2016, the most significant difference between economically active men and women was the age category 25–29 years (22.2 points), and 30–34 years (18.4 points). After this, differences decrease reaching its minimum (3.8 points) in the age category of 40–49 years (SSSU 2017: 60). The first two age categories represent an imbalanced distribution of reproductive labour among Ukrainian families where the gender stereotypes of "typical" man and women behaviour seriously affected social and economic roles. Data on household labour show that Ukrainian women spend a considerable

---

[3] In Ukrainian universities, just 51% female professors have degree of candidate or Doctor of Science in comparison with 79% of male professors.

amount of time on household work in all of Europe (without regard to childcare) at approximately 25 hours per week (Strelnyk 2017: 75).[4]

The government has played an active role in the monetization of reproductive labour. Indeed, this model was a core feature of the Soviet era, established under socialism, where regular child support payments were not just a form of financial support for families with children, but also a way to sustain women's income for a period of 3 years following childbirth. By 2000, reproductive financial support was set around 70% of the minimum wage for the first child and progressed accordingly with every child thereafter. Payments for the third and following children reflected a comparable full salary. This mechanism of compensating reproduction labour was particularly crucial in the rural areas of Ukraine, where unemployment is traditionally higher. This model of reproductive support encouraged women to stay out of the formal labour market while strengthening their position in the family. Nonetheless, by 2014–2015, social payments such as this dropped by as much as 43–69% per family. By 2016 monthly payments for the firstborn were only 17% of the minimum wage. In the same year, 85% of families with three children and 87% of families with four children were trapped in poverty (SSSU 2016: 260–261).

In conditions of economic crisis, all of the factors specified above have resulted in a clear and significant reduction of governmental and social support for female labour, particularly relative to reproductive labour. As a result, Ukrainian women persistently receive smaller earnings with diminishing prospects for decent retirement plans for the most vulnerable groups. Among these, the most deeply affected are elderly women and women with children, living in rural parts of Ukraine and female caregivers.

Gender, the Informal Economy, and Remittances

Harnessing the development potential of remittances and diasporic mobilization to support property rights, good governance and direct investment was an ongoing challenge for the Ukrainian government, even before the Maidan. Much of the research on remittances from foreign

---

[4]On average, a Ukrainian woman spends 15 hours cooking compared to the 9 hours spent by a Ukrainian man. In one year, the Ukrainian woman spends 32 days (or almost 49 days with break on sleep) on cooking food for the family (Dutchak 2018).

workers focuses on middle-income countries, where positive findings such as that by Vaaler (2011) show they enhance capital access and business creation and increase economic openness (see also Ketkar and Ratha 2009). Nevertheless, remittances may be less effective in fragile and conflict affected states where sovereignty is contested, the economy is stalled or underperforming, and in the presence of heavy debt loads. In a country such as Ukraine, increasing fragility motivates households to become overly reliant on remittances, leading to greater dependency, migration outflows, a hollowing out of the economy, and low growth due to a lack of investment opportunities.

Furthermore, remittances are said to be "counter-cyclical", meaning they flow to receiving countries during times of dire need, economic contraction and crisis. In contrast, FDI and other investment flows tend to be in short supply when market conditions are unfavourable and in fragile states more generally. This weakness is particularly true for Ukraine, which has a recent yet significant shortfall in capital inflows. Moreover, by virtue of its exposure to sizeable IMF Bank loans, it must find alternatives to pay off this debt. Another problem, particularly evident in the Ukraine case, is the potential unevenness and potential for the inequitable distribution of such flows within the local economy.

This is partly because the Ukrainian government has had a relatively weak strategy for engaging its diaspora. For example, the Ukrainian diaspora engage in average levels of investment activity and do not contribute significantly to strengthening property rights. Property rights are essential for signalling confidence in the market and for building government legitimacy. In 2012, 8.7% of Ukraine's FDI stock (approximately US$4.7 billion) was received from the then top diaspora host countries (Russia, United States, Kazakhstan), suggesting that the diaspora were at best making modest contributions to capital investment. However, low capacity to secure property rights made such investing risky even before the war. By 2015, Ukraine received a low rank of 109th out of 129 countries in securing property rights; the lowest ranking in the region (Carment and Calleja 2018).

According to Nikolko and Carment (2014: 3), Ukraine "suffers from a negligible understanding of property rights that helps perpetuate a large informal sector". Ukraine's diaspora has only an average involvement in trade promotion and low engagement in enhancing social capital and developing MSMEs. However, at the beginning of the war, trade between Ukraine and its three largest diaspora host states was stable at 12.5%.

Groups like the Ukrainian-Canadian Congress worked to promote trade relations. When we examine data before 2014, we see that the Ukrainian diaspora had, at best, a mixed influence on Ukraine's political and economic structures (Carment and Calleja 2018). On a global basis, the Ukrainian diaspora provided moderate remittance flows relative to GDP (valued at 5.6% in 2011). The degree to which remittance transfers were actively utilized by the state for development is low. For example, prior to 2014, Ukraine's remittance-receiving households were spending remittances on consumption (72%) and developing human capacity through education (12.4%). Approximately 13% of Ukraine's remittances flowed through informal channels in 2011 (Kupets 2012).

This variation is partly explained by differences in the form of transmission with bank accounts losing ground more recently to international money transfers. Over half of remittance-receiving households are located in Western Ukraine with less than 20% located in Eastern Ukraine. Ukraine migrants use a wide array of formal and informal mechanisms to remit money, ranging from electronic transfers through banks and money transfer. Female, unmarried, young, highly skilled individuals whose families live in urban areas have a lower propensity to remit than their counterparts. Overall, remittances received from Ukrainian migrants are spent on essential consumption needs, the purchase of durable goods, improving housing conditions, education, and, less often, on repayment of debt, accumulation of savings, and medical treatment.

The 2014 crisis had important impacts on both intra-state and international Ukrainian migration patterns. Forced migration was a major driver for more than one and a half million internally displaced persons from the Autonomous Republic of Crimea and Sevastopol city as well as the Donetsk and Luhansk oblasts (IOM 2016b). Poland replaced Russia as the state with the most border crossings of Ukrainian citizens, leaving Ukraine with 0.8 million more crossings in 2013 and almost 3 million more than Russia in 2014 (IOM 2016b). The Center for Economic Strategy based in Kyiv estimates that approximately 4 million Ukrainians exited Ukraine in search for employment between 2015 and 2017, of which around a third were seasonal workers, 70% came from Western Ukraine (CES 2018).

Despite the growing need for remittances with the doubling of the poverty headcount ratio (percentage of the population living under $5.50 USD adjusted for 2011 PPP) from 3.6% in 2014 to 7.8% in 2015 and various other macroeconomic indicators, remittances dropped in 2014.

Moreover, net FDI skyrocketed, signalling increased capital flight from Ukraine despite the need for greater funds. The drop in remittances was largely attributable to blockages in remittances via Russian bank transfers that persist today (Talant 2018), notably from Russia with remittances from the country to Ukraine dropping from 5 billion USD in 2013 to 3.8 billion USD in 2014 (World Bank 2017).

What is not typically reported is the diversity of payments within informal networks. Informal networks are important because they shed light on gender dynamics within the region. However, it is essential to note the absence of clear information as to the gender dynamics at play. For example, a broad array of determinants to remittances exists, spanning from socioeconomic conditions, to social ties, to recipient needs and many more (Carling 2008). In the case of Ukraine, the largest portion of remittances are aimed at savings (42.4% on average), consumption for daily needs (24.8%), and investment in property (17.0%) according to the IOM (2016a). It is thought that the high savings rate was a response to the crisis in the event the household underwent economic hardship.

Although women tend to have lower earnings on average, their remitted sums to Ukraine are of similar proportion to their male counterparts. Women are also known to remit more frequently, though they remit lower overall sums (IOM 2016a). Furthermore, women are more likely to send back in-kind remittances and gifts (IOM 2016a).

The feminization of migration clusters and increased attention to gender (Carling 2005) in migration studies are important in understanding shifts in migratory patterns. For example, with male migration to EU states and an expansion in the predominantly male military, Ukrainian women have become a crucial part of the informal economy, dependent on remittances but also present in informal activities previously dominated by men. The Russia-Ukraine border was, until recently, estimated to be the second largest remittance corridor in the World (Ratha 2016). In 2014, two-thirds of Ukrainian migrants abroad remitted funds back to Ukraine (IOM 2016a).

Although women are just as likely to remit as men, in non-family unification situations, women's remittances average 6046 USD per year, whereas men remitted 7391 USD. This gender gap persists due to women's lower wages and homemaker roles taking care of the home and its dependents. However, women were more likely to remit in-kind remittances, namely food supplies, cleaning supplies and clothing and shoes (IOM 2016a). Additionally, women generally remit for their household rather than themselves or for investment purposes (IOM 2016a; Solari 2010). Women, who are predominantly engaged in the household care and services sectors, are as ambitious as men regarding savings despite earning lesser incomes. This supportive household role and high savings is said to promote the diffusion of household caring norms or social remittances centred around the family (Vianello 2013).

For its part, the Ukrainian government does not have a firm policy on the informal economy, choosing instead to focus on making private sector development a priority. Ukraine's extensive informal sector has key implications for the development of the private sector. These activities evade the tax and pension system and therefore undercut efforts aimed at strengthening Ukraine's private sector. Ukraine's informal sector is estimated to be quite large, standing at around 55–70% of GDP. Of this amount, over 42% are women despite the definition only including paid work and excluding household care activities in which swathes of women are involved. Furthermore, these statistics often oversee the differentiated gender roles within this sector, especially when it comes to non-remunerated, sex trafficking or other illegal activities. For this reason, a broader definition of informality through the inclusion of non-remunerated work, household care duties, sex trafficking and other illicit activities to gain a more holistic view of labour is needed for donor countries like Canada. This broader definition is composed of a more substantial female representation that largely embraces household subsistence tasks that have kept many households afloat during, and prior to, the Ukrainian crisis.

A Role for Canada?

During the first years of independence in the early 1990s, aid from the diaspora for the multiplicity of Ukrainian causes seemed mainly to take the form of cash. Now it is common for support from the diaspora to take the form of technical services and advice, goods purchased in the west and shipped to Ukraine, and stipends for Ukrainian students as well as exchange programmes. The Canada–Ukraine relationship is unique in that the two countries have a Free Trade Agreement. Ukraine also receives Official Development and Military Assistance. As noted, the positionality of the Ukrainian diaspora aligns with state interests confirming the strength of state-to-state linkages that tend to de-emphasize remittance flows as a primary conduit for supporting the home state.

Ukrainian diaspora appear not to view money transfers across the Canada–Ukraine corridor as the main benefit of living in Canada (Carment et al. 2020). Most of them are spending or intend to spend significant shares of their savings in Canada, such as purchasing a house or investing in their own education. Some of the newer arrivals and temporary workers contemplate and discuss their return to Ukraine. Significant challenges, such as their changing status in Canada, and long waiting times for reuniting with families, cause significant stress and weigh heavily on new migrants, detracting from their ability and willingness to support the homeland.

A clue on how Canada might redefine its gender-driven policy on Ukraine can be found in how women use different strategies to migrate to Canada compared to men (Carment et al. 2020). Among the most popular migration female strategies: educational migration, family migration (in 92% cases, the husband is the primary applicant) and marriage to a Canadian citizen. The woman migration strategy is less financially focused (health, safety, and a prosperous future for children are among the most popular response for leaving Ukraine among women). As a result, newly arrived Ukrainian women in Canada tend to remit more often and in greater amounts relative to their share of personal income. These remittances combine with the regular gifts, presents and aid to people in need (Carment et al. 2020). In an ideal situation, these transnational elements (in the form of remittances) mostly exhibited by seasonal workers and recent migrants should produce effective outcomes for women. Nevertheless, our macro-level analysis above shows that this is not the case. Ukrainian women still face several structural obstacles to their full and equal participation in the labour force. In essence Canada's current diaspora strategy towards Ukraine is not nearly as effective as it could be.

Recent research on socioeconomic aspects of migration to Canada from post-Soviet space provides a second clue on how policy can be improved. Although this research operates within a broader regional migrant dimension, the Ukrainian share of Post-Soviet migration is very significant, so we consider this data to be relevant to our study. Research shows that the segment of female immigrants to Canada increased from 52% in the 1990s to 56% in the early 2010s (Hou and Yan 2020: 378). In the 2010s, the 18–39 age immigration group consisted of 58% of women. This trend continues upward. Although post-Soviet migrants usually successfully integrate into Canadian society (with 97% speaking one of the official languages at work after ten years), in the 25–44 age group post-Soviet immigrants had lower employment rates than their Canadian-born counterparts. For all educational levels combined, the most important was for women regardless of level of education (Hou and Yan 2020: 382–383). In brief, young well-educated female migrants from Ukraine are struggling to find their place in Canada longer than men and this in turns affects their financial connection with the home-country and more importantly their ability to influence gender-driven inequalities in Ukraine.

Overall, Canada's impact on Ukraine's gender dynamics is not as strong as it could be. First, proportionally Canada's diaspora, though quite influential, is not as sizeable in comparison to the top three—Poland, Russia and the United States. Second, based on our preceding analysis we now know that, far from inducing structural changes, large remittances are contributing to increasing social inequality to the extent they are unable to sufficiently move women out of the informal sector. Third, remittances are no substitute for FDI, especially FDI in US dollars which is necessary to pay off Ukraine's sizeable sovereign debt. This has implications for the support of MSMEs where women are more likely to find employment or play a leadership role. Finally, diaspora strategies need to focus on addressing the underlying structural weaknesses of Ukraine's fragile state status, such as poor governance and a corruption-free economy.

More importantly, there is a disconnect between Canada's stated goals and its actions. The Canadian government launched its first explicit commitment to a feminist foreign policy agenda through its Feminist International Assistance Policy (FIAP) framework over three years ago. At a time when the Liberals took over from the incumbent Conservative government, Justin Trudeau was quick to declare that "Canada is back" as an active middle power reminiscent of the Pearsonian era of Canadian politics. FIAP's primary objective, as publicly stated, is a contribution to global efforts to eradicate poverty worldwide by addressing inequality and focusing on the empowerment of women and girls. The policy also suggests an approach based on human rights with vague hints at intersectionality by addressing numerous other forms of discrimination. The shift towards such a framework supports the Liberal government's internationalist approach in supporting an array of different international development goals, most notably the Sustainable Development Goals.

The government has employed numerous tools in the application of FIAP. One such tool is its Gender-based Analysis Plus (GBA+) tool that is now mandated to be integrated into federal policies and proposals, both domestic and foreign. In the 2018 federal budget, the government committed to increases in the application of the GBA+ tool to trade agreements. As an analytical tool, it provides a framework for the assessment of equity factors in policymaking processes. Predating the Liberal government, the former Conservative Minister for the Status of Women, Rona Ambrose, promoted efforts to "building capacity for the use of Gender-based Analysis Plus (GBA+), a method for examining the intersection of sex and gender with other identity factors".[5]

FIAP has given rise to important debates about the benefits and limitations of such an approach. Although the official formalization and institutionalization of a more gendered approach should be seen as a significant improvement in expanding the analytical lens of policymakers, it has suffered from numerous oversights such as the frequent conflation of gender and women as well as the limited incorporation of concepts of intersectionality compounding inequalities (Tiessen et al. 2020). Mason (2019) documents the disconnects between civil society understandings of intersectionality and those of Canada's diplomatic and international development officials. Eventually, intersectionality is only a "buzzword" if not clearly and consistently conceptualized to further the analysis of foreign policy (Mason 2019). Within the contexts of this research, although the focus is more narrowly on women than gender more broadly, intersectionality is critical in understanding how socioeconomic hardship, violence, a more vulnerable immigration status, and various other facets of potential discrimination not included in this chapter compound the alienation women and diaspora members face.

FIAP and the internationalist approach of the current Liberal government have not escaped political criticism. In contrast to the Conservatives under former Prime Minister Stephen Harper, often described as hampering Canadian foreign efforts at exploiting soft power and instrumentalizing foreign aid (Brown 2016), the government under Justin Trudeau could be accused of similar political goals and advancing their political brand (Nimijean and Carment 2020). The decline of official development assistance as a percentage of national income during the

---

[5] See https://cfc-swc.gc.ca/trans/account-resp/pr/rpp/1314/01-eng.html.

current government's tenure is largely documented and contradicts, or at least competes with, its claim of embracing a more internationalist view.

However, as further explored in Rebecca Tiessen's chapter in this edited volume, the contrasts between the current Liberal government and the former Conservative government, albeit stark in some areas, may be overblown in others. Despite key differences in contraception and abortion for instance, where Conservative Minister of International Cooperation Bev Oda withdrew abortion funding despite reversing initial plans to also withdraw contraception funding, other differences in international development programmes often came down to differentiated brands.

Furthermore, both Conservative and Liberal governments have emphasized the importance of Canadian development assistance in countries with important diasporic ties and large bases of voters in Canada—namely Ukraine and Haiti (Brown 2018). During the Ukraine Reform Conference 2019, the Government of Canada announced over $45 million in support for Ukraine, more than half of this sum ($25 million) assigned "to help implement inclusive and gender-responsive reforms in Ukraine".[6] Our analysis suggests that more should be done through diaspora connections. In sum, many differences exist among both political approaches to foreign affairs, but the decline in Canadian international development efforts is a broader trend in foreign policy rather than the responsibility of any single political party.

Despite the criticism of the current government and its implementation of FIAP, it remains to be seen if this could be extended to apply to diaspora outreach initiatives. Engaging with diaspora groups has the potential to unlock vital resources that could incentivize diaspora to mobilize long-term social, human and physical capital that could break existing patterns of subsistence remittances aimed at consumption. Furthermore, easing diaspora mobilization away from Ukrainian dependency on foreign migrants could be leveraged to reassert women's roles beyond household work and a constrained reproductive role centred around subsistence. Diasporas remain a largely untapped source for economic and social development that could fuel Canadian development efforts—and potentially at low cost since, as is the case with remittances, costs are often borne by diaspora members. International development efforts need not be

---

[6] Details could be found here: https://www.canada.ca/en/global-affairs/news/2019/07/canada-strengthens-commitment-to-ukraine.html.

limited to the disbursement of funds for far-away projects implemented by numerous non-governmental organizations overseas and could start in Canada's own backyard.

CONCLUSION

While gender inequities affect all areas of informal employment, informal self-employment is of particular concern as these activities, such as in the most appalling cases of street economies, human trafficking, growing international surrogacy and providing routine domestic services, are mostly performed by women. They all carry some risk, limited job security, and most importantly, do little to enhance Ukraine's overall economic and human development record. Household surveys and aggregate statistics seldom incorporate measures of women's contributions or their informal work both within and outside the home.

The broadening scope and growing research base related to gender-related issues offers alternatives to better measure women's participation in the economy and the various policy implications to harness this potential. Looking ahead, Canada's Feminist International Assistance Policy should sharpen its understanding of how diaspora can contribute to gender-driven dynamics between development and long-term investments. Frameworks for the inclusion of informal activities are objects of interest for foreign and local development stakeholders and are likely to achieve other intrinsically tied goals including bridging gender and socioeconomic inequities. Canada's diaspora can help encourage Ukrainian women to take on a more significant role in the formal economy, and more coordinated host-state diaspora policies intertwined with its current Gender-Based Analysis framework could be adapted to provide the necessary nudge.

REFERENCES

Aidis, Ruta, Friederike Welter, David Smallbone, and Nina Isakova. 2007. "Female Entrepreneurship in Transition Economies: The Case of Lithuania and Ukraine." *Feminist Economics* 13(2): 157–183.

Brown, Stephen. 2016. "The Instrumentalization of Foreign Aid Under the Harper Government." *Studies in Political Economy* 97 (1): 18–36.

Brown, Stephen. 2018. "All About That Base? Branding and the Domestic Politics of Canadian Foreign Aid." *Canadian Foreign Policy Journal* 24 (2): 145–164.

Carling, Jørgen. 2005. "Gender Dimensions of International Migration." *Global Migration Perspectives* 35: 1–26.

Carling, Jørgen. 2008. "The Determinants of Migrant Remittances." *Oxford Review of Economic Policy* 24 (3): 581–598.

Carment, David, and Ariane Sadjed (eds.). 2017. *Diaspora as Cultures of Cooperation: Global and Local Perspectives.* New York, NY: Palgrave.

Carment, David, and Joseph Landry. 2017. "Diaspora and Canadian Foreign Policy." In *The Harper Era in Canadian Foreign Policy*, edited by Adam Chapnick and Christopher Kukucha. Vancouver: University of British Columbia Press.

Carment, David, and Rachael Calleja. 2018. "Diasporas and Fragile States: Beyond Remittances Assessing the Theoretical and Policy Linkages." *Journal of Ethnic and Migration Studies* 44 (8): 1270–1288.

Carment, David, Milana Nikolko, and Dani Belo. 2019. "Gray Zone Mediation in the Ukraine Crisis: Comparing Crimea and Donbas." In *Research Handbook on Mediating International Crises*, edited by J. Wilkenfeld, K. Beardsley, and D. Quinn, 124–141. Cheltenham: Edward Elgar Press.

Carment, David, Milana Nikolko, and Samuel MacIsaac. 2020. "Mobilizing Diaspora During Crisis: Ukrainian Diaspora in Canada and the Intergenerational Sweet Spot." *Diaspora Studies*, 1–23.

CES. 2018. *Ukrainian Economic Migration.* Presentation at the 12th Europe-Ukraine Forum. https://ces.org.ua/en/wp-contentfkyiv/uploads/2018/04/migration_pres.pdf.

Dutchak, Oksana 2018. *"Genderna nerivnist' ta rezim zhorstkoy ekonomiy."* In Ukrainian. https://commons.com.ua/uk/genderna-nerivnist-ta-rezhim-zhorstkoyi-ekonomiyi/).

Hou, F., and X. Yan. 2020. "Immigrants from Post-Soviet States: Socioeconomic Characteristics and Integration Outcomes in Canada." In *Migration from the Newly Independent States. Societies and Political Orders in Transition*, edited by Mikhail Denisenko, Salvatore Strozza, and Matthew Light. Cham: Springer. https://doi.org/10.1007/978-3-030-36075-7_17.

IOM. 2016a. *Migration as an Enabler of Development in Ukraine: A Study on the Nexus Between Development and Migration-Related Financial Flows to Ukraine.* The International Organisation for Migration.

IOM. 2016b. *Migration in Ukraine. Facts and Figures.* The International Organisation for Migration.

Ketkar, Suhas, and Dilip Ratha. 2009. "New Paths to Funding." *Finance and Development* 46 (2): 43–45.

Kupets, Olga. 2012. *The Development and the Side Effects of Remittances in the CIS Countries: The Case of Ukraine*. CARIM-East Research Report 2012/02.

Kymlicka, Will, and Keith Banting. 2006. "Immigration, Multiculturalism, and the Welfare State." *Ethics & International Affairs* 20 (3): 281–304.

Mason, Corinne L. 2019. "Buzzwords and Fuzzwords: Flattening Intersectionality in Canadian Aid." *Canadian Foreign Policy Journal* 25 (2): 203–219.

Nikolko, Milana. 2016. "Political Narratives of Victimization Among Ukrainian Canadian Diaspora." In *Diaspora as Cultures of Cooperation: Global and Local Perspectives*, edited by David Carment and Ariane Sadjed, 131–149. New York, NY: Palgrave Macmillan.

Nikolko, Milana. 2019. "Diaspora Mobilization and the Ukraine Crisis: Old Traumas and New Strategies." *Ethnic and Racial Studies* 42 (11): 1870–1889.

Nikolko, Milana, and David Carment. 2014. "Canada Has a Key Role to Play in Ukraine's Future." *Globe and Mail*, February 27. https://www.theglobea ndmail.com/opinion/canada-has-arole-to-play-in-ukraines-future/article17 131989/.

Nimijean, Richard, and David Carment (eds.). 2020. *Canada, Nation Branding and Domestic Politics*. Routledge.

Prasad, Shubha Kamala and Filip Savatic. 2018. "Diasporic Foreign Policy Interest Groups in the US: Conflict, Democracy, and Political Entrepreneurship." Conference Paper, International Studies Association, Toronto, 2018.

Ratha, D. 2016. *Migration and Remittances Factbook 2016*. The World Bank.

Smallbone, David, and Friederike Welter. 2001. "The Distinctiveness of Entrepreneurship in Transition Economies." *Small Business Economics* 16 (4): 249–262.

Solari, Cinzia. 2010. "Resource Drain vs. Constitutive Circularity: Comparing the Gendered Effects of Post-Soviet Migration Patterns in Ukraine." *Anthropology of East European Review* 28 (1): 215–235.

State Statistics Service of Ukraine. 2015. "Economic Activity of Population in Ukraine 2014." Kyiv.

State Statistics Service of Ukraine. 2016. "Economic Activity of Population in Ukraine 2015." Kyiv.

State Statistics Service of Ukraine. 2017. "Economic Activity of Population in Ukraine 2016." Kyiv.

Strelnyk, Olena 2017. "Mothering and Care for Children in a Risk Society." *Ukrainian Socium* 1 (60): 72–83.

Talant, B. 2018. "Remittances from Russia Go Unofficial Amid Ukraine's Ban on Russian Money Transfers." *KyivPost*, October 2018. https://www.kyivpost.com/business/remittances-from-russia-go-unofficial-amid-ukraines-ban-on-russian-money-transfers.html.

Tiessen, Rebecca, Heather Smith, and Liam Swiss. 2020. "Canada's Evolving Feminist Foreign Policy: Lessons Learned from 2017 to 2020." *International Journal*.

Vaaler, Paul M. 2011. "Immigrant Remittances and the Venture Investment Environment of Developing Countries." *Journal of International Business Studies* 42 (9): 1121–1149.

Vianello, Francesca Alice. 2013. "Ukrainian Migrant Women's Social Remittances: Contents and Effects on Families Left Behind." *Migration Letters* 10 (1): 91.

World Bank. 2017. *Migration and Remittances*. November 16. https://www.worldbank.org/en/topic/migrationremittancesdiasporaissues/brief/migration-remittances-data.

World Bank. 2019. *World Development Indicators*. Accessed on March 23, 2019. https://datacatalog.worldbank.org/dataset/world-development-indicators.

Young, Mary M., and Susan J. Henders. 2012. "Other Diplomacies and the Making of Canada–Asia Relations." *Canadian Foreign Policy Journal* 18 (3): 375–388.

PART IV

Conclusions

CHAPTER 15

Will Canada Forge Its Own Path in a Turbulent World?

Richard Nimijean, David Carment, and Sydney Stewart

INTRODUCTION

The underlying premise of this volume of *Canada Among Nations* is that disunity in Canada affects how Canada engages with an increasingly turbulent world. As our contributors were writing, three interrelated

R. Nimijean (✉)
Department of English and American Studies,
Masaryk University, Brno, Czech Republic
e-mail: richard.nimijean@carleton.ca

School of Indigenous and Canadian Studies,
Carleton University, Ottawa, ON, Canada

D. Carment · S. Stewart
Norman Paterson School of International Affairs,
Carleton University, Ottawa, Canada
e-mail: david.carment@carleton.ca

S. Stewart
e-mail: sydneystewart3@cmail.carleton.ca

© The Author(s), under exclusive license to Springer Nature
Switzerland AG 2021
D. Carment and R. Nimijean (eds.), *Political Turmoil
in a Tumultuous World*, Canada and International Affairs,
https://doi.org/10.1007/978-3-030-70686-9_15

issues deepened this turbulence: the COVID-19 pandemic, the American presidential election, and the Black Lives Matters movement. These issues will affect Canada in deep and unique ways. The pandemic revealed that Canada has failed to adequately address discrimination and socioeconomic inequality. Growing tensions between China and the United States expose Canadian economic and security vulnerabilities, limiting opportunities for autonomous foreign policy decision-making. At the same time, ethnonationalism and populism continue to challenge established political orders. It should come as no surprise that when a liberal democracy seeks to protect and advance individual dignity and rights, it is doing so at the expense of a collective identity that is necessary to unite the country. Nowhere is this truer than in Canada, a country where the Liberal government continues to position itself as the expositor of Canadian values, often in juxtaposition to the United States. With Donald Trump having vacated the Oval Office, the foil against which Justin Trudeau could match his "better" and more "advanced" progressive values has evaporated. A values-driven rhetorical approach to engaging the world no longer provides the platform upon which to build a country, let alone an effective foreign policy.

The idea that Canadian foreign policy is mostly a branding exercise raises uncomfortable and perhaps irreconcilable questions, most significantly "what is Canada?" and "what does Canada stand for?" It is not enough, for example, to posit that "The promotion and protection of human rights is an integral part of Canadian efforts abroad (Government of Canada 2020)". The test of a country in relation to the values it proclaims involves how it deals with uncomfortable situations and truths, such as the Afghan detainee scandal, Omar Khadr's mistreatment at the hands of CSIS, Canada's relationship with Saudi Arabia, or the sacrifice of the human rights of the "two Michael's" due to a political rejection of "hostage diplomacy". More than 150 years after Confederation, Canada is perhaps still not mature or secure enough as a democratic nation to deal with such uncomfortable truths.

Uncomfortable Truths

A tumultuous 2020 also shed light on the fact that issues of human rights and systemic racial, ethnic and gender inequality are not simply problems elsewhere; they are persistent features of Canadian society as well. The disproportionate impact of COVID-19 on African Americans, coupled with growing unemployment and the flexibility of working from home that prevented protestors from having to make a choice between "protesting for a better tomorrow and earning a paycheck", granted the Black Lives Matter movement greater urgency and a broader base of active participants (Nakhaie and Nakhaie 2020). Shortly after the initial protests in the United States, Black Lives Matter protests took place in solidarity all across Canada. This reminded Canadians of the systemic racism in their own country, dispelling the belief that racial injustice was a uniquely American phenomenon. While Canadians looked on with horror at the violent nature of racism in the United States, Canada has been forced to confront its own legacy of racism which, combined with the authoritarian populism noted by Frank Graves, suggest that socioeconomic turmoil will continue for years to come.

Canadians also need to address ongoing expressions of racism and discrimination against Asian Canadians, which have increased during the pandemic, reflecting a historic racism towards Asian Canadians going back to the construction of the first transcontinental railway. Meanwhile, there were more cases of police violence towards Indigenous peoples and a dispute against Mi'kmaq lobster fishers in Nova Scotia, with accusations that the RCMP has not done enough to stem the violence. The pandemic revealed the depths of Canadian inequality despite the Trudeau government's political messaging on revitalizing the middle class and breaking down barriers. Women, racial and ethnic minorities, and new Canadians have all been disproportionately affected by the pandemic (Hou et al. 2020; Wright 2020) and the pandemic also exposed the mistreatment of migrant farmworkers (Pazzano 2020).

Thus, not only has Canada faced challenges in responding to the pandemic; it is not prepared to address the challenges emerging from 2020. Canadian disunity has been aggravated by the lack of a strategic vision for the country.

The Lack of a Strategic Vision

If there is cause for concern, it is simply that political power is deeply concentrated at the federal level; the prime minister is arguably the most powerful actor in Canadian foreign policy. The concentration of power and the idea that the prime minister is himself the repository of core Canadian values reinforces "domestic brand politics", in which the structure and power of the state enable and reward the rhetorical articulation of values without governments necessarily acting in support of them (Nimijean 2014). In turn, this discounts the important role of diverse influences on foreign policy. Provinces, civil society, cities, and ordinary citizens reflect a diversity of interests and values that must be considered in the making and implementation of foreign policy.

While Canada has received international praise for its response to the pandemic (Farkas 2020), COVID-19 has not proven to be the catalyst for re-engaging the world in a constructive and cooperative way. Climate change commitments, development assistance, and trade relations have all weakened under the Liberals since the pandemic hit. Canada's defeat in its bid for a seat on the United Nations Security Council was spearheaded by a formidable opposition, including the Swedish teenage climate activist Greta Thunberg, a pro-Palestinian coalition (CBC News 2020) and developing countries in Africa Asia and Latin America. That should be a clear signal to the Trudeau government that the values it espouses are hardly universal and will be continually challenged by the very people, groups, and nations it claims to speak for. Given that multilateral institutions contributed to an extended period of relative prosperity and security for Canada, its ability to counterbalance US hegemony and choose an independent path is now cast in doubt. Coming to terms with a highly unequal and dependent relationship is hard. Breaking free from that dependency is even harder.

The contributors to this volume demonstrate how Canada is not necessarily well prepared to address these issues. A unifying thread is the Trudeau government's ongoing tendency to appear concerned and engaged rather than undertake actions that reflect the liberal internationalist values that Trudeau regularly conveys to global audiences. Canada is a country that continues to believe that values substitute for interests. That is a luxury most countries cannot afford in these difficult times.

The question is whether those transcendent values that one might describe as "historically" if not "uniquely" Canadian can continue to shape and inform discourse on Canadian foreign policy in an era of disruption and instability. By privileging values over interests, the Liberal government is lacking in strategic foresight; it reacts to popular opinion rather than providing effective statecraft and focused diplomacy, as seen in its handling of the case of the "two Michael's". The Trudeau government would have us believe they lead Canada with both conviction and clarity, but the evidence presented in this volume contradicts such lofty claims. The Liberals' 2015 election platform was premised on a set of propositions about those values that define Canada's place in the world: a commitment to multilateralism, a respect for human rights, a long-standing support for rule of law and its global position as a middle power with influence and pride of place. The chapters in this volume suggest that many Liberal goals remain out of reach or are contradicted by their record.

After years of struggling with the question of Canada's place in the world, Canada's path forward remains undefined. Stephen Harper's election in 2006 was touted as a major shift in Canadian politics and foreign policy, highlighting significant dissatisfaction with "big L" liberal policies and public ambivalence towards "small l" liberalism. This has not changed since Trudeau's 2015 election. While Trudeau enjoys considerable popularity with many Canadians, due in no small part to the collapse of the NDP under Jagmeet Singh, there is a growing ferocity expressed by those who oppose his policies and brand. Erin O'Toole, the new Conservative leader, seeks to capitalize on this, picking up where Harper left off while adopting key elements of the Trump playbook: attacking elites and vowing to take the country "back" by promoting Canada "first". O'Toole is channelling an increasing disenchantment with elitist, progressive and centralised politics that were key to Trump's success as a politician. Prominent Conservative MP Pierre Poilievre, tapping into the perceived alienation of many Canadians with the Liberal agenda, even warns Canadians of Trudeau's support for a "Great Reset" that conspiracy theorists suggest will empower global elites to the detriment of "the people" (Boutilier 2020).

This personalization of Canadian foreign policy—Harper's "warrior nation" versus Trudeau's liberal internationalism—cheapens debate about the substance and direction of foreign policy. Trudeau's attacks on Harper's policies and his declaration that Canada was back after a decade of Harper contradicted his promise of less partisan politics by effectively implying that Conservative voters were less than Canadian. Conservative efforts to link Canadian foreign policy to Trudeau's brand and political style have the same effect. While leaders try to score political points, Canada is in desperate a need of a strategic vision of its place in the world. Statecraft typically emanates from building stability through linking domestic opportunities (e.g. a strong economy) with international constraints (finding reliable trade partners). This is now more important than ever, given the turbulent times we live in.

VACCINE NATIONALISM

The COVID-19 pandemic has led to growing questioning of global economic relations and supply chains, which in turn feeds into populism and nationalism. The second wave of the pandemic in autumn 2020 has produced "Corona fatigue". While most people follow government measures, we have seen ongoing protests which in many ways received tacit approval from Donald Trump. Many members of his family (including the president himself), inner circle, and administration tested positive for the virus, reflecting their general disdain of mask and social distancing measures. In Germany, anti-government protests against new pandemic measures have been connected to the Alternative for Germany and the far right and in Italy on the far left and far right. Canada has had protests as well. For example, Montreal has witnessed a number of "anti-mask" protests denouncing government regulations (Montpetit and MacFarlane 2020) and in Vancouver almost 1000 people marched in protest of lockdowns, masks and potential vaccines (Miljure 2020).

Lost in the pandemic is concern for developing countries. The world rejoiced when they heard that several vaccines targeting the virus could be available by the end of 2020. However, despite pleas from the United Nations and aid organizations to provide more support for the less well-off, the *Economist* (2020) magazine estimated that wealthy countries, with Canada leading the pack by far (nearly double the number of doses per citizen as second-place Australia), had secured "advanced market commitments" to buy more than 50% of the doses expected to be produced by the end of 2021. Provincial health ministers began telling their citizens that a vaccine was on the way soon. However, while vaccine nationalism may make for good politics at home, it does not address a global problem. Much of the world needs to wait for a vaccine. While wealthy countries anticipate an economic rebound once vaccines emerge, the developing world faces a bleaker economic future, giving lie to the claim that prosperity will only follow resolution of the health crisis. This may be true for wealthy countries, but the global crisis will remain. While Prime Minister Trudeau and Minister of International Development Karina Gould (2020) have called on countries to work together to address the health and economic consequences of the pandemic, it remains that Canada can do much more, as Stephen Brown noted in this volume. In short, the virus has been a stress test for the status quo.

Challenges with securing protective personal equipment and other urgent supplies during the pandemic have led to a questioning of globalization. There have been policy proposals to develop industrial policies that rethink global supply chains and minimize how Canada is affected by disruptions such as those caused by the pandemic (Speer et al. 2020). Deputy Prime Minister Freeland echoed this sentiment. Historically, calls for industrial policy came from the Left, to reduce dependence on the United States and increase Canadian sovereignty. This therefore seems like the right time to have a wide-ranging debate on Canada's future, but Canada does not seem prepared to have a debate on next steps. The Liberals prorogued parliament, ostensibly to offer a post-pandemic vision for Canada, yet the September 2020 Speech from the Throne largely recycled old promises. The opposition, meanwhile, seems more intent on scoring political points than offering a new vision. With a renegotiated NAFTA and the Liberal government's increasing hard-line vis-à-vis China, short-term moves to renationalize supply chains are likely to increase Canada's reliance on the United States, given the deep integration of the economic and defence relationship.

The Need for a New Strategy for Dealing with the United States and China

As a staples-based trading economy, Canada requires predictable trade and constant inflows of foreign direct investment to sustain its economy. This predisposes Canada towards dependent relations with global superpowers—once the United Kingdom, now the United States and, increasingly, China. The current tensions between China and the United States are therefore not simply something that affect Canada as they do other countries; Canada's fate will be affected by the tensions and how Canada chooses to deal with them.

This is concerning, given America's hardening position towards China. Politically, Donald Trump used China for transactional and political goals. However, he was also confrontational, favouring a security-driven agenda over a diplomatic one. This fit into his America first agenda, though he could also continue economic relations with China in public relations terms favourable to him, namely that he was a master negotiator. Economically, however, his policies could be considered a failure. The high tariff policy, while perhaps leading American firms to produce less in China, led many firms to relocate to other low-cost countries, and the policy has actually increased the United States's trade deficit with China (Carr 2020). Meanwhile, the policy's anticipated "reshoring" of jobs has instead increased plant closings (Economic Policy Institute 2020).

Trump's trade and political agendas dragged Canada deeper into the American orbit. The Meng Wanzhou extradition case, and in particular the timing of the request, is a prime example of how Canada was party to Trump's desire to secure an advantage over China (Garossino 2020). In the process, the lives of Canadians have been imperilled and Canadian economic actors (farmers, for example) have been hurt, worsened by the government's refusal to consider an exchange for the two Michael's. More pointedly, while China is the focal point of US policy, Canada has not dealt very well with that shift in strategic orientation. For example, despite the repeated call for trade diversification, the Liberals agreed to a non-market economy clause in the 2018 USMCA deal that makes it near-impossible for Canada to negotiate a trade deal with China. If anything, Canada is now more tightly bound to the continent.

In response, the Liberals tweaked their brand—taking a hard-nosed approach on China with respect to Meng Wanzhou stands out as the most important example, encouraged by media commentary that suggests that Canada is weak if it does not stand up to China (Burney 2020) and wants Canada to support America's China agenda (Burton 2020). But like Trump, much of the Liberals' posturing is public relations as it seeks to find a path that minimizes pressure from the Americans and the Chinese. Canada has yet (as of late March 2021) to take a decision on American insistence that they not use Huawei as a supplier for the development of its 5G network and threatening to block conductors used by Huawei if they did (Simpson 2020; Wintour 2020). Critics believe this is because the Liberals and their business supporters wish to deepen economic ties with China and do not wish to antagonize China further. This has only contributed to a further politicization of thinking about Canada's relationship with China, not a debate on what is in Canada's interest. Thus, opposition members of the Special Committee on Canada–China Relations bolstered by polls and overt pressure tactics from the United States work to both embarrass and corner the government. In November 2020, opposition parties combined to pass a non-binding motion requiring that the government develop plans within 30 days for deciding the fate of Huawei and 5G and for dealing with Chinese aggression. In response the Liberals have let the private sector determine the fate of Huawei in Canada with each of the major telcos rendering their own decision prior to public debate (Fife and Chase 2020). Foreign Affairs Minister Champagne meanwhile cautioned that "tough talk" on China could hurt Canada in its efforts to secure the release of the two Michael's. This did not prevent the opposition from introducing a non-binding motion "that a genocide is currently being carried out by the People's Republic of China against Uyghurs and other Turkic Muslims." The motion also called for the 2022 Olympic Games to be moved from China. Even as they talk past each other, both Conservative leader O'Toole and minister Champagne claim that their own approach is an "'eyes wide open' approach to relations with China" (Bryden 2020).

It is important to note that China sees Canada's current behaviour as an irritant and nothing more, as the economic behemoth gets on with strengthening its economy and building trading and investment partnerships. As a much smaller trading economy itself, Canada needs China more than China needs Canada. Thus, while Canada should not condone the violation of human rights and aggressive and provocative foreign policy statements and actions, Canada still needs to find a way to balance its economic and security interests. For example, Japan and Australia, who are more immediately vulnerable to China, nevertheless did just that by joining the Regional Comprehensive Economic Partnership (RCEP), the November 2020 trade deal between China and 14 other Asia–Pacific countries creating the world's largest free trade alliance. Canada's failure to join will only increase Canada's reliance on the United States. The much-touted Comprehensive and Progressive Agreement for Trans-Pacific Partnership cannot serve as substitute, since most of its signatories excluding Canada are part of the more important RCEP agreement.

This will only create more uncertainty for Liberal government. While Trudeau was very diplomatic towards the Trump administration and was careful not to comment on the 2020 presidential election, Canadians overwhelmingly wanted a Biden victory. However, while relations between new President Biden and Prime Minister Trudeau will no doubt be friendlier, this does not fundamentally change the dynamics at play. Supporters of Bernie Sanders and Elizabeth Warren will pressure the Biden administration to enact measures that favour American interests and workers first and foremost. Historic trade tensions between Canada and the United States will not disappear. Biden's predisposition towards a more progressive climate change agenda will be welcomed by many, though Trudeau and Alberta Premier Kenney will not be fans of Biden's decision to terminate the Keystone XL pipeline once and for all.

While the tone of Biden's foreign policy is more conciliatory and suggests a return to multilateralism and working with allies, the pressures for an America first agenda embedded in the American political culture will not go away. Biden is more likely to work with allies to weaken China rather than confront it directly. Though candidate Biden called Premier Xi a "thug" who did not have a democratic bone in his body, he also stated that China must "play by the rules" (see The Global Herald 2020). To do that, he will need to counter the RCEP while not alienating the 14 other countries that are part of that deal.

We can therefore expect President Biden—like Trudeau—to continue talking tough towards China, given the state of public opinion and Republican control of the Senate. The Biden presidency will target human rights, democracy, and labour issues more so than the military containment strategies espoused by his predecessor. However, given his history, Biden will do so in a multilateral way while he builds back American diplomatic credentials and makes good with wayward and suspicious allies and trade partners.

If Biden holds this course, then America's China agenda will fall into Canada's areas of interests and self-professed expertise, such as human rights advocacy and democracy promotion. In many respects, Canada could end up having a longer-term, hard-line policy on China to satisfy both American and domestic interests. However, Canada's ability to engage constructively is already diminished significantly. Not only will Canada's influence with China take a hit; it will depend on allies to help Canada with its sticky diplomatic relations, an approach that has not worked to date as the two Michael's enter their third year of captivity. Without a major rethinking of Canada's foreign policy, Canada risks being isolated from much of the world while being more dependent on the United States, a country that has its own interests to protect and promote.

CANADA AT A CROSSROADS

Canada is now at a crossroads. It became evident early in the pandemic that Canada would need to rethink its relationship with the United States (Nimijean and Carment 2020). This must continue, even with a Biden presidency. The Canadian government continues to severely limit cross-border traffic between the two countries. Given the deep ties between the countries, this will have a profound impact on Canada, especially since, at the time of writing, it is expected that despite creative workarounds (O'Hara 2020) the border could be closed to non-essential cross traffic until well into 2021.

The growing duration of the pandemic sheds light on how governments are responding to the crisis and managing public health but also planning for a post-pandemic future. Domestically, federal-provincial tensions are re-emerging, primarily over the funding of healthcare, but there is also a political dimension to this: for example, the Trudeau government's musing about regulating homes for the elderly may convey to Canadians that the Liberals are listening, though it ignores the constitutional division of powers and the unequal nature of fiscal federalism, as Nelson Michaud notes, and has brought to light the inadequate provision of resources to long-term care homes.

Uncertainty defines the current geopolitical context. However, this should not serve to paralyse Canadian domestic and foreign policy. Indeed, it should propel us to do just the opposite. As Lloyd Axworthy concludes in his chapter, "Canadians must rise to the occasion, seize the moment to set out on a voyage of discovery...heading into the unknown by putting their ears to the currents and their eyes on a new horizon". The authors in this book have risen to the task, exploring Canada's position in the world and how the current unknowns must be navigated. In some instances, current global contexts, and the pandemic in particular, are fundamentally transforming international relations. This is certainly the case with Canada-China relations, as discussed by Duane Bratt and Kari Roberts. In other cases, COVID-19 presents new opportunities for Canada's engagement on the international stage, as outlined in Michael Manulak's chapter on informal institutions and Robert Huish's analysis of Canadian global health policy. Yet, there are still areas where the status quo is likely to prevail as Stephen Brown asserts in relation to Canadian development assistance.

The COVID-19 pandemic is illustrative of the unpredictable nature of global affairs. Rigorous analyses and thoughtful reflections help us to understand the international environment in which Canada operates; however, uncertainty abounds, and Canada will need foreign, defence, and national security policies that are flexible and nimble enough to respond to constantly evolving trends and threats. The chapters of this book have presented compelling explanations of and suggestions for manoeuvring dynamic domestic and international realities, which can inform Canada's efforts to navigate the months and years to come. This suggests that Canada needs to have a serious reflection on its strategic choices for dealing with a dangerous world while simultaneously dealing with political disunity at home.

Looking ahead, Canada must adjust to a post-Trump world. Biden's first course of action will be to build back diplomacy, so some items on the Canadian agenda will likely have greater traction, including climate change, working with democracies, and re-invigorating poverty-focused aid and investment policies and programmes in Africa as suggested by Stephen Brown. However, Biden is also committed to some potentially destabilising policies, such as increased pressure on Russia and Venezuela (by ramping up sanctions) while withdrawing some troops out of both Afghanistan and Iraq. These are not necessarily bad choices, but they do have the potential to contribute to further regional instability if not achieved through consensus and multilateralism. On balance, Biden will pursue a security-first agenda that will pressure Canada to spend more on defence. As Kari Roberts notes, the Arctic stands out as place where tensions between Canada and United States could deepen; border security management and trade frictions will also not magically disappear either.

The core issue as always is whether deeper integration with the US hampers Canada in striking an independent foreign policy path. Appealing to the past is not a good platform on which to build Canada's future, as the UNSC election loss showed. Inconsistent international conduct has hurt international perceptions of Canada; it increasingly looks like a country whose influence and impact are in serious decline (notwith-standing surveys that always show what a great country Canada is). Strategic reflection is the first step to changing such perceptions, followed by concrete actions in support of clearly defined interests.

Thus, we need to go beyond the daily political skirmishing over how to manage the pandemic and relations with China and the United States, informed by punditry that encourages kneejerk reactions. Debates over the "great reset" are a prime example. The Conservative party's attempt to score political points against the prime minister by hinting at conspiracy theories (Gilmore 2020) has been called out by the very same pundits, though they are dismissive of the idea of a major rethink of how Canada and the rest of the world need to address the pandemic and its aftermath (Coyne 2020; Wells 2020).

Domestically, the pandemic has exposed long-standing socioeconomic inequalities. Coupled with the wave of protest stemming from police brutality in the United States, greater attention was afforded to issues of social injustice within Canada's borders including anti-black racism, mistreatment of Indigenous populations and inequalities in the immigration system (Aljazeera 2020; Kalvapalle 2020). While COVID-19 fuelled activity in regard to social inequalities, it has disrupted the economic sphere. Growing tensions between the United States and China, and Canada's uneasy position in the crossfire, has exposed the economy to new vulnerabilities. A volatile business environment threatened the economic security of many Canadians, particularly of women and members of visible minority communities. Canada has the ability to pursue economic recovery that will engender a more equitable and sustainable future, yet it is this reorientation of the economy that is entangled in the aforementioned conspiracy theories. The Liberal government's stimulus policies seek to help Canadians survive the crisis. However, its November economic statement was timid in addressing pressing socioeconomic inequalities such as a national daycare program. It also ignored important realities such as the Canadian economy's decreasing competitiveness and productivity, tightening markets as countries react to the pandemic, and the lack of a strategy for dealing with countries such as China that hold different values.

The domestic politics of the pandemic does not mean that Canada should ignore the needs of the rest of the world. Furor over the lack of a domestic capacity to produce vaccines has led to complaints that other countries will get the vaccine first. While Canada calls for more global cooperation, its focus is inwards. A number of countries are fragile and more are on the verge of becoming failed states. Looking inwards means not only that Canada will not work to prevent this; it will also be affected by the resultant global instability marked by political turmoil, not to mention ongoing challenges of migration and climate change. With or without a "global reset", Canada is in dire need of strategic direction.

Indeed, since the end of the Cold War, Canada's commitment to and involvement in multilateralism and international institutions has weakened due to changes in the global political economy. The multilateralism that Canada helped develop and increased its influence as a middle power does not work the same way today. As the confrontation with China clearly shows, Canada must engage states with different value systems; leaders must figure out how to make compromises in shaping a new international order without conflict. Canada's role as a traditional middle power has been challenged by new powers wishing to reform international institutions. Canada cannot simply appeal to its past record to maintain its status. It must think *and* act. Canada can no longer afford to be a status quo player in a world so deeply divided.

References

Aljazeera. 2020. "Canada Aims to Bring in Over 1.2 Million Immigrants Over 3 Years." *Aljazeera*, October 20. https://www.aljazeera.com/news/2020/10/30/canada-aims-to-bring-in-over-1-2-immigrants-over-next-3-years.

Boutilier, Alex. 2020. "A Conservative MP Warns That Justin Trudeau Wants a 'Great Reset.' Conspiracy Theorists Are Worried, Too." *The Star*, November 20. https://www.thestar.com/politics/federal/2020/11/19/a-conservative-mp-warns-that-justin-trudeau-wants-a-great-reset-conspiracy-theorists-are-worried-too.html.

Bryden, Joan. 2020. "Champagne Warns Tough Talk on China Could Hurt Efforts to Free Kovrig, Spavor." *National Newswatch*, November 23. https://www.nationalnewswatch.com/2020/11/23/champagne-warns-tough-talk-on-china-could-hurt-efforts-to-free-kovrig-spavor/#.X7_7DhNKg0o.

Burney, Derek H. 2020. "Derek H. Burney on COVID-19: It's Hard for Canada to Stand Up to China While It's Bowing." *National Post*, May 14. https://nationalpost.com/opinion/derek-h-burney-on-covid-hard-for-canada-to-stand-up-to-china-while-its-on-its-knees-bowing.

Burton, Charles. 2020. "America Shouldn't Go It Alone in Containing China." *Globe and Mail*, August 6. https://www.theglobeandmail.com/opinion/article-america-shouldnt-go-it-alone-in-containing-china/.

Carr, Earl. 2020. "Reshoring Jobs to the US Versus Made in China." *Forbes*, August 4. https://www.forbes.com/sites/earlcarr/2020/08/04/reshoring-jobs-to-the-us-versus-made-in-china/?sh=1adfc32785e1.

CBC News. 2020. "Canada Rebuts UN Security Council Critics as Champagne Heads to NYC for Final Push." *CBC News*, June 12. https://www.cbc.ca/news/politics/champagne-nyc-security-council-1.5610109.

Coyne, Andrew. 2020. "The 'Great Reset' Conspiracy Theory Is a Great Embarrassment for All Involved – Including Ottawa." *Globe and Mail*, November 25. https://www.theglobeandmail.com/opinion/article-the-great-reset-conspiracy-theory-is-a-great-embarrassment-for-all/.

Economic Policy Institute. 2020. "Trump's Trade Policies Have Cost Thousands of U.S. Manufacturing Jobs." https://www.epi.org/press/trumps-trade-policies-have-cost-thousands-of-u-s-manufacturing-jobs-action-is-urgently-needed-to-rebuild-the-manufacturing-sector-after-the-coronavirus-pandemic/.

Farkas, Uri. 2020. "Handling of Health Crises Impacts Overall Favorability Towards Nations." *Ipsos,* August 25. https://www.ipsos.com/en-us/handling-health-crises-impacts-overall-favorability-towards-nations.

Fife, Robert and Steven Chase. 2020. "Telus to Build Out 5G Network Without China's Huawei." *Globe and Mail,* November 23. https://www.theglobeandmail.com/politics/article-telus-to-build-out-5g-network-without-chinas-huawei/.

Garossino, Sandy. 2020. "U.S. Strong-Armed Canada into Calamitous Meng Strategy." *National Observer,* June 30. https://www.nationalobserver.com/2020/06/30/opinion/canada-got-hoodwinked-meng-wanzhou-shakedown-and-show-trial.

Gilmore, Rachel. 2020. "'Playing with Fire': How Politicians Can Perpetuate Baseless Conspiracy Theories." *Global News,* November 26. https://globalnews.ca/news/7473149/the-great-reset-conspiracy-theory-tory-twitter/.

Gould, Karina. "Address by Minister Gould to Canadian International Council." *Global Affairs Canada,* November 9. Available at https://www.canada.ca/en/global-affairs/news/2020/11/address-by-minister-gould-to-canadian-international-council.html.

Government of Canada. 2020. "Canada's Approach to Advancing Human Rights." September 1. https://www.international.gc.ca/world-monde/issues_development-enjeux_developpement/human_rights-droits_homme/advancing_rights-promouvoir_droits.aspx?lang=eng.

Hou, Feng, Kristyn Frank and Christoph Schimmele. 2020. "Economic Impact of COVID-19 Among Visible Minority Groups." *Statistics Canada,* July 6. https://www150.statcan.gc.ca/n1/pub/45-28-0001/2020001/article/00042-eng.htm.

Kalvapalle, Rahul. 2020. "'This Is a Canadian Problem, Too': U of T's Maydianne Andrade on Finding the will to Address Anti-Black Racism." *U of T News,* September 11. https://www.utoronto.ca/news/canadian-problem-too-u-t-s-maydianne-andrade-finding-will-address-anti-black-racism.

Miljure, Ben. 2020. "Anti-Mask Protesters, Conspiracy Theorists March Through Downtown Vancouver." *CTV News,* October 17. https://bc.ctvnews.ca/anti-mask-protesters-conspiracy-theorists-march-through-downtown-vancouver-1.5149905.

Montpetit, Jonathon and John MacFarlane. 2020. "Anti-Mask Protest in Montreal Draws Large Crowd, Propelled by U.S. Conspiracy Theories." *CBC News,* September 12. https://www.cbc.ca/news/canada/montreal/anti-mask-protest-montreal-1.5722033.

Nakhaie, Reza and F. S. Nakhaie. 2020. "Black Lives Matter Movement Finds New Urgency and Allies Because of COVID-19." *The Conversation,* July 5. https://theconversation.com/black-lives-matter-movement-finds-new-urgency-and-allies-because-of-covid-19-141500.

Nimijean, Richard. 2014. "Domestic Brand Politics and the Modern Publicity State." In *Publicity and the Canadian State*, edited by Kirsten Kozolanka, 172–194. Toronto: University of Toronto Press.

Nimijean and Carment. 2020. "Rethinkig the Canada–US Relationship After the Pandemic." *Policy Options*, May 7. https://policyoptions.irpp.org/fr/magazines/may-2020/rethinking-the-canada-us-relationship-after-the-pandemic/.

O'Hara, Clare. 2020. "Snowbirds Take to the Air to Cross Closed Canada–U.S. Land Border, Despite Government Warnings." *Globe and Mail*, November 23. https://www.theglobeandmail.com/business/article-snowbirds-take-to-the-air-to-cross-closed-canada-us-land-border/.

Pazzano, Jasmine. 2020. "Coronavirus: Canada's Migrant Farm Workers Face Fatal COVID-19 Outbreaks, Alleged Mistreatment." *Global News*, August 28. https://globalnews.ca/news/7301324/coronavirus-canadas-migrant-farm-workers-alleged-mistreatment/.

Simpson, Katie. 2020. "State Department Says U.S. Will Reassess Intelligence-Sharing with Canada If It Lets Huawei into 5G." *CBC News*, June 4. https://www.cbc.ca/news/politics/huawei-5g-state-department-trudeau-china-1.5598548.

Speer, Sean, Robert Asselin, and Royce Mendes. 2020. "New North Star II: A Challenge-Driven Industrial Strategy for Canada." *Public Policy Forum*. https://ppforum.ca/wp-content/uploads/2020/04/NewNorthStarII-PPF-APRIL2020-EN.pdf.

The Economist. 2020. "Rich Countries Grab Half of Projected COVID-19 Vaccine Supply." November 12. https://www.economist.com/graphic-detail/2020/11/12/rich-countries-grab-half-of-projected-covid-19-vaccine-supply

The Global Herald. 2020. "Joe Biden Calls China's Xi Jinping a 'Thug.'" February 26. https://theglobalherald.com/politics/joe-biden-calls-chinas-xi-jinping-a-thug/.

Wells, Paul. 2020. "The Great Reset Is Mostly Just Liberals Blowing Off Steam. Mostly." *Maclean's*, November 23. https://www.macleans.ca/politics/ottawa/the-great-reset-is-mostly-just-liberals-blowing-off-steam-mostly/.

Wintour, Patrick. 2020. "UK Should Revisit 5G Ban Now Trump Is Defeated, Says Huawei." *The Guardian*, November 16. https://www.theguardian.com/technology/2020/nov/16/uk-should-revisit-5g-ban-now-trump-is-defeated-says-huawei.

Wright, Teresa. 2020. "Feds Probing Ways to Address COVID-19 Impact on Women." *CTV News*, May 23. https://www.ctvnews.ca/politics/feds-probing-ways-to-address-covid-19-impact-on-women-1.4951560.

CPSIA information can be obtained
at www.ICGtesting.com
Printed in the USA
LVHW011049141021
700426LV00003B/327